Differential Games in Industrial Economics

Game theory has revolutionised our understanding of industrial organisation and the traditional theory of the firm. Despite these advances, industrial economists have tended to rely on a restricted set of tools from game theory, focussing on static and repeated games to analyse firm structure and behaviour. Luca Lambertini, a leading expert on the application of differential game theory to economics, argues that many dynamic phenomena in industrial organisation (such as monopoly, oligopoly, advertising and R&D races) can be better understood and analysed through the use of differential games. After illustrating the basic elements of the theory, Lambertini guides the reader through the main models, spanning from optimal control problems describing the behaviour of a monopolist through to oligopoly games in which firms' strategies include prices, quantities and investments. This approach will be of great value to students and researchers in economics and those interested in advanced applications of game theory.

Luca Lambertini is Professor of Economics at the University of Bologna. He is a member of the International Federation of Automatic Control, collaborator of the Dynamic Systems Program at the International Institute for Applied Systems Analysis and associate editor of *Dynamic Games and Applications*. He has published extensively in international journals, including *Automatica, Journal of Economic Theory, European Journal of Operational Research* and *Journal of Economic Dynamics and Control*.

Differential Games in Industrial Economics

LUCA LAMBERTINI

University of Bologna

CAMBRIDGE
UNIVERSITY PRESS

University Printing House, Cambridge CB2 8BS, United Kingdom

One Liberty Plaza, 20th Floor, New York, NY 10006, USA

477 Williamstown Road, Port Melbourne, VIC 3207, Australia

314-321, 3rd Floor, Plot 3, Splendor Forum, Jasola District Centre, New Delhi - 110025, India

79 Anson Road, #06-04/06, Singapore 079906

Cambridge University Press is part of the University of Cambridge.

It furthers the University's mission by disseminating knowledge in the pursuit of
education, learning and research at the highest international levels of excellence.

www.cambridge.org
Information on this title: www.cambridge.org/9781107164680
DOI: 10.1017/9781316691175

© Luca Lambertini 2018

First published 2018

A catalogue record for this publication is available from the British Library

Library of Congress Cataloging in Publication data
Names: Lambertini, Luca, author.
Title: Differential games in industrial economics / Luca Lambertini.
Description: 1 Edition. | New York : Cambridge University Press, 2018. |
Includes bibliographical references and index.
Identifiers: LCCN 2017042299 | ISBN 9781107164680 (Hardback) | ISBN 9781316616499 (Paperback)
Subjects: LCSH: Industrial organization (Economic theory) | Industrial management. |
BISAC: BUSINESS & ECONOMICS / Industrial Management.
Classification: LCC HD2326 .L356 2018 | DDC 330.01/51932–dc23 LC record
available at https://lccn.loc.gov/2017042299

ISBN 978-1-107-16468-0 Hardback
ISBN 978-1-316-61649-9 Paperback

To Monica, just because

Contents

Preface

The main aim of this volume is to do justice to a literature which has developed itself at the intersection of several disciplines but, unlike others using similar formal instruments (as, for example, growth theory), has not yet been given a systematic reconstruction. To avoid misunderstandings, I want to point out that the material contained in this volume covers the literature using continuous time models in industrial economics, i.e., either *optimal control problems* or *differential games*. Covering also dynamic models in discrete time would require at least the same space, or transforming the book into a large survey. Either way, the volume would become hardly useful.

After the adoption of the game theory approach, the analysis of oligopolistic competition has taken a completely new angle as compared to the previous view of industrial economics prevailing until the early 1970s. The revolution generating what we now call the theory of industrial organization (IO) has shed light on topics which had remained at the margin of the discipline for decades, creating from scratch a number of research strands. Some of the topics addressed in these fields of IO – if not all – have an explicit and intuitive dynamic nature. Capacity accumulation, research & development (R&D) and advertising are obvious examples. Yet, the game theory toolkit has included static (often multistage) and repeated games, and Markovian games in discrete time. In static multistage games, time is blackboxed, while repeated games take a time invariant constituent stage game and typically insert time and time discounting to look at critical thresholds of the latter (as in folk theorems investigating the stability of implicit collusion in prices or outputs).

Proper dynamic games in either discrete or continuous time have been seldom used. This is apparent from dominant textbook in IO at different levels (Tirole, 1988; Martin, 1993, 2002; Shy, 1995; Belleflamme and Peitz, 2010), where dynamics in continuous time is usually confined to the exposition of models dealing with R&D races. Even in Fudenberg and Tirole (1986), a relevant portion of the text treats repeated games while most of the remainder looks at R&D competition. A relevant exception is Fudenberg and Tirole (1991), in which differential game theory is presented and complemented with an illustration of oligopoly games with capacity accumulation games. However, for a wider perspective on differential games in IO and related fields (environmental and resource economics and trade theory), the choice is confined to Dockner *et al.* (2000), Erickson (2003), Jørgensen and Zaccour (2004), Long (2010), Lambertini (2013), and discrete time models (Sorger 2015).

In a nutshell, the difference between a static game (whether one-shot, repeated, or multistage) and a truly dynamic game is the presence of at least one state variable whose motion is governed by its own dynamic equation hosting the players' controls and – in turn – affecting the players' performance at any time during the game. To grasp intuitively the implications of the presence of state variables, it suffices to note that this is exactly what is lost for good when one builds up a multistage game to investigate, say, the interplay between a long-run variable (say, R&D or product quality/location and, *a fortiori*, the stock of natural resources or environmental damages) and a short-run one (prices or quantities). As mentioned earlier, this approach is usually thought of as blackboxing a dynamic process which remains behind the curtains of the static model. The latter, including any policy implications it may produce, is indeed reliable if and only if the results are consistent with those one would find solving the dynamic version of the same problem. For instance, to be more explicit, if the limit of the dynamic model coincides with the equilibrium of the static one. In other words, is the static equilibrium always an accurate snapshot of the steady state equilibrium of its truly dynamic version? Even if the answer is affirmative, it is still true that the static model is silent about the transition to the equilibrium.

Moreover, the equilibria of static (and often multistage) games are built to be subgame perfect and therefore credible. This raises another crucial question as to whether and when the limit of a dynamic game confirms the predictions of its static version. One of the pieces of common wisdom about differential games – not entirely justified in itself – holds that the open-loop solution is (quasi-)static. In fact, what usually happens is that the limit of the open-loop equilibrium coincides with the equilibrium of the static game, for instance when discounting is absent. However, this is almost never the case when feedback effects are operating, unless the game features specific properties. Whenever the subgame perfect equilibria of the static and dynamic version of a game do not coincide (even in the limit), the descriptive and normative powers of the static model are compromised and potentially counterproductive.

The foregoing considerations motivate revisiting anew a consolidated theory using the alternative lens of differential game theory, so as to

- deliver a coherent view of the existing research on the dynamics of competition along several dimensions associated with market and non-market variables;
- offer a forward-looking perspective on future developments concerning topics which have recently entered the picture (e.g., portfolio race games) or largely disregarded because of technical difficulties but representing obvious candidate to be investigated with these instruments (e.g., collusive games featuring trigger strategy equilibria); and
- establish a connection with fields in which differential game theory has been extensively applied, but which are traditionally considered as external to IO (e.g., environmental and resource economics and trade theory and even macroeconomic growth models).

Additionally, brief digressions towards discrete time games are also present at some points, as this approach has been intensively used to construct a general framework for the numerical and empirical analysis of the evolution of an industry (Doraszelski and Pakes, 2007).

Aims and Style

Given the nature of the subject matter and the level of the mathematics involved, this book is aimed at PhD students carrying out their research in the field of optimal control and differential game theory with applications to industrial economics and related fields, and as a reference for professional researchers working in the same area. Although, at least in line of principle, the ideal reader could be expected to be familiar with the theory of optimal control and dynamic programming, technical aspects will be duly illustrated in Chapters 1 and 9 as well as throughout the volume, where necessary.

The book may be of interest to PhD students and researchers in other areas, such as business and management, engineering, applied mathematics and operations research. Indeed, as mentioned earlier, many contributions – including crucial ones – have been produced by colleagues in all of these areas.

Writing a really exhaustive and self-contained book is hardly possible, if at all. At least this is my sincere opinion. What I had in mind when my ideas about this venture took shape was to produce an instrument using which a reader endowed with some essential skills in optimal control and dynamic programming could understand some important differential games top to bottom. As will become apparent reading the book, I have used (hopefully not abused) my personal judgement in devoting some additional space to core models that, in view of their relevance and/or didactical properties, are illustrated in deeper details than others, which are instead more briefly sketched.

Structure of the Book

Chapter 1 provides the coordinates of the required mathematics, obviously without replicating in full what the reader can find in Dockner *et al.* (2000) and without offering a detailed exposition of the theory of differential equations and stability analysis of dynamic systems. In particular, the chapter illustrates Bellman's dynamic programming principle against Pontryagin's maximum principle, in connection with open-loop, closed-loop and feedback information. Then it also explains the conditions for strong time consistency (i.e., subgame perfection) to arise in differential games, and singles out the classes of differential games where subgame perfection is attained under open-loop information. The latter is an important feature, as many relevant games contained in the chapters to follow indeed share this property. Finally, it paves the way for the analysis of time consistency in Stackelberg differential games, which is the focus of Chapter 9.

The material appearing in Chapter 2 serves the threefold objective of (1) motivating the whole book through the simplest setting – monopoly – in which strategic inter-action is absent but time does affect a firm's performance and therefore its strategies;

(2) illustrating the fact that, under monopoly, the open-loop solution via the Hamiltonian technique (indeed, a single-agent optimal control problem) and the feedback solution via the Bellman equation may not coincide even if no strategic interaction takes place; and (3) offering an overview of those themes (from capacity accumulation and environmental issues to optimal pricing for durables and the impact of network externalities) which will appear again in proper differential games.

Chapter 3 is the largest of the book, as it reviews oligopoly games where firms use market variables only. The exposition sets out with the paradigmatic Cournot game under price stickiness, which is given a careful look as it offers the possibility of comparing open-loop, closed-loop and feedback solutions in detail, using linear and nonlinear demands and also nonlinear feedback strategies. This is followed by the opposite problem posed by sluggish demand and then by the illustration of Bertrand and Cournot games with capacity accumulation dynamics, either à la Solow–Swan or à la Ramsey. The survey of oligopoly games is complemented by those featuring price competition with costly price adjustment and durable or addictive goods. The remainder of the chapter is devoted to a reconstruction of the debate about conjectural variations, best reply functions and potential functions in differential games, as well as the little we avail of about the use of trigger strategies and, as mentioned earlier, to the growing literature on the empirical analysis of the intertemporal evolution of industries.

Chapter 4 deals with advertising games. A large portion of the extant material in this subfield has been produced either in industrial economics or in marketing and management, but also in operations research and engineering. Bluntly speaking, this literature stipulates that firms' advertising efforts modify either market size or market shares or goodwill (also labelled as brand equity). The resulting literature is teeming with games which lend themselves to a fully analytical solution under any information structure, and has attracted a considerable amount of empirical research.

Product differentiation based on discrete choice models (Anderson et al., 1992) is the subject matter of Chapter 5. The incentive for firms to invest in product differentiation in order to soften price competition has been investigated IO in full details and for several decades by now. Conversely, the space devoted to this issue in differential game theory is still limited. This might sound surprising, given the inherently dynamic nature of this theme, and the discussion carried out in this chapter is also meant to illustrate the reasons for this apparent lack of activity, in connection with the lack of tractability of discrete choice models when these are translated into continuous time frameworks.

Chapter 6 summarises stochastic and deterministic games of innovation. The first part offers a reconstruction of the transformation of R&D races with exogenous efforts into proper differential games with firms using R&D investments as controls, influencing the expected innovation date in a really strategic way. The second part accounts for games in which uncertainty plays no role and firms invest in either process or product innovation, or both. Here we will come back to the issue of whether the limit properties of differential games coincide with those of their static counterparts. Learning by doing, the use of technological knowledge as a barrier to entry and catching-up in portfolio races are complementary issues also treated in this chapter.

Differential oligopoly games in environmental and resource economics are illustrated in Chapter 7, where the benchmark Cournot games with either polluting emissions or renewable resource extraction are described in detail, including nonlinear feedback strategies and the voracity effect possibly leading to resource extinction. A large amount of space is devoted to the behaviour of cartels extracting nonrenewables, as well as to R&D for green or backstop technologies.

Chapter 8 deals with intraindustry trade, reviewing dynamic reformulations of intraindustry trade with tariffs, quotas and voluntary export or import restraints in frameworks appearing in Chapter 3, based on either price stickiness or capacity accumulation. This exposition is then complemented by the material pertaining to the intersection between trade theory and environmental economics, in which trade impacts pollution and global warming.

Chapter 9 is a mix of theory and applications meant to illustrate the delicate nature of the Stackelberg solution in differential games. Actually, I might simply say 'games' without any further qualification, since the chapter sets out with a compact illustration of the original Cournot-Stackelberg model (Stackelberg, 1934) we are accustomed to from introductory textbooks in microeconomics, in order to outline the concept of time (in)consistency. This is then extensively discussed in the remainder of the chapter by illustrating the property of uncontrollability and the requirements for subgame perfect Stackelberg equilibria to arise under open-loop and feedback information. This discussion is complemented by examples based on games with sticky prices, advertising or taxation of polluting emissions in monopoly. A relatively wider space is for a theme which is widespread in the business and management literature, supply chain coordination, as this is a natural candidate for the analysis of the Stackelberg solution.

At the end of each chapter, there appears a short paragraph offering suggestions for further readings.

Acknowledgments

A book is never the outcome of a one-man-band effort. I would like to warmly thank Roberto Cellini, Luca Colombo, Flavio Delbono, Davide Dragone, Paola Labrecciosa, Andrea Mantovani and Arsen Palestini for many fruitful suggestions and comments and for carefully reading each chapter. Needless to say, the responsibility for the contents and any remaining errors or omissions remains with me only. Special thanks to five reviewers for their constructive comments and suggestions on the initial book proposal, and to Phil Good, my editor at Cambridge University Press, who accompanied me most friendly and efficiently throughout the gestation of the book. Last but by no means least, I would like to express my most sincere gratitude and affection to George Leitmann, with a hug to him and Nancy.

During the editorial process of the book, Engelbert Dockner passed away. He largely contributed to the development of differential game theory and its applications in several directions, including the areas treated here. This volume is also a modest tribute to his memory.

Bibliography

Anderson, S., A. de Palma and J.-F. Thisse (1992), *Discrete Choice Theory of Product Differentiation*, Cambridge, MA, MIT Press.

Belleflamme, P. and M. Peitz (2010), *Industrial Organization*, Cambridge, Cambridge University Press.

Dockner, E.J., S. Jørgensen, N.V. Long and G. Sorger (2000), *Differential Games in Economics and Management Science*, Cambridge, Cambridge University Press.

Doraszelski, U. and A. Pakes (2007), "A Framework for Applied Dynamic Analysis in IO", in M. Armstrong and R. Porter (eds), *Handbook of Industrial Organization*, vol. 3, 1887–966.

Erickson, G. (2003), *Dynamic Models of Advertising Competition. Second Edition*, Dordrecht, Kluwer.

Fudenberg, D. and J. Tirole (1986), *Dynamic Models of Oligopoly*, Chur, Harwood Academic Publishers.

Fudenberg, D. and J. Tirole (1991), *Game Theory*, Cambridge, MA, MIT Press.

Jørgensen, S. and G. Zaccour (2004), *Differential Games in Marketing*, Dordrecht, Kluwer.

Lambertini, L. (2013), *Oligopoly, the Environment and Natural Resources*, London, Routledge.

Long, N.V. (2010), *A Survey of Dynamic Games in Economics*, Singapore, World Scientific.

Martin, S. (1993), *Advanced Industrial Economics*, Oxford, Blackwell.

Martin, S. (2002), *Advanced Industrial Economics. Second Edition*, Oxford, Blackwell.

Shy, O. (1995), *Industrial Organization*, Cambridge, MA, MIT Press.

Sorger, G. (2015), *Dynamic Economic Analysis. Deterministic Models in Discrete Time*, Cambridge, Cambridge University Press.

Stackelberg, H. von (1934), *Marktform und Gleichgewicht*, Berlin and Vienna, Springer-Verlag.

Tirole, J. (1988), *The Theory of Industrial Organization*, Cambridge, MA, MIT Press.

1 Elements of Optimal Control, Dynamic Programming and Differential Game Theory

The aim of this chapter is to offer a synthetic introduction to optimal control models and differential games, covering the outline of their structure as well as a compact exposition of the solution methods used in applications in the field of industrial organization which appear in the remainder of the book.

Setting out with a summary of a simple dynamic problem featuring a single variable, the exposition is expanded to account for optimal control models with a single agent, and then it is further extended to encompass strategic interaction between at least two players with conflicting objectives, transforming the model into a differential game. Throughout the chapter, the illustration is restricted to noncooperative games; cooperative games are not dealt with, as they are a special case of optimal control models with a single agent controlling several variables.

The concept of Nash equilibrium for differential games is defined. In connection to it, the nature and role of information are discussed under open-loop, closed-loop and feedback rules, to outline the related notions of subgame perfection and weak vs. strong time consistency in differential games. This discussion prompts the analysis of Stackelberg differential games, where the source of time inconsistency, widely known in the macroeconomic policy literature, is identified and a time-consistent solution is outlined.

A summary of the elements of stability analysis based on the properties of the state-control dynamic system and the trace and determinant of the associated Jacobian matrix is also included. More on stability analysis will appear in the context of specific models throughout the book.

For obvious reasons – as is always the case with introductory tutorials about mathematical methods preparatory to the illustration of their applications in any scientific field – this single chapter necessarily falls short of supplying an exhaustive overview of the whole theoretical background, for which the interested reader is referred to the large literature mentioned at the end of the chapter itself.

1.1 Preliminaries: The Simplest Dynamic Problem

The point of departure is a dynamic problem with a single object, whose specific nature for the moment is irrelevant, evolving over continuous time. Consider a generic variable $x(t) \in \mathcal{X} \subseteq \mathbb{R}^n$ (which represents a 'state') evolving over continuous time t according to the following ordinary differential equation:

$$\frac{dx}{dt} \equiv \dot{x}(t) = f(x(t), t) \tag{1.1}$$

where $f(x(t), t)$ is continuously differentiable in $x(t)$ and t. Such equation is *auto-nomous* if $\dot{x} = f(x(t))$, i.e., if the time argument does not appear explicitly. If $x(t)$ satisfies (1.1), then it is a solution or an *integral* of the above differential equation. The so-called *Cauchy problem* obtains when we require such a solution to take a specific value $x(0) = x_0$ at the initial instant t_0:

$$\begin{cases} \dot{x} = f(x(t), t) \\ x(0) = x_0 \end{cases} \tag{1.2}$$

where $x(0) = x_0$ identifies the *initial condition*. A specific and relevant example of the Cauchy problem describes the evolution of a population, species or, in general, a renewable natural resource as in the Verhulst–Lotka–Volterra model (Verhulst, 1838; Lotka, 1925; Volterra, 1931). Indeed, the presence of the undisturbed resource is in Verhulst (1838). Since we will encounter it in Chapters 2 and 7, the evolution of the model and its basic features can be usefully illustrated here. Suppose the resource is not disturbed by any harvesting activity (i.e., in the traditional jargon of the model, there is no predator), so that its population follows a logistic growth:

$$\dot{x}(t) = zx(t)[1 - vx(t)] \tag{1.3}$$

where v and z are positive parameters. Differential equation (1.3) is in separable variables, and can be easily manipulated to write

$$\frac{dx}{x[1 - vx]} = zdt \Leftrightarrow \frac{dx}{x} + \frac{dx}{\varsigma - x} = zdt \tag{1.4}$$

in which $\varsigma = 1/v$. The next step consists in resorting to logarithms, whereby $\ln(x/x_0) - \ln[(\varsigma - x)/(\varsigma - x_0)] = zt$. As a result, solving (1.3) yields

$$x^*(t) = \frac{\varsigma e^{zt} x_0}{\varsigma + (e^{zt} - 1)x_0} \tag{1.5}$$

with the asymptotic limit of the population size being $\lim_{t \to \infty} x^*(t) = \varsigma = 1/v$.

If n state variables $\{x_1(t), x_2(t), ...x_n(t)\}$ are present, the Cauchy problem is defined by the dynamic systems

$$\begin{cases} \dot{x}_1 = f_1(x_1(t), x_2(t), ..., x_n(t)) \\ \dot{x}_2 = f_2(x_1(t), x_2(t), ..., x_n(t)) \\ \quad\quad ... \\ \dot{x}_n = f_n(x_1(t), x_2(t), ..., x_n(t)) \end{cases} \tag{1.6}$$

accompanied by a set of n initial conditions $x_i(0) = x_{i0}$, one for each state. Its solution at a generic time t is a vector $\{x_1^*(t), x_2^*(t), ...x_n^*(t)\}$, and a *steady-state equilibrium point* of system (1.6) – which, in general, may not be unique – is identified by coordinates

$$x^{ss} = \left(x_1^{ss}, x_2^{ss}, ...x_n^{ss}\right) \tag{1.7}$$

If there are only two states, we have a planar system whose phase curves can be drawn in the phase plane (x_1, x_2).

Now admit the presence of a predator harvesting the resource, which has thus become a prey. This extension yields the Lotka-Volterra *prey-predator model* (Lotka, 1925; Volterra, 1931). The variable attached to the prey is x_1 while that attached to the predator is x_2:

$$\begin{cases} \dot{x}_1 = x_1 (\varpi - \beta x_2) \\ \dot{x}_2 = x_2 (\upsilon x_1 - \delta) \end{cases} \tag{1.8}$$

where constants $\{\beta, \delta, \upsilon, \varpi\}$ capture, respectively, (1) the impact of predation (or harvesting activity) on the prey (or resource), (2) the decay rate of the predators; (3) the growth rate of predators given the size of the resource at any time; and (4) the natural growth rate of the resource. The foregoing system has two solutions: $(0, 0)$, involving the extinction of both the preys and predators; and $(x_1^* = \delta/\upsilon, x_2^* = \beta/\varpi)$, with the two species coexisting in a sustainable way in the long run. The peculiar feature of the prey-predator model is that here neither population literally 'controls' anything, the interaction taking place between two state variables only: it is the pressure exerted by the predators' population onto the preys' one that drives the system towards its steady state, reflecting the idea that here what matters is animal instinct or biology rather than choice. As soon as human beings (and firms) assume the role of predators, conscious and deliberate choices take place and at least a control variable must be added to the model. This is what we will see in Chapters 1 and 7.

1.2 Optimal Control Theory

The next step consists in envisaging the realistic possibility that the evolution of states be affected by other variables manoeuvred by one or more agents pursuing explicit objectives. For simplicity, suppose there exist (a) a single state $x(t)$ and (b) a single agent manipulating a single variable; then, (c) define the latter as a *control*, say, $u(t) \in \mathcal{U}$, where $\mathcal{U} \subseteq \mathbb{R}^n$ is the control domain. Additionally, define as (1) $\pi(x(t), u(t), t)$ the instantaneous payoff of the agent controlling $u(t)$, and (2) $f(x(t), u(t), t)$ the function describing the kinematics of state $x(t)$. In the remainder of the chapter, I stipulate that the nature of the model at hand makes it a maximization problem, and that the problem itself is constructed in such a way to meet the concavity conditions.

If the agent controlling $u(t)$ does not discount future payoffs, the control problem defined over a finite time horizon $t \in [0, T]$ consists in

$$\max_{u(t)} \Pi \equiv \int_{t_0}^{T} \pi(x(t), u(t), t) \, dt, \tag{1.9}$$

subject to the state equation

$$\dot{x} = f(x(t), u(t), t) \tag{1.10}$$

and the initial condition $x(t_0) = x_0$, while the terminal condition $x(T)$ is left free, for the moment. Here, $\pi(x(t), u(t), t)$ and $f(x(t), u(t), t)$ are continuously differentiable in $x(t)$, $u(t)$ and t. If the relevant time interval is $[t_0, \infty)$, then the optimal control problem is defined over an infinite time horizon.

We can then define the *Hamiltonian function* as

$$\mathcal{H}(x(t), u(t), \mu(t), t) = \pi(x(t), u(t), t) + \mu(t)f(x(t), u(t), t) \tag{1.11}$$

in which $\mu(t)$ is known as the *costate* or *adjoint variable*. The constrained maximisation problem (1.9–1.10) is formally equivalent to maximising Hamiltonian (1.11) s.t. the initial condition $x(t_0) = x_0$. The solution relies on Pontryagin's *Maximum principle* (Pontryagin et al., 1962; Pontryagin, 1966):[1]

> **The maximum principle** If $(x^*(t), u^*(t))$ is an optimal couple, then there exists a trajectory $\mu : [t_0, T] \to \mathbb{R}$, not identically equal to zero, such that
>
> • $\dot{\mu} = -\partial\mathcal{H}/\partial x$ where $u^*(t)$ is continuous, and
> • the following transversality condition $\mu(T) \geq 0$; $\mu(T)x^*(T) = 0$ is satisfied.

In plain words, solving the Hamiltonian problem requires identifying the optimal instantaneous control $u^*(t)$ and the associated state trajectory. The pair $(x^*(t), u^*(t))$ is called an *optimal couple*. The equation $\dot{\mu} = -\partial\mathcal{H}/\partial x$ is the costate or *adjoint equation*, describing the evolution of the costate. As is the case for the Lagrangian multiplier in static constrained optimization problems, $\mu(t)$ can be thought of as a shadow value (or price). This may be – although not systematically – a sound interpretation of the costate variable that indeed helps intuition in optimal control problems (i.e., with a single agent involved). However, one should refrain from extending this interpretation to differential games, where costates are not, in general, a correct measure of shadow values. More on this very important aspect below.

In general, the value attached to future payoffs is not the same as that of current ones. This is equally true in both economics and politics, and the current debate on environmental values is there to prove the relevance of time discounting.[2] If discounting matters, the constrained optimization problem becomes

$$\max_{u(t)} \Pi \equiv \int_{t_0}^{T} \pi(x(t), u(t), t) e^{-\rho t} dt \tag{1.12}$$

s.t. the same state equation and initial condition as above. In expression (1.12), the payoff flow is discounted at the rate $\rho > 0$. This requires rewriting the Hamiltonian as follows:

---

[1] Parallel to the work of Pontryagin and associates, Isaacs indentified an equivalent instrument, the *tenet of transition* (Isaacs, 1954, 1965), while working at the RAND Corporation.

[2] See, e.g., Stern (2007, 2009). Although the most common notion of discounting holds that the future counts less than the past – which may be intuitive for firms' profits – there are cases in which it would be wise to think the opposite. And this is not only true for environmental issues, in which the welfare of future generations is at stake. It may also apply when it comes to firms' profits (think of the long-run consequences of advertising campaigns of finite duration) and political parties, who could or should attach a value to the aftermath of electoral campaigns. One such example is presented in Chapter 4.

$$\mathcal{H}\left(x\left(t\right),u\left(t\right),\mu\left(t\right),t\right) = \pi\left(x\left(t\right),u\left(t\right),t\right)e^{-\rho t} + \mu\left(t\right)f\left(x\left(t\right),u\left(t\right),t\right) \tag{1.13}$$

or – as it will consistently appear throughout the volume – in its *current value* formulation:

$$\mathcal{H}\left(x\left(t\right),u\left(t\right),\mu\left(t\right),t\right) = e^{-\rho t}\left[\pi\left(x\left(t\right),u\left(t\right),t\right) + \lambda\left(t\right)f\left(x\left(t\right),u\left(t\right),t\right)\right] \tag{1.14}$$

in which $\lambda(t) = \mu(t)e^{\rho t}$ is the *capitalised costate variable*. As a result, the adjoint equation becomes

$$\dot{\lambda}\left(t\right) = -\frac{\partial\mathcal{H}\left(\cdot\right)}{\partial x\left(t\right)} + \rho\lambda\left(t\right) \tag{1.15}$$

while the first-order condition (FOC) w.r.t. the control variable is

$$\frac{\partial\mathcal{H}\left(\cdot\right)}{\partial u\left(t\right)} = e^{-\rho t}\left[\frac{\partial\pi\left(\cdot\right)}{\partial u\left(t\right)} + \lambda\left(t\right)\cdot\frac{\partial f\left(\cdot\right)}{\partial u\left(t\right)}\right] = 0 \tag{1.16}$$

The solution derived from conditions (1.15–1.16) must satisfy the transversality condition $\lim_{t\to\infty} x(t)\lambda(t)e^{-\rho t} = 0$.

Before proceeding, a short digression on games played over a finite horizon is in order. If $t \in [0, T]$, the terminal payoff at date T becomes relevant. Call it the *salvage value* and define it as $\mathcal{S}\left(x\left(T\right)\right)$, continuous and differentiable w.r.t. the state. The transversality condition becomes

$$\mu\left(T\right) = \frac{\partial\mathcal{S}\left(\cdot\right)}{\partial x}\cdot x\left(T\right) \tag{1.17}$$

and becomes $\mu\left(T\right) = 0$ if the salvage value is nil or, in the limit, as T tends to infinity. Condition (1.17) tells that the costate cannot be nil at T if there exists a *bequest*, whose interpretation depends on the nature of the specific problem being modelled. For instance, firms may activate investment projects of finite duration, either in advertising, capacity or R&D. Another evident example is that political parties cyclically invest in electoral campaigns whose duration is fixed and known to everybody, including voters. Chapter 4 contains a game of advertising for sale expansion based on this idea.

We can revert to the solution of the optimal control problem. Henceforth I will drop the explicit indication of the time argument, to shorten expressions and simplify the exposition. Manipulating appropriately necessary conditions (1.15–1.16) and the state equation (1.10), one can obtain the control equation

$$\dot{u} = g\left(x, u\right) \tag{1.18}$$

describing the evolution of $u\left(t\right)$. Taken together, (1.10) and (1.18) constitute the state-control system

$$\begin{cases} \dot{x} = f\left(x, u\right) \\ \dot{u} = g\left(x, u\right) \end{cases} \tag{1.19}$$

describing the dynamics of the optimal control model, and solving (1.19) yields the trajectories of state and control variables in the (x, u) space (plane, if – as here – we have two variables only). If (1.19) is not integrable, one has to linearise the system around the steady state(s) and study the properties of the following 2×2 *Jacobian matrix*:

$$
J =
\begin{bmatrix}
\dfrac{\partial f\,(\cdot)}{\partial x} & \dfrac{\partial f\,(\cdot)}{\partial u} \\[2ex]
\dfrac{\partial g\,(\cdot)}{\partial x} & \dfrac{\partial g\,(\cdot)}{\partial u}
\end{bmatrix}
\tag{1.20}
$$

1.2.1　Sketch of the Stability Analysis

The stability properties of the state-control system (1.19) and its stationary points depend on two characteristics (sign and size) of the trace $\mathcal{T}\,(J)$ and determinant $\Delta\,(J)$ of the Jacobian matrix (1.20). If

$$
\Delta\,(J) = \frac{\partial f\,(\cdot)}{\partial x} \cdot \frac{\partial g\,(\cdot)}{\partial u} - \frac{\partial f\,(\cdot)}{\partial u} \cdot \frac{\partial g\,(\cdot)}{\partial x} < 0
\tag{1.21}
$$

we have a saddle. That is, the negativity of the determinant is a sufficient condition for the dynamic system to produce a saddle, independently of the sign of the trace of the Jacobian matrix,

$$
\mathcal{T}\,(J) = \frac{\partial f\,(\cdot)}{\partial x} + \frac{\partial g\,(\cdot)}{\partial u}
\tag{1.22}
$$

The assessment of stability (or instability) is a slightly more involved exercise when the determinant is positive. In this case, a stationary point can be

- a stable node, if $\mathcal{T}\,(J) < 0$ and $\Delta\,(J) \in \left(0, \mathcal{T}^2\,(J)\,/4\right]$;
- an unstable node, if $\mathcal{T}\,(J) > 0$ and $\Delta\,(J) \in \left(0, \mathcal{T}^2\,(J)\,/4\right]$;
- a stable focus, if $\mathcal{T}\,(J) < 0$ and $\Delta\,(J) > \mathcal{T}^2\,(J)\,/4$;
- an unstable focus, if $\mathcal{T}\,(J) > 0$ and $\Delta\,(J) > \mathcal{T}^2\,(J)\,/4$.

The above list includes the most frequent cases (which we will encounter in the remainder of the book) but is not exhaustive. A center is an additional type of steady state, whose nature is such that the characteristic polynomial of the Jacobian matrix admits two complex eigenvalues whose real part is nil. An example of center is one of the steady-state points generated by the Verhulst–Lotka–Volterra model, with coordinates $\left(x_1^* = \delta/\upsilon, x_2^* = \beta/\varpi\right)$.

1.3　Dynamic Programming

The alternative technique characterising the *dynamic programming approach* is due to the work of Bellman (1957). This approach permits to solve the entire family of control problems by solving one of them. It does so by introducing the so-called *optimal value function*, assigning the optimal value to each one of many control problems belonging to the same family, and using a solution method based on Bellman's *optimality principle*. To understand the optimality principle, consider the following argument.

Examine a dynamic problem defined over $t \in [0, T]$. Then eliminate part of the time horizon, say, $[0, \tilde{t}]$, with $\tilde{t} < T$. If the solution (or trajectory of the system) solving the initial problem defined for $t \in [0, T]$ is indeed optimal, its portion concerning the residual time interval $[\tilde{t}, T]$ must remain optimal when evaluated anew over such residual time horizon, from $\tilde{t}$ onwards. This means two related and equally important things:

- the optimal solution (trajectory) has to be independent of initial conditions,
- and must be *strongly time consistent*, i.e., robust to a change in the values of initial conditions.

These two requirements, which indeed are satisfied by the dynamic programming approach, amount to saying that the solutions engendered by the optimality principle are subgame (or Markov) perfect. In fact, one can use strong time consistency, Markov perfection or subgame perfection to indicate the same property.

Now we can turn to the solution method. Take $t \in [\tilde{t}, T]$ and consider the same objective functional as in the Hamiltonian we have examined earlier, $\Pi = \int_{\tilde{t}}^{T} \pi(x(s), u(s), s) e^{-\rho s} ds$. Then define $V(x, t)$ as the value function of the problem at hand. The optimal value function $V^*(x, t)$ must solve the Hamilton–Jacobi–Bellman (HJB) equation

$$-\frac{\partial V(\cdot)}{\partial t} + \rho V(\cdot) = \max_u \left\{ \pi(\cdot) + \frac{\partial V(\cdot)}{\partial x} \cdot f(\cdot) \right\} \qquad (1.23)$$

which, more often than not, is simply labelled as the *Bellman equation*. If the time horizon stretches to doomsday $(T \to +\infty)$, one only needs to find $V^*(x)$ and the Bellman equation becomes[3]

$$\rho V(\cdot) = \max_u \left\{ \pi(\cdot) + \frac{\partial V(\cdot)}{\partial x} \cdot f(\cdot) \right\} \qquad (1.24)$$

The solution procedure consists in writing the FOC w.r.t. the control variable,

$$\frac{\partial [\pi(\cdot) + f(\cdot) \cdot \partial V(\cdot) / \partial x]}{\partial u} = 0 \qquad (1.25)$$

which (possibly implicitly) identifies the optimal control, $u^*(x)$. If equation (1.25) is explicitly solvable, one can then substitute the expression of the optimal control into either (1.23) or (1.24), so that the Bellman equation is now a function of the state variable only, if the problem is autonomous (otherwise, also, the time argument will pop up explicitly).

In general, we cannot expect to attain a fully analytical solution of either (1.23) or (1.24), unless a reasonable guess about the functional form of the value function can be made. One class of problems in which this is the case is that consisting of linear-quadratic (LQ) models. These are identified by checking that (1) the instantaneous payoff $\pi(\cdot)$ be quadratic in state and control variables, and (2) the evolution of the state (i.e., $f(\cdot)$) be linear in state(s) and control(s). If so, then we may guess that the

---

[3] This holds only if the problem at hand is time-autonomous (as will consistently be the case throughout the book). This requires the functional forms of both $\pi(\cdot)$ and $f(\cdot)$ to be independent of time.

value function itself is linear-quadratic in the state variable, and can be written as $V(x) = \epsilon_1 x^2 + \epsilon_2 x + \epsilon_3$ – where, if the problem is autonomous, the time argument does not explicitly appear.

If the problem is autonomous and the model is linear-quadratic, the Bellman equation will contain the vector of undetermined parameters $\{\epsilon_1, \epsilon_2, \epsilon_3\}$ appearing in the value function and the state variable x, so that the Bellman equation (1.23) can be rewritten in the following form:

$$x^2 \cdot g(\epsilon) + x \cdot h(\epsilon) + \ell(\epsilon) = 0 \qquad (1.26)$$

where polynomials $g(\epsilon)$, $h(\epsilon)$ and $\ell(\epsilon)$ contain the vector of undetermined parameters (or just some of them, not necessarily all). Equation (1.26) generates a system of three equations

$$g(\epsilon) = 0; \; h(\epsilon) = 0; \; \ell(\epsilon) = 0 \qquad (1.27)$$

which has to be solved w.r.t. $\{\epsilon_1, \epsilon_2, \epsilon_3\}$. Given a model defined in LQ form, the above system yields two solutions consisting of two different triples $\{\epsilon_{1i}^*, \epsilon_{2i}^*, \epsilon_{3i}^*\}$, $i = I, II$, one stable and the other unstable, although both strongly time consistent. Both of them will be linear in the state x, and therefore are usually labelled as *linear feedback solutions*, the meaning of feedback being that they account for the feedback effect of state(s) onto optimal control(s) at any time t of the relevant time span.[4] Each of these feedback solutions can also be differentiated w.r.t. time to yield the control dynamics.

Once the stable solution has been singled out and the corresponding triple $\{\epsilon_{1i}^*, \epsilon_{2i}^*, \epsilon_{3i}^*\}$ has been substituted back into the value function, this identifies the optimal value function $V^*(x)$, and the Bellman equation is satisfied. Then, the last step consists in solving the differential equation governing the motion of the state variable to fully characterise the steady state point(s).

Before proceeding to the description of differential games, an additional remark is in order concerning the correspondence between the alternative solutions of the same dynamic model with a single agent through optimal control theory and dynamic programming, respectively. To help visualize ideas, suppose the model has a linear-quadratic form. One of the linear feedback solutions generated by the Bellman equation will reproduce the open-loop one generated by the Hamiltonian, but this is not necessarily the stable one. Indeed, we will see both cases in the models reviewed in the next chapter. Now, the problem here is that if the solution of the optimal control problem based on the Hamiltonian function is unstable, this does not imply that the model as such is affected by instability, as there may exist another solution delivered by the dynamic programming approach which is stable but remains out of reach when solving the Hamiltonian formulation of the same problem. I will say more on this and related matter in the remainder of the chapter.

---

[4] As far as I know, the source of this terminology has a lot to do with electrical and electronical engineering. Feedback is used in audio amplifiers by creating loops feeding back the signal from the power section to the preamplifier section, so as to improve the control of the signal reaching the loudspeakers. As we shall see, loops and feedbacks are extremely relevant as soon as it comes to differential games, where I will carefully discuss the meaning of this terminology in order to avoid risky misunderstandings.

1.4 Differential Games with Simultaneous Play

When the model admits the presence of several agents, it becomes a dynamic game – specifically, since we are considering differential equations, a differential game. Let $\mathcal{N} \equiv \{1, 2, 3, ...n\}$ identify the set of players, and suppose $t \in [0, \infty)$.[5] Additionally, $x_i(t) \in \mathcal{X}$ and $u_i(t) \in \mathcal{U}$ define, respectively, player i's state and control variables. The dynamics of $x_i(t)$ is described by the ith state equation

$$\dot{x}_i(t) = f_i(\mathbf{x}(t), \mathbf{u}(t)) \tag{1.28}$$

where $\mathbf{x}(t) \equiv \{x_1(t), x_2(t), ...x_n(t)\}$ and $\mathbf{u}(t) \equiv \{u_1(t), u_2(t), ...u_n(t)\}$ are the vectors of state and control variables at any instant t. Equation (1.28) says that, in general case, one may expect the dynamics of the ith state variable to be affected by all states and controls. Of course, this does not consistently hold true throughout the entire spectrum of games formalising relevant issues in economics, politics and the social sciences in general. Then, one can easily define the vector of initial conditions as $\mathbf{x}(0) \equiv \{x_1(0), x_2(0), ...x_n(0)\} = \mathbf{x}_0$.

Let the instantaneous payoff function of player i be

$$\pi_i(t) = \pi_i(x_i(t), \mathbf{x}_{-i}(t), u_i(t), \mathbf{u}_{-i}(t), t), \tag{1.29}$$

where $\mathbf{x}_{-i}(t)$ and $\mathbf{u}_{-i}(t)$ are, respectively, the vectors of the $n-1$ states and $n-1$ controls pertaining to each player $j \neq i$. Player i's objective is then to maximise the discounted flow of payoffs

$$\Pi_i \equiv \int_0^\infty \pi_i(\cdot)e^{-\rho t}dt \tag{1.30}$$

w.r.t. $u_i(t)$, subject to the set of n constraints (1.28), given the vector of initial conditions $\mathbf{x}_0$ on states, which is assumed to be known to all players alike. All of them use the common and constant discount rate $\rho > 0$.

The optimal strategy defined by each player depends on the information structure characterising the game. To avoid misunderstandings, note that, in general, we will examine games with symmetric and complete information, and 'information structure' has a meaning which is specific to the context and nature of dynamic analysis.

We will consider three different information structures, to which three different equilibrium concepts are associated:

Definition 1.a (Open-loop information)   *Under open-loop information, the optimal control is $u_i^* = u_i^*(t)$. This means that it is conditional on current time only, and depends on initial conditions $\mathbf{x}_0$.*

In plain words, the adoption of open-loop rules implies that the player decides what to do on the basis of calendar time, regardless of the game's past history and the current values of state variables.

---

[5] The game can be reformulated in discrete time without significantly affecting its qualitative properties. For further details, see Başar and Olsder (1982, 1995[2]).

Definition 1.b (Closed-loop memoryless information)   *Under closed-loop memoryless information, $u_i^* = u_i^*(t, \mathbf{x}(t), \mathbf{x}_0)$. This means that the closed-loop memoryless control depends on time, states and initial conditions. Additionally, $u_i^* = u_i^*(t, \mathbf{x}(t), \mathbf{x}_0)$ must be continuous in t and uniformly Lipschitz in the state vector at any t during the game.*

Definition 1.c (Feedback information)   *Under feedback information, $u_i^* = u_i^*(t, \mathbf{x}(t))$. This means that the feedback strategy depends on time and states at any instant $t > 0$, but not initial conditions $\mathbf{x}_0$. Additionally, the feedback control must be continuous in t and uniformly Lipschitz in $\mathbf{x}(t)$ throughout the game.*

Now consider the difference between open-loop, memoryless closed-loop and feedback information. The first implies that a player decides the entire plan of actions at the initial date and then strictly follows it throughout the time horizon of the game. This implies that one must rely on some commitment device (or technology) to fulfil this sort of requirement, without looking at the evolution of the system to see whether the initial plan remains indeed optimal at any intermediate date $\hat{t} \in [0, \infty)$. I'm asking for a little patience on the part of the reader, before delving into the implications of this aspect of open-loop rules.

Apparently, memoryless closed-loop information solves this problem by requiring players to take into account the states (or stocks) at any point in time. However, the resulting strategy still depends on initial conditions, and therefore any change in the latter implies changes in the resulting closed-loop strategies.

This is where feedback information kicks in, by removing the requirement concerning the role of initial conditions in the design of players' strategies. This might seem a matter of detail, but it is not, as it renders feedback strategies subgame perfect while open-loop and memoryless closed-loop ones are not so, in general (the special cases where this, instead, is true, will be reviewed later here).

I would also like to draw your attention to a terminological misunderstanding affecting here and there the extant literature (in particular, applications of differential game theory), where 'feedback' and 'closed-loop' attributes are somewhat liberally used as synonymous, while in fact they are not if one wants to stick to the appropriate definitions of these two types of information structures. Strictly speaking, feedback strategies are those characterised by solving the HJB equation of a dynamic problem, while closed-loop strategies are all those incorporating loops between states and controls. Hence, a feedback strategy is a closed-loop one, while the opposite is not necessarily true.[6]

Now we can look at the solution concept. Suppose players enjoy complete, symmetric and imperfect information at any point in time, but information becomes complete between any two points in time, i.e., instant after instant. Hence, we are saying that moves are simultaneous at any time t, and at that instant all players correctly observe the past history of the game. The resulting definition of Nash equilibrium for a differential game is the following:

---

[6] Moreover, observe that closed-loop information may take several forms, more or less sophisticated and not equivalent to each other. Here I am only considering the memoryless specification, but there also exist perfect and imperfect closed-loop rules (see Başar and Olsder, 1982, chapter 5).

Definition 1.d (Nash equilibrium) *Given the information structure, a strategy profile $\left(u_1^N, u_2^N, ...u_i^N, ...u_n^N\right)$, with $u_i^N \in \mathcal{U}$ for all $i \in \mathcal{N}$, is a Nash equilibrium if and only if*

$$\Pi_i \left(u_1^N, u_2^N, ...u_i^N, ...u_n^N\right) \geq \Pi_i \left(u_1^N, u_2^N, ...u_i, ...u_n^N\right)$$

for all $u_i \neq u_i^N, u_i \in \mathcal{U}$ and for all $i \in \mathcal{N}$.

Hence, the definition is analogous to the one we are accustomed with in static games, except that the Nash equilibrium will be an open-loop, a closed-loop or a feedback one according to the nature of the information stipulated in the initial definition of the setup.

Now we can go back to the implications of open-loop rules and the necessity to sustain the resulting plan through commitments, as this is a key aspect to understand subgame perfection in differential games. This brings us to the discussion of the concept of *time consistency*. In a nutshell, a strategy profile is time consistent if none of the players has any incentive, at any date during the game, to deviate from the strategy previously chosen for that date. At a closer look, one discovers that subgame perfection is equivalent to *strong* time consistency. To understand why, we have to examine the definitions of *weak* and *strong* time consistency:

Definition 1.e (Weak time consistency) *Consider a game $\mathfrak{G}(0, \infty)$ played over $t = [0, \infty)$ and examine the trajectories of the state variables $x(t)$ generated by the vector of Nash equilibrium strategies $u^N(t)$. If the truncated plans $u^N(T)$ pertaining to the time interval $t = [T, \infty)$, with $T \in (0, \infty)$, identify a Nash equilibrium also for the truncated game $\mathfrak{G}(T, \infty)$ starting from $t = T$ and from the set of initial conditions x_T, then the equilibrium $u^N(t)$ is weakly time consistent.*

Definition 1.f (Strong time consistency) *Consider a game $\mathfrak{G}(0, \infty)$ played over $t = [0, \infty)$ and examine the trajectories of the state variables $x(t)$ generated by the vector of Nash equilibrium strategies $u^N(t)$. If the truncated plans $u^N(T)$ pertaining to the time interval $t = [T, \infty)$, with $T \in (0, \infty)$, identify a Nash equilibrium also for the truncated game $\mathfrak{G}(T, \infty)$ starting from $t = T$, regardless of the set of initial conditions x_T, then the equilibrium $u^N(t)$ is strongly time consistent.*

From Definition 1.f, it appears that an equilibrium is strongly time consistent only if all players take into account their rival's actions at all times. This is indeed the requirement posed by feedback information and subgame perfection. Conversely, in general, Definition 1.e covers the cases of open-loop and memoryless closed-loop information, where initial conditions – no matter whether for the complete game or any truncation thereof – do matter in evaluating the robustness of the players' plans. As a result, open-loop and closed-loop rules give rise to weakly time-consistent equilibria which – again, in general – will not be subgame perfect.

Another way of reading the requirements contained in the above definitions is to note that while weak time consistency requires the truncated plan $u^N(T)$ to be a Nash equilibrium plan along the equilibrium trajectory of states from T onwards, strong time consistency requires $u^N(t)$ to accomplish the same task along any other possible trajectory of states as well. Using the jargon of static multistage games, $u^N(t)$ is weakly time consistent if it just produces a Nash equilibrium in the subgame (or, subhistory) starting at T, while it is also strongly time consistent if it does so in any possible subgame (or, subhistory) starting at the same date. In the latter case, $\mathbf{u}^N(t)$ is subgame perfect.

More can be grasped about the relationship between time consistency and subgame perfection in differential games under simultaneous moves, by looking at the methods one should follow to solve them under different information structures. If the solution concept is the open-loop Nash equilibrium, the current value Hamiltonian of player i writes as follows:

$$\mathcal{H}_i(\cdot) \equiv e^{-\rho t}\left[\pi_i\left(x_i(t), \mathbf{x}_{-i}(t), u_i(t), \mathbf{u}_{-i}(t)\right) + \lambda_{ii}(t) \cdot f_i\left(\mathbf{x}(t), \mathbf{u}(t)\right)\right.$$

$$\left. + \sum_{j \neq i} \lambda_{ij}(t) \cdot f_j\left(\mathbf{x}(t), \mathbf{u}(t)\right)\right], \tag{1.31}$$

where $\lambda_{ij}(t) = \mu_{ij}(t)e^{\rho t}$ is the capitalised costate variable pertaining to the state variable $x_j(t)$. Here we have the vector of initial conditions $\mathbf{x}_0$ and n transversality conditions $\lim_{t \to \infty} x(t)\lambda_{ij}(t)e^{-\rho t} = 0$.

The solution follows the same steps as in Section 1.2, with the same FOC, adjoint and transversality conditions, except that we have n FOCs on controls, n^2 costate equations and n transversality conditions. Manipulating necessary conditions, one derives the set of control dynamics, and if the model admits the imposition of symmetry across the population of players, one may end up with a state-control system consisting of two differential equations. This seemingly large amount of simplicity does not imply that the open-loop game has to be labelled as simplistic, and we should also refrain from the temptation of thinking that it is essentially non-strategic or 'static', an impression which also pops up sometimes in relation to open-loop solutions. It may be 'quasi-static' in the sense that the open-loop Nash equilibrium (or one of them, as there can be many) replicates the one delivered by the static version of the same game. There are cases where this happens literally, or taking appropriate limits of equilibrium controls w.r.t. time discounting, for instance. However, we have to keep in mind that, even under naive open-loop rules, the differential game describes the consequences of players' actions on states via the set of differential equations (1.28), which, by definition, do not appear in static games. We will encounter examples of quasi-static differential games and these will allow us to appreciate in much deeper details the meaning of this synthetic defense of their dignity.

The adoption of the closed-loop memoryless information structure leaves the FOC on player i's control unmodified, of course, while affecting the whole set of adjoint equations:

$$-\frac{\partial \mathcal{H}_i}{\partial x_j} - \sum_{\ell \neq j} \frac{\partial \mathcal{H}_i}{\partial u_\ell} \cdot \frac{\partial u_\ell^*}{\partial x_j} = \frac{d\lambda_{ij}}{dt} - \rho\lambda_{ij}, \forall j = 1, 2, \dots n; \tag{1.32}$$

these being accompanied by initial conditions $\mathbf{x}_0$ and transversality conditions. Each of the state-control loops

$$\frac{\partial \mathcal{H}_i}{\partial u_\ell} \cdot \frac{\partial u_\ell^*}{\partial x_j} \tag{1.33}$$

in (1.32) grasps the effect of a change in every single state onto every control variables at any time t. Observe that the term $(\partial \mathcal{H}_i/\partial u_i) \cdot (\partial u_\ell^*/\partial x_j)$ is enveloped out thanks to the FOC. The relevant expression of the optimal instantaneous control $u_\ell^*(t)$ to be differentiated w.r.t. x_j obtains from the solution of FOCs.

If the game structure is such that the expression in (1.33) is zero for all ℓ, because either $\partial \mathcal{H}_i/\partial u_\ell = 0$ or $\partial u_\ell^*/\partial x_j = 0$, then the closed-loop memoryless solution coincides with the open-loop one. However, this fact does not imply that either the former or the latter qualify as Markov or subgame perfect (i.e., strongly time consistent), as they still depend on initial conditions and therefore do not generate feedback controls.

1.4.1   Feedback Solutions under Open-Loop Information

The possible arising of subgame perfect controls under open-loop information has intuitively attracted a large amount of efforts. Indeed, that the identification of classes of differential games delivering strongly time-consistent open-loop equilibria is of the highest value becomes evident as soon as one dwells upon the problem posed by solving feedback games whose form is not linear-quadratic. Taken together, all of these classes fall into the group of *perfect games* (Mehlmann, 1988, pp. 129–39).

The first class of games endowed with this property is that of gathering *trilinear games*, identified by Clemhout and Wan (1974). A differential game is trilinear iff each player's Hamiltonian is linear in states and costates, and the payoff function in the Hamiltonian is also linear (cf. Dockner *et al.*, 1985). This implies "that the state variables are absent from the costate system and the choice of controls is independent of the value of $\mathbf{x}$ (the state variables)" (Clemhout and Wan, 1979, p. 19).

The second class is that of *linear state games*, where the Hamiltonian function is linear in the state variables but not in controls. This suffices to ensure that states will not appear in adjoint equations. But there is more to it, as state linearity entails, by the way, a very important consequence that will emerge several times in the next chapters: a linear-quadratic game may simultaneously be a linear state one. To see why, consider the following two-player game. Player i's instantaneous payoff function is $\pi_i = \left(1 - u_i \pm u_j\right) u_i$ – the sign in front of the rival's control is irrelevant here – and there exists a single state whose dynamics is $\dot{x} = u_i + u_j - \delta x$, where $\delta > 0$ is its constant decay rate. Now, the payoff and state equations being, respectively, quadratic in controls (only) and linear in state and controls, the present structure qualifies as both a linear state game and a linear-quadratic one at the same time. This fact, in turn, has an important implication as to the solutions, because the open-loop equilibrium is a degenerate feedback one, but not the only feedback equilibrium, as there will be others generated by the Bellman equation. Finally, the open-loop solution, although subgame perfect, may be unstable, in which case the stable one must be characterised solving through the method of dynamic programming. In the remainder of this section, to simplify the matter, I will assume there exists a single state variable. The extension of the ensuing arguments to the general case of several states is quite straightforward.

The third class with the same property contains exponential games (Reinganum, 1982), where the state equation is $\dot{x} = f(\mathbf{u})$, i.e., the state dynamics depends on controls but not on the state itself, which instead appear in the discounted payoff flow:

$$\Pi_i = \int_0^T e^{-x} \pi_i(\mathbf{u}) \, e^{-\rho t} dt \qquad (1.34)$$

Although at first sight this may sound counterintuitive, this structure is equivalent to a linear state game. To check that this is true, it suffices to pose $e^{-x} \equiv y$, which becomes the new state variable, and then observe that $\dot{y} = -y\dot{x} = -yf(\mathbf{u})$, so that (1.34) rewrites as follows:

$$\Pi_i = \int_0^T y\pi_i(\mathbf{u}) \, e^{-\rho t} dt \qquad (1.35)$$

which has a state linear form, and therefore ensures subgame perfection under open-loop rules. As we shall see in Chapter 6, this setup is very important in the analysis of innovation races.

The fourth class of perfect games is that of the so-called *state-separable games* (Dockner *et al.*, 1985) which satisfy the following properties:

$$\left. \frac{\partial^2 \mathcal{H}_i}{\partial u_i \partial x} \right|_{\frac{\partial \mathcal{H}_i}{\partial u_i} = 0} = 0 \qquad (1.36)$$

$$\frac{\partial^2 \mathcal{H}_i}{\partial x_j^2} = 0 \qquad (1.37)$$

Condition (1.36) says that the cross effect (i.e., the loop between state and control) must be nil in correspondence of the optimal control obtained from the FOC. Essentially, it requires that the maximised Hamiltonian be independent of the state variable. Condition (1.37) requires the Hamiltonian to be state-linear. Obviously, this class encompasses (but is not limited to) trilinear and linear state games.

The largest and, in a sense, most loosely defined class is that of *state-redundant games* (Fershtman, 1987), imposing the requirement

$$\left. \frac{\partial^2 \mathcal{H}_i}{\partial u_i \partial x} \right|_{\lambda_i = \lambda_i^*} = 0 \qquad (1.38)$$

That is, the FOC on player i's control must not depend on the state after plugging back into the Hamiltonian itself the expression of the optimal costate λ_i^*, which, in such a case, qualifies as the 'real' shadow price. That is, the shadow price is correctly measured by both the costate variable and the partial derivative of the value function, as the they coincide.[7] For more on this aspect, see also Caputo (2007). As shown by Mehlmann and Willing (1983), any perfect game either is state-redundant or can be transformed into a state-redundant form. Examples of state-separable and state-redundant games

---

[7] For an example meeting this property, see the exposition concerning the existence and construction of potential functions in differential games contained in Chapter 3.

possessing properties (1.36–1.37) or (1.38) are illustrated in Chapters 2 and 4, as well as elsewhere in the book.

1.4.2   The Main Route: Feedback Games

In most of the cases, open-loop, closed-loop memoryless and feedback solutions differ from each other. When this happens, using the dynamic programming approach is the only way of attaining strongly time-consistent or subgame perfect strategies. Assuming the problem is autonomous, player i's Bellman equation is the following

$$\rho V_i(\mathbf{x}) = \max_{u \in \mathcal{U}} \left\{ \pi(\cdot) + \frac{\partial V_i(\mathbf{x})}{\partial x_i} \cdot f_i(\cdot) + \sum_{j \neq i} \frac{\partial V_i(\mathbf{x})}{\partial x_j} \cdot f_j(\cdot) \right\}. \tag{1.39}$$

If, additionally, it is linear-quadratic, then we may guess the form

$$V_i(\mathbf{x}) = \epsilon_{1ii} x_i^2 + \sum_{j \neq i} \epsilon_{1ij} x_j^2 + \sum_{j \neq i} \epsilon_{2ij} x_i x_j + \epsilon_{3ii} x_i + \sum_{j \neq i} \epsilon_{3ij} x_j + \epsilon_{4i} \tag{1.40}$$

for the value function, and then follow the same method illustrated above for the single-agent problem. In the linear-quadratic case, if the model can accomodate full symmetry, this method yields a couple of feedback controls which are linear in state(s) and therefore are labelled as *linear feedback strategies*. Intuitively, should the game be a linear state one, then the obvious and correct guess would be to conjecture a linear value function and then verify that it works. Yet, the linear form can be appropriate even in cases where the model is not state linear and, nonetheless, the game is state-redundant. One such framework is an oligopoly with advertising for goodwill which appears in Chapter 4.

There exists a special framework (Sethi and Thompson, 1981) in which we can formulate a correct guess, for which we actually lack a convincing explanation. This case envisages a model where the instantaneous payoff is linear in a state common to all players and quadratic in the control of player i, something like $\pi_i = ax - bu_i^2$, with parameters $a, b > 0$, while the state equation is

$$\dot{x} = \sqrt{x} \sum_{i=1}^{n} u_i + u_2 - \delta x \tag{1.41}$$

For simplicity, we may set $n = 2$. The conjecture about the value function is $V_i = \epsilon_{1i} x + \epsilon_{2i}$, $i = 1, 2$, and it works. Imposing symmetry on controls after the derivation of FOCs, and substituting the Nash equilibrium control $u^N = \epsilon_1 \sqrt{x}/(2b)$, the Bellman equation of the individual player simplifies as follows:

$$\frac{4b\epsilon_1 \left[(\delta + \rho) x + \epsilon_2 \rho \right] - x \left(4ab + \epsilon_1^2 \right)}{4b} = 0 \tag{1.42}$$

which, indeed, is linear in the state variable and requires the solution of the system

$$4b\epsilon_2 \rho = 0$$
$$4ab + \epsilon_1 \left[3\epsilon_1 - 4b(\delta + \rho) \right] = 0 \tag{1.43}$$

delivering $\epsilon_2 = 0$ and

$$\epsilon_1 = \frac{2\left[b\left(\delta + \rho\right) \pm \sqrt{b\left(b\left(\delta + \rho\right)^2 - 3a\right)}\right]}{3} \tag{1.44}$$

Clearly, $\epsilon_1 \in R$ for all $a < b\left(\delta + \rho\right)^2/3$. This example is 'trivial', since $\epsilon_2 = 0$, but the present structure has a major role in a dominant stream of research on advertising, as we shall see in Chapter 4.

To appropriately conclude this brief illustration of the technique at the basis of the solution of feedback games, one has to account for the existence of infinitely many *nonlinear feedback solutions*, whose presence is revealed through the following method. Consider a differential two-player game in which a single state evolves following

$$\dot{x} = u_i + u_2 - \delta x \tag{1.45}$$

and the individual payoff function is $\pi_i = \left(a - u_i - u_j\right)u_i - bx^2$. As a result, the Bellman equation of i is

$$\rho V_i(x) = \max_{u \in \mathcal{U}} \left\{\left(a - u_i - u_j\right)u_i - bx^2 + V_i'(x) \cdot (u_i + u_2 - \delta x)\right\} \tag{1.46}$$

where $V_i'(x) = \partial V_i(x)/\partial x$, and the FOC w.r.t. u_i is

$$a - 2u_i - u_j + V'(x) = 0 \tag{1.47}$$

Now, given the linear quadratic form of the model, one might take the route outlined above, guess a linear-quadratic form for the value function and characterise linear feedback strategies. However, there is an alternative route allowing one to discover nonlinear ones. This consists in imposing symmetry on controls and solve the above FOC w.r.t. the partial derivative of the value function. Plugging $V'(x) = 3u - a$ back into (1.46), the Bellman equation becomes

$$\rho V(x) - a(u + \delta x) + u(2u + 3\delta x) + bx^2 = 0 \tag{1.48}$$

and this can be solved w.r.t. the control variable, to obtain

$$u_{NLF}^* = \frac{a - 3\delta x}{4} \pm \frac{\sqrt{a(a + 2\delta x) + x^2\left(9\delta^2 - 8b\right) - 8rV(x)}}{4} \tag{1.49}$$

The expression in (1.49) is the sum of two components, one linear and the other nonlinear in x. The latter generates a continuum of nonlinear feedback strategies, and this fact is independent of discounting, as even assuming it away (which implies that the value function does not appear in the square root), the nonlinear component remains there. A detailed analysis of the game without discounting is in Haurie *et al.* (2012, pp. 271–74). Nonlinear strategies with discounting are characterised in games illustrated in Chapters 2 and 7.

1.5   Stackelberg Games

The literature in economics and the social sciences in general is teeming with hierarchical solutions à la Stackelberg (1934), where the best reply of the follower enters the optimization problem of the leader as a constraint. The drawback of this sequential play structure is that it is bound to generate time inconsistency in most cases. Note that this is already evident in static games: in the linear Cournot duopoly model, the Stackelberg solution is the tangency point between the leader's most profitable isoprofit curve and the follower's linear reaction function, but this entails that the leader has an incentive to deviate towards her/his own reaction function. That is, the Cournot–Stackelberg outcome is unstable, and this fact – if one stretches the static model to get a hint of the underlying dynamics – directly points at the arising of time inconsistency. This argument can be rephrased in the following terms. Subgame perfection requires a strategy profile yielding a Nash equilibrium in each and every proper subgame of the game under examination, attained through backward induction under perfect information. In turn, the attainment of a Nash equilibrium requires all players to be along their respective best reply functions. Now, the Stackelberg framework is one in which there are both sequential play (and therefore perfect information, the leader's action being visible to the follower before the latter chooses a strategy) and backward induction. Yet, the last requirement is not fulfilled, as the leader locates oneself along the rival's best reply. Hence, the Stackelberg outcome is not a Nash equilibrium, a feature which clarifies the source of its instability (in static games) and time inconsistency (in dynamic ones, regardless of whether we treat time as discrete or continuous).

When it comes to differential games, the relationship between the nature of information and time consistency under sequential play becomes even more crucial than it is under simultaneous play. In fact, with a few relevant exceptions which will be explored in Chapter 9, open-loop Stackelberg games are systematically affected by *time inconsistency*, and therefore are not credible. To see why, consider the simplest setup with two players, 1 and 2, interacting over an infinite horizon. Each of them has a single control $u_i(t)$, and the model features just one state, $x(t)$. Suppose 1 is the leader and 2 is the follower. At $t = 0$, the leader chooses the control path $u_1(t)$. Assuming that the follower believes $u_1(t, x_0)$ will actually be implemented by the leader, she/he has to choose $u_2(t)$ to maximise the discounted payoff flow

$$\Pi_2 = \int_0^\infty \pi_2(\bar{u}_1, u_2, x)e^{-\rho t}dt \tag{1.50}$$

under the constraint $\dot{x} = f(\bar{u}_1, u_2, x)$, where the upper bar mnemonics for the fact that the leader's control plan is *given* and *observable*. Under open-loop information, this means that the relevant Hamiltonian function of the follower is

$$\mathcal{H}_2 = e^{-\rho t}\left[\pi_2(\bar{u}_1, u_2, x) + \lambda_2 f(\bar{u}_1, u_2, x)\right] \tag{1.51}$$

from which we have

$$\frac{\partial \mathcal{H}_2}{\partial u_2} = 0 \tag{1.52}$$

$$\dot{\lambda}_2 = -\frac{\partial \mathcal{H}_2}{\partial x} + \rho \lambda_2 \tag{1.53}$$

both entering the leader's problem together with the state equation, as additional constraint. In particular, the solution to (1.52), i.e., the follower's best reply $u_2^* (\bar{u}_1, \lambda, x)$, must be substituted into the leader's Hamiltonian, while (1.53) is added up to the leader's problem and is indeed treated as an additional state equation. Hence, the leader must choose u_1 to maximise

$$\mathcal{H}_1 = e^{-\rho t} \left[\pi_1 (u_1, u_2^*, x) + \lambda_{11} f \left(u_1, u_2^*, x \right) + \lambda_{12} \lambda_2 \right] \tag{1.54}$$

where λ_{12} is the costate variable attached by the leader to the follower's adjoint equation. Initial conditions now include also $\lambda_{12} (0) = 0$, since $\lambda_2 (0)$ is unrestricted.

This very fact is a key factor (not the only one) explaining the emergence of time inconsistency of Stackelberg play under open-loop rules. Suppose first the leader writes the set of necessary conditions deriving from (1.54). The FOC will yield a plan u_1^L defining the leader's actions over $t \in [0, \infty)$. Then, suppose the leader dwells upon the possibility of designing the control path anew at some later date, say, $\widehat{t} \in (0, \infty)$. Call the resulting new path $\widehat{u}_1 (\widehat{t})$. This, in turn, requires solving the maximization of the relevant Hamiltonian over the truncated time span $[\widehat{t}, \infty)$, with a new initial condition $\lambda_{12} (\widehat{t}) = 0$, which, in general, will not coincide with the value of $\lambda_{12} (\widehat{t})$ generated by the solution u_1^L (joint with the paths of the state x and the follower's best reply u_2^*) at the same date $\widehat{t}$.

It takes little thinking for the leader to find out that this deviation from the path u_1^L initially decided upon for the entire duration of the game is indeed convenient, because u_1^L is not optimal at any intermediate date between the initial instant and doomsday. Put differently (but equivalently), the leader's incentive to deviate at any date from the initial control path is the consequence of the fact that any arbitrary instant can be taken as the initial one and the value of the additional costate λ_{12} must be nil at any date if taken as the initial one. This, in turn, goes along with the fact that $u_1^L \neq u_1^N$, which tells the same thing from another standpoint: the leader's open-loop plan decided upon at $t = 0$ differs, in general, from the one generated by the leader's best reply at any point in time (i.e., it is not part of a Nash equilibrium).

This problem is well known in differential game theory ever since Simaan and Cruz (1973a,b) and Kydland (1977), and has generated a very important discussion about macroeconomic policy games in which the policy makers' announcements try to condition agents' expectations about inflation, taxation or other relevant variables. The resulting debate on the time (in)consistency and credibility of optimal fiscal and monetary policies opened by Kydland and Prescott (1977) and Calvo (1978) is exhaustively accounted for in Persson and Tabellini (2000). Needless to say, Stackelberg play makes the need for commitment devices even more important than it is under simultaneous play. Such devices may not exist or may just be too hard to implement; however, the Stackelberg open-loop model cannot be disregarded in those cases in which reoptimising is enormously costly in terms of either the amount of money or the time span needed to design and carry out the deviation.

To conclude the discussion of open-loop Stackelberg games, it is worth noting that the time inconsistency of this solution is due to the presence of the leader's control either in the follower's FOC or in the follower's costate dynamics, coupled with the appearance of the same costate in the follower's FOC. When this happens, the open-loop Stackelberg game is *controllable* by the leader (Xie, 1997), since he or she can manipulate the follower's FOC as well as the evolution of the state-control system, and has a clear incentive to do so. If the game structure is such that neither the first nor the second condition applies, the game is *uncontrollable* by the leader, and the open-loop Stackelberg equilibrium is time consistent. Still, it may not be expected to be strongly so, as all controls may indeed depend on state(s), and open-loop rules do not ensure their subgame perfection, as is usually the case for the open-loop Nash equilibrium. There exists, however, a class of state-redundant games where open-loop Nash and feedback Stackelberg equilibria coincide, yielding strong time consistency (Rubio, 2006; Bacchiega *et al.*, 2010). Interestingly, this class encompasses some relevant oligopoly models, whose illustration appears in Chapter 9, preceded by a brief illustration of the technique used for detecting uncontrollability.

Now we can reformulate the same problem in terms of the dynamic programming approach, in two different ways. The first is one in which the leader enjoys the *first mover advantage instant by instant*. Note that this is not what happens under open-loop rules, as there the plan is decided upon by the leader at $t = 0$. Here, the advantage is stagewise and (should) produce a *feedback Stackelberg equilibrium*.

The best reply of the follower, $u_2^* (\overline{u}_1, x)$, solves

$$\frac{\partial \pi_2}{\partial u_2} + \frac{\partial V_2}{\partial x} \cdot \frac{\partial f}{\partial u_2} = 0 \tag{1.55}$$

and can be substituted back into the leader's HJB equation to be differentiated w.r.t. u_1. The equilibrium strategy pair at any time t is

$$u_1^L = \arg\max_{u_1} \left\{ \pi_1 \left(u_1, u_2^*, x\right) + \frac{\partial V_1}{\partial x} \cdot f \left(u_1, u_2^*, x\right) \right\} \tag{1.56}$$
$$u_2^F = u_2^* \left(u_1^L, x\right)$$

but the solution of the leader's HJB equation remains out of reach.[8]

A partial way out, which has something in common with the open-loop model, is the alternative route consisting in the so-called *global Stackelberg equilibrium*. In this case, once again, the follower solves her/his FOC to obtain $u_2^* (\overline{u}_1, x)$, and the leader designs the entire control plan at $t = 0$, but the resulting control is specified as a linear function of the state, $u_1^L = \alpha x + \beta$, the constants α and β being determined by the leader at the outset. This method yields time consistency, but it is conceptually close to an open-loop solution, since the leader's plan is defined once and for all, over the whole time horizon of the game. Yet, the manageability of the global Stackelberg equilibrium has encouraged its adoption in characterising several problems in economics and elsewhere.

---

[8] One should add 'almost always'. Indeed, a relevant exception is, intuitively, the class of state-redundant uncontrollable games, where, however, one can rely on the open-loop formulation.

Relevant examples of Stackelberg games concerning environmental economics, the sticky price model and vertical relations are in Chapters 7 and 9. Chapter 9 also provides additional formal details about the concepts of controllability and time inconsistency in the immediate vicinity of applications to differential games in the field of industrial organization.

Further Reading

Extensive and detailed expositions of optimal control theory are in Chiang (1967, 1992), Intriligator (1971), Kamien and Schwartz (1981, 1991[2]), Leitmann (1981) and Léonard and Long (1992), *inter alia*, while for differential game theory, see Blaquière *et al.*, (1969), Friedman (1971), Leitmann (1974), Başar and Olsder (1982, 1995[2]), Krasovskii and Subbotin (1988), Mehlmann (1988), Clemhout and Wan (1994), Dockner *et al.* (2000), Cellini and Lambertini (2003), Engwerda (2005), Long (2010) and Haurie *et al.* (1012). On transversality in optimal control problems over infinite time horizons, see Aseev and Kryazhimskiy (2004, 2007). For more on degenerate feedback Nash and Stackelberg equilibria attained under open-loop information, in addition to the aforementioned sources, see Cellini *et al.* (2005). A direct method for finding extremal in optimal control problems and open-loop differential games relies on Leitmann (1967) and is illustrated in Leitmann (2001), Dockner and Leitmann (2001) and Carlson and Leitmann (2008), among others; see also Malinowska and Torres (2010) and the references therein. An alternative method for the characterization of subgame perfect equilibria in differential games is in Rincon-Zapatero *et al.* (1998). The analysis of uncontrollable open-loop Stackelberg games has been extended by Karp and Lee (2003) and Cellini and Lambertini (2007). For a detailed analysis of second-order conditions, which I have left aside, see Mangasarian (1966), Arrow (1968) and Stalford and Leitmann (1973), among others.

Bibliography

Arrow, K. (1968), "Applications of Control Theory to Economic Growth", in G.B. Dantzig and A.F. Veinott, Jr. (eds), *Mathematics of the Decision Sciences, Part 2*, Providence, American Mathematical Society.

Aseev. S. and A. Kryazhimskiy (2004), "The Pontryagin Maximum Principle and Transversality Conditions for a Class of Optimal Control Problems with Infinite Time Horizons", *SIAM Journal on Control and Optimization*, **43**, 1094–119.

Aseev. S. and A. Kryazhimskiy (2007), *The Pontryagin Maximum Principle and Optimal Economic Growth Problems*, Proceedings of the Steklov Institute of Mathematics, vol. 257, Heidelberg, Springer.

Bacchiega, E., L. Lambertini and A. Palestini (2010), "On the Time Consistency of Equilibria in a Class of Additively Separable Differential Games", *Journal of Optimization Theory and Applications*, **145**, 415–27.

Başar, T. and G.J. Olsder (1982, 1995[2]), *Dynamic Noncooperative Game Theory*, San Diego, CA, Academic Press.

Bellman, R.E. (1957), *Dynamic Programming*, Princeton, NJ, Princeton University Press.

Blaquière, A., F. Gérard and G. Leitmann (1969), *Quantitative and Qualitative Games*, New York, Academic Press.

Carlson, D.A. and G. Leitmann (2008), "Fields of Extremals and Sufficient Conditions for the Simplest Problem of the Calculus of Variations", *Journal of Global Optimization*, **40**, 41–50.

Calvo, G. (1978), "On the Time Consistency of Optimal Policy in a Monetary Economy, *Econometrica*, **46**, 1411–28.

Caputo, M. (2007), "The Envelope Theorem for Locally Differentiable Nash Equilibria of Finite Horizon Differential Games", *Games and Economic Behavior*, **61**, 198–224.

Cellini, R. and L. Lambertini (1998), "A Dynamic Model of Differentiated Oligopoly with Capital Accumulation", *Journal of Economic Theory*, **83**, 145–55.

Cellini, R. and L. Lambertini (2003), "Differential Oligopoly Games", in P. Bianchi and L. Lambertini (eds), *Technology, Information and Market Dynamics: Topics in Advanced Industrial Organization*, Cheltenham, Edward Elgar, 173–207.

Cellini, R. and L. Lambertini (2007), "Time Consistent Fiscal Policies in a Ramsey Economy", *Mathematical Social Sciences*, **53**, 296–313.

Cellini, R., L. Lambertini and G. Leitmann (2005), "Degenerate Feedback and Time Consistency in Differential Games", in E.P. Hofer and E. Reithmeier (eds), *Modeling and Control of Autonomous Decision Support Based Systems. Proceedings of the 13th International Workshop on Dynamics and Control*, Aachen, Shaker Verlag, 185–92.

Chiang, A.C. (1967), *Fundamental Methods of Mathematical Economics*, New York, McGraw-Hill.

Chiang, A.C. (1992), *Elements of Dynamic Optimization*, New York, McGraw-Hill.

Clemhout, S. and H.Y. Wan, Jr. (1974), "A Class of Trilinear Differential Games", *Journal of Optimization Theory and Applications*, **14**, 419–24.

Clemhout, S. and H.Y. Wan, Jr. (1979), "Interactive Economic Dynamics and Differential Games", *Journal of Optimization Theory and Applications*, **27**, 7–30.

Clemhout, S. and H.Y. Wan, Jr. (1994), "Differential Games. Economic Applications", in R.J. Aumann and S. Hart (eds), *Handbook of Game Theory*, vol. 2, Amsterdam, North-Holland.

Dockner, E.J. and G. Leitmann (2001), "Coordinate Transformations and Derivation of Open-Loop Nash Equilibria", *Journal of Optimization Theory and Applications*, **110**, 1–15.

Dockner, E.J., G. Feichtinger and S. Jørgensen (1985), "Tractable Classes of Nonzero-Sum Open-Loop Nash Differential Games: Theory and Examples", *Journal of Optimization Theory and Applications*, **45**, 179–97.

Dockner, E.J., S. Jørgensen, N. Van Long and G. Sorger (2000), *Differential Games in Economics and Management Science*, Cambridge, Cambridge University Press.

Engwerda, J. (2005), *Linear-Quadratic Dynamic Optimization and Differential Games*, New York, Wiley.

Fershtman, C. (1987), "Identification of Classes of Differential Games for Which the Open-Loop Is a Degenerate Feedback Nash Equilibrium", *Journal of Optimization Theory and Applications*, **55**, 217–31.

Friedman, A. (1971), *Differential Games*, New York, Wiley.

Haurie, A., J. Krawczyk and G. Zaccour (2012), *Games and Dynamic Games*, Singapore, World Scientific.

Intriligator, M.D. (1971), *Mathematical Optimization and Economic Theory*, Englewood Cliffs, NJ, Prentice-Hall.

Isaacs, R. (1954), "Differential Games, I, II, III, IV", Reports RM-1391, 1399, 1411, 1486, RAND Corporation.

Isaacs, R. (1965), *Differential Games*, New York, Wiley.

Kamien, M.I. and N.L. Schwartz (1981, 1991[2]), *Dynamic Optimization: The Calculus of Variations and Optimal Control in Economics and Management*, Amsterdam, North-Holland.

Karp, L. and I.H. Lee (2003), "Time-Consistent Policies", *Journal of Economic Theory*, **112**, 353–64.

Krasovskii, N.N. and A.I. Subbotin (1988), *Game-Theoretical Control Theory*, Heidelberg, Springer.

Kydland, F. (1977), "Equilibrium Solutions in Dynamic Dominant-Player Models", *Journal of Economic Theory*, **15**, 307–24.

Kydland, F. and E. Prescott (1977), "Rules Rather than Discretion: The Inconsistency of Optimal Plans", *Journal of Political Economy*, **85**, 473–92.

Leitmann, G. (1967), "A Note on Absolute Extrema of Certain Integrals", *International Journal of Nonlinear Mechanics*, **2**, 55–59.

Leitmann, G. (1974), *Cooperative and Non-Cooperative Many Players Differential Games*, Heidelberg, Springer.

Leitmann, G. (1981), *The Calculus of Variations and Optimal Control*, New York, Plenum Press.

Leitmann, G. (2001), "On a Class of Direct Optimization Problems", *Journal of Optimization Theory and Applications*, **108**, 467–81.

Léonard, D. and N.V. Long (1992), *Optimal Control Theory and Static Optimization in Economics*, Cambridge, Cambridge University Press.

Long, N.V. (2010), *A Survey of Dynamic Games in Economics*, Singapore, World Scientific.

Lotka, A.J. (1925), *Elements of Physical Biology*, Philadelphia, Williams and Wilkins.

Malinowska, A.B. and D.F.M. Torres (2010), "Leitmann's Direct Method of Optimization for Absolute Extrema of Certain Problems of the Calculus of Variations on Time Scales", *Applied Mathematics and Computation*, **217**, 1158–62.

Mangasarian, O.L. (1966), "Sufficient Conditions for the Optimal Control of Nonlinear Systems", *SIAM Journal on Control*, **4**, 139–52.

Mehlmann, A. (1988), *Applied Differential Games*, New York, Plenum Press.

Mehlmann, A. and R. Willing (1983), "On Nonunique Closed-Loop Nash Equilibria for a Class of Differential Games with a Unique and Degenerate Feedback Solution", *Journal of Optimization Theory and Applications*, **41**, 463–72.

Persson, T. and G. Tabellini (2000), *Political Economics. Explaining Economic Policy*, Cambridge, MA, MIT Press.

Pontryagin, L.S. (1966), "On the Theory of Differential Games", *Advances in Mathematical Sciences*, **21**, 219–74.

Pontryagin, L.S., V.G. Boltyanskii, R.V. Gamkrelidze and E.F. Mishchenko (1962), *The Mathematical Theory of Optimal Processes*, New York, Interscience.

Reinganum, J. (1982), "A Class of Differential Games for Which the Closed Loop and Open Loop Nash Equilibria Coincide", *Journal of Optimization Theory and Applications*, **36**, 253–62.

Rincon-Zapatero, J.P., J. Martinez and G. Martin-Herran (1998), "New Method to Characterize Subgame Perfect Nash Equilibria in Differential Games", *Journal of Optimization Theory and Applications*, **96**, 377–95.

Rubio, S.J. (2006), "On the Coincidence of Feedback Nash Equilibria and Stackelberg Equilibria in Economic Applications of Differential Games", *Journal of Optimization Theory and Applications*, **128**, 203–21.

Sethi, S. and G. Thompson (1981), *Optimal Control Theory: Applications to Management Science*, Boston, MA, Nijhoff.

Selten, R. (1965), "Spieltheoretische Behandlung eines Oligopolmodells mit Nachfrageträgheit", *Zeitschrift für die gesamte Staatswissenschaft*, **121**, 301–24.

Selten, R. (1975), "Re-Examination of the Perfectness Concept for Equilibrium Points in Extended Games", *International Journal of Game Theory*, **4**, 25–55.

Simaan, M. and J.B. Cruz Jr. (1973a), "On the Stackelberg Strategy in Nonzero Sum Games", *Journal of Optimization Theory and Applications*, **11**, 533–55.

Simaan, M. and J.B. Cruz Jr. (1973b), "Additional Aspects of the Stackelberg Strategy in Nonzero Sum Games", *Journal of Optimization Theory and Applications*, **11**, 613–26.

Stackelberg, H. von (1934), *Marktform und Gleichgewicht*, Berlin-Wien, Springer.

Stalford, H. and G. Leitmann (1973), "Sufficiency Conditions for Nash Equilibria in N-Person Differential Games", in A. Blaquiere (ed.), *Topics in Differential Games*, North-Holland, Amsterdam, pp. 345–76.

Stern, N. (2007), *The Economics of Climate Change: The Stern Review*, Cambridge, Cambridge University Press.

Stern, N. (2009), *A Blueprint for a Safer Planet. How to Manage Climate Change and Create a New Era of Progress and Prosperity*, London, Random House.

Verhulst, P.H. (1838), "Notice sur la loi que la population poursuit dans son accroissement", *Correspondance mathématique et physique*, **10**, 113–21.

Volterra, V. (1931), "Variations and Fluctuations of the Number of Individuals in Animal Species Living Together", in R.N. Chapman (ed.), *Animal Ecology*, New York, McGraw-Hill, pp. 31–113.

Xie, D. (1997), "On Time Consistency: A Technical Issue in Stackelberg Differential Games", *Journal of Economic Theory*, **76**, 412–30.

2 Monopoly

This chapter contains the review of a selection of dynamic monopoly models in continuous time. As such, these are not proper differential games (although one may consider them as games *with a single player*). So, why monopoly? Because the purpose of this survey is in fact to illustrate the potential of dynamic analysis abstracting from the explicitly strategic motives characterising games.

In the remainder of the chapter, I will tune the illustration of the dynamic behaviour of monopolistic firms so as to highlight the qualitative and quantitative differences between the properties of different versions of the same models and therefore also between the predictions drawn from dynamic versus static setups dealing with issues like capacity accumulation, polluting emissions, natural resource exploitation, advertising, network externalities and the supply of durable goods. The latter case, more than the others, is one in which the intrinsically dynamic nature of the problem at hand, closely connected with the Coase conjecture (Coase, 1972), calls for a dynamic analysis.

For the aforementioned reasons, and in order to provide a gym where exercising with the tools of dynamic analysis in continuous time is not complicated by the presence of strategic interaction, I will lay out the ensuing models using a high degree of detail, commenting crucial passages wherever appropriate and useful.

Last but not least, the ensuing optimal control models have been selected as they constitute special cases of differential games on which we will dwell more extensively in the following chapters.

2.1 Monopoly *à la* Solow–Swan

To set the stage, let us think of a static monopoly where the firm has to choose capacity k. The demand function is $p = a - Q$, where p is market price, $a > 0$ is the reservation (or choke) price and Q is the output. To simplify the matter, we can stipulate that the monopolist, knowing market demand, has in mind to operate at full capacity, so that $Q = k$ and $p = a - k$. Then, assuming a constant marginal production cost set equal to zero, the profit function is $\pi = (a - k)k - rk$, where $r \in (0, a)$ is the rental price of a unit of capacity or physical capital. It takes little algebra to ascertain that, *mutatis mutandis*, this is the profit of a monopolist operating at a marginal and average cost equal to r, and therefore the equilibrium output is $k^M = (a - r)/2$, where superscript M denotes the monopoly optimum.

Now, this evidently simplistic line of reasoning tells us that (1) the investment process is instantaneous (or 'blackboxed away') and costless, except for the rental cost of capacity, and (2) the equilibrium outcome is observationally hardly distinguishable from that arising from a textbook model in which a firm free of capacity constraints exploits its market power to maximise its profits w.r.t. either market variable. Shall we take this message at face value?

Verifying that this is not the case amounts to (1) invoking an explicit role for calendar time and (2) reformulating the acquisition of capacity as the outcome a dynamic investment plan, in which investment becomes the firm's control variable. The resulting pure monopoly version of the growth model with costly capacity accumulation of Solow (1956) and Swan (1956) is a single-agent dynamic optimization problem endowed with a manifold of interesting properties which may help illustrate the difference between the solution arising under open-loop and feedback information even in absence of strategic interaction. The present formulation dates back to Eisner and Strotz (1963) and Gould (1968). We will encounter the same setup, properly reformulated as a strategic game, at the beginning of the next chapter, dealing with the oligopoly version of the model due to Reynolds (1987, 1991).

A single firm operates in the market, over $t \in [0, \infty)$. The monopolist sells a single good, whose demand function is $p(t) = a - k(t)$ at any instant t; $a > 0$ is the time-invariant choke price, and $k(t) > 0$ is the firm's physical capital or productive capacity, which is supposed to be fully used at all times. Capacity is the state variable, and evolves over time following

$$\dot{k}(t) = I(t) - \delta k(t) \qquad (2.1)$$

where $\delta > 0$ is its constant depreciation rate, and $I(t)$ is the instantaneous investment, which is the firm's unique control variable. Investment involves the instantaneous cost function $C(t) = cI(t) + bI^2(t)/2$, where $b, c \geq 0$ are time-invariant parameters. Ruling away for the sake of simplicity, any production costs, the monopolist's profit function at any time t is

$$\pi(t) = p(t)k(t) - C(t) = [a - k(t)]k(t) - cI(t) - \frac{bI^2(t)}{2}. \qquad (2.2)$$

The monopolist must

$$\max_{I(t)} \Pi = \int_0^\infty \pi(t)e^{-\rho t}dt \qquad (2.3)$$

where $\rho > 0$ is the time-invariant discount rate, s.t. the dynamic constraint (2.1), the initial condition $k(0) = k_0 > 0$ and the appropriate transversality condition. To begin with, we may formulate the optimal control problem by constructing the Hamiltonian function.

2.1.1   Solving the Optimal Control Problem

The current-value Hamiltonian function of the firm is:

$$\mathcal{H}\left(k(t), I(t), \lambda(t)\right) = e^{-\rho t} \left\{ [a - k(t)] k(t) - cI(t) - \frac{bI^2(t)}{2} + \lambda(t) \left[I(t) - \delta k(t) \right] \right\}$$

$$(2.4)$$

where $\lambda(t) = \mu(t)e^{\rho t}$ is the 'capitalised' costate variable associated with the state dynamics. The first order condition (FOC) is[1]

$$\frac{\partial \mathcal{H}(\cdot)}{\partial I(t)} = -c - bI(t) + \lambda(t) = 0$$

$$(2.5)$$

and the costate equation is

$$-\frac{\partial \mathcal{H}(\cdot)}{\partial k(t)} = \dot{\lambda}(t) - \rho\lambda(t) \Rightarrow \dot{\lambda}(t) = 2k(t) - a + \lambda(t)(\delta + \rho)$$

$$(2.6)$$

The transversality condition is $\lim_{t \to \infty} e^{-\rho t} \lambda(t) k(t) = 0$.

FOC (2.5) yields the optimal instantaneous expression of the costate variable as a function of the control, $\lambda(t) = c + bI(t)$, and can be differentiated w.r.t. time to deliver the control equation:

$$\dot{I}(t) = \frac{\dot{\lambda}(t)}{b} = \frac{2k(t) - a + \lambda(t)(\delta + \rho)}{b}$$

$$(2.7)$$

which, using $\lambda(t) = c + bI(t)$, can be rewritten in its final form as

$$\dot{I}(t) = \frac{2k(t) - a + [c + bI(t)](\delta + \rho)}{b}$$

$$(2.8)$$

Taken together, the simultaneous differential equations (2.1) and (2.8) form the state-control system, which is linear in $k(t)$ and $I(t)$. Its unique steady state point is identified by

$$k_H^M = \frac{a - c(\delta + \rho)}{2 + b\delta(\delta + \rho)} \; ; \; I_H^M = \delta k_H^M$$

$$(2.9)$$

where, again, superscript M stands for monopoly, while subscript H reminds us that the solution has been generated by the Hamiltonian function. Now we may pause to compare the expression of k_H^M in (2.9) with the static solution $k^M = (a - \rho)/2$, where I have intentionally set $r = \rho$ to imply that it would be reasonable for the (static) rental price of capacity r to equal intertemporal discounting ρ. It is easy to ascertain that

$$\lim_{\rho \to 0} \left(k^M - k_H^M \right) = \frac{\delta(ab\delta + 2c)}{2(2 + b\delta^2)}$$

$$(2.10)$$

and then

$$\lim_{\delta \to \infty} \frac{\delta(ab\delta + 2c)}{2(2 + b\delta^2)} = 0$$

$$(2.11)$$

These two limits jointly prove the following:

[1] Exponential discounting is omitted for brevity.

Remark 2.1 *Take $r = \rho$. In the limit, as both time discounting and depreciation drop to zero, the steady state capacity generated by the dynamic model tends to coincide with the equilibrium capacity generated by the static model.*

In general, for any $r = \rho > 0$ and $\delta > 0$, this is not true. A fortiori, it is not true if $r \neq \rho$. In such a case,

$$k^M \gtrless k_H^M \ \forall \ r \lessgtr \frac{(ab\delta + 2c)(\delta + \rho)}{2 + b\delta(\delta + \rho)} \tag{2.12}$$

Back to the optimal control model, we see that the following property of the unique steady state can be easily shown to hold:

Proposition 2.2 *The steady state monopoly equilibrium (k_H^M, I_H^M) is a saddle point.*

This fact can be appreciated by looking at the 2×2 Jacobian matrix associated with the state-control system:

$$J_H^M = \begin{bmatrix} \dfrac{\partial \dot{k}(t)}{\partial k(t)} = -\delta & \dfrac{\partial \dot{k}(t)}{\partial I(t)} = 1 \\[3mm] \dfrac{\partial \dot{I}(t)}{\partial k(t)} = \dfrac{2}{b} & \dfrac{\partial \dot{I}(t)}{\partial I(t)} = \delta + \rho \end{bmatrix} \tag{2.13}$$

whose trace and determinant are

$$T\left(J_H^M\right) = \frac{\partial \dot{k}(t)}{\partial k(t)} + \frac{\partial \dot{I}(t)}{\partial I(t)} = \rho > 0 \tag{2.14}$$

$$\Delta\left(J_H^M\right) = \frac{\partial \dot{k}(t)}{\partial k(t)} \cdot \frac{\partial \dot{I}(t)}{\partial I(t)} - \frac{\partial \dot{k}(t)}{\partial I(t)} \cdot \frac{\partial \dot{k}(t)}{\partial I(t)} = -\frac{2 + b\delta(\delta + \rho)}{b} < 0 \tag{2.15}$$

The negativity of $\Delta\left(J_H^M\right)$ suffices to prove the saddle point stability of (k_H^M, I_H^M).

The same property can be easily grasped by looking at the phase diagram appearing in Figure 2.1, where the loci

$$\dot{k}(t) = 0 \Leftrightarrow I(t) = \delta k(t) \tag{2.16}$$

and

$$\dot{I}(t) = 0 \Leftrightarrow I(t) = \frac{a - 2k(t) + c(\delta + \rho)}{b(\delta + \rho)} \tag{2.17}$$

are drawn. The arrows illustrate the dynamics of state and control, and show the presence of a stable branch driving the firm towards (k_H^M, I_H^M).

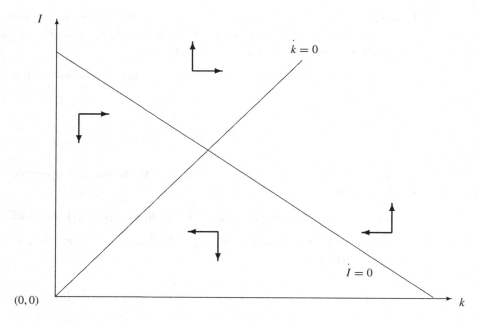

Figure 2.1 The Solow–Swan monopoly model: phase diagram

2.1.2   Solving the Feedback Problem

Now suppose the firm relies on feedback information, and solves the following Hamilton–Jacobi–Bellman equation:

$$\rho V (k (t)) = \max_{I(t)} \left\{ [a - k (t)] k (t) - cI (t) - \frac{bI^2 (t)}{2} + V' (k (t)) [I (t) - \delta k (t)] \right\}$$

(2.18)

in which $V (k (t))$ is the value function and $V' (k (t)) = \partial V (k (t)) / \partial k (t)$ is its partial derivative w.r.t. the state variable. The FOC taken w.r.t. $I (t)$ is

$$- c - bI (t) + V' (k (t)) = 0$$

(2.19)

which is solved by $V' (k (t)) = c + bI (t)$, suggesting that, since $V' (k (t)) = \lambda (t)$ at all times, then the feedback solution and the solution of the above optimal control problem indeed coincide.

As we shall see in the remainder of the book, solving the FOC taken on the r.h.s. of the Bellman equation w.r.t. the partial derivative of the value function is a route often chosen to characterise linear feedback controls. Here, we may confine our attention to the traditional method, whereby (2.19) delivers the optimal control[2]

$$I^* = \max \left\{ 0, \frac{V' (k) - c}{b} \right\}$$

(2.20)

---

[2] Henceforth, the explicit indication of the time argument is omitted for the sake of brevity.

Provided $V'(k) > c$, $I^* = [V'(k) - c]/b$ can be substituted into (2.18), so that the Bellman equation simplifies as follows:

$$\frac{2b[\rho V(k) - k(a - k)] + 2b\delta kV'(k) - [V'(k) - c]}{2b} = 0 \qquad (2.21)$$

Now, given the linear quadratic form of (2.18), one may conjecture that the value function be linear quadratic in the state variable, and pose $V(k) = \varepsilon_1 k^2 + \varepsilon_2 k + \varepsilon_3$, so that $V'(k) = 2\varepsilon_1 k + \varepsilon_2$, where the undetermined coefficients $\{\varepsilon_1, \varepsilon_2, \varepsilon_3\}$ can be identified as follows. Plugging these expressions into (2.21) generates the following system of three equations:

$$4\varepsilon_1 - 2b[1 + \varepsilon_1(2\delta + \rho)] = 0$$
$$ab - 2c\varepsilon_1 + \varepsilon_2[2\varepsilon_1 - b(\delta + \rho)] = 0 \qquad (2.22)$$
$$(c - \varepsilon_2)^2 - 2b\rho\varepsilon_3 = 0$$

The above system can be solved w.r.t. $\{\varepsilon_1, \varepsilon_2, \varepsilon_3\}$. From the third equation in (2.22), we obtain $\varepsilon_3 = (c - \varepsilon_2)^2 / (2b)$, while the second equation is satisfied by

$$\varepsilon_2 = \frac{2c\varepsilon_1 - ab}{2\varepsilon_1 - b(\delta + \rho)} \qquad (2.23)$$

The first has, obviously, two solutions:

$$\varepsilon_1^{\pm} = \frac{b(2\delta + \rho) \pm \sqrt{b[8 + b(2\delta + \rho)^2]}}{4} \qquad (2.24)$$

Since we are looking for a maximum, the intuitive candidate is the smaller one, i.e., ε_1^{-}. As we are about to see, this *a priori* intuition is correct. Nonetheless, it is useful to characterise both solutions. Taking $\varepsilon_1 = \varepsilon_1^{-}$, the expression of the optimal control $I^* = [V'(k) - c]/b$ becomes

$$I_{-}^* = \frac{2[a - c(\delta + \rho)] + k\left[\delta\sqrt{b(8 + b(2\delta + \rho)^2)} - 4 - b\delta(2\delta + \rho)\right]}{b\rho + \sqrt{b(8 + b(2\delta + \rho)^2)}} \qquad (2.25)$$

while using $\varepsilon_1 = \varepsilon_1^{+}$, we have

$$I_{+}^* = \frac{-2[a - c(\delta + \rho)] + k\left[\delta\sqrt{b(8 + b(2\delta + \rho)^2)} + 4 + b\delta(2\delta + \rho)\right]}{\sqrt{b(8 + b(2\delta + \rho)^2)} - b\rho} \qquad (2.26)$$

Using either one or the other, the steady state point remains (k_H^M, I_H^M). However, while $\partial I_{-}^*/\partial k < 0$, $\partial I_{+}^*/\partial k > 0$ over the whole parameter space. The two solutions, together with the locus $\dot{k} = 0$ in (2.16), are drawn in Figure 2.2. The arrows appearing along I_{-}^* and I_{+}^* account for the dynamics of k in the state-control space, and show that I_{-}^* is stable while I_{+}^* is not.

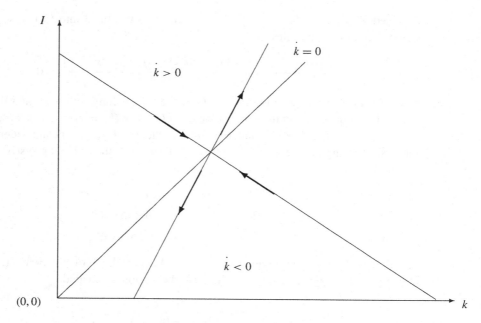

Figure 2.2 The Solow–Swan monopoly model: phase diagram, feedback solutions

So far so good, seemingly, as we have a stable solution being attained under open loop rules which appears again under feedback rules. In the latter case, another solution also obtains, but it can be disregarded as it is unstable in view of the state dynamics. Relying solely on the present monopoly problem, one could be tempted to conclude that the Hamiltonian formulation offers a more compact way of characterising the stable solution, overlooking the unstable one.[3] But this turns out not to be the case, as there is a lot more to it which the Solow–Swan model does not reveal. To understand why one should always solve the dynamic programming problem, we may turn our attention to environmental and resource economics.

2.2   Polluting Emissions and Resource Extraction

This time we can set out using the dynamic problem. As above, the time horizon is infinite. Let $p(t) = a - Q(t)$ be the instantaneous demand for a nondurable good supplied by the monopolistic firm, whose technology operates at constant returns to scale and is summarised by the cost function $C(t) = cQ(t)$ at any instant t, with $c \in [0, a)$. Production may (1) entail an environmental damage due to polluting emissions,

---

[3] Here, for expositional purpose, the firms is not subject to any policy measure. The analysis of the distortionary effect of taxation on the accumulation of installed capacity or other forms of physical capital dates back to Jorgenson (1963) and Hall and Jorgenson (1967), where, however, firms' market behaviour is not exlicitly formalised. In Chapter 3 I will briefly dwell upon the effect of taxation in an oligopoly with capital accumulation.

and/or (2) require the extraction of a natural resource, either renewable or not. Let us consider each scenario in turn.

In the first case, the relevant state variable is the stock of emissions $S(t)$, which evolves according to the following dynamics:

$$\dot{S}(t) = Q(t) - \delta S(t),\tag{2.27}$$

where $\delta > 0$ is the constant decay rate characterising the natural carbon sinks and the rate of CO_2-equivalent emissions per unit of output is normalised to one, for the sake of simplicity, so that the instantaneous amount of pollutants is $S(t) = Q(t)$. In absence of any environmental policy (such as emission taxes, environmental standards or the costly acquisition of pollution permits), the monopolist chooses $Q(t)$ to maximise the discounted profit flow

$$\Pi = \int_0^\infty [a - Q(t) - c] Q(t) e^{-\rho t} dt,\tag{2.28}$$

under the constraints posed by the state equation (2.27) and the initial condition $S(0) = S_0 \geq 0$.

In the second case, the firm exploits a natural resource, whose dynamic behaviour is described by the following state equation:

$$\dot{X}(t) = F(X(t)) - Q(t)\tag{2.29}$$

where[4]

$$F(X(t)) = \begin{cases} \eta X(t) & \forall X(t) \in (0, X_y] \\ \eta X_y \left(\dfrac{X_{max} - X(t)}{X_{max} - X_y} \right) & \forall X(t) \in (X_y, X_{max}] \end{cases}\tag{2.30}$$

In (2.30), $X(t)$ is the resource stock, $\eta \geq 0$ is its *implicit* growth rate when the stock is at most equal to X_y and ηX_y is the maximum sustainable yield. Looking at (2.29–2.30), we can appreciate that if the resource stock is sufficiently small, the population grows at an exponential rate, while beyond X_y the asset grows at a decreasing rate. Moreover, X_{max} measures the *carrying capacity* of the habitat of this resource or species. For any $X(t) > X_{max}$, the growth rate of the resource drops below zero, being limited by the available amounts of food and space. Clearly, if $\eta > 0$ the resource is renewable (e.g., fish or woods); if instead $\eta = 0$, it is non-renewable (e.g., oil or mineral ores). The extant literature very often considers a linear approximation $F(X(t)) = \eta X(t)$, so that (2.29) becomes

$$\dot{X}(t) = \eta X(t) - Q(t)\tag{2.31}$$

---

[4] The nonlinear version of the growth rate appearing in (2.30),

$$\dot{X}(t) = zX(t) \left[1 - \frac{X(t)}{X_{max}} \right]$$

with $z > 0$, dates back to the model of Verhulst (1838), Lotka (1925) and Volterra (1931). It appears again in the remainder, in the analysis of advertising campaigns.

This is very common when dealing with differential games, as the above linear dynamics yields a linear-quadratic form. Therefore, the monopolist has to maximise (2.28) w.r.t. $Q(t)$ under the constraint (2.31) and the initial condition $X(0) = X_0 \geq 0$.

In both scenarios, the problem of the firm is quadratic in its control (the output level or extraction rate) and linear in the state variable (polluting emissions or the resource stock). However, as we are about to see, the dynamic properties of the solutions are totally different.

2.2.1   The Optimal Control Problem

When the relevant state equation is the stock of pollution, the firm's Hamiltonian function is

$$\mathcal{H}(t) = e^{-\rho t} \{(a - Q(t) - c) Q(t) + \lambda(t) [Q(t) - \delta S(t)]\} \tag{2.32}$$

in which $\lambda(t) = e^{\rho t} \mu(t)$ is the costate variable in current value associated with the dynamics of CO_2-equivalent emissions. The set of necessary conditions generated by (2.32) is:

$$\frac{\partial \mathcal{H}}{\partial Q} = a - c - Q + \lambda = 0 \tag{2.33}$$

$$\dot{\lambda} = -\frac{\partial \mathcal{H}}{\partial S} + \rho \lambda \Leftrightarrow \dot{\lambda} = (\delta + \rho) \lambda \tag{2.34}$$

Since (2.34) is a differential equation in separable variables admitting the solution $\lambda = 0$ at all times, this illustrates that the quasi-static pure monopoly output $Q^M = (a - c)/2$ is indeed chosen at any instant t. The required transversality condition $\lim_{t \to \infty} e^{-\rho t} \lambda S = 0$ is met. The resulting level of pollution at the steady state is $S^M = Q^M / \delta = (a - c) / (2\delta)$.

On the basis of the dynamic properties of the state variable S and the associated Jacobian matrix, it is also easily verified that the steady state equilibrium (S^M, Q^M) is a saddle point. This property is highlighted in Figure 2.3, in which the arrows drawn along the flat line of Q^M illustrate the convergence towards the steady state equilibrium.

Now consider the scenario describing the extraction of a renewable natural resource (i.e., take $\eta > 0$). Here, the state equation is (2.31), and the monopolist chooses $Q(t)$ to maximise

$$\mathcal{H}(t) = e^{-\rho t} \{(a - Q(t) - c) Q(t) + \lambda(t) [\eta X(t) - Q(t)]\} \tag{2.35}$$

Before delving into the details of the solution, it is worth stressing that, although it may indeed look strange at first sight, a situation in which a firm exploits a natural resource without taking into account explicitly the constraint $X(t) > 0$ in fact allows us to intuitively describe the so-called *tragedy of commons* (Hardin, 1968) as the consequence of such a myopic behaviour. That is, behaving in a quasi-static way, a single firm may cause the exhaustion of the resource (or the extinction of the species) precisely because its residual stock is never accounted for. As we are about to see, the (in)stability

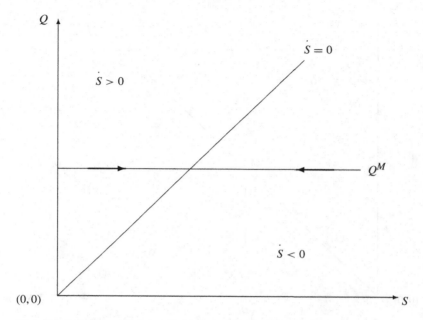

Figure 2.3 Polluting emissions: phase diagram in the (S, Q) space

properties of the dynamic system and the initial stock also play a role in setting the stage for the tragedy.

We will extensively come back to this issue in Chapter 7, where the tragedy of commons is discussed in relation with industry structure (i.e., the numerosity of firms). There, it will become apparent that increasing the intensity of competition increases the pressure on the resource. However, a plausible way of interpreting the following monopoly problem is that the exhaustion of a natural resource is not necessarily the outcome of free access.

Going back to the model, the necessary conditions generated by (2.35) are:

$$\frac{\partial \mathcal{H}}{\partial Q} = a - c - 2Q - \lambda = 0 \tag{2.36}$$

$$\dot{\lambda} = -\frac{\partial \mathcal{H}}{\partial X} + \rho \lambda \Leftrightarrow \dot{\lambda} = (\rho - \eta) \lambda \tag{2.37}$$

Also in this case, the costate equation admits the solution $\lambda = 0$, and the same quasi-static monopoly output (or extraction rate) $Q^M = (a - c)/2$ is selected at all times. The resulting steady state resource stock *would be* $X^M = Q^M/\eta$. However, as it appears from the arrows drawn along the flat line at Q^M in Figure 2.4, the reversal in signs characterising the state dynamics (2.31) as compared to (2.27) makes the point (X^M, Q^M) unstable. In particular, the fate of the natural resource or species will depend on the initial condition X_0 of the resource itself. For all $X_0 \in (0, X^M)$, the resource stock will disappear; conversely, for all $X_0 > X^M$, the stock will grow up to reach the carrying capacity of its habitat. Hence, it appears that a myopic or 'careless' firm may

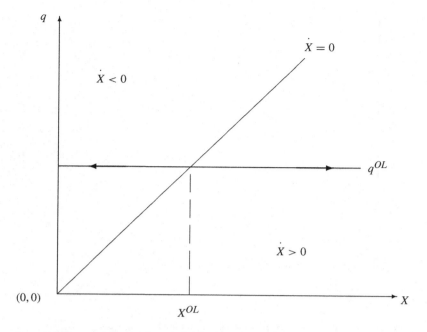

Figure 2.4 Resource extraction: phase diagram in the (X, Q) space

cause the tragedy of commons to arise whenever the initial stock is sufficiently small. Or, *monopoly may be enough to cause extinction*.

A simple numerical example is useful to help grasping the intuition of what may happen. Imagine a scenario in which $X_0 = (a - c) / (3\eta)$. If $Q = Q^M$, solving the state equation yields

$$X(t) = \frac{a - c}{2\eta} + e^{\eta t} C \tag{2.38}$$

at any generic instant t. The integration constant C can then be determined by solving the above equation at $t = 0$, obtaining $C = -(a - c)/\eta$, in such a way that (2.38) becomes

$$X(t) = \frac{(a - c)(3 - e^{\eta t})}{6\eta} \tag{2.39}$$

which is non-negative for all $t \in \left[0, \widehat{t}\,\right]$, with $\widehat{t} \cong 5.493$ for $\eta = 1/5$. That is, if the instantaneous natural reproduction rate of the resource is 20%, the clock will announce extinction at $\widehat{t} \cong 5.493$. Obviously, this will also imply the disappearance of the market for the final product and the sharp drop of the unaware firm's profits to zero at the same date.

The foregoing analysis deserves a few additional comments. A noteworthy aspect of the unregulated dynamic monopoly model with polluting emissions is that its solution via the Hamiltonian formulation replicates the same control as in the static model. This feature, which we will encounter again in several differential games, might induce us to question the dynamic nature of a model with these characteristics. Indeed, I have labelled the monopoly output as quasi-static for two related reasons. The first is that, although it does look like a perennial replication of a static choice, strictly speaking the problem remains properly dynamic because of the state equation. The second is that the infinite replication of the static monopoly output is possible, in principle, only in the pollution model. As we have seen, the exploitation of a natural resource which is exhaustible even when it is renewable may prevent the firm from perpetually repeating the static extraction rate simply because the stock might get entirely depleted in finite time if its initial volume is low. This is where the dynamic programming (or feedback) solution kicks in to tell a very different story.

2.2.2 Dynamic Programming

The HJB equation of the polluting monopolist is

$$\rho V(S) = \max_{Q} \left\{ (a - Q - c) Q + V'(S)(Q - \delta S) \right\} \tag{2.40}$$

with the FOC

$$a - 2Q - c + V'(S) = 0 \tag{2.41}$$

Plugging its solution $Q^* = \left[a - 2Q - c + V'(S) \right]/2$ (under the assumption $Q^* > 0$) into (2.40) and adopting the linear quadratic form $V = \varepsilon_1 S^2 + \varepsilon_2 S + \varepsilon_3$ for the value function, we obtain the following system of equations:

$$
\begin{aligned}
\varepsilon_1 (2\delta + \rho - \varepsilon_1) &= 0 \\
\varepsilon_2 (\delta + \rho - \varepsilon_1) - \varepsilon_1 (a - c) &= 0 \\
4\rho\varepsilon_3 - (a - c + \varepsilon_2)^2 &= 0
\end{aligned}
\tag{2.42}
$$

which is solved by

$$\varepsilon_3 = \frac{(a - c + \varepsilon_2)^2}{4\rho}; \; \varepsilon_2 = \frac{(a - c)\varepsilon_1}{\delta + \rho - \varepsilon_1} \tag{2.43}$$

$$\varepsilon_1 = \left\{ \begin{array}{l} 0 \\ 2\delta + \rho \end{array} \right. \tag{2.44}$$

Now, clearly, combining (2.43) with $\varepsilon_1 = 0$ replicates the same picture obtaining from the Hamiltonian version of the problem, and we already know that the resulting steady state is a saddle point equilibrium. Using instead (2.43) with $\varepsilon_1 = 2\delta + \rho$, the resulting optimal control is

$$Q^*(S) = \frac{2S\delta (2\delta + \rho) - (a - c)(\delta + \rho)}{2\delta} \tag{2.45}$$

which appears in Figure 2.5 together with $Q^M = (a - c)/2$ and the locus $\dot{S} = 0$. The dynamic properties of state S, together with the fact that $\partial Q^*(S)/\partial S > 0$ everywhere, imply that the alternative solution identified under dynamic programming, $Q^*(S)$, is indeed unstable.

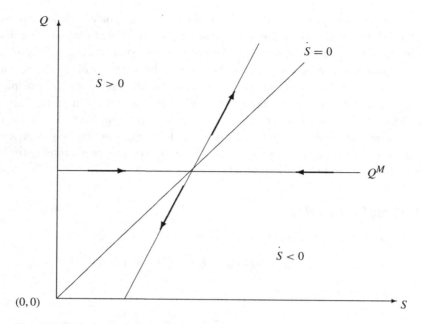

Figure 2.5 Polluting emissions: feedback solution

We may now look at the resource extraction problem. In this case, the relevant HJB equation is

$$\rho V(X) = \max_Q \left\{ (a - Q - c)Q + V'(X)(\eta X - Q) \right\} \qquad (2.46)$$

so that the FOC is

$$a - 2Q - c - V'(X) = 0 \qquad (2.47)$$

Using again a linear quadratic form $V = \varepsilon_1 X^2 + \varepsilon_2 X + \varepsilon_3$, the system of three equations to be used to determine the vector of parameters $\{\varepsilon_1, \varepsilon_2, \varepsilon_3\}$ is

$$\varepsilon_1(\rho - 2\eta - \varepsilon_1) = 0$$
$$\varepsilon_2(\varepsilon_1 + \eta - \rho) - \varepsilon_1(a - c) = 0 \qquad (2.48)$$
$$4\rho\varepsilon_3 - (a - c - \varepsilon_2)^2 = 0$$

which is solved by

$$\varepsilon_3 = \frac{(a - c - \varepsilon_2)^2}{4\rho} \; ; \; \varepsilon_2 = \frac{(a - c)\varepsilon_1}{\varepsilon_1 + \eta - \rho} \qquad (2.49)$$

$$\varepsilon_1 = \begin{cases} 0 \\ \rho - 2\eta \end{cases} \qquad (2.50)$$

While $\varepsilon_1 = 0$ replicates the quasi-static solution (which is unstable), $\varepsilon_1 = \rho - 2\eta$ yields

$$Q^*(X) = \frac{(a - c)(\rho - \eta) + 2X\eta(2\eta - \rho)}{2\eta} \qquad (2.51)$$

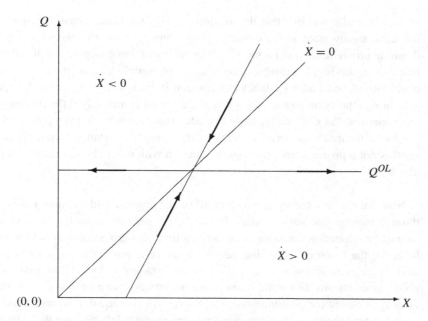

Figure 2.6 Resource extraction: stable feedback solution

whose slope w.r.t. S is positive (resp., negative) for all $\rho \in (0, 2\eta)$ (resp., $\rho \in (2\eta, \infty)$). If discounting is low enough, the relevant picture appears in Figure 2.6, where the feedback control associated with $\varepsilon_1 = \rho - 2\eta$ is stable. In this regard, note that any $\rho \in (0, 2\eta)$ implies $\varepsilon_1 < 0$, which in turn ensures the concavity of the value function $V(X)$. Therefore, here the concavity condition is necessary and sufficient to generate a stable feedback solution to the resource extraction model which the Hamiltonian method is unable to identify.

Of course, if $\rho \in (2\eta, \infty)$, the additional solution $Q^*(X)$ becomes unstable (its graphical representation, which is elementary, is omitted). However, it is appropriate to briefly comment on this case, as it arises when discounting is significantly higher than the natural growth rate of the resource, and this is the driver of the instability of both solutions alike. As a result, coupling the monopolist's shortsightedness with a sufficiently low initial stock, the resource is bound to deplete altogether in finite time. This issue will appear again in differential games dealing with the exploitation of common pool resources, combined with the companion problem of determining the optimal number of firms (or group size) in the commons.

The take-home message delivered by the analysis of pollution and natural resource exploitation can be then formulated in the following terms:

Remark 2.3 *In general, the Hamiltonian approach to a single-agent optimal control problem does not identify all existing solutions. In particular, it may overlook stable solutions which are instead identified by solving the HJB equation.*

That is, while it is true that the maximization of the Hamiltonian function identifies the same steady state as the dynamic programming version of the same single-agent dynamic problem, relying on the Hamiltonian method one might be induced to believe that the equilibrium is unstable when this is not entirely true, as the same steady state could be reached under feedback information in such a way that a stable equilibrium path brings the agent to the very same place with a completely different perception of its properties. Put differently, these considerations amounts to saying that, in general, *the use of feedback information can be of the utmost importance even if the problem at hand is not a proper game*, strategic interaction with other similar agents being totally absent.

Now we can ask ourselves whether all of the above could be more easily obtained through manageable static models. The answer is negative in both cases (pollution and resource exploitation), not simply because of limit properties (which could be replicated here, for the resource extraction case), but, more importantly, for reasons pertaining to the procedure followed to construct the two static problems. Take first the case of polluting emissions. In a static framework, one thinks of an emission volume increasing linearly in output (or consumption), i.e., $S = Q$. All else equal, this static version of the model indeed produces the same conclusion as above solely because the solution of the optimal control problem based on the Hamiltonian function (2.32) is indeed stable and is being replicated forever in a quasi-static way by the firm. But this no longer holds if any environmental policy enters the picture (see Chapter 7). Moreover, it is not true for the alternative version of the model, in which the exploitation of a renewable resource is at stake. Disregarding the reproduction of the resource (which, in itself, would be sufficient to reject a static formulation), what matters the most is the fact that the static formulation replicates the solution of the Hamiltonian problem, which is unstable. Hence, the static formulation is not conducive to a proper understanding of the subject matter, the caveat concerning the intrinsically dynamic nature of the topic having been already stressed more than enough.

2.3   Advertising Campaigns

Ever since Dorfman and Steiner's (1954) pioneering analysis of advertising in a monopolistic industry, we are accustomed to the notion that the optimal ratio between advertising effort k and revenues $R = pQ$ must equal the ratio between the elasticities of demand w.r.t. advertising and price,

$$\frac{k}{pQ} = \frac{\epsilon_k}{|\epsilon_p|} \tag{2.52}$$

which is known as the *Dorfman–Steiner condition*.

Nerlove and Arrow (1962) provide a confirmation as well as an extension of this condition in a dynamic monopoly model where revenues are boosted by *goodwill* or *brand equity*, $G(t)$, constituting the state variable of the problem. Its dynamics is described by

$$\dot{G}(t) = k(t) - \delta G(t) \tag{2.53}$$

where $\delta > 0$ is the instantaneous and constant decay rate of goodwill. Output is then stipulated to depend on goodwill and price, $Q(G(t), p(t))$. Production costs are $C(Q(G(t), p(t)))$, and the monopolist aims at maximising the discounted flow of profits

$$\pi(t) = p(t) Q(G(t), p(t)) - C(Q(G(t), p(t))) - k(t) \tag{2.54}$$

under (2.53), the initial condition being $G(0) = G_0 > 0$. Here I rely on the formulation of the model in Sethi (1977, pp. 688–90) and Jacquemin (1972), as in the original paper the authors do not use optimal control theory.

Controls are price $p(t)$ and the advertising investment $k(t)$. Obviously, the Hamiltonian

$$\mathcal{H}(t) = e^{-\rho t} \{ p(t) Q(G(t), p(t)) - C(Q(G(t), p(t))) - k(t) + \lambda(t) [k(t) - \delta G(t)] \} \tag{2.55}$$

where $\rho > 0$ is the usual discount rate, generates a quasi-static solution for the market price, $p^M(t) = |\epsilon_p| C'(\cdot) / (|\epsilon_p| - 1)$, which obeys the familiar elasticity rule. The adjoint equation

$$\dot{\lambda} = -\frac{\partial \mathcal{H}}{\partial G} + \rho \lambda = \tag{2.56}$$

$$(\delta + \rho) \lambda - p(t) \cdot \frac{\partial Q(\cdot)}{\partial G} + \frac{\partial C(\cdot)}{\partial G} = (\delta + \rho) \lambda - \frac{\partial \pi(\cdot)}{\partial G}$$

reveals that the optimal value of the costate variable λ corresponds to the sum of the capital gain measured by the time derivative of the same variable and marginal profit, discounted at the cumulative rate $\delta + \rho$.

Using the optimal price and (2.56), one can establish that

$$G^M = \frac{\epsilon_G p^M Q^M}{|\epsilon_p| \left[(\delta + \rho) \lambda - \dot{\lambda} \right]} \iff \tag{2.57}$$

$$\frac{G^M}{p^M Q^M} = \frac{\epsilon_G}{|\epsilon_p| \cdot \partial \pi(\cdot) / \partial G} \tag{2.58}$$

must hold. Given the linear form of the state equation (2.53), $G^M = k^M/\delta$ and therefore the above condition rewrites as follows:

$$\frac{k^M}{p^M Q^M} = \frac{\delta \epsilon_G}{|\epsilon_p| \cdot \partial \pi(\cdot) / \partial G} \tag{2.59}$$

where $\epsilon_G = \partial Q / \partial G \cdot (G/Q) > 0$. In any of its three alternative but equivalent formulations (2.57–2.59), this finding conveys a well defined message:

Proposition 2.4 *The optimal ratio between the stock of goodwill (or the advertising effort) and sales revenues is proportional to the ratio between the elasticities of market* demand w.r.t. goodwill and price, respectively, appropriately adjusted to account for capital gains and depreciation.

This model is an evident example of a dynamic setup reproducing a familiar result initially derived on the basis of a static approach, and adding the appropriate ingredients related with time. The extension of this setup to the oligopoly case will be discussed in Chapter 4.

An earlier, equally important but a bit less user-friendly formulation of the same advertising problem is that of Vidale and Wolfe (1957). While having in mind the objective of finding a theoretical explanation of empirical data on the matter, these authors in fact opened a fruitful stream of theoretical research parallel to that on goodwill, gathering *sales-advertising response* models.

Vidale and Wolfe (1957) use the following state equation:

$$\dot{Q}(t) = zk(t)\left[1 - \frac{Q(t)}{Q_{\max}}\right] - \delta Q(t) \tag{2.60}$$

where $Q_{\max}$ is the exogenous saturation level of demand (the *carrying capacity* of the market), δ is a 'forgetting rate' measuring the amount of individual demand lost at any instant, and $z > 0$ is a constant parameter measuring the effectiveness of advertising efforts. This, indeed, is borrowed from the literature on resource extraction, being a modified form of the Verhulst–Lotka–Volterra equation (see fn. 4). The Vidale–Wolfe approach to modelling the impact of advertising on sales drastically differs from the Nerlove-Arrow one as it features the *diffusion term* $zk_i(t)\left[1 - Q(t)/Q_{\max}\right]$ in place of the purely linear effect of the effort $k(t)$. Additionally, the presence of this multiplicative effect between state and control causes (2.60) to be nonlinear, which in turn implies that the analytical treatment of this problem is restricted to the monopoly case, as the oligopoly game does not lend itself to a closed-form solution under feedback information. As we shall see in Chapter 4, however, there exist other similar ways of approaching the problem of advertising in oligopoly which do allow for a feedback solution although state equations are not linear.

2.4   Network Externalities

Several markets are characterised by network externalities. Typically, a network effect operates whenever a consumer's utility does not depend solely on the intrinsic properties of a good or service, but also on the number of other consumers buying or using it. This is evidently true of telephones and computers.[5]

---

[5] In the earliest days of the telephone industry, a telephone only produced a network effect (or, its intrinsic utility could not be distinguished from the externality). Nowadays, smart phones can be used as an agenda, a playstation, a music device or a digital camera, so they also produce an intrinsic utility independently of the network size. Instead, both components contributed to define the total utility produced by a PC back in the 1980s before the beginning of the internet age.

Starting from the early 1970s, industrial economics has developed static and dynamic models investigating network effects and the optimal price policy of firms operating in network industries. This section illustrates both versions of the baseline model of this literature.

2.4.1   The Original Static Model

As a starting point, I briefly summarise the basic elements of the so-called uniform calling model. This model was introduced by Artle and Averous (1973) in the context of the telephone system, and then further explored by Rohlfs (1974).[6] A unit mass of consumers is uniformly distributed over $[0, 1]$, i.e., the analogous of Hotelling's (1929) linear city, in decreasing order w.r.t. their willingness to pay in order to enter the network. A network externality appears in the generic consumer's utility or net surplus function U, as the value of joining the network is increasing in the size of the network itself:

$$U = w - p = q(1 - m) - p \qquad (2.61)$$

In (2.61), the overall willingness to pay for the good or service provided by the monopolist to a consumer located at point $m \in [0, 1]$ is $w = Q(1 - m)$, where Q measures the size of the network, i.e., the market demand for that good or service; and p is market price. Note that the willingness to pay of the consumer located at 1 is nought, which immediately implies that the network will not involve the whole population. In order to determine demand Q, the firm must identify the marginal consumer at $m = Q$ and then choose the price level extracting the entire surplus from the marginal consumer's pockets, $p_M(Q) = Q(1 - Q)$.

Noting that the gross surplus of the marginal consumer $\widehat{w} = Q(1 - Q)$ is concave in the network size Q, with $\max \widehat{w} = 1/4$ in correspondence of $Q = 1/2$, we see that, for any given price $\overline{p} < 1/4$, there are two economically admissible network sizes of the network. This fact is represented in Figure 2.6.

Supposing, for simplicity, that marginal cost is negligible, the monopolist's profit function coincides with revenues, and using the optimal price p_M, it can be written as

$$\pi = p_M(Q) \cdot Q = \widehat{w} \cdot Q = Q^2(1 - Q) \qquad (2.62)$$

which is now defined in terms of the network size (or quantity) only.

First and second order conditions are

$$\frac{\partial \pi}{\partial Q} = Q(2 - 3Q) = 0 \qquad (2.63)$$

$$\frac{\partial^2 \pi}{\partial Q^2} = 1 - 3Q \leq 0 \qquad (2.64)$$

The first solution of (2.63), $Q = 0$, can be disregarded as the corresponding profits are nil. The monopoly equilibrium is instead reached at $Q_M = 2/3$, which of course

---

[6] A summary of which also appears in Shy (1998, pp. 256–69).

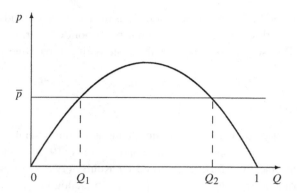

Figure 2.7 Monopoly with network externality

also strictly satisfies the concavity requirement (2.64). The bottom line of Rohlf's (1974) analysis is that the optimal policy of the monopolist is to cover the market only partially, due to the ambiguous nature of the network effect, whereby the increase in the willingness to pay it generates has a nonlinear effect on the price imposed onto the marginal consumer, which does not coincide with the last one locates at the end of the main street, so to speak.

Another extremely relevant aspect of the model is the coordination problem accompanying the (blackboxed) underlying dynamic process whereby consumers enter sequentially the network, starting from the individual located at left boundary of the linear street of unit length. The adjustment process towards the equilibrium is driven by the assumption that Q increases for all $p < Q(1 - Q)$, and conversely for all $p > Q(1 - Q)$. Hence, as soon as the network takes size Q_1 in correspondence of price $\widehat{p}$, the market immediately jumps into point $(Q_2, \widehat{p})$ through a sudden expansion of the network. This reveals that the point $(Q_1, \widehat{p})$ is unstable. Such instability notwithstanding, the relevance of $(Q_1, \widehat{p})$ can be found in the fact that Q_1 is the so-called *critical mass*. Once it has been reached, the start-up problem has been solved: the product has proven to be successful and its sales will necessarily expand to reach Q_2.

2.4.2   The Dynamic Problem

Now we can open up the black box used by Artle and Averous (1973) and Rohlfs (1974) to examine the properly dynamic version of the monopoly model with network externalities due to Dhebar and Oren (1985). The market exists over $t \in [0, \infty)$. The basic ingredients of the model are the same as in the static setup. At any time t, monopoly profits are $\pi(t) = p(t)Q(t)$, and the generic consumer's net utility is defined as in (2.61), with the appearance of the time argument.

What Dhebar and Oren (1985) add to the model is essentially the dynamics of the network size, by assuming that

$$\dot{Q}(t) = b\left[1 - \frac{p(t)}{Q(t)} - Q(t)\right] \tag{2.65}$$

which implies that the instantaneous growth rate of the network is a function of the difference between unsatisfied demand and the current network size. Hence, the firm must choose its price path to maximise

$$\Pi = \int_0^\infty p(t) Q(t) e^{-\rho t} dt \tag{2.66}$$

s.t. (2.65); $Q(0) = Q_0 \geq 0$; and $p(t) \in [0, Q(t)(1 - Q(t))]$. The resulting Hamiltonian function is

$$\mathcal{H}(t) = e^{-\rho t} \left\{ p(t) Q(t) + \lambda(t) b \left[1 - \frac{p(t)}{Q(t)} - Q(t) \right] \right\} \tag{2.67}$$

which is linear in the control variable, price $p(t)$. As we are about to see, this does not jeopardise the solvability of this optimal control problem. The FOC is

$$\frac{\partial \mathcal{H}}{\partial p} = Q - \frac{b\lambda}{Q} = 0 \tag{2.68}$$

yielding $\lambda = Q^2/b$. The costate equation is

$$\dot{\lambda} = -\frac{\partial \mathcal{H}}{\partial Q} + \rho \lambda \Leftrightarrow \dot{\lambda} = (b + \rho)\lambda - p \left(1 + \frac{b\lambda}{Q^2} \right) \tag{2.69}$$

which, using $\lambda = Q^2/b$, can be rewritten as follows:

$$\dot{\lambda} = \frac{Q^2 (b + \rho)}{b} - p \tag{2.70}$$

The necessary conditions (2.68–2.69) are accompanied by the transversality condition $\lim_{t \to \infty} e^{-\rho t} \lambda Q = 0$. Now it is worth noting that the state dynamics is in fact

$$\dot{Q} = \frac{b}{Q} \left[Q(1 - Q) - p \right] \tag{2.71}$$

which implies that $\dot{Q} \geq 0$ for all $p \in [0, Q(1 - Q)]$. This amounts to saying that the network expands for any admissible price level, reaching its steady state volume at $p_M(Q) = Q(1 - Q)$. Treating (2.69) as an additional state equation and imposing stationarity, one obtains the steady state network size

$$Q_M = \frac{2b}{3b + \rho} \tag{2.72}$$

which can be substituted into $p_M(Q)$ to compute the steady state equilibrium price

$$p_M = \frac{2b(b + \rho)}{(3b + \rho)^2} \tag{2.73}$$

Looking at (2.72–2.73), together with

$$\frac{\partial p_M}{\partial \rho} = \frac{2b(b - \rho)}{(3b + \rho)^3} \gtrless 0 \,\forall\, \rho \lessgtr b; \quad \frac{\partial Q_M}{\partial \rho} = -\frac{2b}{(3b + \rho)^2} < 0 \,\forall\, b, \rho \tag{2.74}$$

one can easily ascertain that the following holds:

Proposition 2.5 *The steady state levels of price and network coincide with their static levels iff $\rho = 0$. As the discount rate increases, the steady state network size decreases, while the steady state price exhibits a non-monotone (concave) shape.*

The first part of the Proposition says that the static outcome can be replicated provided the monopolist attaches the same value to a dollar gained today or on doomsday, otherwise the slightest myopia causes the equilibrium network size to shrink as compared to the prediction of the static version of the problem. An interesting detail of the second part of the Proposition is that $\lim_{\rho \to \infty} Q_M = 0$, which, in addition to reinforcing the first part of the claim, tells that the transversality condition will be surely met.

2.5   Durable Good Monopoly, the Coase Conjecture and Optimal Durability

The problem of the intertemporal price pattern of a durable good supplied by a monopolist is intimately connected with the so-called *Coase conjecture* (Coase, 1972). The conjecture can be formulated as follows: since a monopolistic firm selling a durable good competes against its future self, it will eventually supply the perfectly competitive output at the perfectly competitive price. 'Eventually' means as soon as the terminal time of the period of commitment not to flood the market – if any – is reached; indeed, if such a period is infinitesimal, monopoly power evaporates and therefore so does the control over price, and the monopolist is forced to immediately supply the competitive output at the competitive price 'in the twinkling of an eye' (Coase, 1972, p. 141).

The source of the unlucky monopolist's curse is the fact that it faces consumers endowed with rational expectations about the price dynamics, who therefore delay their purchases since they correctly anticipate that price will go down and – sooner or later – fall to marginal production cost. An appealing way of appreciating the twofold nature of the Coase conjecture is that (1) the key to preserving the profitability of standing alone on the market place is possessing a credible commitment device, and (2) product durability reduces or completely eliminates the difference between monopoly and perfect competition, thereby making the issue of industry structure immaterial, in the limit case in which commitment technologies are altogether absent.

The long-standing discussion about the Coase conjecture has focussed on the construction of dynamic models constructed either to prove it or to single out factors that could discard it. In a nutshell, the elements which might cause its failure are the presence of depreciation (Bond and Samuelson, 1984, 1987), capacity constraints (Bulow, 1982) or convex variable costs of production (Khan, 1986).

The essential elements of this debate can be outlined relying on Driskill (1997). His analysis may be reconstructed via a linear quadratic representation of the monopolist's problem, which is a special and illustrative case of the more general exposition contained in his paper.

The monopoly market for a durable good exists over $t \in [0, \infty)$. The representative consumer derives an instantaneous utility

$$U(t) = Q(t) \left[a - \frac{Q^2(t)}{2} \right] \tag{2.75}$$

from the services generated by the durable good, whose stock at any instant t is $Q(t) \geq 0$; a is a positive constant. At any t, the firm produces $u(t) \geq 0$ units of the durable, $u(t)$ being the control variable. The stock depreciates at an invariant rate $\delta \geq 0$, so that the state dynamics is

$$\dot{Q}(t) = u(t) - \delta Q(t) \tag{2.76}$$

The presence of depreciation is important in that it makes room for a regenerating rent for the monopolist. For future reference, note that (2.76) is analogous to the Solow–Swan dynamics of capacity in (2.1), except for a change of labels. Consumers and the firm share the same discount rate $\rho > 0$, at which consumers can either borrow or lend money. Hence, defining as $p(t)$ the unit price of the durable, an intuitive indifference condition establishes that the representative consumer has in mind the following expected price dynamics:

$$E\left[\dot{p}(t)\right] = (\delta + \rho)\,p(t) - \frac{\partial U(t)}{\partial Q(t)} \tag{2.77}$$

as marginal utility must equal the difference between marginal cost (the sum of depreciation and discounting) and the expected capital gain at all times, that is,

$$\frac{\partial U(t)/\partial Q(t)}{p(t)} = \delta + \rho - \frac{E\left[\dot{p}(t)\right]}{p(t)} \tag{2.78}$$

where $E[\cdot]$ is the expectation operator. If the price expectation function is linear in $Q(t)$, e.g., $\dot{p}(t) = \beta + \gamma Q(t)$, with $\beta > 0$ and $\gamma \in (0, 1)$, from (2.75) and (2.77) one obtains the demand function expressed by the representative consumer:

$$p(t) = \frac{a + \beta - (1 - \gamma)\,Q(t)}{\delta + \rho} \tag{2.79}$$

which explains the restriction on γ, in order to have a decreasing demand schedule. Before proceeding, a remark is in order concerning the price dynamics implicitly defined by (2.79): $\dot{p}(t) < 0$ whenever $\dot{Q}(t) > 0$, revealing that price falls if the stock is lower than its steady state volume, and vice versa. This happens because the high marginal utility attached to a small stock must be compensated for by a negative capital gain, and vice versa.

The monopolist sells instead of renting. Assuming the firm's production technology is characterised by decreasing returns, e.g., $C(t) = bu^2(t)/2$, $b \geq 0$, the instantaneous profit function is $\pi(t) = \left[p(t) - bu(t)/2\right]u(t)$, and the monopolist must

$$\max_{u(t)} \Pi = \int_0^\infty \left[p(t) - \frac{bu(t)}{2}\right]u(t)\,e^{-\rho t}dt \tag{2.80}$$

s.t. (2.76), the initial condition $Q(0) = Q_0 \geq 0$ and the appropriate transversality condition. The current-value Hamiltonian function is

$$\mathcal{H}(\cdot) = e^{-\rho t}\left\{\left[\frac{a + \beta - (1 - \gamma)\,Q(t)}{\delta + \rho} - \frac{bu(t)}{2}\right]u(t) + \lambda(t)\left[u(t) - \delta Q(t)\right]\right\}$$
$$\tag{2.81}$$

which generates the FOC

$$\frac{\partial \mathcal{H}}{\partial u} = \frac{a + \beta - (1 - \gamma) Q}{\delta + \rho} - bu + \lambda = 0 \tag{2.82}$$

and the costate equation

$$-\frac{\partial \mathcal{H}}{\partial k} = \dot{\lambda} - \rho \lambda \Rightarrow \dot{\lambda} = \frac{(1 - \gamma) u}{(\delta + \rho)} + \lambda (\delta + \rho) \tag{2.83}$$

The transversality condition is $\lim_{t \to \infty} e^{-\rho t} \lambda Q = 0$.

From (2.82) we obtain the optimal value of the costate variable,

$$\lambda = bu - \frac{a + \beta - (1 - \gamma) Q}{\delta + \rho} \tag{2.84}$$

and the control equation

$$\dot{u} = \frac{(\delta + \rho) \dot{\lambda} - (1 - \gamma) \dot{q}}{b (\delta + \rho)} \tag{2.85}$$

which, using (2.76) and (2.84), can be rewritten as follows:

$$\dot{u} = \frac{\delta (1 - \gamma) q + (\delta + \rho) \left[b (\delta + \rho) u + (1 - \gamma) q - a - \beta \right]}{b (\delta + \rho)} \tag{2.86}$$

On the basis of (2.76) and (2.86), we learn two relevant pieces of information, namely,

- the determinant of the 2×2 Jacobian matrix of the state-control system is

$$\Delta (J) = \frac{\partial \dot{Q}}{\partial Q} \cdot \frac{\partial \dot{u}}{\partial u} - \frac{\partial \dot{Q}}{\partial u} \cdot \frac{\partial \dot{u} (t)}{\partial Q} = \frac{(1 - \gamma) (2\delta + \rho)}{b (\delta + \rho)} - \delta (\delta + \rho) < 0 \tag{2.87}$$

and therefore the steady state equilibrium is a saddle point iff

$$1 - \gamma < \frac{b\delta (\delta + \rho)^2}{2\delta + \rho} \tag{2.88}$$

and

- the locus $\dot{u} = 0$, i.e.,

$$u = \frac{(a + \beta) (\delta + \rho) - (1 - \gamma) (2\delta + \rho) Q}{b (\delta + \rho)^2} \tag{2.89}$$

is a negatively sloped line in the state-control space; as a result, the phase diagram looks exactly the same as in Figure 2.1 (the capacity accumulation model).

The unique steady state point is

$$Q^M = \frac{(a + \beta) (\delta + \rho)}{b\delta^2 (\delta + 2\rho) + \delta \left[2 (1 - \gamma) + b\rho^2 \right] - \rho (1 - \gamma)} \; ; u^M = \delta Q^M \tag{2.90}$$

both expressions being positive if condition (2.88) is satisfied. This proves the following:

Proposition 2.6 *If the coordinates of the steady state equilibrium* (Q^M, u^M) *are positive, then such a steady state is a saddle point, and conversely.*

Studying the properties of (2.86) and (2.90), we may now easily derive the main result of Driskill's (1997, p. 146) analysis:

Proposition 2.7 *The steady state stock of the monopolist selling the durable to consumers endowed with rational expectations is lower than the steady state stock associated with the socially efficient outcome (or, the perfectly competitive level).*

This conclusion, however, has two relevant ancillary conclusions, also highlighted by Driskill (1997, p. 146). The first derives from

$$\lim_{\delta \to 0} Q^M = \frac{\alpha + \beta}{1 - \gamma} \tag{2.91}$$

which implies:

Corollary 2.8 *If production is characterised by an increasing marginal cost and the durable good does not depreciate, the monopoly steady state is socially efficient.*

This replicates Kahn's (1986) conclusion, assuming the durable does not depreciates and marginal cost is increasing. Yet, it also shows that the perfect equilibrium outcome is only one in the continuum of equilibria generated by the presence of depreciation (more about this aspect in Section 2.5.2). The second property is generated by the limit of the control dynamics $\dot{u}$ as $b \to 0$:

Corollary 2.9 *If $b = 0$, the adjustment to the steady state is instantaneous, and the monopolist supplies the socially efficient stock 'in the twinkling of an eye'.*

This corollary replicates the result in Bond and Samuelson (1984), assuming the presence of depreciation and a constant marginal cost. Hence, Driskill's (1997) analysis nicely encompasses two cornerstones of the previous debate on the Coase conjecture as special cases of a more general picture.[7]

2.5.1   The Finite Horizon Case

Additionally, the same model produces a turnpike property emerging when the monopolist's planning horizon becomes finite, with a terminal time T. The turnpike theorem proven by Driskill (1997, p. 148) establishes that choosing a sufficiently long time horizon drives the equilibrium path of the finite horizon case arbitrarily close to that of the infinite horizon setting.

Given $t \in [0, T]$, the firm's maximand is

$$\max_{u} \Pi = \int_0^T \left[p(t) - \frac{bu(t)}{2} \right] u(t) e^{-\rho t} dt \tag{2.92}$$

---

[7] Karp (1993, 1996a) illustrate the failure of the Coase conjecture when durables are based on the extraction of non-renewable resources. Again Karp (1996b) shows that monopoly power may not be so appealing in the same situation. On the relationship between market power (or industry structure) and the extraction of natural resources, see Chapter 7.

under the same constraints as above, except that the demand function and the firm's control are defined in terms of time-varying parameters:

$$p(t) = h(t) + \ell(t) Q(t) \tag{2.93}$$

$$u(t) = m(t) + r(t) Q(t) \tag{2.94}$$

and the transversality condition accompanying the FOC and the costate equation is now $\lambda_T = 0$.

To prove the turnpike property, Driskill (1997) manipulates the necessary conditions to generate

$$\dot{m} = \frac{h - h(\delta + \rho)}{b} - m\rho \tag{2.95}$$

$$\dot{r} = r(2\delta + \rho - r) - \frac{\ell(2\delta + \rho) + \dot{\ell}}{b} \tag{2.96}$$

and the rational expectations requirement to find that the latter is satisfied iff

$$\dot{\ell} = 1 + \ell(2\delta + \rho - r) \tag{2.97}$$

and

$$\dot{h} = h(\delta + \rho) - \ell m - a \tag{2.98}$$

and the critical values of ℓ and r solving $\ell = r = 0$ are the values of the autonomous, infinite-horizon problem price and control function p and u. The vector of terminal values $\{h_T, \ell_T, m_T, r_T\}$ is then determined by the terminal conditions $\lambda_T = p_T = 0$, the FOC evaluated at T and the initial condition Q_0, and turns out to be independent of T. This yields the following result, whose full proof in in Driskill (1997, appendix C):

Proposition 2.10 *Define as Q_T the equilibrium stock of the durable good in the finite horizon problem and Q_∞ the equilibrium stock of the good in the infinite-horizon problem. For any $t > 0$ and any arbitrarily small $\varepsilon > 0$, there exists a finite horizon of length $T > t$ such that $|Q_T - Q_\infty| < \varepsilon$.*

The interest of this turnpike theorem emerging from the analysis of the finite horizon setting lies in an aspect highlighted by Tsutsui and Mino (1990) in the sticky price oligopoly game which is illustrated in detail in the next chapter, and whose relevance has been stressed by Karp (1996) in the context of the present monopoly model. He shows that if the good depreciates there exists a continuum of equilibria, so that the Coase conjecture may not hold, as the competitive equilibrium is just one out of infinitely many. This fact also appears in Bond and Samuelson (1987), Ausubel and Deneckere (1989) and, as we already know, Driskill (1997, see the limit in (2.91) above).

The point is that the common wisdom in connection with the folk theorem literature is that a repeated game unravelling over a finite horizon does differ from a repeated game unravelling over an infinite horizon, given the same constituent stage game. The turnpike property outlined in Proposition 2.10 demonstrates that the equilibrium paths of the dynamic monopoly problem in the two cases can become arbitrarily close to each other by choosing an appropriately long time horizon, and the competitive outcome emerges in the limit.

The extension of the model to allow for the presence of many players, thus giving rise to a differential game (Driskill, 2001), can be found in the next chapter. Here, to complete the treatment of the durable good monopolist, we have to go through a few implications of the foregoing discussion, pointing at an issue directly connected with the role of depreciation.

2.5.2   Optimal Durability

The depreciation of a durable good has triggered a parallel discussion about optimal durability or planned obsolescence, as depreciation/durability affects the firm's intertemporal rent. This literature dates back at least to Martin (1962), Kleiman and Ophir (1966), Levhari and Srinivasan (1969) and Schmalensee (1970), all of these preceding Coase (1972) and showing that if production costs increase in durability, a monopolist will find it optimal to choose a lower durability than a perfectly competitive firm operating with an analogous technology. Swan (1970, p. 884) argues that this might no be the case as

the choice of durability by a monopolist is essentially one of minimizing the cost of the provision of any given service flow from a stock of durable goods. The decision is independent of demand or revenue conditions. It follows that a monopolist will produce goods of the same durability as competitive firms

That is, according to Swan (1970), the durability of goods is unaffected by industry structure or the intensity of market competition. What follows offers a synthetic account of this debate, using a sketch of the linear quadratic version of the model investigated by Kamien and Schwartz (1974), where a time-invariant industry structure with $n \geq 1$ firms is assumed, durability (i.e., the depreciation rate) and plant size are both chosen once and for all at the initial instant, while the individual production rate is controlled over the entire time horizon. Hence, the setup used by Kamien and Schwartz (1974), unlike most of the classical literature on the Coase conjecture and optimal durability, is indeed an oligopoly game, whose limits are pure monopoly and perfect competition. What these authors analyse is a scenario in which firms maximise profits w.r.t. their production rates in a properly dynamic fashion, and then by backward induction choose capacities and depreciation rates in order to maximise the present value of their firms' profit flows calculated on the basis of the aforementioned maximization, treating capacity and depreciation as long-run variable that cannot be changed during the game (which, in fact, requires the presence of some commitment device remaining hidden behind the curtains of the model).

The instantaneous demand function is $p(t) = a - Q(t)$, with $Q(t) = \sum_{i=1}^{n} q_i(t)$. The dynamics of firm i's stock of durable good is

$$\dot{q}_i(t) = u_i(t) - \delta q_i(t) \tag{2.99}$$

The assumption concerning the technology common to all firms alike has it that the short-run average production cost is convex, while long-run average cost is constant. The total cost function of the individual firm is $C_i(t) = u_i(t)[u_i(t) + f(\delta) - 2k_i] + k_i^2$, where k_i is the plant size and $f(\delta)$ is monotonically decreasing in the decay rate δ and must satisfy $2\partial f(\delta)/\partial\delta + (\delta + \rho)\partial^2 f(\delta)/\partial\delta^2 > 0$.[8] Both $f(\delta)$ and k_i are constant throughout the optimization interval, as they are decided upon by the firm before starting production at time zero. In Kamien and Schwartz (1974), firms retains the ownership of their shares of the durable good and collect rental fees. The resulting Hamiltonian function of firm i is

$$\mathcal{H}(\cdot) = e^{-\rho t}\left\{p(Q)q(t) + \lambda(t)\left[u_i(t) - \delta q_i(t)\right]\right\} \tag{2.100}$$

which reveals the assumption that each firm takes the rival's aggregate stock as given and therefore disregard their $n - 1$ state equations. The firm chooses $u(t)$ to maximise (2.100), with the initial condition $q_i(0) = q_{i0} = 0$.

From the system of necessary conditions, there emerges that the optimal control and the individual state at any t are

$$u^* = u^{ss}\left(1 - e^{-\varpi t}\right)$$
$$q^* = q^{ss}\left[\delta + (\varpi - \delta)e^{-\varpi t}\right] \tag{2.101}$$

where superscript ss stands for steady state and

$$\varpi = \frac{\sqrt{(2\delta + \rho)^2 + 2(n + 1)} - \rho}{2} \tag{2.102}$$

$$q^{ss} = \frac{a - (\delta + \rho)[f(\delta) - 2k]}{2\delta(\delta + \rho) + n + 1} \tag{2.103}$$

The phase diagram is analogous to the Solow–Swan model (i.e., Figure 2.1, changing the labels of state and control variables) and produces a saddle path departing from the vertical axis (starting at some $u(0) > u^{ss}$) and going eastward to reach the steady state equilibrium point (q^{ss}, u^{ss}).

Once the optimal control path and the steady state have been characterised, one can write the maximum present value of the individual firm's profit flow, given the symmetric plant size k and $f(\delta)$ as

$$\rho V = (q^{ss})^2 w^2\left[1 - \frac{n - 1}{(\rho + \varpi)(\rho + 2\varpi)}\right] - 2k \tag{2.104}$$

which takes its maximum at

$$k^* = \frac{[a - f(\delta)(\delta + \rho)](\delta + \rho)\vartheta}{2[(\rho + \varpi)^2 - \vartheta(\delta + \rho)^2]}, \quad \vartheta = 1 - \frac{n - 1}{(\rho + \varpi)(\rho + 2\varpi)} \tag{2.105}$$

Then it can be checked that such plant size can be thought of as being chosen in order to minimise the average production cost.

---

[8] This shape of the cost function means that the long-run cost function is $C(t) = f(\delta)u(t)$, while the optimal scale of production satisfies $\partial C(t)/\partial k_i = 0$, which in turn implies that the firm must operate at full capacity.

As for optimal durability, let's introduce an explicit (and simplifying) assumption absent in Kamien and Schwartz (1974), whereby $f(\delta) = 1/\delta$. If $n = 1$ and the industry is a monopoly, we have $\partial V/\partial \delta = 0$ in

$$\delta_M^* = \frac{1 - a - 2\rho k + \sqrt{8\rho k + (a + 2\rho k - 1)^2}}{4k} > 0 \qquad (2.106)$$

while if $n \to \infty$, we have that $\partial V/\partial \delta = 0$ is equivalent to requiring $f(\delta) + (\delta + \rho)f'(\delta) = 0$, which, using $f(\delta) = 1/\delta$, entails that $\lim_{n \to \infty} \partial V/\partial \delta < 0$, whereby an arbitrarily large population of perfectly competitive firms will choose infinite durability (or, a decay rate equal to zero). This exercise proves the following:

Proposition 2.11 *The optimal decay rate (durability) under monopoly is higher (lower) than the optimal decay rate under perfect competition.*

Once again, a quasi-static investigation of the problem (in this case, optimal durability) is doomed to fall short of the target. The reason is that one may construct for this purpose a multi-period model in discrete time, where the monopoly operates, say, for T periods and discounting matters. But this (1) makes the model intrinsically dynamic and (2) calls for the analysis of the limit case in which $T \to \infty$.

Further Reading

Probably the earliest dynamic analyses of monopoly are in Evans (1924) and Tintner (1937). For more, see Mussa (1977) and Sobel (1984). The cornerstone of the intertemporal exploitation of natural resources is Hotelling (1931), while an exhaustive overview of acquired wisdom is in Dasgupta and Heal (1979). The monopoly model with advertising has been extended by Jacquemin (1972), among others, to include the possibility that advertising may enter explicitly the definition of the market demand function. The role of uncertainty in the same goodwill model is investigated by Tapiero (1978). On the solution of the Vidale and Wolfe (1957), see Sethi (1973). A modified version of the same setup, with a different state equation, is in Ozga (1960). For a survey of the related debate, see Sethi (1977), Feichtinger *et al.* (1994), Erickson (2003) and Jørgensen and Zaccour (2004). A monopoly model with advertising and spatial differentiation is in Lambertini (2005). In Hörner and Kamien (2004), the Coase conjecture and Hotelling's intertemporal pricing rule are treated as the dual of each other, in the spirit of Sonnenschein (1968). For more on the theory of network esternalities, see Shy (2000). For further investigations of monopoly with network effects, see Rabenau and Stahl (1974), Oren and Smith (1981) and Olsen (1992). Recent reformulations of the role of network externalities interacting with product quality in a dynamic monopoly are in Markovich (2008) and Lambertini and Orsini (2010). Additional insights on the Coase conjecture and optimal durability or planned obsolescence in monopoly can be found in Stokey (1981), Bulow (1986), Gul *et al.* (1986), Ausubel and Deneckere (1989), Bagnoli *et al.* (1989), Malueg and Solow (1990) and Karp and Perloff (1996), among several others. An argument which I haven't treated here is that of R&D for process and product innovation (see Lambertini and Mantovani, 2009), but this topic will be extensively treated in Chapter 6, including monopoly as a special case.

Bibliography

Artle, R. and C. Averous (1973), "The Telephone Systems as a Public Good: Static and Dynamic Aspects", *Bell Journal of Economics*, **4**, 89–100.

Ausubel, L. and R. Deneckere (1989), "Reputation and Bargaining in Durable Goods Monopoly", *Econometrica*, **57**, 511–32.

Bagnoli, M., S. Salant and J. Swierzbinski (1989), "Durable Goods Monopoly with Discrete Demand", *Journal of Political Economy*, **97**, 1459–78.

Bond, E. and L. Samuelson (1984), "Durable Good Monopolies with Rational Expectations and Replacement Sales", *Journal of Economics*, **15**, 336–45.

Bond, E. and L. Samuelson (1987), "The Coase Conjecture Need Not Hold for Durable Good Monopolies with Depreciation", *Economics Letters*, **24**, 93–97.

Bulow, J. (1982), "Durable-Goods Monopolists", *Journal of Political Economy*, **90**, 314–32.

Bulow, J. (1986), "The Economic Theory of Planned Obsolescence", *Quarterly Journal of Economics*, **101**, 729–49.

Coase, R. (1972), "Durability and Monopoly", *Journal of Law and Economics*, **15**, 143–49.

Dasgupta, P. and G. Heal (1979), *Economic Theory and Exhaustible Resources*, Cambridge, Cambridge University Press.

Dhebar, A. and S. Oren (1985), "Optimal Dynamic Pricing for Expanding Networks", *Marketing Science*, **4**, 336–51.

Dorfman, R. and P. Steiner (1954), "Optimal Advertising and Optimal Quality", *American Economic Review*, **44**, 826–36.

Driskill, R. (1997), "Durable Goods Monopoly, Increasing Marginal Cost and Depreciation", *Economica*, **64**, 137–54.

Driskill, R. (2001), " Durable Goods Oligopoly", *International Journal of Industrial Organization*, **19**, 391–413.

Eisner, R. and R. Strotz (1963), "Determinants of Business Investment", in Commission on Money and Credit, *Impacts of Monetary Policy*, Englewood Cliffs, NJ, Prentice-Hall.

Erickson, G. (2003), *Dynamic Models of Advertising Competition*, Dordrecht, Kluwer.

Evans, G.C. (1924), "The Dynamics of Monopoly", *American Mathematical Monthly*, **31**, 75–83.

Feichtinger, G., R. Hartl and S. Sethi (1994), "Dynamic Optimal Control Models in Advertising: Recent Developments", *Management Science*, **40**, 195–226.

Gould, J.P. (1968), "Adjustment Costs in the Theory of Investment of the Firm", *Review of Economic Studies*, **35**, 47–55.

Gul, F., H. Sonnenschein and R. Wilson (1986), "Foundations of Dynamic Monopoly and the Coase Conjecture", *Journal of Economic Theory*, **39**, 155–90.

Hall, R.E. and D.W. Jorgenson (1967), "Tax Policy and Investment Behaviour", *American Economic Review*, **57**, 391–414.

Hardin, G. (1968), "The Tragedy of the Commons", *Science* **162**, 1243–48.

Hörner, J. and M. Kamien (2004), "Coase and Hotelling: A Meeting of the Minds", *Journal of Political Economy*, **112**, 718–23.

Hotelling, H. (1929), "Stability in Competition", *Economic Journal*, **39**, 41–57.

Hotelling, H. (1931), "The Economics of Exhaustible Resources", *Journal of Political Economy*, **39**, 137–75.

Jacquemin, A. (1972), "Market Structure and the Firm's Market Power", *Journal of Industrial Economics*, **20**, 122–34.

Jorgenson, D.W. (1963), "Capital Theory and Investment Behaviour", *American Economic Review*, **53** (Papers & Proceedings), 247–59.

Jørgensen, S. and G. Zaccour (2004), *Differential Games in Marketing*, Kluwer, Dordrecht.

Kahn, C. (1986), "The Durable Goods Monopolist and Consistency with Increasing Costs", *Econometrica*, **54**, 275–94.

Kamien, J. and N. Schwartz (1974), "Product Durability under Monopoly and Competition", *Econometrica*, **42**, 289–301.

Karp, L. (1993), "Monopoly Extraction of a Durable Nonrenewable Resource: Failure of the Coase Conjecture", *Economica*, **60**, 13–26.

Karp, L. (1996a), "Depreciation Erodes the Coase Conjecture", *European Economic Review*, **40**, 473–90.

Karp, L. (1996b), "Monopoly Power Can Be Disadvantageous in the Extraction of a Durable Nonrenewable Resource", *International Economic Review*, **37**, 825–49.

Karp, L. and J. Perloff (1996), "The Optimal Suppression of a Low-Cost Technology by a Durable-Good Monopoly", *RAND Journal of Economics*, **27**, 346–64.

Kleiman, E . and T. Ophir (1966), "The Durability of Durable Goods", *Review of Economic Studies*, **33**, 165–78.

Lambertini, L. (2005), "Advertising in a Dynamic Spatial Monopoly", *European Journal of Operational Research*, **166**, 547–56.

Lambertini, L. and A. Mantovani (2009), "Process and Product Innovation by a Multiproduct Monopolist: A Dynamic Approach", *International Journal of Industrial Organization*, **27**, 508–18.

Lambertini, L. and R. Orsini (2010), "R&D for Quality Improvement and Network Externalities", *Networks and Spatial Economics*, **10** 113–24.

Levhari, D. and T.N. Srinivasan (1969), "Durability of Consumption Goods: Competition versus Monopoly", *American Economic Review*, **59**, 102–07.

Lotka, A.J. (1925), *Elements of Physical Biology*, Philadelphia, Williams and Wilkins.

Malueg, D. and J. Solow (1990), "Monopoly Production of Durable Exhaustible Resources", *Economica*, **57**, 29–47.

Markovich, S. (2008), "Snowball: A Dynamic Oligopoly Model with Network Externalities", *Journal of Economic Dynamics and Control*, **32**, 909–38.

Martin, D.D. (1962), "Monopoly Power and the Durability of Durable Goods", *Southern Economic Journal*, **28**, 271–77.

Mussa, M. (1977), "External and Internal Adjustment Costs and the Theory of Aggregate and Firm Investment", *Economica*, **44**, 163–78.

Nerlove, M. and K.J. Arrow (1962), "Optimal Advertising Policy under Dynamic Conditions", *Economica*, **29**, 129–42.

Olsen, T.E. (1992), "Durable Goods Monopoly, Learning by Doing and the Coase Conjecture", *European Economic Review*, **36**, 157–77.

Oren, S. and S. Smith (1981), "Critical Mass and Tariff Structure in Electronic Communications Markets", *Bell Journal of Economics*, **12**, 467–87.

Ozga, S. (1960), "Imperfect Markets Through Lack of Knowledge", *Quarterly Journal of Economics*, **74**, 29–52.

Rabenau, B. and K. Stahl (1974), "Dynamic Aspects of Public Goods: A Further Analysis of the Telephone System", *Bell Journal of Economics*, **5**, 651–69.

Reynolds, S.S. (1987), "Capacity Investment, Preemption and Commitment in an Infinite Horizon Model", *International Economic Review*, **28**, 69–88.

Reynolds, S. (1991), "Dynamic Oligopoly with Capacity Adjustment Costs", *Journal of Economic Dynamics and Control*, **15**, 491–514.

Rohlfs, J. (1974), "A Theory of Interdependent Demand for a Communications Service", *Bell Journal of Economics*, **5**, 16–37.

Schmalensee, R. (1970), "Regulation and the Durability of Goods", *Bell Journal of Economics*, **1**, 54–64.

Sethi, S. (1973), "Optimal Control of the Vidale-Wolfe Advertising Model", *Operations Research*, **21**, 998–1013.

Sethi, S. (1977), "Dynamic Optimal Control Models in Advertising: A Survey", *SIAM Review*, **19**, 685–725.

Shy, O. (1998), *Industrial Organization. Theory and Applications*, Cambridge, MA, MIT Press.

Shy, O. (2000), *The Economics of Network Industries*, Cambridge, Cambridge University Press.

Sobel, J. (1984), "The Timing of Sales", *Review of Economic Studies*, **51**, 353–68.

Solow, R. (1956), A Contribution to the Theory of Economic Growth", *Quarterly Journal of Economics*, **70**, 65–94.

Sonnenschein, H. (1968), "The Dual of Duopoly Is Complementary Monopoly: Or, Two of Cournot's Theories Are One", *Journal of Political Economy*, **76**, 316–18.

Stokey, N. (1981), "Rational Expectations and Durable Goods Pricing", *Bell Journal of Economics*, **12**, 112–28.

Swan, P.L. (1970), "Durability of Consumption Goods", *American Economic Review*, **60**, 884–94.

Swan, P.L. (1972), "Optimum Durability, Second Hand Markets, and Planned Obsolescence", *Journal of Political Economy*, **80**, 575–85.

Swan, T.W. (1956), "Economic Growth and Capital Accumulation", *Economic Record*, **32**, 334–61.

Tapiero, C. (1978), "Optimum Advertising and Goodwill under Uncertainty", *Operations Research*, **26**, 450–63.

Tintner, G. (1937), "Monopoly over Time", *Econometrica*, **5**, 160–70.

Tsutsui, S. and K. Mino (1990), "Nonlinear Strategies in Dynamic Duopolistic Competition with Sticky Prices, *Journal of Economic Theory*, **52**, 136–61.

Verhulst, P.H. (1838), "Notice sur la loi que la population poursuit dans son accroissement", *Correspondance mathématique et physique*, **10**, 113–21.

Vidale, M. and H. Wolfe (1957), "An Operations Research Study of Sales Response to Advertising", *Operations Research*, **5**, 370–81.

Volterra, V. (1931), "Variations and Fluctuations of the Number of Individuals in Animal Species Living Together", in R.N. Chapman (ed.), *Animal Ecology*, New York, McGraw–Hill.

Waldman, M. (1993), "A New Perspective on Planned Obsolescence", *Quarterly Journal of Economics*, **108**, 273–83.

3 Oligopoly

This chapter reviews differential games of different natures, sharing, however, a common feature: firms are assumed to control either quantities or prices and nothing else. Note that the evolution of applications of differential games has not been linear, so to speak. What I mean here is that while industrial economics has slowly moved away from basic oligopoly models describing quantity or price competition to account for richer and more sophisticated strategy spaces, differential games in IO left aside proper characterisation of what we are accustomed to consider as Bertrand and Cournot competition for quite some time, taking as departure points either models including several different control spaces at the same time or models where firms are indeed choosing output levels but never shoot right at the correct price level except asymptotically at equilibrium. Industrial economists started learning about differential oligopoly games thanks to Clemhout et al. (1971), where such things as consumer loyalty and market shares are already taken to be the relevant objects of analysis. And in the 1970s a large literature flourishes on themes connected with marketing and management, like advertising, which are reviewed in the next chapters. Then, Simaan and Takayama (1978) investigate the role of demand dynamics in the form of price stickiness, with many productive follow-ups.

Their model, frequently revisited, lends itself to be used as a ductile and malleable tool for the illustration of solution techniques as well as for helping us to understand properly how a state dynamics may condition the strategic behaviour of firms, and why it is relevant to adopt such a dynamic view. Put differently, in addition to its intrinsic value, the sticky price game allows one to grasp the difference between a static and a dynamic approach to a 'simple' oligopoly game, where 'simple' means that firms are just choosing output levels. This is the subject matter of Section 3.1, where quantity competition under price stickiness is investigated using several solution concepts, including nonlinear feedback strategies, also considering the case (empirically relevant but seldom considered in the theoretical literature) of hyperbolic demand functions.

Section 3.2 examines the opposite case, where demand is sluggish, while Section 3.3 illustrates games of capacity accumulation, where physical capital is a state variable for each firm and the structure is a strategic reinterpretation of dominant growth models in macroeconomics. The little we avail of about price competition appears in Section 3.4. Section 3.5 covers oligopoly games with durable and addictive goods.

The remainder of the chapter discusses themes which have been largely debated in IO and have been treated also in dynamic settings, although not necessarily differential games. The first is the nature of strategic competition as we recognise it observing the slope of reaction functions or thinking about conjectural variations (Section 3.6). This subject ultimately leads to one of the current frontiers of game theory, known as potential games. The second theme is collusion, a terrain on which little has been done in terms of applications (in any field, not only IO), although the toolkit does exist and is waiting for researchers to take it up. Collusion sustained by trigger strategies defined anew in a differential game is illustrated in Section 3.7, where a summary of the general model illustrates the difficulties affecting the replication in the field of differential oligopoly games of a line of research which has been intensively and extensively explored using the theory of supergames. Finally, Section 3.8 summarises a long and solid debate about the evolution of an industry over time, with firms joining and quitting the market at different points in time, and a relatively old but elegant stream of research on limit pricing dating back to the 1970s, complemented by the modern literature on optimal stopping decisions and the discrete time approach to the construction of Markovian equilibria lending themselves to empirical evaluation.

3.1   Sticky Prices

The Cournot game with price stickiness has a long tradition in differential oligopoly games, as it dates back to Simaan and Takayama (1978),[1] and has been subsequently extended in several directions by Fershtman and Kamien (1987, 1990), Dockner (1988), Tsutsui and Mino (1990) and Cellini and Lambertini (2004), among others. As we are about to see, this game has a paradigmatic value, since it offers the possibility of analytically characterising several types of solutions, including the open-loop, closed-loop memoryless and linear feedback Nash equilibria, plus the continuum of nonlinear feedback solutions, all of which lend themselves to an intuitive interpretation and can be easily compared. In particular, the possibility of solving the game under nonlinear feedback strategies is due to the presence of a single state variable common to all firms. Additionally, the game allows one to single out some drawbacks of a purely static approach to modelling strategic market behaviour.

For future reference, consider first the static setup. The model describes a homogeneous good duopoly in which fully symmetric firms (1) have a common linear-quadratic cost function $C_i = cq_i + q_i^2/2$, where q_i is the output of firm $i = 1, 2$; and (2) face a linear market demand $p = a - q_1 - q_2$, where p is price and the vertical intercept a is larger than c.

The Cournot–Nash output is

$$q^{CN} = \frac{a - c}{4} \tag{3.1}$$

---

[1] Indeed, the earliest formulation of competition with slow price adjustment is in Roos (1925, 1927). The contribution of Simaan and Takayama (1978), however, has started a fertile literature on this subject.

and delivers equilibrium profits

$$\pi^{CN} = \frac{3\,(a-c)^2}{32} \tag{3.2}$$

If instead firms collude to maximise joint profits – so as to replicate the performance of a monopolist manoeuvring two identical production plants – their task consists in choosing output levels to maximise $\pi^M = \pi_1 + \pi_2$. The FOC of firm i is

$$\frac{\partial \pi^M}{\partial q_i} = a - c - 3q_i - 2q_j = 0 \tag{3.3}$$

which, under symmetry, yields the jointly optimal output $q^M = (a-c)/5$ for each firm.

It is also useful to reconstruct the perfectly competitive equilibrium (although, admittedly, it may look a bit weird in a duopoly game). The marginal cost of firm i being $\partial C_i/\partial q_i = c + q_i$, marginal cost pricing yields an individual equilibrium output $q^{pc} = (a-c)/3$.

Now suppose the duopoly exists over $t \in [0, \infty)$ and market price evolves according to the following dynamics:

$$\dot{p}(t) = s\left[\widehat{p} - p(t)\right] \tag{3.4}$$

where $\widehat{p} = a - q_1(t) - q_2(t)$ is the 'notional' price and parameter $s \in [0, \infty)$ measures the speed of price adjustment. Hence, s is an inverse measure of price stickiness, black-boxing menu costs or other similar mechanism which remain behind the curtains of the model. The instantaneous profit function of firm i is

$$\pi_i(t) = \left[p(t) - c - \frac{q_i(t)}{2}\right] q_i(t) \tag{3.5}$$

and firm i must

$$\max_{q_i(t)} \Pi_i = \int_0^\infty \left[p(t) - c - \frac{q_i(t)}{2}\right] q_i(t)\, e^{-\rho t} dt \tag{3.6}$$

subject to (3.4) and the initial condition $p(0) = p_0 > 0$ (in line of principle, $p(t)$ may fall below c at some point in time, including the initial instant, but not forever – see discussion that follows). The discount rate $\rho > 0$ is common to both firms and time-invariant.

3.1.1   The Open-Loop Solution

What follows summarises the essential elements of the open-loop analysis in Simaan and Takayama (1978), Fershtman and Kamien (1987) and Cellini and Lambertini (2004). Under open-loop information, each firm chooses its whole production plan at $t = 0$ and then sticks to it forever. The Hamiltonian is

$$\mathcal{H}_i\left(p(t), q_i(t), q_j(t), \lambda(t)\right) = e^{-\rho t}\left\{\left[p(t) - c - \frac{q_i(t)}{2}\right] q_i(t) + \lambda_i(t) s\left[\widehat{p} - p(t)\right]\right\} \tag{3.7}$$

where $\lambda_i(t)$ is the capitalised costate variable. The FOC on control is

$$\frac{\partial \mathcal{H}_i(\cdot)}{\partial q_i(t)} = p(t) - c - q_i(t) - \lambda_i(t)s = 0 \tag{3.8}$$

while the costate equation is

$$-\frac{\partial \mathcal{H}_i(\cdot)}{\partial p(t)} = \dot{\lambda}_i(t) - \rho \lambda_i(t) \Rightarrow \dot{\lambda}_i(t) = \lambda_i(t)(s + \rho) - q_i(t) \tag{3.9}$$

The transversality condition is $\lim_{t \to \infty} e^{-\rho t} \lambda(t) p(t) = 0$.

From (3.8), the optimal instantaneous control is (the time argument is dropped henceforth):

$$q_i^* = \max\{p - c - \lambda_i s, 0\} \tag{3.10}$$

and, for all $p > c + \lambda_i s$, the optimal costate is $\lambda_i = (p - c)/s$. Moreover, if $p > c + \lambda_i s$, q_i^* can be differentiated w.r.t. time to yield the following control equation:

$$\dot{q}_i = \dot{p} - \dot{\lambda}_i s, \tag{3.11}$$

which, imposing the symmetry condition $q_1 = q_2 = q$ and then using the state dynamics (3.4), the adjoint equation (3.9) and the expression for λ_i, takes its final form

$$\dot{q} = s(a - c - 2p) - \rho(p - c - q) \tag{3.12}$$

The final step required to characterise the steady state output strategy consists in imposing the stationarity condition $\dot{q} = 0$ to obtain:

$$q^{OL} = \frac{p^{OL}(2s + \rho) - as - c(s + \rho)}{\rho} \tag{3.13}$$

where the steady state level of the market price is

$$p^{OL} = \frac{a(2s + \rho) + 2c(s + \rho)}{4s + 3\rho} > c \tag{3.14}$$

everywhere. Using (3.14), q^{OL} simplifies as follows:

$$q^{OL} = \frac{(a - c)(s + \rho)}{4s + 3\rho} \tag{3.15}$$

It is easily checked that the open-loop equilibrium is a saddle point. The Jacobian matrix is

$$J = \begin{bmatrix} \dfrac{\partial \dot{p}}{\partial p} = -s & \dfrac{\partial \dot{p}}{\partial q} = -2s \\[4mm] \dfrac{\partial \dot{q}}{\partial p} = -2s - \rho & \dfrac{\partial \dot{q}}{\partial q} = \rho \end{bmatrix} \tag{3.16}$$

whose determinant is

$$\Delta\left(J\right) = \frac{\partial \dot{p}}{\partial p} \cdot \frac{\partial \dot{q}}{\partial q} - \frac{\partial \dot{p}}{\partial q} \cdot \frac{\partial \dot{q}}{\partial p} = -s\left(4s + 3\rho\right) < 0 \qquad (3.17)$$

and this implies saddle point stability.

More interesting are the limit properties of the open-loop steady state equilibrium. Look at the following limits taken on output (3.15):

$$\lim_{\rho \to 0} q^{OL} = \lim_{s \to \infty} q^{OL} = \frac{a - c}{4} = q^{CN} \qquad (3.18)$$

$$\lim_{\rho \to \infty} q^{OL} = \lim_{s \to 0} q^{OL} = \frac{a - c}{3} = q^{pc} \qquad (3.19)$$

That is, (3.18) tells that the open-loop equilibrium reproduces the static Cournot–Nash outcome in the limit, provided either the speed of adjustment is infinitely high or there is no discounting at all: $s \to \infty$ means that market price *always* coincides with its 'notional' level, and therefore firms *always* produce the 'correct' quasi-static Cournot equilibrium outputs; the same holds if firms attach the same value to profits irrespective of the date at which they gain such profits. Conversely, for any $s, \rho \in (0, \infty)$, $q^{OL} > q^{CN}$: open-loop rules drive a firm to produce more than in the static case, for all positive and finite values of the two key parameters (in the remainder, we shall see that this is not robust to substantial changes in the structure and interpretation of the dynamic Cournot model).

Conversely, (3.19) says that the perfectly competitive outcome is attained if either discounting shoots up to infinity or market price becomes infinitely sticky. All of these properties can be shown to extend to the case of an oligopoly with n firms (see Cellini and Lambertini, 2004).

Summing up, the open-loop game yields a unique steady state with positive output levels, which is a saddle point and encompasses the static Nash equilibrium as well as perfect competition under intuitive conditions about the two key parameters of the model, i.e., discounting and the speed of price adjustment. All of this sounds good, but the open-loop solution is not subgame perfect (or strongly time consistent), and properties (3.18–3.19) do not carry over to feedback solutions.

To see that open-loop rules do not deliver subgame perfection, it suffices to observe that q_i^* in (3.10) is a linear function of p for all $p > c + \lambda_i s$, so that its dynamics is also explicitly affected by price, as it appears from (3.11). These facts call for the analysis of the game under feedback rules, both linear and nonlinear.

3.1.2   Linear Feedback Strategies

In the feedback game, firm i solves the following problem:

$$\rho V_i\left(p\right) = \max_{q_i} \left\{ \left(p - c - \frac{q_i}{2}\right) q_i + V_i'(p) s\left(\widehat{p} - p\right) \right\} \qquad (3.20)$$

where $V_i'(p) = \partial V_i(p)/\partial p$. The FOC is

$$p - c - q_i - sV_i'(p) = 0, \tag{3.21}$$

solving which one obtains the optimal feedback strategy identified by[2]

$$q_i^* = \begin{cases} 0 & \text{if } p - c - sV_i'(p) \leq 0 \\ p - c - sV_i'(p) & \text{otherwise} \end{cases} \tag{3.22}$$

Then, if indeed $p - c - sV_i'(p) > 0$ for all firms, imposing $q_1 = q_2 = p - c - sV'(p)$, one can rewrite the Bellman equation (3.20) as follows:

$$\rho V(p) - \frac{(p-c)^2 + s^2 \left[V'(p)\right]^2 + 2sV'(p)\left[a + 2c - 3p + sV'(p)\right]}{2} = 0 \tag{3.23}$$

Given the linear quadratic shape of the model, one may adopt a linear quadratic value function $V = \varepsilon_1 p^2 + \varepsilon_2 p + \varepsilon_3$, whereby solving (3.23) amounts to solving the system

$$-12\varepsilon_1^2 s^2 + 2\varepsilon_1 (6s + \rho) - 1 = 0$$
$$c - 2\varepsilon_1 s (a - 2c) + \varepsilon_2 \left[\rho + 3s (1 - 2\varepsilon_1 s)\right] = 0 \tag{3.24}$$
$$2 (\varepsilon_3 \rho - a\varepsilon_2 s) - (c + \varepsilon_2 s)(c + 3\varepsilon_2 s) = 0$$

w.r.t. the undetermined coefficients $\{\varepsilon_1, \varepsilon_2, \varepsilon_3\}$. System (3.24) is solved by

$$\varepsilon_3 = \frac{c (c + 4\varepsilon_2 s) + \varepsilon_2 s (2a + 3\varepsilon_2 s)}{2\rho} \tag{3.25}$$

$$\varepsilon_2 = \frac{2\varepsilon_1 s (a + 2c) - c}{\rho + 3s (1 - 2\varepsilon_1 s)} \tag{3.26}$$

$$\varepsilon_1^{\pm} = \frac{6s + \rho \pm \sqrt{(6s + \rho)^2 - 12s^2}}{12s} \tag{3.27}$$

the latter roots being real as $(6s + \rho)^2 - 12s^2 > 0$ for all $s, \rho > 0$. Since $V'(p) = 2\varepsilon_1 p + \varepsilon_2$, (3.27) gives rise to two linear feedback strategies, identified by

$$q_{\pm}^{LF} = p - c - s \left(2\varepsilon_1^{\pm} p + \varepsilon_2\right) \tag{3.28}$$

with q_-^{LF} (resp., q_+^{LF}) being stable (resp., unstable). More on stability will emerge below, when we will be in a position to describe graphically all of the relevant solutions in the space (p, q).

---

[2] Tsutsui (1996) adds capacity constraints $\bar{k}$ to the model, whereby (3.22) becomes

$$q_i^* = \begin{cases} 0 & \text{if } p - c - sV_i'(p) \leq 0 \\ \bar{k} & \text{if } p - c - sV_i'(p) \geq \bar{k} \\ p - c - sV_i'(p) & \text{otherwise} \end{cases}$$

and proves that, under feedback rules, firms voluntarily restrict steady state equilibrium outputs more than it is strictly required by the exogenous constraint. This fact has a quasi-collusive flavour which will also emerge in the analysis of nonlinear feedback strategies in absence of dimensional constraints.

For the moment, we may confine our attention to the stable solution, q_-^{LF}. Plugging it into the price dynamics, solving for the steady state price and then substituting the latter into q_-^{LF}, we obtain

$$q_-^{LF} = \frac{(a-c)\left(6s + 5\rho + \sqrt{(6s+\rho)^2 - 12s^2}\right)}{3\left(8s + 5\rho + \sqrt{(6s+\rho)^2 - 12s^2}\right)} \qquad (3.29)$$

and we easily discover that $q_-^{LF} > q^{OL}$ everywhere. In particular,

$$\lim_{\rho \to 0} q_-^{LF} = \lim_{s \to \infty} q_-^{LF} > q^{CN} \qquad (3.30)$$

and

$$\lim_{\rho \to \infty} q_-^{LF} = \lim_{s \to 0} q_-^{LF} = q^{pc} \qquad (3.31)$$

which amounts to saying that perfect competition is replicated in the limit as under open-loop rules, while the Cournot–Nash outcome is not. Overproduction at the stable linear feedback equilibrium is the consequence of firms being fully aware of strategic interaction and therefore trying hard to preempt each other. Intuitively, this has negative consequence on profits, which fall short of the level attained at the open-loop equilibrium.

3.1.3   Nonlinear Feedback Strategies

Under feedback rules, the game also produces a continuum of infinitely many nonlinear solutions, whose characterization can be carried out using two different but equivalent procedures, both of which depart from imposing symmetry across firms in the FOC (3.21), and then solving it w.r.t. $V'(p)$. The first method, used by Tsutsui and Mino (1990), uses auxiliary variables $y = V'(p)$ and $y' = V''(p)$ to generate an auxiliary equation which can be manipulated to solve the original HJB equation (3.20). By doing so, Tsutsui and Mino (1990) construct something similar to a folk theorem for this sticky price Cournot game, in the sense that they show that

for each price between a competitive stationary price and a near collusive stationary price, there exists some stationary Markov feedback equilibrium which supports it as its stationary price ... [and] ... when there exists more than one equilibrium, the payoff of an equilibrium is positively related to the level of its supporting stationary price. (Tsutsui and Mino, 1990, p. 138)

Their analysis hinges on restrictions on the state space, i.e., on a price ceiling, relying on which they find out that they evaluate short-run deviations against the incentive to raise long-run profits. Their findings illustrate that, in portions of the state space, starting prices do not allow firms to reach targeted prices. The task of the restriction to a subdomain of the state space is therefore to remove a portion of subgames from the game tree to guarantee subgame perfection.

Here I will outline nonlinear feedback strategies by summarising their method. I will come back to the characterisation of nonlinear solutions in more detail in Chapter 7, relying instead on the approach initiated by Rowat (2007), where no restrictions on the state space are imposed.[3]

Consider $p - c - sV'(p) \geq 0$. Solving (3.21), substituting $q^* = p - c - sV'(p)$ into the Bellman equation (3.20) and then differentiating it w.r.t. p yields

$$\rho V'(p) = p - csV''(p)\left[a + 2c - 3p + 2sV'(p)\right] - 3psV'(p) + 2s^2 V'(p) V''(p) \tag{3.32}$$

Now define $V'(p) = y$ and $V''(p) = y'$, so that (3.32) can be rewritten as

$$y' = \frac{(3s + \rho)y - p + c}{s\left[a + 2c - 3(p - sy)\right]} \tag{3.33}$$

Then, using the transformations $\mathbf{P} = p - \alpha$ and $\mathbf{Y} = y - \beta$, (3.33) becomes

$$\frac{d\mathbf{Y}}{d\mathbf{P}} = G(\mathbf{Y}/\mathbf{P}) \equiv \frac{(\rho + 3s)(\mathbf{Y}/\mathbf{P}) - 1}{3s\left[s(\mathbf{Y}/\mathbf{P}) - 1\right]} \tag{3.34}$$

with

$$\alpha = \frac{a(3s + \rho) + c(3s + 2\rho)}{3(2s + \rho)} \; ; \; \beta = \frac{a - c}{3(2s + \rho)} \tag{3.35}$$

and (3.34), posing $\mathbf{Y} = \mathbf{ZP}$, is equivalent to

$$\frac{d\mathbf{P}}{\mathbf{P}} = \frac{d\mathbf{Z}}{G(\mathbf{Z}) - \mathbf{Z}} \tag{3.36}$$

whose general solution is $\mathbf{P} = (\mathbf{Z} - z_I)^{-\gamma_I}(\mathbf{Z} - z_{II})^{-\gamma_{II}}/\mathbf{K}$. Here, $\mathbf{K}$ is an integration constant, $z_I < z_{II}$ solve

$$1 + 3s^2 z^2 - (6s + \rho) = 0 \tag{3.37}$$

and

$$\gamma_I = \frac{1 - sz_I}{z_{II} - z_I} \; ; \; \gamma_{II} = \frac{sz_{II} - 1}{z_{II} - z_I} \tag{3.38}$$

Hence, for all price levels satisfying the condition $p \geq c + sV'(p)$, the continuum of solutions of (3.33) is identified by

$$\mathbf{K} = \left[y - \beta - z_I(p - \alpha)\right]^{\gamma_I}\left[y - \beta - z_{II}(p - \alpha)\right]^{\gamma_{II}} \tag{3.39}$$

The special cases $\mathbf{K} = 0$ and $(p_0, y_0) = (\alpha, \beta)$ identify the following singular solutions:

$$y_{I,II} = \begin{cases} \beta + z_I(p - \alpha) \\ \beta + z_{II}(p - \alpha) \end{cases} \tag{3.40}$$

---

[3] For an illustration of the use of Tsutsui and Mino's (1990) method to characterise the *continuum* of nonlinear feedback strategies in a resource extraction game, see Colombo and Labrecciosa (2015). They adopt product differentiation as in Singh and Vives (1984) to solve the Cournot and Bertrand games, to single out novel results on the welfare consequences of Bertrand and Cournot competition. I will come back to their contribution in Chapter 7.

The resulting picture appears in Figure 3.1, in which the space (p, y) is divided in two regions by the positively sloped line $y = V'(p) = (p - c)/s$. The two singular solutions y_I and y_{II} are also drawn, intersecting each other in (α, β). The admissible region is identified by all pairs (p, y) such that $y \leq (p - c)/s$, ensuring the non-negativity of output levels. The hyperbolic curves identify some of the infinitely many non-singular solutions generated by $\mathbf{K}$.

Now note that, the stationarity condition being

$$\dot{p} = s(a - 2q^* - p) = 0, \tag{3.41}$$

the steady state line is $y^* = [3p - a - 2c]/(2s)$, which is the fourth straight line appearing in Figure 3.1. This line intersects the horizontal axis at $p = (a + 2c)/3 = p^{pc}$, i.e., the perfectly competitive price, and is tangent to a single curve (the thick one in the graph) in correspondence of the price level

$$p^{tg} = \frac{a(3s + 2\rho) + 2c(s + 2\rho)}{5s + 6\rho} \tag{3.42}$$

where the superscript tg mnemonics for *tangency*.

Given that $\dot{p} > 0$ for all $y > y^*$, and conversely, the segment AT along the steady state locus identifies the set of stable nonlinear feedback equilibria, while the segment TB identifies unstable ones. A few features of the set AT can be usefully outlined.

At the tangency point, the steady state output is

$$q^{tg} = \frac{a - p^{tg}}{2} = \frac{(a - c)(s + 2\rho)}{5s + 6\rho} \tag{3.43}$$

The limits of (3.43) are easily computed:

$$\lim_{\rho \to 0} q^{tg} = \lim_{s \to \infty} q^{tg} = \frac{a - c}{5} = q^M \tag{3.44}$$

$$\lim_{\rho \to \infty} q^{tg} = \lim_{s \to 0} q^{tg} = \frac{a - c}{3} = q^{pc} \tag{3.45}$$

The above limits deserve a few comments, as they show that the individual volume of production associated to the tangency point ranges from the fully collusive output to the perfectly competitive one. The first property, in particular, illustrates the point made by Tsutsui and Mino (1990) about the possibility of reconstructing collusive outcomes through the nonlinear feedback solution of the game. But there is more to it. Indeed, as it appears from Figure 3.1, there are infinitely many nonlinear solutions which are stable and arbitrarily close to reproducing the behaviour of a static joint-profit maximising cartel.

Additionally, it is worth comparing the output levels associated with the tangency point, the stable steady state generated by the linear feedback strategy $q^{LF} = p - c - s(2\varepsilon_1^- p + \varepsilon_2)$, the open-loop equilibrium, and the cooperative equilibrium of the dynamic game in which firms maximise joint profits s.t. (3.4). The steady state

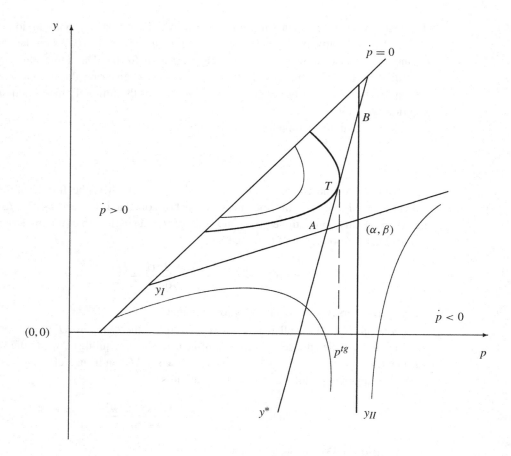

Figure 3.1 Linear and nonlinear feedback solutions in the (p, q) space

equilibrium of this case, whose calculations are omitted for brevity, has the following coordinates:

$$p^M(s, \rho) = \frac{a(3s + \rho) + 2c(s + \rho)}{5s + 3\rho} \; ; \; q^M(s, \rho) = \frac{(a - c)(s + \rho)}{5s + 3\rho} \tag{3.46}$$

The limits of $q^M(s, \rho)$ are the same as in (3.44–3.45), and $q_-^{LF} > q^{tg} > q^M(s, \rho)$ for all $s, \rho \in (0, \infty)$. However, the limits of the difference

$$q^{tg} - q^M(s, \rho) = \frac{2(a - c)s\rho}{(5s + 3\rho)(5s + 6\rho)} \tag{3.47}$$

for s and ρ tending to either zero or infinity are all equal to zero. By continuity, infinitely many stable equilibria whose output levels are slightly higher than q^{tg} asymptotically approach the cartel solution of the dynamic game, although $q^M(s, \rho)$ remains out of reach for all positive and finite values of the speed of price adjustment and the discount rate.

3.1.4   Closed-Loop Memoryless Strategies

Another case remains to be illustrated, that in which feedback effects appear in the solution of the Hamiltonian function (3.7) of the problem, in the form of state-control loops appearing in the costate equation. The FOC (3.8) remaining unmodified, the relevant adjoint equation becomes now

$$-\frac{\partial \mathcal{H}_i}{\partial p} - \frac{\partial \mathcal{H}_i}{\partial q_j} \cdot \frac{\partial q_j^*}{\partial p} = \dot{\lambda}_i(t) - \rho\lambda_i(t) \qquad (3.48)$$

where $\partial \mathcal{H}_i / \partial q_j - s\lambda_i$ and, if $p > c + \lambda_j s$, the rival's optimal output is $q_j^* = p - c - \lambda_i s$ and therefore $\partial q_j^* / \partial p = 1$. The additional term appearing on the l.h.s. of (3.48) accounts for the cross effect exerted by the current state on the rival's optimal control, feeding back into firm i's costate variable at any time t. Since λ_i influences firm i's optimal instantaneous output and its dynamic evolution, the loop in the costate equation allows the individual firm to become aware of the interplay between state and control(s) at any time during the game and adjust its production plan accordingly, something which, by construction, does not happen under open-loop rules. What emerges from the adoption of (3.48) is the so-called *closed-loop memoryless solution* (it is without memory because the loop involves the current values of the state and controls but not their history).

The procedure follows the same steps as under open-loop information. The unique and stable steady state point reached in this case is

$$p^{CL} = a - 2q^{CL} ; \; q^{CL} = \frac{(a-c)(2s+\rho)}{7s+3\rho} \qquad (3.49)$$

Output q^{CL} is larger than q_-^{LF} everywhere, with the exceptions of the limits for $s \to 0$ and $\rho \to \infty$. That is, the presence of loops in the costate equations induces firms to produce in excess of the output associated with the equilibrium output engendered by the proper linear feedback solution. Additionally, this also shows, with no need of further calculations, that (1) the associated equilibrium value of λ does not coincide with the partial derivative of the value function, $V'(p)$, and therefore is not a correct measure of the shadow value attached to the state variable; and (2) the closed-loop no-memory equilibrium does not belong to the subset of feedback equilibria identified by the segment AT in Figure 3.1, since $q^{CL} > q_-^{LF} > q^{tg}$. Putting all of these pieces of information together, this closed-loop solution and others equally relying on the Hamiltonian function are not, in general, subgame perfect, even though they explicitly incorporate the players' awareness concerning the relationship between state(s) and control(s) as compared to the open-loop solution.

3.1.5   Hyperbolic Market Demand

Now allow me to take a point which will intentionally sound a bit paradoxical and provocative. Most of the existing literature on oligopoly theory uses linear demand functions, for two reasons: the first is simplicity and the second is concavity (of profits).

Sometimes, strictly concave demands are also adopted (see the next section for more), but usually convex demands are avoided or explicitly excluded to eliminate the risk of non-concavity (see, e.g., Dixit, 1986). Instead, convex demand functions are familiar in microeconomics, where the Marshallian demands resulting from the representative consumer's maximisation of a Cobb–Douglas utility function defined of the consumption basket are indeed hyperbolic.[4] So, one studies the perfectly competitive model in general equilibrium accepting convex demands with no objections, and then forgets about them as soon as the topic becomes the theory of industrial organization (which is itself a subset of microeconomics). The typical example usually brought forward to illustrate the reason for leaving aside convex demand functions is the fact that a monopolist might find it impossible to identify the optimal point along a hyperbolic demand because all rectangles identified by any points along the hyperbola have the same area.

Relying on Lambertini (2010), it can be shown that the differential game approach to oligopolies with convex demand functions offers a way out to some of the problems affecting the static formulations, and also some additional insights (and drawbacks, to be honest).

Also in this case, a brief reconstruction of the static Cournot game will be useful to fix ideas. The industry consists of n single-product firms supplying a homogeneous good; individual quantity is q_i, $i = 1, 2, 3, ...n$. Each firm bears total costs $C_i = cq_i^2$, $c > 0$, and chooses q_i so as to maximise the profit $\pi_i = (p - cq_i) q_i$. Market demand $p = a/Q$, $Q = \sum_{i=1}^{n} q_i$ is generated by solving the constrained maximum problem of a representative consumer whose preferences are described by the logarithmic utility function $U = \log [Q] + m$, where m is a numeraire good whose price is normalized to one.

The FOC for profit maximisation is:

$$\frac{\partial \pi_i}{\partial q_i} = \frac{aQ_{-i}}{(q_i + Q_{-i})^2} - 2cq_i = 0, \tag{3.50}$$

where $Q_{-i} \equiv \sum_{j \neq i} q_j$. The unique fully symmetric Cournot–Nash equilibrium takes place at

$$q^{CN} = \frac{1}{n} \sqrt{\frac{a(n-1)}{2c}}, \ p^{CN} = \frac{\sqrt{2ac(n-1)}}{n-1}, \tag{3.51}$$

per-firm profits amounting to $\pi^{CN} = a(n+1) / (2n^2)$. On the basis of (3.51), it is evident that the monopoly case must be ruled out because the price is indeterminate. The perfectly competitive equilibrium has coordinates $p^{pc} = 2cq^*$ and $q^* = \sqrt{a/(2cn)}$. Additionally, both the oligopolistic equilibrium with $n \geq 2$ and the perfectly competitive outcome appears to be defined for strictly positive values of c.

The Open-Loop Game

Now we can turn to the dynamic version of the oligopoly game, with sticky price dynamics as in (3.4), over $t \in [0, \infty)$. To begin with, observe that the shape of the game is no

---

[4] Moreover, they often emerge from the empirical analysis of market demands. In this regard, see Hausman (1981) and Varian (1982), among others.

longer linear quadratic, and the presence of a hyperbolic demand prevents guessing an intuitive form for the value function.[5] Moreover, the closed-loop memoryless solution can be pursued but does not ensure subgame perfection. Hence, this is a typical setting where one must come to terms with open-loop information, at least if a fully analytical solution is desired.

Firm i's Hamiltonian function is:

$$\mathcal{H}_i = e^{-\rho t} \left[(p - cq_i) q_i + \lambda_i s \left(\frac{a}{q_i(t) + Q_{-i}(t)} - p(t) \right) \right], \tag{3.52}$$

which produces the following set of necessary conditions:

$$\frac{\partial \mathcal{H}_i}{\partial q_i} = p - 2cq_i - \frac{\lambda_i as}{(q_i + Q_{-i})^2} = 0, \tag{3.53}$$

$$-\frac{\partial \mathcal{H}_i}{\partial p} = \dot{\lambda}_i - \rho \lambda_i \Leftrightarrow \dot{\lambda}_i = \lambda_i (\rho + s) - q_i, \tag{3.54}$$

accompanied by the transversality condition $\lim_{t \to \infty} e^{-\rho t} \lambda_i p = 0$.

The dynamics of individual output is:

$$\dot{q} = \frac{n^2 q \left[p(2s + \rho) - 2cq(s + \rho) \right] - as(n + 1)}{2n^2 (p - 3cq)}. \tag{3.55}$$

Stationarity obtains at $p^{OL} = a/\left(nq^{OL}\right), \dot{q} = 0$ yielding

$$q_I = 0, \quad q_{II} = -\frac{1}{n} \sqrt{\frac{a[n(s + \rho) - s]}{2(s + \rho)c}} < 0, \quad q_{III} = \frac{1}{n} \sqrt{\frac{a[n(s + \rho) - s]}{2(s + \rho)c}} > 0, \tag{3.56}$$

among which q_I and q_{II} can intuitively be disregarded. In correspondence of $q^{OL} = q_{III}$, the steady state price is $p^{OL} = \sqrt{2a(s + \rho)c/[n(s + \rho) - s]}$, which is higher than marginal cost $2cq^{OL}$ for any value of s and, more importantly, for any $n \geq 1$. Additionally, q^{OL} is defined for any $n \geq 1$. The steady state profits are

$$\pi^{OL} = \frac{a[N(s + \rho) + s]}{2N^2(s + \rho)}. \tag{3.57}$$

The stability analysis reveals that $\left(p^{OL}, q^{OL}\right)$ is a saddle point for all $n \geq 3$ and all $s \in (0, \infty)$. Otherwise, if $n \in \{1, 2\}$, saddle point stability requires $s \in (0, \rho/2)$, that is, a high degree of price stickiness. If $s \geq \rho/2$, the monopolistic equilibrium is unstable (in particular, an unstable focus), while the duopolistic one is stable (either a stable node or a stable focus). The source of the instability in the monopoly case can be identified by assessing the second-order condition for the concavity of the Hamiltonian w.r.t. output, which, at $n = 1$, simplifies as follows:

$$-\frac{2c(\rho - 2s)}{\rho} \leq 0 \; \forall s \leq \frac{\rho}{2} \tag{3.58}$$

---

[5] See Lambertini (2010, pp. 116–17) for a sketch of the feedback problem where there clearly emerges that the partial derivative of the value function cannot coincide with the optimal value of the costate variable in the open-loop formulation, since the game is not state-redundant.

which illustrates that, if the industry is a monopoly, the lack of concavity goes hand in hand with the arising of instability.

As for the limit behaviour of $\left(p^{OL}, q^{OL}\right)$, we have

$$\lim_{s \to \infty} p^{OL} = \lim_{\rho \to 0} p^{OL} = \frac{\sqrt{2ac(n-1)}}{n-1},$$

$$\lim_{s \to \infty} q^{OL} = \lim_{\rho \to 0} q^{OL} = \frac{1}{n}\sqrt{\frac{a(n-1)}{2c}}, \tag{3.59}$$

which is the static Cournot–Nash equilibrium, and

$$\lim_{s \to 0} p^{OL} = \lim_{\rho \to \infty} p^{OL} = \sqrt{\frac{2ac}{n}}, \ \lim_{s \to 0} q^{OL} = \lim_{\rho \to \infty} q^{OL} = \sqrt{\frac{a}{2nc}}, \tag{3.60}$$

$$\lim_{s \to 0} \pi^{ss}_{OL} = \lim_{\rho \to \infty} \pi^{ss}_{OL} = \frac{a}{2n} \tag{3.61}$$

reproducing the perfectly competitive equilibrium of the static game.

This version of the game illustrates that, in general, the problems emerging from the static setup based on a hyperbolic demand function must not be expected to arise if price does not strike its notional equilibrium level at all times, as implied by the sticky dynamics – keeping in mind the limits of the latter, which 'mimics' the presence of menu costs or some other mechanisms hindering firms' ability to adjust prices optimally instant by instant, without modelling them properly.

3.2   Sluggish Demand

The opposite (and complementary) case is that where firms adjust supplies to a sluggish or viscous demand, as in Wirl (2010), where the dynamics of market demand $D(t)$ is

$$\dot{D}(t) = \frac{Q(p(t)) - D(t)}{\tau} \tag{3.62}$$

in which $\tau \in [0, \infty)$ is the time constant of demand adjustment (the lower is τ, the faster is demand adjustment)[6] and the instantaneous demand function is linear, $Q(p(t)) = a - p(t)$. This demand viscosity may capture some relevant aspects of energy (oil) markets, where sluggishness is engendered by the fact that goods (cars) and equipment (installed capacity, pipelines) are long-lasting and not easily adjustable, which causes also individual supplies $y_i(t)$ to be viscous. In a sense, this setup may be considered as a dynamic version of models describing supply function competition, in the vein of Klemperer and Meyer (1989) and Vives (2011), *inter alia*.

Each firm i exerts an instantaneous investment $I_i(t)$ to increase supply $y_i(t)$, which evolves linearly, following

$$\dot{y}_i(t) = I_i(t) \tag{3.63}$$

---

[6] Hence, one could rewrite (3.62) using $s = 1/\tau$ as a direct measure of the speed of demand adjustment.

and this investment involves an instantaneous cost $C_i(t) = cI(t) + bI^2(t)/2$, where $b, c \geq 0$ are constant parameters.

Imposing market clearing at every instant amounts to requiring $D(t) = \sum_{i=1}^{n} y_i(t)$ and therefore also $\dot{D}(t) = \sum_{i=1}^{n} \dot{y}_i(t) = \sum_{i=1}^{n} I_i(t)$, i.e.,

$$\frac{a - p(t) - D(t)}{\tau} = \frac{1}{\tau}\left[a - p(t) - \sum_{i=1}^{n} y_i(t)\right] = \sum_{i=1}^{n} I_i(t) \qquad (3.64)$$

which univocally determines the market clearing price

$$p(t) = a - \sum_{i=1}^{n} y_i(t) - \tau \sum_{i=1}^{n} I_i(t) \qquad (3.65)$$

at every instant. Then, firm i's problems amount to choose investment $I_i(t)$ to maximise the discounted profit flow

$$\Pi_i = \int_0^{\infty}\left[p(t)y_i(t) - cI(t) + \frac{bI^2(t)}{2}\right]e^{-\rho t}dt \qquad (3.66)$$

s.t. the state equation (3.63). Wirl (2010) characterises the static Cournot–Nash equilibrium, as well as the noncooperative open-loop and linear feedback Nash equilibria[7] and the cartel solution, the latter being included in the picture in view of the applicability of the model to energy markets.

3.2.1   The Open-Loop Solution and the Static Equilibrium

This can be dealt with quickly: the open-loop equilibrium is not subgame perfect and is derived as a useful benchmark. The set of necessary conditions delivers the control equation

$$I = \frac{\lambda - \tau y}{b} \qquad (3.67)$$

and the unique steady state

$$y^{OL} = \frac{a - c\rho}{n + 1 + \rho\tau} \; ; \; I^{OL} = 0 \qquad (3.68)$$

admissible for all $a > c\rho$, is a saddle point. In the static game, the Cournot–Nash supply is $y^{CN} = (a - c\rho)/(n+1)$.

3.2.2   The Linear Feedback Solution

Under feedback information, firm i solves the following HJB equation:

$$\rho V_i(\mathbf{y}) = \max_{u_i}\left\{py_i - cI - \frac{bI^2}{2} + V_i'(\mathbf{y})\dot{y}_i\right\} \qquad (3.69)$$

in which $\mathbf{y}$ is the vector of states and $V_i'(\mathbf{y}) = \partial V(\mathbf{y})/\partial y_i$.

---

[7] The nonlinear feedback strategies cannot be characterised, due to the presence of n state variables.

The guess for the value function is

$$V_i(\mathbf{y}) = \frac{\varepsilon_1 y_i^2 + \varepsilon_2 y_{-i}^2 + 2\varepsilon_3 y_i y_{-i}}{2} + \varepsilon_4 y_i + \varepsilon_5 y_{-i} + \varepsilon_6 \tag{3.70}$$

where y_{-i} represents the supply of any rival of firm i. Using (3.70), the optimal investment determined by the FOC is

$$I^* = \frac{\varepsilon_4 - c}{b} + \frac{2(\varepsilon_1 - \tau) y_i + \varepsilon_3 y_{-i}}{2b} \tag{3.71}$$

while the Bellman equation (3.69) generates a system of six equations whose solution (accounting for the stability requirement) is the following:[8]

$$\varepsilon_6 = \frac{(\varepsilon_4 - c)^2}{2b\rho} \;;\; \varepsilon_4 = \frac{ab - c(\varepsilon_1 - n\tau)}{b\rho + n\tau - \varepsilon_1} \tag{3.72}$$

$$\varepsilon_3 = \frac{2(n-1)(b - \tau^2)}{b\rho + n\tau - \varepsilon_1} \;;\; \varepsilon_5 = -\frac{2(n-1)(a - c\rho)(b - \tau^2)}{\rho\left[b(4 + \rho(b\rho + 2n\tau)) + 2\tau^2(n^2 - 1) + b\rho\Psi\right]} \tag{3.73}$$

$$\varepsilon_2 = \frac{4(n-1)^2(b - \tau^2)^2}{b\rho(b\rho + \Psi)^2} \;;\; \varepsilon_1 = \frac{b\rho + 2n\tau - \Psi}{2} \tag{3.74}$$

where $\Psi \equiv \sqrt{4(2b - \tau^2) + (b\rho + 2n\tau)}$. As a result, the feedback steady state supply for each individual firm is

$$y^F = \frac{2b(a - c\rho)}{b(n+1)(2 + \rho\tau) + (n-1)\tau(2n\tau - \Psi)} \tag{3.75}$$

3.2.3   The Cartel Solution

The behaviour of the cartel is investigated relying on the assumption of explicit cooperation among the n firms – as is the case of OPEC – so that stability against unilateral deviations and the deterrence thereof, a *leitmotiv* in repeated games with implicit collusion, is not an issue here. Hence, the objective common to all firms alike is to choose the vector $\mathbf{I}$ of investments s.t. the dynamics of supplies, and this translates into an optimal control problem with a single agent (the cartel, or a multiplant monopolist) manoeuvring n symmetric controls at all times.

The steady state per-firm collusive supply turns out to be

$$y^M = \frac{a - c\rho}{n(2 + \rho\tau)} \tag{3.76}$$

3.2.4   Comparing Equilibria

The properties of the spectrum of different steady state equilibria can be now assessed. First of all, cartel behaviour implies an output restriction as compared to the static Cournot–Nash behaviour, $y^M < y^{CN}$, but this is much less than surprising.

---

[8] However, note that I^* is determined using only three of these coefficients.

More interesting is the comparison conducted across $\{y^M, y^{CN}, y^{OL}, y^F\}$ using parameter τ. To begin with, observe these limits:

$$\lim_{\tau \to \infty} y^F, y^{OL} y^M = 0 \tag{3.77}$$

$$\lim_{\tau \to 0} y^F, y^{OL} = \frac{a - c\rho}{n + 1} = y^{CN} \tag{3.78}$$

The first says that if demand is infinitely sluggish, steady state supplies are bound to drop to zero irrespective of the regime which generated them.[9] The second reveals that if demands adjusts instantaneously, then feedback and open-loop steady state supply coincide with the static one. The latter result is at odds with the conclusion reached in the sticky price model, where only the static Cournot–Nash output can be reached in the limit only under open-loop plans (and the associated commitment, which may not be credible in many circumstances).

Moreover,

- $y^F > y^{OL} > y^M$ for all positive values of τ; and,
- while y^{CN} is obviously flat w.r.t. τ, $\partial y^M/\partial \tau, \partial y^{OL}/\partial \tau < 0$ while y^F is non-monotone and concave in τ, and crosses y^{CN} from above in correspondence of

$$\tau = \frac{\sqrt{b(n-1)\left[n\left(2 + b\rho^2\right) - 2\right]} - bn\rho}{n - 1} > 0 \tag{3.79}$$

Hence, unlike what happens under price stickiness, in presence of a sluggish demand, the linear feedback strategy may be less aggressive that the static one, although not of the open-loop one, as usual. Bluntly speaking, this amounts to saying that if demand is sufficiently viscous, too much information drives a firm to choose supplies that, in a static world, would look collusive, even though no collusion or cooperation is taking place in the feedback Nash game.

The explanation for this seemingly counterintuitive inverted-U shape of y^F w.r.t. demand viscosity can be found in the interplay between this feature of the model and the classical feedback motive for preemption. Observe that, using the expression of ε_1, the coefficient multiplying the product $y_i y_{-i}$ in the HJB equation simplifies as follows:

$$\varepsilon_3 = -\frac{4(n-1)\left(b - \tau^2\right)}{b\rho - \Psi} \tag{3.80}$$

which is real and negative whenever the solution (3.72–3.75) is real and stable. So, the coefficient in (3.80) grasps the impact of feedback information on dynamic Cournot competition and illustrates the resulting incentive to preempt rivals by expanding output. As long as this strategic effect prevails on demand viscosity (i.e., as long as the latter is low enough and demand adjusts fastly), feedback equilibrium supplies are increasing in τ. The opposite applies as soon as τ is high enough to more than offset the output expansion triggered by the preemption instinct, thereby generating a non-monotone feedback supply.

---

[9] Here, marginal production cost being nil, zero is the perfectly competitive individual output.

An even more striking reversal emerges by looking at the open-loop equilibrium output being lower than the static Cournot quantity, which is exactly the opposite of what we are aware of under sticky prices.

3.3   Capacity Accumulation

Our approach to modelling the behaviour of firms accumulating capacity over time is twofold, and in both cases it is indebted with the dominant models in the theory of economic growth: Ramsey (1928) and then Solow (1956) and Swan (1956). The former is usually considered as the general equilibrium version of the latter. In the Solow–Swan model, capacity adjustment involves an explicit cost accounted for in the instantaneous profit function, while in Ramsey, capital or capacity accumulation involves an implicit cost of consumption/sales postponement. For this reason, it is often labelled as a corn-corn model.

The analysis of costly capacity adjustment starts in Spence (1979), Fershtman and Muller (1984), Reynolds (1987, 1991), Driskill and McCafferty (1989) and Dockner (1992). All of them illustrate the open-loop equilibrium; Driskill and McCafferty (1989) also investigate the closed-loop memoryless one, which, once again, is not subgame perfect.[10] Reynolds outlines the feedback solution of the Bellman equation for a duopoly (1987) and an oligopoly (1987, 1991) using trigonometric functions and some numerical analysis, even if the game is in LQ form.

Bluntly speaking, this approach describes a capacity-constrained Cournot oligopoly in which firm incur costly investments to increase capacity and the latter is fully exploited at any point in time. Hence, capacity and output being the same, quantity is not a strategic variable but a state one, controls being instantaneous investment efforts. As a consequence, this model has also much in common with the Nerlove and Arrow (1962) view of advertising campaigns, which is the topic covered in the next chapter.

An additional implication of this approach is that the oligopolistic version of the Solow–Swan model – although possessing a Cournot flavour – does not, in general, closely replicate the typical Cournot equilibrium we are accustomed to from static games. The main message generated by this strand of literature is essentially that increasing the amount of information intensifies strategic interaction in the form of a preemption incentive for all firms that end up being bigger and selling more under closed-loop rules than under open-loop ones.

Notwithstanding its intrinsic appeal and the uncountably many (potential) applications, the model with costly capacity adjustment has not been employed to investigate anything else than its basic features. Why? One plausible answer is that the feedback solution in Reynolds (1987, 1991) cannot be easily replicated as soon as sensible and

---

[10] Driskill and McCafferty (1989, p. 325 and elsewhere) state that the closed-loop no-memory equilibrium attained through the necessary conditions taken on the Hamiltonian is subgame perfect. This claim appears repeatedly in the related literature on applications of differential games, especially in the 1980s. As explained in Chapter 1, this is an indicator of the lack of a clearcut definition of subgame perfection in dynamic games in the early literature on the matter.

relatively simple extensions are added up (say, taxation, mergers, externalities, etc.). The only notable exceptions consist in the analysis of conjectural variations in Dockner (1992) and the relationship between capacity accumulation and entry threats (Kort and Wrzaczek, 2015). For both issues, see Sections 3.6 and 3.8.

What follows is a brief reconstruction of the approach adopted by Reynolds (1987, 1991), complemented by an alternative one where the limit properties of the Cournot model based on Novshek (1980) are used to solve the feedback game without resorting to either trigonometry or numerical simulations.

Unexpectedly, in some sense, the general equilibrium version of the oligopoly game with capacity accumulation based on Ramsey (1928) is somewhat simpler, as it is state-redundant and therefore capable of delivering subgame perfection under open-loop rules. This strand of research begins with Cellini and Lambertini (1998) and has been developed along several directions, to account, e.g., for polluting emissions and intraindustry trade. Indeed, these extensions can be found in Chapters 7 and 8, respectively.

3.3.1   The Solow–Swan Game

In addition to being an oligopoly version of the Solow–Swan model, the setup considered by Driskill and McCafferty (1989) and Reynolds (1987, 1991) can also be viewed as the extension of the Eisner and Strotz's (1963) model we have encountered in Chapter 1 to the n-firm case. The following exposition relies on Reynolds (1987, 1991).[11]

As already mentioned earlier, the main interest of this partial equilibrium oligopoly model with costly capacity accumulation is that it singles out the emergence of preemption incentives on the part of firms in building up their capacity endowments as a result of feedback information, which intensifies strategic interaction (or the firms' awareness thereof). The market exists over $t \in [0, \infty)$, served by $n \geq 1$ firms selling a homogeneous good whose demand function is:

$$p(t) = a - K(t), \quad K(t) \equiv \sum_{i=1}^{n} k_i(t) \tag{3.81}$$

Individual capacity $k_i(t)$ evolves according to:

$$\frac{dk_i(t)}{dt} \equiv \dot{k}_i(t) = I_i(t) - \delta k_i(t), \tag{3.82}$$

where $I_i(t)$ is the investment of firm i at t. Marginal production cost is zero for simplicity, while the instantaneous investment cost is $C_i(t) = cI_i(t) + bI_i^2(t)/2$, with $b, c \geq 0$. Instantaneous profits are:

$$\pi_i(t) = \left[a - \sum_{j=1}^{n} k_j(t) \right] k_i(t) - cI_i(t) - \frac{bI_i^2(t)}{2} \tag{3.83}$$

---

[11] The reason is the derivation of feedback equilibria, which is not present in Driskill and McCafferty (1989). Spence's (1979) approach focusses on the industry evolution influenced by the entry process in continuous time, a theme treated in the last section of this chapter.

and firm i chooses $I_i(t) \geq 0$ so as to maximise the discounted profit flow under the set of dynamic constraints and initial conditions. In view of its structure, as in Driskill and McCafferty (1989), one could as well read the model as a game in which firms incur adjustment or advertising costs to modify outputs or sales, rather than investing to expand a capacity which is fully used but subject to depreciation.

This game is in LQ form and can be solved via the Bellman equation to characterise the feedback equilibrium (Reynolds, 1987, 1991). It is nonetheless interesting to derive the open-loop equilibrium.

The Hamiltonian of firm i is

$$\mathcal{H}_i(t) = e^{-\rho t}\left[\pi_i(t) + \lambda_{ii}(t)\,\dot{k}_i(t) + \sum_{j=1}^{n} \lambda_{ij}(t)\,\dot{k}_j(t)\right] \tag{3.84}$$

and, from the necessary conditions, we obtain

$$\dot{\lambda} = \lambda(\delta + \rho) - a + (n+1)k \tag{3.85}$$

$$\lambda = bI + c;\ \dot{I} = \frac{\dot{\lambda}}{b} \tag{3.86}$$

where symmetry has been imposed across firms, so that $\lambda_{ii} = \lambda$, $k_i = k$ and $I_i = I$ for all i. The unique steady state reached under open-loop information has coordinates

$$k^{OL} = \frac{a - c(\delta + \rho)}{n + 1 + b\delta(\delta + \rho)};\ I^{OL} = \delta k^{OL} \tag{3.87}$$

provided $a > c(\delta + \rho)$. The trace and determinant of the Jacobian matrix of the state-control system show that (3.87) is a saddle point, as in the monopoly case illustrated in Chapter 2. Obviously, if $n = 1$, (3.87) reproduces the monopoly equilibrium; moreover,

$$\lim_{n\to\infty} k^{OL} = \lim_{n\to\infty} I^{OL} = \lim_{n\to\infty} \pi^{OL} = 0 \tag{3.88}$$

and

$$\frac{a}{n+1} - k^{OL} = \frac{[ab\delta + c(n+1)](\delta + \rho)}{(n+1)[n+1+b\delta(\delta + \rho)]} > 0 \tag{3.89}$$

for any finite number of firms, which imply

Lemma 3.1 *Under open-loop information, steady state equilibrium capacities, investments and profits tend to zero as the number of firms increases towards infinity. For any finite n, steady state capacity (and therefore also output) is below the Cournot equilibrium output of the static game with the same linear demand.*

Now we can go back to Reynolds (1987, 1991) relying on the LQ form of the game to investigate the analytics of the feedback solution. What follows illustrates the oligopoly game in Reynolds (1991).

Firm i's Bellman equation is:

$$\rho V_i(\mathbf{k}) = \max_{I_i} \left[\pi_i + \frac{\partial V_i(\mathbf{k})}{\partial k_i} \dot{k}_i + \sum_{j \neq i} \frac{\partial V_i(\mathbf{k})}{\partial k_j} \dot{k}_j \right] \tag{3.90}$$

where $\mathbf{k}$ is the vector of state variables, and the form of the value function is

$$V_i(\mathbf{k}) = \frac{\varepsilon_1}{2} k_i^2 + \varepsilon_2 \sum_{j \neq i} k_j^2 + \varepsilon_3 k_i \sum_{j \neq i} k_j + \varepsilon_4 k_i + \varepsilon_5 \sum_{j \neq i} k_j + \varepsilon_6, \tag{3.91}$$

and the feedback game is solved in the special case $\delta = 0$ (see Reynolds, 1991, p. 495). The FOC is

$$\frac{\partial \pi_i}{\partial I_i} + \frac{\partial V_i(\mathbf{k})}{\partial k_i} \cdot \frac{\partial k_i}{\partial I_i} = 0 \tag{3.92}$$

or, equivalently,

$$-c - bI_i + \frac{\partial V_i(\mathbf{k})}{\partial k_i} = 0 \tag{3.93}$$

so that the optimal instantaneous control is

$$I_i^* = \max \left\{ 0, \frac{\partial V_i(\mathbf{k})/\partial k_i - c}{b} \right\} \tag{3.94}$$

The resulting feedback equilibrium is summarised in

Proposition 3.2 *Take* $\delta = 0$. *If* $\rho \in (0, \overline{\rho})$, *stable linear feedback Nash strategies generate state trajectories converging to*

$$k^F = \frac{(a - c\rho)\left[\varepsilon_1^* + (n-2)\varepsilon_3^* - b\rho\right]}{(n+1)\left[\varepsilon_1^* + (n-2)\varepsilon_3^* - b\rho\right] - (n-1)\varepsilon_3^*}$$

where $\varepsilon_1^* < \varepsilon_3^* < 0$ *are the optimal values of* ε_1 *and* ε_3.

Comparing k^F with (3.87) under the same conditions on parameters (in particular, posing $\delta = 0$), Reynolds (1991) shows that $k^F > k^{OL}$ for any industry configurations, with the obvious exceptions of monopoly and perfect competition. Hence, the preemption effect associated with the firms' awareness of strategic interaction under feedback rules can be spelled out in

Corollary 3.3 *Feedback information generates overinvestment as compared to open-loop information. As a consequence, the steady state equilibrium capacity and output is larger under feedback information then under open-loop information.*

The solution of the game specified as in (3.90–3.91) requires using trigonometric functions to establish a relationship between some of the undetermined parameters appearing in the value function $V_i(\mathbf{k})$ (see Reynolds, 1987, Appendix 1, p. 84).

An alternative method relying on some appropriate amount of symmetry across firms and sensible properties which must apply in equilibrium can be used to produce a more "user-friendly" feedback solution without *a priori* ruling out capacity depreciation, i.e., for all $\delta \geq 0$, as in Dragone *et al.* (2011). There, the following form of $V_i(\mathbf{k})$ is used:

$$V_i(\mathbf{k}) = \frac{\varepsilon_1}{2}k_i^2 + \varepsilon_3 k_i \sum_{j \neq i} k_j + \varepsilon_4 k_i + \varepsilon_5 \sum_{j \neq i} k_j + \varepsilon_6, \tag{3.95}$$

disregarding quadratic terms k_j^2 for all $j \neq i$, as they do not appear in firm i's problem. From the first order condition, we obtain the analogous of (3.91), which in this case is

$$q + cI_i = \frac{\partial V_i(\mathbf{k})}{\partial k_i} \implies I_i^* = \frac{\varepsilon_1 k_i + \varepsilon_1 \sum_{j \neq i} k_j + \varepsilon_4 - c}{b} \tag{3.96}$$

Then, simplifying the Bellman equation of the individual firm under full symmetry on states and controls, we obtain a set of three equations:

$$\Lambda(\varepsilon_1, \varepsilon_3) = 0$$
$$\Theta(\varepsilon_1, \varepsilon_3, \varepsilon_4, \varepsilon_5) = 0 \tag{3.97}$$
$$\Upsilon(\varepsilon_4, \varepsilon_5, \varepsilon_6) = 0$$

with five unknown parameters $(\varepsilon_1, \varepsilon_3, \varepsilon_4, \varepsilon_5, \varepsilon_6)$. Dragone *et al.* (2011) solve (3.97) w.r.t. three of these parameters, $(\varepsilon_1, \varepsilon_4, \varepsilon_6)$. This leaves parameters ε_3 and ε_5 to be identified. This is where Dragone *et al.* (2011) depart from Reynolds (1987, 1991) by considering that the equilibrium solution must deliver a capacity which (1) generates the optimal monopoly endowment if $n = 1$ and (2) reproduces the atomistic outcome of perfect competition as $n \to \infty$.

The first requirement is used to determine ε_5. Take the monopoly steady state capacity:

$$k^M = \frac{a - c(\delta + \rho)}{2 + b\delta(\delta + \rho)} \tag{3.98}$$

and imposing stationarity on the state equation to obtain an expression $k(\varepsilon_3, \varepsilon_5)$ that must be equal to k_M in correspondence of $n = 1$. Hence, imposing $n = 1$ and solving $k(\varepsilon_3, \varepsilon_5) = k_M$ delivers $\varepsilon_5(\varepsilon_3)|_{n=1}$.

The determination of β relies on the property whereby, in the limit, the steady state plant size or capacity endowment must shrink to zero. This fact can be exploited by calculating $\lim_{N \to \infty} k(\varepsilon_3, \varepsilon_5(\varepsilon_3)) = 0$ and then finding the expression of ε_3 which indeed nullifies such a limit. The five parameters can finally be plugged recursively into one another as well as in $k(\varepsilon_3, \varepsilon_5)$ to obtain:

$$\widehat{k}^F = \frac{4b[A - c(\delta + \rho)](2\Omega + c\rho)}{(2\Theta + b\rho)[4\Theta\Omega - b(4(N-1) + \rho(2(\Omega - \Theta) + b\rho))]} \tag{3.99}$$

where

$$\Omega \equiv \frac{1}{2}\sqrt{b(b(2\delta + \rho)^2 + 8)}$$

$$\Theta \equiv \frac{1}{2}\sqrt{b\left(b(2\delta + \rho)^2 + 8n + \frac{16b(n-1)^2}{(2\Omega + b\rho)^2}\right)} \tag{3.100}$$

The corresponding equilibrium investment is $\widehat{I}^F = \delta \widehat{k}^F$, and $\widehat{k}^F > k^{OL}$ for all $n \geq 2$, confirming the presence of a preemption effect induced by feedback rules. However, in general, $\widehat{k}^F \neq k^F$ for all n: the two solution methods are not equivalent, and this is reaffirmed by the fact that the equilibrium value functions do not coincide either, $V\left(\widehat{k}^F\right) \neq V\left(k^F\right)$.

3.3.2   The Ramsey Game

This is the general equilibrium model 'completed' by the assumption that unsold output is reinvested to become additional capacity for the future. Its first formulation as a differential oligopoly game is in Cellini and Lambertini (1998), and the model turns out to lend itself to several extensions, either summarised later here or presented in Chapters 8 and 9.

Since its general formulation is not linear quadratic, unless the production technology is linear, the model is usually solved under open-loop information – which, however, turns out to be strongly time consistent, as shown in Calzolari and Lambertini (2007) and Cellini and Lambertini (2008).

The Ramsey model can be treated explicitly as both a Cournot or a Bertrand game, and yields market-driven equilibria replicating the static ones in addition to the Ramsey golden rule. The market exists over $t \in [0, \infty)$, served by n Cournot firms with demand function:

$$p(t) = a - Q(t), \quad Q(t) \equiv \sum_{i=1}^{n} q_i(t) \tag{3.101}$$

Capacity $k_i(t)$ evolves over time according to

$$\frac{dk_i(t)}{dt} \equiv \dot{k}_i(t) = f(k_i(t)) - q_i(t) - \delta k_i(t) \tag{3.102}$$

where $f(k_i(t)) = y_i(t)$ denotes output of firm i at t. This technology is concave, with $f' \equiv \partial f(k_i(t))/\partial k_i(t) > 0$ and $f'' \equiv \partial^2 f(k_i(t))/\partial k_i(t)^2 < 0$ (cf. Blanchard and Fischer, 1989, chapter 2). Capacity accumulates as a result of intertemporal relocation of unsold output, whenever $y_i(t) > q_i(t)$. Each firm sets its unique control $q_i(t)$ to maximise discounted profits,

$$\Pi_i = \int_0^\infty e^{-\rho t} \left[p(t) - c\right] q_i(t) dt, \tag{3.103}$$

under the set of dynamic constraints (3.102), the initial conditions $\mathbf{k}\,(0) = [k_1\,(0),\, k_2\,(0),\ldots k_i\,(0),\ldots k_N\,(0)]$ and the appropriate transversality conditions $\lim_{t \to \infty} e^{-\rho t}$ $\lambda_{ij}\,(t)\,k_j\,(t) = 0\,\forall\,i,j$.

The FOC on the control variable is

$$\frac{\partial \mathcal{H}_i(\cdot)}{\partial q_i(t)} = a - 2q_i(t) - Q_{-i}(t) - c - \lambda_{ii}(t) = 0 \tag{3.104}$$

while the costate equations are

$$-\frac{\partial \mathcal{H}_i(\cdot)}{\partial k_i(t)} = \dot{\lambda}_{ii}(t) - \rho\lambda_{ii}(t) \Rightarrow \dot{\lambda}_{ii}(t) = \lambda_{ii}(t)\left[\delta + \rho - f'(k_i(t))\right],$$ (3.105)

and

$$-\frac{\partial \mathcal{H}_i(\cdot)}{\partial k_j(t)} = \dot{\lambda}_{ij}(t) - \rho\lambda_{ij}(t) \Rightarrow \dot{\lambda}_{ij}(t) = \lambda_{ij}(t)\left[\delta + \rho - f'(k_l(t))\right]$$ (3.106)

Now note that the system of adjoint equations (3.105–3.106) consists of n differential equations in separable variables, admitting the solutions $\lambda_{ii}(t) = \lambda_{ij}(t) = 0$ at all times and for all i, j. Hence, although the present game is not a linear state one, it is indeed state redundant and produces a subgame perfect equilibrium under open-loop information, optimal controls delivered by (3.104) being independent of states at every instant.

Yet, imposing stationarity under full symmetry, in addition to the static Cournot–Nash solution we also find the equilibrium output generated by the Ramsey golden rule which we are accustomed with from the original macroeconomic growth model:

$$\dot{q} = 0 \text{ at } \begin{cases} q^{CN} = \dfrac{a-c}{n+1} \\ f'(k) = \delta + \rho \end{cases}$$ (3.107)

The phase diagram of the present model can be drawn in the space $\{k, q\}$. The locus $\dot{q} \equiv dq/dt = 0$ is given by the solutions in (3.107). These loci partition the state-control space $\{k, q\}$ into four regions, where the dynamics of q is summarised by the vertical arrows. The locus $\dot{k} = 0$ as well as the dynamics of k, depicted by horizontal arrows, derive from (3.102). Steady state equilibria, denoted by $E1$, $E2$ along the horizontal arm and $E3$ along the vertical one, are identified by the intersections between loci.

Figure 3.2 describes only one out of five possible configurations, since the position of the vertical line $f'(k) = \rho + \delta$ is independent of demand parameters, while the locus $q = (a-c)/(n+1)$ shifts upwards as market size $a - c$ increases or the number of firms n decreases (and conversely). Therefore, we obtain one out of five possible regimes:

1. There exist three steady state points, with $k_{E1} < k_{E2} < k_{E3}$ (this is the scenario depicted in Figure 3.2).
2. There exist two steady state points, with $k_{E1} = k_{E2} < k_{E3}$.
3. There exist three steady state points, with $k_{E2} < k_{E1} < k_{E3}$.
4. There exist two steady state points, with $k_{E2} < k_{E1} = k_{E3}$.
5. There exists a unique steady state equilibrium point, corresponding to $E2$.

The vertical locus $f'(k) = \rho + \delta$ is a constraint on optimal capital, determined by firms' intertemporal preferences, i.e., their common discount rate, and depreciation. This identifies the *optimal capital constraint* k_{GR}, subscript GR standing for *golden rule*. The corresponding 'Ramsey output' $q(k_{GR})$ is determined by the intersection between loci $f'(k) = \rho + \delta$ and $\dot{k} = 0$. If market size $a - c$ is very large (or n is low), points $E1$ and $E3$ either do not exist (regime 5) or fall to the right of $E2$ (regimes 2, 3 and 4).

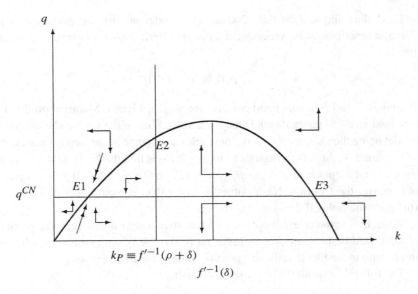

$$k_P \equiv f'^{-1}(\rho + \delta)$$

$$f'^{-1}(\delta)$$

Figure 3.2 The phase diagram of the Cournot–Ramsey game

In such a case, the capital constraint is operative and firms choose the capital accumulation corresponding to $E2$.

The detailed stability analysis of the dynamic system can be found in Cellini and Lambertini (1998, 2003). Here, I will confine myself to stressing two related facts, namely, that

- whenever $q^{CN} < q(k_{GR})$, the static Cournot–Nash equilibrium is a saddle point, while the Ramsey equilibrium is unstable (as is the case in Figure 3.2), while the opposite applies if $q^{CN} > q(k_{GR})$; and
- the industry may reach the golden rule along a saddle path in two very different ways. The first is the consequence of a sufficiently large increase in market size or industry concentration, causing $q^{CN} > q(k_{GR})$. The second is the consequence of free entry, which, in the limit, reproduces perfect competition as q^{CN} drops to zero. If the horizontal locus coincides with the horizontal axis, the model fully coincides with the macroeconomic model based on the assumption of perfect competition, and the golden rule is obviously reproduced.[12] The former implication says, however, that even a monopoly might deliver the golden rule, which does not go hand in hand with perfect competition. Of course, the welfare performances of these two outcomes largely diverge.

In addition to the aforementioned extensions, the model has been used to investigate horizontal mergers in markets with a nonlinear demand (Cellini and Lambertini, 2007a) and the impact of profit taxation on managerial firms (Baldini and Lambertini, 2010).

---

[12] The dynamic properties of the system, highlighted in the phase diagram, also imply that $q^{CN} = 0$ is unstable.

In Cellini and Lambertini (2007a), the model admits the presence of nonlinear demand functions, as in Anderson and Engers (1992, 1994). The inverse market demand function

$$p(t) = [a - Q(t)]^{\frac{1}{\beta}} \tag{3.108}$$

is convex for all $\beta \in (0, 1)$ and concave for all $\beta \in (1, \infty)$. Marginal production cost is assumed away, to guarantee the analytical solvability of the game. The remainder of the model being the same as above, the only relevant change in the steady state configuration of the game – which is analogous to Figure 3.2 – is that the horizontal locus identifying the Cournot output is at $q^{CN} = a\beta / (\beta n + 1) \gtrless a / (n + 1)$ for all $\beta \gtrless 1$, i.e., if demand is concave, the Cournot–Nash output is larger than it would be with a linear demand (the opposite holds if demand is convex).

When q^{CN} is the relevant output both before and after the merger, the profit incentive is calculated in the same way as in Salant et al. (1983), with similar conclusions. More interesting is the fact that the merger may indeed entail $q^{CN} > q_{GR}$.

The following result is then easily established:

Proposition 3.4 *A sufficiently large horizontal merger may drive the industry from the static Cournot–Nash equilibrium into the golden rule. This task becomes easier to accomplish the higher is β.*

The intuition is as follows. Suppose q^{CN} yields a saddle point equilibrium. Any increase in β and any decrease in n bring about an increase in q^{CN}. Hence, the horizontal merger of size $2 \leq m \leq n - 1$, coupled with a sufficiently high value of β, shifts the horizontal locus upwards, and this shift may be sufficiently large to drive q^{CN} above q_{GR}.

With no need of increasing industry concentration, the convergence of the Cournot–Nash equilibrium to the golden rule can be attained through the separation between ownership and control, with firms' strategies being delegated to managers. The dynamic analysis of firms' growth by Penrose (1955, 1959) and Slater (1980) has singled out the limits imposed by managerialization. Instead, using the strategic delegation model dating back to Fershtman (1985), Vickers (1985), Fershtman and Judd (1987) and Sklivas (1987), Baldini and Lambertini (2010) illustrate a scenario where the opposite applies.

The instantaneous reward of manager of firm i is proportional to

$$M_i(t) = \pi_i(t) + \theta q_i(t) \tag{3.109}$$

where $\theta > 0$ measures the extent of delegation in the form of output expansion, and the manager chooses $q_i(t)$ to maximise

$$\mathcal{M}_i(t) = \int_0^\infty M_i(t) e^{-\rho t} dt \tag{3.110}$$

under the set of n dynamic constraints (3.102) and the vector of initial conditions concerning the state variables, $k_i(0) = k_{i0}$, $i = 1, 2, 3, ...n$. Once again, open-loop strategies are strongly time consistent as the game is state-redundant. Following the same procedure as above, the market-driven optimal output is

$$q^N(\theta) = \frac{a - c + \theta}{n + 1} \tag{3.111}$$

appearing as a horizontal line in the phase diagram, which has the same shape as in Figure 3.2. However, since $q^N(\theta) > q^{CN}$ for all $\theta > 0$, the horizontal line is higher if all firms are managerial, and therefore the market-driven equilibrium is closer to the golden rule than in the pure profit-seeking oligopoly case, *all else equal*. In particular, noting that $q_{GR} = f(k_{GR}) - \delta k_{GR}$, the golden rule is reached for all

$$\theta \geq \max\left\{0, \frac{f(k_{GR}) - \delta k_{GR}}{n + 1} - a + c\right\} \tag{3.112}$$

keeping industry structure unmodified. This implies the following:

Proposition 3.5 *By going fully managerial, an oligopoly with any given number of firms may reproduce the Ramsey golden rule.*

In Baldini and Lambertini (2011), the effect of profit taxation is also accounted for, and the instantaneous profit function becomes

$$\pi_i = (a - q_i - Q_{-i} - c)(1 - \tau)q_i \tag{3.113}$$

This allows to single out the distortionary effects of taxation and the possibility of neutralising the latter through an appropriated choice of the delegation parameter θ. Clearly, this becomes even more evident if production production is being taxed, in such a way that $\pi_i = (a - q_i - Q_{-i} - c - \tau)q_i$, as then $\theta = \tau$ fully offsets the tax rate and the model is observationally equivalent to the pure profit-seeking Cournot oligopoly in Cellini and Lambertini (1998).

The oligopolistic version of the Ramsey (1928) model has also been used in Lambertini *et al.* (2016) to produce the dynamic version of the Cournot duopoly with CSR investigated in Lambertini and Tampieri (2015), showing that, provided market size is sufficiently large, a CSR firm internalising polluting emissions and consumer surplus sells more, installs a larger productive capacity and earns higher profits than its profit-seeking rival in the market-driven steady state equilibrium. This and several other extensions of the setup illustrated earlier (sometimes not explicitly admitting a role for managers) show that the IO reinterpretation of a classical macroeconomic growth model is very versatile, and is most likely to hide additional routes for research, still unexplored.

3.4   Price Competition with Adjustment Costs

In Jun and Vives (2004) we find a compendium of dynamic oligopolistic competition under capacity accumulation or sticky prices, and the complementary analysis of both cases under Bertrand competition, using product differentiation as in Singh and Vives (1984), so that the duopoly setting has two single product firms facing the following system of demand functions at every instant:

$$q_i(t) = \frac{a}{1+\gamma} - \frac{p_i(t)}{1-\gamma^2} + \frac{\gamma p_j(t)}{1-\gamma^2} \tag{3.114}$$

in which the constant $\gamma \in [-1, 1]$ measures the degree of complementarity (if negative) or substitutability (if positive) between the two varieties. This parameter captures the likings of the representative consumer, or, her/his *taste for variety*.

Consider first the case of costly price adjustment, whereby prices are states evolving along the kinematics

$$\dot{p}_i(t) = I_i(t) \tag{3.115}$$

where effort $I_i(t)$ is firm i's control and involves the same linear-quadratic instantaneous cost $C_i(t) = cI_i(t) + bI_i^2(t)/2$ as in Reynolds (1987). Solving this game under linear feedback strategies, Jun and Vives (2004) find that the steady state price is quasi-collusive (although not fully so), in the sense that it is above its open-loop equilibrium level and lower than the static Bertrand–Nash price. This result is driven by the property that $\partial I_i^*(t)/\partial p_j(t) > 0$ along the optimal path to the equilibrium.

Now turn to the alternative scenario in which it is costly to adjust capacity, and firms are supposed to always operate at full capacity, so that $q_i(t) = k_i(t)$ at all times. Here, demand functions remain as in (3.114), except for the new label of a variable, and individual capacity follows the differential equation

$$\dot{k}_i(t) = \alpha p_j(t) - \delta p_i(t) \tag{3.116}$$

in which α and δ are positive parameters. The cost of adjusting capacity (or output) is $C_i(t) = c\left[\dot{k}_i(t)\right]^2/2$. The feedback solution of this second version of the game leads to a steady state price which lies below its equilibrium value under open-loop rules. We will come back to these properties and their intuitive explanation below.

3.5   Durability and Addiction

Driskill (2001) extends the traditional durable good models, usually assuming monopoly (as in Driskill, 1997), to an oligopolistic setup with n firms treated as a differential game with stock decay. On the demand side, as in Chapter 1, the representative consumer's utility is $U(t) = aQ(t) - Q^2(t)/2$, where $Q(t)$ is the stock of the durable good and a is a positive constant; and the stock follows $\dot{Q} = \sum_{i=1}^{n} u_i(t) - \delta Q(t)$, in which $u_i(t)$ is the instantaneous production rate of firm i. Price expectations are

$$E\left(\dot{p}\right) = (\delta + \rho)p(t) - \frac{\partial U(t)}{\partial Q(t)} = (\delta + \rho)p(t) - a + Q(t) \tag{3.117}$$

At any time during the game, the consumer can get funds from debt to increase income $R(t)$ faces the flow budget constraint

$$p(t) \sum_{i=1}^{n} u_i(t) + \Upsilon(t) = R(t) + \rho B(t) \qquad (3.118)$$

where $\Upsilon(t)$ measures flow purchases or sales of debt, and $B(t)$ is the amount of bond holding, evolving along $\dot{B} = \Upsilon(t)$. From the necessary conditions generated by the Hamiltonian of the consumer, one indeed obtains (3.117). To close the demand side of the model and prepare the ground for the analysis of firms' behaviour, Driskill (2001) specifies the feedback (i.e., state-dependent) expectation function

$$E\left(\dot{p}\right) = h + mQ(t) \qquad (3.119)$$

where h and m are positive parameters. Hence, the instantaneous demand faced by firms is

$$p(t) = \frac{a + h + (m - 1)Q(t)}{\delta + \rho} \qquad (3.120)$$

Firms are identical and use a technology characterised by decreasing returns, the cost function being $C_i(t) = cu_i(t) + nbu_i^2(t)$, where c and b are positive parameters.[13] Hence, firm i's aim is

$$\max_{u_i(t)} \Pi_i = \int_0^{\infty} u_i(t) \left[p_i(t) - c - nu_i(t)\right] e^{-\rho t} dt \qquad (3.121)$$

subject to the stock dynamics and the initial condition $Q_0 > 0$. The characterization of the equilibrium behaviour of firms says that the resulting stock is lower than the efficient one, irrespective of the number of firms, including the monopoly case which reflects the model exposed in Chapter 1. However, the gap decreases monotonically in the number of firms. in the cost parameter b and in the decay rate δ. This implies

Proposition 3.6 *Free entry (perfect competition) drives oligopolists to supply the socially efficient stock of durable goods. The same happens for any finite number of firms if marginal production cost is constant or the stock does not depreciate.*

Rational expectations formulated by farsighted consumers also fit the formulation of other problems, such as the consumption of addictive goods. This topic is taken up in Driskill and McCafferty (2001), where, at any given time, the representative consumer's utility function

$$U(t) = q(t) \left[a - q(t)\right] + k(t) \left[\alpha + \beta z(t)\right] + q(t) k(t) \qquad (3.122)$$

is characterised by a *consumption capital* deriving from past consumption:

$$k(t) = \int_0^T q(t) e^{\delta(T-t)} dt \qquad (3.123)$$

---

[13] The appearance of n in $C_i(t)$ is due to the assumption that each firm owns a fraction $1/n$ of the stock of capacity installed in the whole industry.

where $q(t)$ is instantaneous consumption and $\delta > 0$ affects the speed at which consumption capital builds up, as well as its dynamic behaviour along the kinematic equation

$$\dot{k} = q(t) - \delta k(t) \tag{3.124}$$

In (3.122), a, α and β are positive constants, and the consumer chooses the consumption path maximising the discounted flow of utility along an infinite horizon, under the budget constraint $p(t) q(t) = R(t)$ and the above state equation. Assuming again price expectations to be linear in the state, in this case $E\left(\dot{p}\right) = h + mk(t)$, it is possible to solve the oligopoly game w.r.t. firms' production strategies to ascertain what follows:

Proposition 3.7 *In steady state, the equilibrium price can be lower than marginal production cost and firms' profits are not monotonically decreasing as the number of firms increases.*

The first result comes from the fact that marginal revenue includes a component related with the consumption stock (that is, addiction matters). The second comes from the balance of two effects generated by any increase in the number of firms: the first is the usual procompetitive effect, the second is the free-riding effect distorting the investment in consumption capital.

3.6   Conjectural Variations, Best Replies and Potential Functions

A recurrent theme in the mainstream of oligopoly theory is the description of what happens in the minds of entrepreneurs (or managers) during the various phases of competition. In its early stage, starting with Bowley (1924), the related literature has discussed the concept of conjectural variations and their consistency (see Bresnahan, 1981; Perry, 1982; Boyer and Moreaux, 1983; Kamien and Schwartz, 1983; and Klemperer and Meyer, 1988, among others). The second phase is driven by a characterisation of the firms' attitude (Fudenberg and Tirole, 1984) and then builds upon the analogy with demand theory leading to the concepts of strategic complementarity and substitutability (Bulow et al., 1985). The main point raised by this approach is that the attitude of firm i in a given static game involving the choice of some strategic variables is equivalently described by the two derivatives

$$\frac{\partial u_i^*(u_j)}{\partial u_j} \; ; \; \frac{\partial^2 \pi_i}{\partial u_i \partial u_j} \tag{3.125}$$

which always have the same sign, since the best reply function $u_i^*(u_j)$ is nothing but another way of writing the FOC of firm i. If the derivatives in (3.125) are negative (positive), strategic variables are strategic substitutes (complements), and the best replies are negatively (positively) sloped. Of course, (1) the mixed case is also admissible, and (2) if the derivatives in (3.125) are nil, then firm i avails of a dominant strategy.

A similar analysis has been developed in the field of differential games, starting with the construction of a dynamic theory of conjectural variations (Dockner, 1992) where open-loop and feedback Nash equilibria are reformulated in the space of consistent conjectures, including as an example the Cournot model with costly adjustment of Driskill and McCafferty (1989). The subsequent step is in Lambertini and Mantovani (2006), who study firms' best replies and their slopes (relying, in this respect, on Bulow et al., 1985) in the sticky price model of Simaan and Takayama (1978) and Fershtman and Kamien (1987) and the capital accumulation game, either à la Solow (as in Reynolds, 1987) or à la Ramsey (as in Cellini and Lambertini, 1998), in the latter case examining both Cournot and Bertrand competition. Lambertini and Mantovani (2006) confine their attention to open-loop and memoryless closed-loop solutions of the Hamiltonian problems, and show that if a firm's Hamiltonian is additively separable w.r.t. all controls, then best replies are orthogonal to one another in the control space, and firms solve the game using dominant strategies at all times. If instead the Hamiltonian function is not additively separable w.r.t. controls, instantaneous best replies can be characterised in terms of strategic substitutability/complementarity.

The frontier of this stream of research is drawn in Figuières (2009),[14] where the concept of Markov substitutability/complementarity is defined as the dynamic counterpart of strategic substitutability/complementarity. The idea behind it is that to single out the mechanisms whereby firms' outputs, prices or investments must be higher or lower under open-loop or closed-loop/feedback information. In other terms, the analytical instruments designed by Figuières (2009) allows us to understand the arising of preemption incentives and understand when and why we may expect firms to behave more or less aggressively. The basic instruments are two partial derivatives. Suppose, for the moment, that the game features n firms, n states and n controls (one for each firm). As in Chapter 1, it is useful to define the control and state pertaining to firm i as u_i and x_i, respectively. If the game is solved under feedback rules, then we can examine the linear feedback strategy $u^{LF}(\mathbf{x})$ at any time t, to learn that

- if $\partial u^{LF}(\mathbf{x})/\partial x_j < 0$ for all $j \neq i$, the game exhibits Markov substitutability; conversely,
- if $\partial u^{LF}(\mathbf{x})/\partial x_j > 0$ for all $j \neq i$, the game exhibits Markov complementarity;
- under Markov complementarity, feedback information softens competition as compared to open-loop information; the opposite holds for Markov substitutability.

So, it all boils down to the cross effects of the states upon any of the firms' controls. Note that the partial derivatives $\partial u^{LF}(\mathbf{x})/\partial x_j$ appears in the costate equations augmented by the loops which one has to calculate in the closed-loop memoryless game. In such a case, the method of Figuières (2009) can be applied to the material investigated in Lambertini and Mantovani (2006) to reconstruct their conclusion using his instruments.

The approach used by Figuières (2009) also produces two ancillary but very relevant results which further help intuition. The first is that (1) under Markov substitutability

---

[14] See also Lapham and Ware (1994) for a Markovian version of the labels proposed by Fudenberg and Tirole (1984).

the steady state level of feedback controls lies above the open-loop level, the latter being higher than the one associated with the cartel solution; while (2) under Markov complementarity, equilibrium feedback controls lie between open-loop and cartel ones (cf. Figuières, 2009, Theorem 6.1, p. 52). The second is that if the limit game exhibits strategic substitutability (complementarity), then the feedback game exhibits Markov substitutability (complementarity) at any finite date (cf. Figuières, 2009, p. 51). Hence, the properties of static competition, as we understand them through the lenses of strategic substitutability/complementarity, tell us in advance what to expect from the solution of the dynamic version of a game, whenever the basic features of the static version are known to arise from some limits of the relevant magnitudes of the differential game. This is the case, for instance, of the sticky price model, as well as the two versions of the capacity accumulation game investigated above.

A related matter is the concept of potential game. Slade (1994) has been the first to ask the fundamental question of "what do oligopolists maximise" in a static Cournot–Nash game. The general question as to whether we can identify a function yielding the same gradient as a given game under examination has received an answer by Monderer and Shapley (1996), borrowing the concept of potential function from physics. In a nutshell, if it exists, the objective function of a single agent replicating the behaviour (or, the system of first order conditions) of the players involved in the actual game is the potential function of that game.

In a differential game the issue is more involved, as necessary conditions include costate equations in addition to the FOCs on controls. The first work outlining the definition of a potential function in a differential game setup is Dragone et al. (2012), where it is shown that the Cournot–Ramsey game based upon the nonlinear demand model in Anderson and Engers (1992, 1994) admits a potential function. After having constructed the potential function of the static game, they perform the same task for the differential game, by transforming the game into an optimal control problem with as many controls and states, complemented by the same number of fictitious costate variables as the original game.

A more general approach is in Dragone et al. (2015), in which open-loop information is considered and sufficient conditions for existence are identified. Moreover, it is illustrated that the task of proving the existence and constructing the potential function in a differential game significantly differs from what one has to do in a static one, since the potential function must also reproduce the same dynamics – in particular, the same costate and control equations, as the state equations are by definition the same – and attain the same solution as the original differential game. Dragone et al. (2015) also prove that, in order to admit a Hamiltonian potential function, an open-loop differential game must satisfy two properties: (1) conservativity, whereby the candidate potential function's first-order partial derivatives w.r.t. all controls and states are the same as those of Hamiltonian functions of the open-loop differential game;[15] and (2) redundancy of a portion of the set of the costate variables pertaining to the original differential game.

---

[15] This property can take a less demanding form, in cases where the game admits a representation in terms of a *best-response potential function* (Voorneveld, 2000).

This property, in turn, happens to be satisfied if the dynamic system of the game is decoupled in such a way to meet it. To perform this latter part of their analysis, Dragone *et al.* (2015) in fact largely rely on ideas and procedures related to the state-redundancy property investigated by Dockner *et al.* (1985), whose illustration is in Chapter 1.

The same authors also offer some preliminary insights about the identification of potential functions in games solved under feedback rules, by constructing the related HJB equation (Dragone *et al.*, 2015, p. 137). Their example is worth reporting here almost in full, as its exposition clarifies an important point. The game envisages n players, each controlling a single strategic variable u_i, and a single state variable x, whose kinematic equations is

$$\dot{x} = \sum_{i=1}^{n} u_i - \delta x \qquad (3.126)$$

Let the instantaneous payoff accruing to player i be $\pi_i = f(x) + g(u_i)$. Note that any effect of $u_j \neq u_i$ upon π_i solely depends on the presence of all controls in the above state dynamics. The individual HJB equation

$$\rho V_i(x) = \max_{u_i} \left\{ f(x) + g_i(u_i) + V_i'(x) \left[\sum_{i=1}^{n} u_i - \delta x \right] \right\} \qquad (3.127)$$

is $\partial g_i(u_i) / \partial u_i = -V_i'(x)$. Then, note that using the function

$$\mathbf{P}(x, \mathbf{u}) = f(x) + \sum_{i=1}^{n} g_i(u_i) \qquad (3.128)$$

one can build the following HJB equation:

$$\rho V_{\mathbf{P}}(x) = \max_{u_1 \ldots u_n} \left\{ \mathbf{P}(x, \mathbf{u}) + V_{\mathbf{P}}'(x) \left[\sum_{i=1}^{n} u_i - \delta x \right] \right\} \qquad (3.129)$$

whose gradient coincides with the system of n FOCs of the original game. Hence, (3.129) is indeed the Bellman equation of the potential representation of the feedback game whose canonical representation is based on (3.127). Moreover, it is also easily shown that the open-loop solution of the same game is strongly time consistent and coincides with the feedback solution produced by either (3.127) or (3.129). Therefore, the Hamiltonian potential function is

$$\mathcal{H}_{\mathbf{P}} = \mathbf{P}(x, \mathbf{u}) + \lambda_{\mathbf{P}} \left(\sum_{i=1}^{n} u_i - \delta x \right) \qquad (3.130)$$

with, intuitively, $\lambda_{\mathbf{P}} = V_{\mathbf{P}}'(x)$ at all times. Since this chapter is about differential *oligopoly* games, one may think of a situation in which firms jointly invest in a public good (or bad, depending on the exact specification of the function $f(x)$), as in Fershtman and Nitzan (1991). The absence of interplay between controls in the instantaneous payoff may fit an industry in which an endogenous market demand is replaced by a regulated price, so that $g_i(u_i) = pu_i - bu_i^2$. Having dealt with expositional details and interpretation, the above example implies that (1) we have a route along which to confidently seek for potential functions under feedback information; and (2) if a state-redundant game admits a representation in terms of a Hamiltonian potential function, then there also exists a HJB equation yielding the feedback potential representation of the same game.

3.7   Collusive Equilibria and Trigger Strategies

The endogenous arising of implicitly collusive equilibria Pareto-dominating the non-cooperative Nash equilibrium is a major theme in the theory of repeated games and industrial organization, and one of the issues traditionally receiving the highest attention is the design of punishment strategies to deter deviations and stabilise the cartel path forever. The building blocks of the related theoretical discussion are Friedman (1971), using the infinite Nash reversion; and Abreu (1986, 1988) and Fudenberg and Maskin (1986), using optimal punishments. In the framework outlined by Friedman (1971), the players' behaviour relies on *grim trigger* strategies.

Trigger strategies and the possibility of using them to sustain perpetually collusive outcomes have also been formalised in the theory of differential games, with, however, extremely scant applications (mainly belonging to the area of resource extraction games, which I will mention in Chapter 7). Yet, the theoretical formulation of the problem is quite well known, and has a lot in common with the theory of supergames, except for a few relevant aspects which I will mention in the ensuing exposition.

To the best of my knowledge, the first to define the notion of trigger strategies in a dynamic game in discrete time is Tolwinski (1982), where trigger strategies are used to enforce a bargaining solution. The same instrument is translated into the language of differential games modelling collusive outcomes by Tolwinski et al. (1988) and Mehlmann (1994), and then thoroughly overviewed in the volume of Dockner et al. (2000, chapter 6), to which I refer the reader interested to additional details.

The setting is a differential game over an infinite horizon with $n \geq 2$ players (each endowed with a control variable $u_i (t)$) and a single state $x (t)$, whose dynamics is

$$\dot{x} (t) = f (x (t), \mathbf{u} (t)) \tag{3.131}$$

Assuming for simplicity that players are identical, one can define the individual instantaneous payoff as $\pi (x (t), \mathbf{u} (t))$ and the individual value of the game under noncooperative (Nash) behaviour as

$$\Pi^N = \int_0^\infty \pi^N \left(x^N (t), \mathbf{u}^N (t) \right) e^{-\rho t} dt \tag{3.132}$$

Now suppose players want to attain a Pareto-superior outcome, targeting a path $\left\{ x^C (t), \mathbf{u}^C (t) \right\}$, where superscript C stands for *collusion*. If this path is followed by all players at all times, the individual value of the game becomes

$$\Pi^C = \int_0^\infty \pi^C \left(x^C (t), \mathbf{u}^C (t) \right) e^{-\rho t} dt > \Pi^N \tag{3.133}$$

As in repeated games, the temptation to defect at some $T \in [0, \infty)$ may disrupt collusion. The deterrence against unilateral deviations is performed by trigger strategies similar to those adopted by grim trigger profiles, except that in a differential game the presence of an evolving state makes the deviation dependent on the entire past history of the game. For this reason, the deviation date is also sensitive to $x(t)$, while in a standard repeated game it is commonly set equal to zero because the underlying stage game is time-invariant. Moreover, a detection lag $\delta > 0$ is explicitly admitted, so that the punishment path starts (if at all) at $t = T + \delta$. The trigger strategy is then defined as follows:

$$u_i(T + \delta) = \begin{cases} u^C(t), \text{ if } u_i(t) = u^C(t) \,\forall i \text{ at } t \leq T + \delta \\ u^{ps}(t), \text{ if } u_i(t) \neq u^C(t) \text{ for at least one player at } t \leq T + \delta \end{cases} \tag{3.134}$$

where superscript ps stands for threat punishment strategy; for instance, the Nash reversion $u^{ps}(t) = u^N(t)$. Moreover, one may think of a deviation taking place along the best reply function of the cheating firm, $u_i^D(t) = u_i^*(\mathbf{u}_{-i}^C(t))$, superscript D standing for *deviation*. If this is the case, the picture is largely analogous to Friedman (1971). The value of the game to the deviator, from T to doomsday, is therefore equal to

$$\Pi^D = \int_T^{T+\delta} \pi_i^D \left(u_i^* \left(\mathbf{u}_{-i}^C(t) \right), \mathbf{u}_{-i}^C(t), x^D(t) \right) e^{-\rho(t-T)} dt + \Pi^N e^{-\rho T} \tag{3.135}$$

Now note that, in the above expression, the trajectory of the state differs from that associated with the collusive game during the initial period preceding the punishment (along which it is denoted by $x^D(t)$), and, in general, will also differ from that associated with the fully noncooperative game from $T + \delta$ onwards, as the initial condition for this continuation game, $x^D(T + \delta)$ will differ from the level of the state $x^N(T + \delta)$ reached along the Nash path generating the value (3.132).

Having said that, collusion is sustainable forever iff $\Pi^C \geq \Pi^D$ at all times (that is, for all $T \in [0, \infty)$) and for all δ *positive but sufficiently small*, i.e., provided the detection delay is short enough (cf. Dockner *et al.*, 2000, Theorem 6.3, p. 156). Also note that the idea of a detection lag is connected with the information coming from the consequences of players' actions on the state of the system, whereby loyal firms realise that someone must have cheated observing the consequence of deviation on $x(t)$ and therefore on profits. The main problem is that dealing with strategies, which depends on the whole history of the game instead of the current state, makes this equilibrium non-Markovian, or, non-subgame perfect. To achieve subgame perfection, one has to construct the so-called δ-strategies, where δ is still positive but arbitrarily small, allowing instantaneous detection of deviations (Tolwinski *et al.*, 1988).

3.8   Entry, Industry Dynamics and Empirical Research

This section covers a spectrum of related issues: the incumbents' attitude towards entry, the evolution of an industry over time admitting firms' entry and exit and the possibility of constructing dynamic models describing this evolution while at the same time offering a framework for the empirical analysis of this process and its key features.

The first topic has quite rapidly attracted the attention of researchers modelling entry and entry barriers through the toolkit of optimal control and differential game theory, responding to the stimulus coming from the early debate about limit pricing behaviour (Bain, 1956; Sylos-Labini, 1957; Modigliani, 1958). The insurgence of interest in this respect is demonstrated by the number of papers offering a dynamic reformulation of this problem in the 1970s and 1980s (Gaskins; 1971; Pyatt, 1971; Kamien and Schwartz, 1971; Flaherty, 1980; Matthews and Mirman, 1983) using continuous time models, and its later persistence in a fully mature literature (Maskin and Tirole, 1987; 1988a,b; 2001) using discrete time models.

With no ambition to cover the debate based on the aforementioned contributions in detail, here I will confine myself to a succinct exposition of Gaskins (1971), whose focus is the characterisation of the bearings of limit pricing on the profit stream of an incumbent facing entry by a generic number of competitors. That is, the interest of his model lies in its close kinship with the original literature on the same issue which appeared in the late 1950s.

The game takes place over an infinite horizon, between an incumbent (firm $\mathbb{I}$) and at least one entrant (the competitive fringe $\mathbb{F}$), and is built in such a way that it is actually an optimal control problem. The instantaneous market price is $p(t)$, while the limit price is p_ℓ, at least equal to marginal cost c. The incumbent aims at maximising

$$\Pi_{\mathbb{I}} = \int_0^\infty \pi_{\mathbb{I}}(t) e^{-\rho t} dt = \int_0^\infty \left[p(t) - c \right] q_{\mathbb{I}}(p(t)) e^{-\rho t} dt \qquad (3.136)$$

The incumbent's instantaneous output level $q_{\mathbb{I}}(p(t))$ is equal to

$$q_{\mathbb{I}}(p(t)) = Q(p(t)) - q_{\mathbb{F}}(t) \qquad (3.137)$$

where $Q(p(t)) - q_{\mathbb{F}}(t)$ is the difference between market demand at price $p(t)$ and the output $q_{\mathbb{F}}(t)$ of the newcomers; i.e., the incumbent's sales are identified in terms of a residual demand curve. The market demand function is downward sloping and continuously differentiable w.r.t. price.

Then, Gaskin (1971, p. 307) argues that

$$\dot{q}_{\mathbb{F}} = \alpha \left[p(t) - p_\ell \right] \qquad (3.138)$$

on the basis of the intuition whereby the incumbent treats the current price as an indication of the market's profitability; in the above differential equation, α is a positive parameter. The initial condition is $q_{\mathbb{F}}(0) \geq 0$ for all $p_\ell \geq c$, so that, if the incumbent adopts the limit price, no further entry occurs. The model is built in such a way that one can actually think of any number of entrants behaving as price takers. Indeed, interpreting it as a description of competition between a dominant firm and a competitive fringe facilitates the interpretation of the state equation (3.138) as something similar to a supply function (cf. Klemperer and Meyer, 1989; Vives, 2011), since the fringe's collective output is increasing in market price.

Hence, (3.138) is the state equation of the problem at hand. As a result, the incumbent's current value Hamiltonian is

$$\mathcal{H}_{\mathrm{I}}\left(q_{\mathbb{F}}\left(t\right),p\left(t\right)\right)=e^{-\rho t}\left\{\left[p\left(t\right)-c\right]\left[Q\left(p\left(t\right)\right)-q_{\mathbb{F}}\left(t\right)\right]+\alpha\lambda\left(t\right)\left[p\left(t\right)-p_{\ell}\right]\right\} \tag{3.139}$$

which has to be maximised using $p\left(t\right)$ as the control variable. This yields the FOC

$$\left(p-c\right)\cdot\frac{\partial Q}{\partial p}+Q-q_{\mathbb{F}}+\alpha\lambda=0 \tag{3.140}$$

and the adjoint equation

$$\dot{\lambda}=p-c+\rho\lambda \tag{3.141}$$

and differentiating (3.140) w.r.t. time, we obtain the control equation

$$\dot{p}=\frac{\dot{q}_{2}-\alpha\dot{\lambda}}{2\partial Q/\partial p+\left(p-c\right)\cdot\partial^{2}Q/\partial p^{2}} \tag{3.142}$$

which, together with (3.138), forms the state-control system of the model, and it implies the existence of a unique saddle point equilibrium, portrayed in Figure 3.3.

The unique steady state point entails $p=p_{\ell}$ with a positive fringe size, and as the graph shows, the limit price can be reached from any initial condition $q_{\mathbb{F}}\left(0\right)$. Of course, the decreasing price path starting from any price $p\left(t\right)>p_{\ell}$ looks more sensible than the alternative increasing path. Moreover, it is also easy to prove that the steady state limit price is lower than the pure monopoly price.

In Kamien and Schwartz (1971), the limit pricing behaviour is further investigated to account for the fact that the incumbent may be aware that its price policy affects the probability of entry, showing that the pre-entry price decreases as discounting decreases.

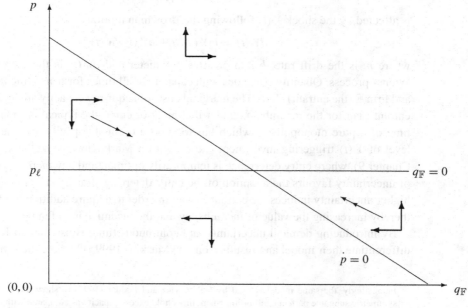

Figure 3.3 The limit price game: phase diagram

Flaherty (1980) takes an approach to the problem which revives the predatory argument in Bain (1956), Sylos-Labini (1957) and Modigliani (1958), showing that if technology is characterised by increasing returns and the latter are sufficiently strong, then the dynamic model produces an equilibrium in which expanding output to deter entry is indeed optimal.

The subsequent literature on strategic entry barriers pivots around the idea that incumbents have an incentive to invest so as to acquire excess capacity to deter entry (see Spence, 1977; Dixit, 1980, *inter alia*). The first dynamic models of this kind (Spence, 1979; Fudenberg and Tirole, 1983) in fact revealed the existence of equilibria characterised by strategic deterrence. The current frontier of research about entry-and-capacity games is the real option approach to entry timing and the endogenous determination of optimal investment in capacity. Following the pioneering contribution of Dixit (1989) on entry and exit decisions under uncertainty, the basic elements of the real option view of the optimal timing of entry *for a given investment level* are in Dixit and Pindyck (1994) and Trigeorgis (1996), while the joint determination of both is a being currently outlined in a lively literature (Dangl, 1999; Pawlina and Kort, 2006; Yang and Zhou, 2007; Thijssen *et al.*, 2012; Huisman and Kort, 2015). In a nutshell, the idea is that in a dynamic game envisaging possible entry at any instant over an arbitrarily long horizon, coupled with a stochastic demand (typically, demand shock following a Brownian motion), expecting entrants to be always deterred sounds quite a bit unrealistic.

In particular, Huisman and Kort (2015) extend the analysis presented in Dangl (1999) and Yang and Zhou (2007) by making the incumbent's investment decisions about the timing of investment and the choice of capacity entirely endogenous to the model, where instantaneous demand

$$p(t) = Y(t)[a - Q(t)] \tag{3.143}$$

is affected by the shock $Y(t)$ following the Brownian motion

$$dY(t) = mY(t)\,dt + bY(t)\,dw(t) \tag{3.144}$$

where m is the drift rate, b is a positive parameter and $dw(t)$ is the increment of a Wiener process. Quantity coincides with capacity at all times for firm $\mathbb{I}$ (the incumbent) and firm $\mathbb{E}$ (the entrant) alike. The marginal costs of acquiring capacity are higher for the entrant than for the incumbent. Under the threat of entry, the typical optimal stopping time of a pure monopolist – which has to choose optimal capacity and the threshold level of $Y(t)$ triggering investment – turns into a Markovian Stackelberg game (see Chapter 9), where entry deterrence is temporarily optimal, and any increase in the level of uncertainty favours the adoption of the entry-deterring strategy. The reason is that a higher uncertainty induces the entrant to wait in order to acquire additional information, thereby increasing the value of incumbency and the incentive to defend it.

By introducing demand uncertainty and continuous time, Huisman and Kort (2015) differentiate their model and results from (1) Maskin (1999),[16] where the setup is static

---

[16] Interestingly, the same model is used by Gabszewicz and Poddar (1997) to show the emergence of a symmetric subgame perfect equilibrium where firms hold excess capacity as compared with the Cournot–Nash certainty equivalent equilibrium.

and uncertainty ultimately makes deterrence less appealing; (2) Dockner and Mosburger (2007), where time is discrete and there is no uncertainty; and (3) Besanko *et al.* (2010), where again time is discrete, while products are imperfect substitutes and uncertainty affects a firm's perception of the rival's benefits from modifying its capacity. In Besanko *et al.* (2010), there emerges that product differentiation makes the adoption of entry-deterring strategies less likely.

To complete the overview contained in this section, two additional areas of research must be mentioned, although neither of them is dealing with proper differential games. The first, whose cornerstones are Jovanovic (1982) and Hopenhayn (1992), refreshing the discussion on industry evolution and the relationship between firms' size, profitability and survival inherited from Gibrat (1931) and the law named after him. According to Gibrat's law (also called the rule of proportionate growth or the law of proportionate effect), a firm's growth rate of growth is independent of its size. Jovanovic (1982) and Hopenhayn (1992) revisit this theme after Adelman (1958), Lucas (1978) and several others, by analysing a dynamic stochastic model describing the evolution of a competitive industry where firms are price takers. Uncertainty caused by productivity shocks (either at the industry or individual level) brings about a selection process among firms, through entry and exit, and in Hopenhayn (1992) the predictions of the model – implying a size distribution of firms by age cohort – prompt for numerical simulations and empirical assessment.

The current frontier of research in this area is based on Ericson and Pakes (1995) and the related literature, reviewed in Doraszelski and Pakes (2007), uses discrete time models describing industry evolution, including investments, entry and exit, and its Markov perfect equilibria, starting from any initial industry structure and offering also the complete characterization of the techniques involved in equilibrium selection, as well as providing a full-fledged framework to conduct numerical and empirical analysis. Having discussed the definition of trigger strategies in differential games, I must refer the interested reader to the analysis of collusion and price wars, based on Ericson and Pakes (1995), in Fershtman and Pakes (2000). I will come back to this approach in the next chapter.

Further Reading

The profitability of horizontal mergers under sticky prices is investigated in Dockner and Gaunersdorfer (2001), Benchekroun (2003) and Esfahani and Lambertini (2012). See also Gowrisankaran (1999). Further extensions account for value-added maximisation (Cellini and Lambertini, 2006) and product differentiation (Cellini and Lambertini, 2007b). The analysis of the bearings of hyperbolic demand functions on market equilibria has a tradition of its own: see Puu (1991, 2011), Lamantia (2011) and the references therein. Other properties of the viscous demand model are identified by Radner and Richardson (2003). The turnpike property of the Solow–Swan game is in Fershtman and Muller (1986). The Ramsey game in Cellini and Lambertini (1998) uses product differentiation as in Singh and Vives (1984) to investigate also Bertrand competition, showing that if varieties are substitutes in demand, the Bertrand case collapses into the Ramsey golden rule in a wider parameter range than the Cournot one. More on capacity accumulation in a feedback oligopoly game can be found in Lambertini and Palestini (2014), where market demand is hyperbolic. Additional non-LQ games are considered in Jun and Vives (2004), Koulovatianos and Mirman (2007) and Dockner and Mosburger (2007). A very good synthesis of the debate about conjectural variations is in Friedman (1983). An extension of the Dixit (1989) model is in Bar-Ilan and Strange (1996). A comprehensive survey of entry and entry barriers is in Gilbert (1989). Relevant insights in the vein of dynamic models with a potential for empirical analysis; see Pakes and McGuire (1994), Besanko and Doraszelski (2004), Besanko et al. (2010a,b) and Doraszelski and Satterthwaite (2010). More on optimal stopping in continuous time models is in Zhang (2017). A survey of the debate on Gibrat's law is in Sutton (1997).

Bibliography

Abreu, D.J. (1986), "Extremal Equilibria of Oligopolistic Supergames", *Journal of Economic Theory*, **39**, 191–225.

Abreu, D.J. (1988), "On the Theory of Infinitely Repeated Games with Discounting", *Econometrica*, **56**, 383–96.

Adelman, I. (1958), "A Stochastic Analysis of the Size Distribution of Firms", *American Statistical Association Journal*, **53**, 893–900.

Anderson, S. and M. Engers (1992), "Stackelberg vs Cournot Oligopoly Equilibrium", *International Journal of Industrial Organization*, **10**, 127–35.

Anderson, S. and M. Engers (1994), "Strategic Investment and Timing of Entry", *International Economic Review*, **35**, 833–53.

Azevedo, A. and D. Paxson (2014) "Developing Real Options Game Models", *European Journal of Operational Research*, **237**, 909–20.

Bain, J. (1956), *Barriers to New Competition*, Cambridge, MA, Harvard University Press.

Baldini, M. and L. Lambertini (2011), "Profit Taxation and Capital Accumulation in a Dynamic Oligopoly Model", *Japan and the World Economy*, **23**, 13–18.

Bar-Ilan, A. and W.C. Strange (1996), "Investment Lags", *American Economic Review*, **86**, 610–22.

Benchekroun, H. (2003), "The Closed-Loop Effect and the Profitability of Horizontal Mergers", *Canadian Journal of Economics*, **36**, 546–65.

Besanko, D. and U. Doraszelski (2004), "Capacity Dynamics and Endogenous Asymmetries in Firm Size', *RAND Journal of Economics*, **35**, 23–49.

Besanko, D., U. Doraszelski, Y. Kriulov and M. Satterthwaite (2010a), "Learning-by-Doing, Organizational Forgetting, and Industry Dynamics", *Econometrica*, **78**, 453–508.

Besanko, D., U. Doraszelski, L.X. Lu and M. Satterthwaite (2010b), "Lumpy Capacity Investment and Disinvestment Dynamics", *Operations Research*, **58**, 1178–93.

Blanchard, O.J. and S. Fischer (1989), *Lectures on Macroeconomics*, Cambridge, MA, MIT Press.

Bowley, A.L. (1924), *The Mathematical Groundworks of Economics*, Oxford, Oxford University Press.

Boyer, M. and M. Moreux (1983), "Consistent versus Non-Consistent Conjectures in Duopoly Theory: Some Examples", *Journal of Industrial Economics*, **23**, 97–110.

Bresnahan, T. (1981), "Duopoly Models with Consistent Conjectures", *American Economic Review*, **71**, 934–45.

Bulow, J., J. Geanakoplos and P. Klemperer (1985), "Multimarket Oligopoly: Strategic Substitutes and Complements", *Journal of Political Economy*, **93**, 488–511.

Calzolari, G. and L. Lambertini (2007), "Export Restraints in a Model of Trade with Capital Accumulation", *Journal of Economic Dynamics and Control*, **31**, 3822–42.

Cellini, R., and L. Lambertini (1998), "A Dynamic Model of Differentiated Oligopoly with Capital Accumulation", *Journal of Economic Theory*, **83**, 145–55.

Cellini, R. and L. Lambertini (2003), "Differential Oligopoly Games", in R. Bianchi and L. Lambertini (eds), *Technology, Information and Market Dynamics: Topics in Advanced Industrial Organization*, Cheltenham, Edward Elgar.

Cellini, R. and L. Lambertini (2004), "Dynamic Oligopoly with Sticky Prices: Closed-Loop, Feedback and Open-Loop Solutions", *Journal of Dynamical and Control Systems*, **10**, 303–14.

Cellini, R. and L. Lambertini (2006), "Workers' Enterprises Are Not Perverse: Differential Oligopoly Games with Sticky Price", *Review of Economic Design*, **10**, 233–48.

Cellini, R. and L. Lambertini (2007a), "Capital Accumulation, Mergers, and the Ramsey Golden Rule", in M. Quincampoix, T. Vincent and S. Jørgensen (eds), *Advances in Dynamic Game Theory and Applications*, Annals of the International Society of Dynamic Games, vol. 8, Boston, Birkhäuser.

Cellini, R. and L. Lambertini (2007b), "A Differential Oligopoly Game with Differentiated Goods and Sticky Prices", *European Journal of Operational Research*, **176**, 1131–44.

Cellini, R. and L. Lambertini (2008), "Weak and Strong Time Consistency in a Differential Oligopoly Game with Capital Accumulation", *Journal of Optimization Theory and Applications*, **138**, 17–26.

Chevalier-Roignant, B. and L. Trigeorgis (2011), *Competitive Strategy: Options and Games*, Cambridge, MA, MIT Press.

Clemhout, S., G. Leitmann and H. Wan (1971), "A Differential Game Model of Duopoly", *Econometrica*, **39**, 911–38.

Colombo, L. and P. Labrecciosa (2015), "On the Markovian Efficiency of Bertrand and Cournot Equilibria", *Journal of Economic Theory*, **155**, 332–58.

Dangl, T. (1999), "Investment and Capacity Choice under Uncertain Demand", *European Journal of Operational Research*, **117**, 415–28.

Dixit, A.K. (1980), "The Role of Investment in Entry Deterrence", *Economic Journal*, **90**, 95–106.

Dixit, A.K. (1986), "Comparative Statics for Oligopoly", *International Economic Review*, **27**, 103–22.

Dixit, A.K. (1989), "Entry and Exit Decisions under Uncertainty", *Journal of Political Economy*, **97**, 620–38.

Dixit, A.K. and R. Pindyk (1994), *Investment under Uncertainty*, Princeton, NJ, Princeton University Press.

Dockner, E.J. (1988), "On the Relation between Dynamic Oligopolistic Competition and Long-Run Competitive Equilibrium", *European Journal of Political Economy*, **4**, 47–64.

Dockner, E.J. (1992), "A Dynamic Theory of Conjectural Variations", *Journal of Industrial Economics*, **40**, 377–95.

Dockner, E.J. and A. Gaunersdorfer (2001), "On the Profitability of Horizontal Mergers in Industries with Dynamic Competition", *Japan and the World Economy*, **13**, 195–216.

Dockner, E.J. and G. Mosburger (2007), "Capital Accumulation, Asset Values and Imperfect Product Market Competition", *Journal of Difference Equations and Applications*, **13**, 197–215.

Dockner, E.J., G. Feichtinger and S. Jørgensen (1985), "Tractable Classes of Nonzerosum Open-Loop Nash Differential Games: Theory and Examples", *Journal of Optimization Theory and Applications*, **45**, 179–97.

Dockner, E.J., S. Jørgensen, N. Van Long and G. Sorger (2000), *Differential Games in Economics and Management Science*, Cambridge, Cambridge University Press.

Doraszelski, U. and A. Pakes (2007), "A Framework for Applied Dynamic Analysis in IO", in M. Armstrong and R. Porter (eds), *Handbook of Industrial Organization*, vol. 3, 1887–966.

Doraszelski, U. and M. Satterthwaite (2010), "Computable Markov-Perfect Industry Dynamics", *RAND Journal of Economics*, **41**, 215–43.

Dragone, D., L. Lambertini and A. Palestini (2011), "On the Feedback Solution of a Differential Oligopoly Game with Capacity Adjustment", in S. Bittanti, A. Cenedese and S. Zampieri (eds), *Proceedings of the IFAC World Congress 2011*, IFAC (in CD-rom, also available online, www.ifac-papersoline.net).

Dragone, D., L. Lambertini and A. Palestini (2012), "Static and Dynamic Best-Response Potential Functions for the Non-Linear Cournot Game", *Optimization*, **61**, 1283–93.

Dragone, D., L. Lambertini, G. Leitmann and A. Palestini (2015), "Hamiltonian Potential Functions for Differential Games", *Automatica*, **62**, 134–38.

Driskill, R. (2001), "Durable Goods Oligopoly", *International Journal of Industrial Organization*, **19**, 391–413.

Driskill, R. and S. McCafferty (1989), "Dynamic Duopoly with Adjustment Costs: A Differential Game Approach", *Journal of Economic Theory*, **49**, 324–38.

Driskill, R. and S. McCafferty (2001), "Monopoly and Oligopoly Provision of Addictive Goods", *International Economic Review*, **42**, 43–72.

Eisner, R. and R. Strotz (1963), "Determinants of Business Investment", in Commission on Money and Credit, *Impacts of Monetary Policy*, Englewood Cliffs, NJ, Prentice-Hall.

Ericson, R. and A. Pakes (1995), "Markov-Perfect Industry Dynamics: A Framework for Empirical Work", *Review of Economic Studies*, **62**, 53–82.

Esfahani, H. and L. Lambertini (2012), "The Profitability of Small Horizontal Mergers with Nonlinear Demand Functions", *Operations Research Letters*, **40**, 370–73.

Fershtman, C. (1985), "Managerial Incentives as a Strategic Variable in a Duopolistic Environment", *International Journal of Industrial Organization*, **3**, 245–53.

Fershtman, C. and K. Judd (1987), "Equilibrium Incentives in Oligopoly", *American Economic Review*, **77**, 927–40.

Fershtman, C. and M. Kamien (1987), "Dynamic Duopolistic Competition with Sticky Prices", *Econometrica*, **55**, 1151–64.

Fershtman, C. and M. Kamien (1990), "Turnpike Properties in a Finite-Horizon Differential Game: Dynamic Duopoly with Sticky Prices", *International Economic Review*, **31**, 49–60.

Fershtman, C. and E. Muller (1984), "Capital Accumulation Games of Infinite Duration", *Journal of Economic Theory*, **33**, 322–39.

Fershtman, C. and E. Muller (1986), "Turnpike Properties of Capital Accumulation Games", *Journal of Economic Theory*, **38**, 167–77.

Fershtman, C. and S. Nitzan (1991), "Dynamic Voluntary Provision of Public Goods", *European Economic Review*, **35**, 1057–67.

Fershtman, C. and A. Pakes (2000), "A Dynamic Oligopoly with Collusion and Price Wars", *RAND Journal of Economics*, **31**, 207–36.

Figuières, C. (2009), "Markov Interactions in a Class of Dynamic Games", *Theory and Decision*, **66**, 39–68.

Flaherty, M.T. (1980), "Dynamic Limit Pricing, Barriers to Entry, and Rational Firms", *Journal of Economic Theory*, **23**, 160–82.

Friedman, J.W. (1971), "A Non-Cooperative Equilibrium for Supergames", *Review of Economic Studies*, **28**, 1–12.

Friedman, J. (1983), *Oligopoly Theory*, Cambridge, Cambridge University Press.

Fudenberg, D. and E. Maskin (1986), "The Folk Theorem in Repeated Games with Discounting or with Incomplete Information", *Econometrica*, **54**, 533–54.

Fudenberg, D. and J. Tirole (1984), "The Fat-Cat Effect, the Puppy Dog Ploy, and the Lean and Hungry Look", *American Economic Review*, **74** (Papers and Proceedings), 361–66.

Gabszewicz, J.J. and S. Poddar (1997), "Demand Fluctuations and Capacity Utilization under Duopoly", *Economic Theory*, **10**, 131–46.

Gaskins, D. (1971), "Dynamic Limit Pricing: Optimal Pricing Under Threat of Entry", *Journal of Economic Theory*, **7**, 306–22.

Gibrat R. (1931), *Les inégalités économiques*, Paris, Librairie du Recueil Sirey.

Gilbert, R. (1989), "Mobility Barriers and the Value of Incumbency", in R. Schmalensee and R. Willig (eds), *Hanbook of Industrial Organization*, vol. I, Amsterdam, North-Holland.

Gowrisankaran G. (1999), "A Dynamic Model of Endogenous Horizontal Mergers", *RAND Journal of Economics*, **30**, 56–83.

Hausman, J. (1981), "Exact Consumer's Surplus and Deadweight Loss", *American Economic Review*, **71**, 662–76.

Hopenhayn, H. (1992), "Entry, Exit, and Firm Dynamics in Long Run Equilibrium", *Econometrica*, **60**, 1127–50.

Huisman, K. and P. Kort (2015), "Strategic Capacity Investment under Uncertainty", *RAND Journal of Economics*, **46**, 376–408.

Jovanovic, B. (1982), "Selection and the Evolution of Industry", *Econometrica*, **50**, 649–70.

Jun, B. and X. Vives (2004), "Strategic Incentives in Dynamic Duopoly", *Journal of Economic Theory*, **116**, 249–81.

Kamien, M. and N. Schwartz (1971), "Limit Pricing and Uncertain Entry", *Econometrica*, **19**, 441–54.

Kamien, M. and N. Schwartz (1983), "Conjectural Variations", *Canadian Journal of Economics*, **16**, 191–211.

Klemperer, P. and M. Meyer (1988), "Consistent Conjectures Equilibria: A Reformulation Showing Non-Uniqueness", *Economics Letters*, **27**, 111–15.

Klemperer, P.D. and M.A. Meyer (1989), "Supply Function Equilibria in Oligopoly under Uncertainty", *Econometrica*, **57**, 1243–77.

Koulovatianos, C. and L. Mirman (2007), "The Effects of Market Structure on Industry Growth: Rivalrous Non-Excludible Capital", *Journal of Economic Theory*, **133**, 199–218.

Kort, P. and S. Wrzaczek (2015), "Optimal Firm Growth under the Threat of Entry", *European Journal of Operational Research*, **246**, 281–92.

Lamantia, F. (2011), "A Nonlinear Duopoly with Efficient Production-Capacity Levels", *Computational Economics*, **38**, 295–309.

Lambertini, L. (2010), "Oligopoly with Hyperbolic Demand: A Differential Game Approach", *Journal of Optimization Theory and Applications*, **145**, 108–19.

Lambertini, L. and A. Mantovani (2006), "Identifying Reaction Functions in Differential Oligopoly Games", *Mathematical Social Sciences*, **52**, 252–71.

Lambertini, L. and A. Palestini (2014), "On the Feedback Solution of Differential Oligopoly Games with Hyperbolic Demand Curve and Capacity Accumulation", *European Journal of Operational Research*, **236**, 272–81.

Lambertini, L. and A. Tampieri (2015), "Incentive, Performance and Desirability of Socially Responsible Firms in a Cournot Oligopoly", *Economic Modelling*, **50**, 40–48.

Lambertini, L., A. Palestini and A. Tampieri (2016), "CSR in Asymmetric Duopoly with Environmental Externality", *Southern Economic Journal*, **83**, 236–52.

Lapham, B. and R. Ware (1994), "Markov Puppy Dogs and Related Animals", *International Journal of Industrial Organization*, **12**, 569–93.

Lucas, R. (1978), "On the Size Distribution of Business Firms", *Bell Journal of Economics*, **9**, 508–23.

Maskin, E. (1999), "Uncertainty and Entry Deterrence", *Economic Theory*, **14**, 429–37.

Maskin, E. and J. Tirole (1987), "A Theory of Dynamic Oligopoly, III: Cournot Competition", *European Economic Review*, **31**, 947–68.

Maskin, E. and J. Tirole (1988a), "A Theory of Dynamic Oligopoly, I: Overview and Quantity Competition with Large Fixed Costs", *Econometrica*, **56**, 549–69.

Maskin, E. and J. Tirole (1988b), "A Theory of Dynamic Oligopoly II: Price Competition, Kinked Demand Curves, and Edgeworth Cycles", *Econometrica*, **56**, 571–99.

Maskin, E. and J. Tirole (2001), "Markov Perfect Equilibrium I. Observable Actions", *Journal of Economic Theory*, **100**, 191–219.

Matthews, S. and L. Mirman (1983), "Equilibrium Limit Pricing: The Effects of Private Information and Stochastic Demand", *Econometrica*, **51**, 981–96.

Mehlmann, A. (1994), "On Differential Games with Markov Perfect Triggering", *Journal of Optimization Theory and Applications*, **80**, 273–88.

Modigliani, F. (1958), "New Developments on the Oligopoly Front", *Journal of Political Economy*, **66**, 215–32.

Monderer, D. and L Shapley (1996), "Potential Games", *Games and Economic Behavior*, **14**, 124–43.

Novshek, W. (1980), "Cournot Equilibrium with Free Entry", *Review of Economic Studies*, **47**, 473–86.

Pakes, A. and P. McGuire (1994), "Computing Markov-Perfect Nash Equilibria: Numerical Implications of a Dynamic Differentiated Product Model", *RAND Journal of Economics*, **25**, 555–89.

Pawlina, G. and P. Kort (2006), "Real Options in an Asymmetric Duopoly: Who Benefits from Your Competitive Disadvantage?", *Journal of Economics and Management Strategy*, **15**, 1–35.

Penrose, E. (1955), "Limits to the Size and Growth of Firms", *American Economic Review*, **45** (Papers & Proceedings), 531–43.

Penrose, E. (1959), *The Theory of the Growth of the Firm*, Oxford, Wiley.

Perry, M. (1982), "Oligopoly and Consistent Conjectural Variations", *Bell Journal of Economics*, **13**, 197–205.

Puu, T. (1991), "Chaos in Duopoly Pricing", *Chaos, Solitons and Fractals*, **1**, 573–81.

Puu, T. (2011), *Oligopoly: Old Ends – New Means*, Berlin, Springer.

Pyatt, G. (1971), "Profit Maximization and the Threat of New Entry", *Economic Journal*, **81**, 242–55.

Radner, R. and T.J. Richardson (2003), "Monopolists and Viscous Demand", *Games and Economic Behavior*, **45**, 442–64.

Ramsey, F.P. (1928), "A Mathematical Theory of Saving", *Economic Journal*, **38**, 543–59.

Reynolds, S. (1987), "Capacity Investment, Preemption and Commitment in an Infinite Horizon Model", *International Economic Review*, **28**, 69–88.

Reynolds, S. (1991), "Dynamic Oligopoly with Capacity Adjustment Costs", *Journal of Economic Dynamics and Control*, **15**, 491–514.

Roos, C.F. (1925), "A Mathematical Theory of Competition", *American Journal of Mathematics*, **46**, 163–75.

Roos, C.F. (1927), "A Dynamic Theory of Economics", *Journal of Political Economy*, **35**, 632–56.

Rowat, C. (2007), "Non-Linear Strategies in a Linear Quadratic Differential Game", *Journal of Economic Dynamics and Control*, **31**, 3179–202.

Salant S., S. Switzer and R. Reynolds (1983), "Losses from Horizontal Merger: The Effects of an Exogenous Change in Industry Structure on Cournot-Nash Equilibrium", *Quarterly Journal of Economics*, **98**, 185–213.

Simaan, M. and T. Takayama (1978), "Game Theory Applied to Dynamic Duopoly Problems with Production Constraints", *Automatica*, **14**, 161–66.

Singh, N. and X. Vives (1984), "Price and Quantity Competition in a Differentiated Duopoly", *RAND Journal of Economics*, **15**, 546–54.

Sklivas, S.D. (1987), "The Strategic Choice of Managerial Incentives", *RAND Journal of Economics*, **18**, 452–58.

Slade, M. (1994), "What Does an Oligopoly Maximize?", *Journal of Industrial Economics*, **42**, 45–61.

Slater, M. (1980), "The Managerial Limitation to the Growth of Firms", *Economic Journal*, **90**, 520–28.

Solow, R. (1956), "A Contribution to the Theory of Economic Growth", *Quarterly Journal of Economics*, **70**, 65–94.

Spence, M. (1977), "Entry, Capacity, Investment and Oligopolistic Pricing", *Bell Journal of Economics*, **8**, 534–44.

Spence, M. (1979), "Investment Strategy and Growth in a New Market", *Bell Journal of Economics*, **10**, 1–19.

Sutton, J. (1997), "Gibrat's Legacy", *Journal of Economic Literature*, **35**, 40–59.

Swan, T.W. (1956), "Economic Growth and Capital Accumulation", *Economic Record*, **32**, 334–61.

Sylos-Labini, P. (1957), *Oligopolio e progresso tecnico*, Torino, Einausi; English edition: *Oligopoly and Technical Progress*, Oxford, Oxford Univerity Press, 1962.

Thijssen, J., K. Huisman and P. Kort (2012), "Symmetric Equilibrium Strategies in Game Theoretic Real Option Models", *Journal of Mathematical Economics*, **48**, 219–25.

Tirole, J. (1988), *The Theory of Industrial Organization*, Cambridge, MA, MIT Press.

Tolwinski, B. (1982), "A Concept of Cooperative Equilibrium for Dynamic Games", *Automatica*, **18**, 431–41.

Tolwinski, B., A. Haurie and G. Leitmann (1986), "Cooperative Equilibria in Differential Games", *Journal of Mathematical Analysis and Applications*, **119**, 182–202.

Trigeorgis, L. (1996), *Real Options: Managerial Flexibility and Strategy in Resource Allocation*, Cambridge, MA, MIT Press.

Tsutsui, S. (1996), "Capacity Constraints and Voluntary Output Cutback in Dynamic Cournot Competition", *Journal of Economic Dynamics and Control*, **20**, 1683–708.

Tsutsui, S. and K. Mino (1990), "Nonlinear Strategies in Dynamic Duopolistic Competition with Sticky Prices", *Journal of Economic Theory*, **52**, 136–61.

Varian, H. (1982), "The Nonparametric Approach to Demand Analysis", *Econometrica*, **50**, 945–73.

Vickers, J. (1985), "Delegation and the Theory of the Firm", *Economic Journal*, **95** (Conference Papers), 138–47.

Vives, X. (2011), "Strategic Supply Function Competition with Private Information", *Econometrica*, **79**, 1919–66.

Voorneveld, M. (2000), "Best-Response Potential Games", *Economics Letters*, **66**, 289–95.

Wirl, F. (2010), "Dynamic Demand and Noncompetitive Intertemporal Output Adjustments", *International Journal of Industrial Organization*, **28**, 220–29.

Wiszniewska-Matyszkiel, A., M. Bodnar and F. Mirota (2015), "Dynamic Oligopoly with Sticky Prices: Off-Steady-State Analysis", *Dynamic Games and Applications*, **5**, 568–98.

Yang, M. and Q. Zhou (2007), "Real Options Analysis for Efficiency of Entry Deterrence with Excess Capacity", *Systems Engineering – Theory and Practice*, **27**, 63–70.

Zhang, Y.-C. (2017), "Entry-Exit Decisions with Underlying Processes Following Geometric Lévy Processes", *Journal of Optimization Theory and Applications*, **172**, 309–27.

4 Advertising

With the material contained in this chapter, we are entering the realm of non-price competition. To be more precise, I should rather say that we are about to extend the models reviewed in Chapter 3 to variables complementing price, quantity and capacity competition. Yet, it is true that the models appearing in the previous chapter boil down to the determination of outputs and prices.

The relevance of non-price instruments is well understood in industrial economics. In particular, the predatory nature of advertising has been recognised at least since Braithwaite (1928), and its impact on market power since Kaldor (1950).

Quite intuitively in view of its intrinsically dynamic nature, advertising is probably the most debated topic in the tradition of optimal control and differential game theory. In fact, understanding advertising campaigns has been the driver of some of the earliest applications of differential game theory to IO and management, in Friedman (1958), Dhrymes (1962), Clemhout et al. (1971) and Leitmann and Schmitendorf (1978). Interestingly, the views on the nature of advertising commonly accepted in IO (see, e.g., Tirole, 1988; Bagwell, 2007) significantly differ from the taxonomy of advertising acquired in the literature dealing with dynamic formulations of the same problems.

Industrial economists stress that advertising is aimed at enhancing a brand's reputation by altering consumer tastes, thereby preventing any welfare assessment. We are aware of this since Dorfman and Steiner (1954) and many others (Dixit and Norman, 1978). Advertising campaigns can be informative, persuasive or complementary (Stigler and Becker, 1977; Becker and Murphy, 1993), the latter property indicating that advertising contributes to define the overall features of a product, and therefore *complements* it. In a sense, complementary advertising can be seen as an extension or reinforcement of the concept of persuasive advertising. In the applications of dynamic techniques to this subject, the attention is focussed on the specific state variable affected by advertising efforts (which are controls), or on the impact of advertising along the product life cycle, in such a way that the taxonomy of advertising commonly used in the applications of differential game theory is somewhat different in terms of both terminology and interpretation.

Consider the instantaneous profit function of an oligopolistic firm (here I am deliberately omitting the time argument for a reason which is about to become evident):

$$\pi_i = (p_i - c)\, q_i - bk_i^2 \tag{4.1}$$

where k_i is the instantaneous advertising effort of the same firm. The remaining variables have the usual meaning, and market price is either endogenously determined as a function of the n firms' output levels, $p_i = a_i - \sum_{j=1}^{n} q_j$, or it is exogenously given (for instance, because the advertising campaigns of all firms start after price lists have been fixed). Also, note that the vertical intercept of demand (the choke price a_i) is firm specific. In (4.1) there are two candidate state variables, a_i and q_i, which can be positively affected by the effort of firm i and possibly negatively affected by those of its rivals. In both cases, the effect sought by firm i is one of (its own) *demand (or output) expansion*. This approach is close to the idea of persuasive advertising, and the literature has investigated this version of the advertising games using alternatively both assumptions concerning prices (or mark-ups).

Suppose instead efforts are targeted at market shares, as in Vidale and Wolfe (1957). In this case, the dynamics of the state is a modified version of the one appearing in Chapter 2. Indeed, the marketing literature distinguishes between *market share* models and *sales response* models, with the latter label largely replicating the interpretation of the one I have used above to define the direct or indirect impact of advertising on output. As we shall see below, market share and sales response models do have much in common.

Another scenario is that in which advertising is targeted at increasing goodwill or brand equity, as in Nerlove and Arrow (1962). Here the individual firm's profit is augmented by a state variable, goodwill G_i, inflating revenues. In fact, goodwill has been modelled in at least two different ways, both illustrated in the remainder of this chapter, with largely different results.

Last but not least, there remains the approach modelling advertising in *market growth* or *product diffusion* models, dating back to Bass (1969), accounting also for word-of-mouth effects across the population of consumers. In this framework, the relevant state variable is a firm's cumulative volume of sales, and the time horizon is typically finite, as the further diffusion of the product is bound to be hindered, sooner or later, by the supply of other goods by existing rivals or new entrants.

4.1   Sales or Market Share Expansion

Here I will offer a compact reconstruction of the large debate on games in which advertising efforts are aimed at increasing outputs or market shares.

Suppose first that in the market we are looking at, there is still some room for an increase in demand, which, in turn, amounts to assuming that the product is not 'mature' yet. As anticipated above, expanding demand may mean two different things. The first is that firms invest to increase market price or the reservation (or choke) prices, thereby shifting the market demand function outwards without affecting its slope. The first example of this type is in Piga (2000), where the sticky price model introduced by Simaan and Takayama (1978) and further developed by Fershtman and Kamien (1987) is augmented by the presence of advertising efforts, in the following way. Suppose n firms supply a homogeneous good. The notional demand function becomes

$$\hat{p} = a + \alpha \sum_{i=1}^{n} k_i(t) - \sum_{i=1}^{n} q_i(t) \tag{4.2}$$

where $\alpha > 0$ is a constant, and $2n$ controls (R&D efforts and outputs) simultaneously affect the price. The price dynamics rewrites, accordingly, as follows:

$$\dot{p} = s \left[a + \alpha \sum_{i=1}^{n} k_i(t) - \sum_{i=1}^{n} q_i(t) - p(t) \right] \tag{4.3}$$

From (4.2), it appears that firms are investing to provide a public good (from their point of view of course), as the good is homogeneous and is sold at a single price, and this feature drives the model to produce results which look largely analogous to Fershtman and Nitzan's (1991): firms invest less under linear feedback rules than under open-loop ones, and consequently price and profits. The rationale behind this conclusion is that open-loop information dilutes strategic interaction and therefore also the free-riding incentive affecting the advertising campaign of each individual firm *vis-à-vis* all of its rivals. Then, following Tsutsui and Mino (1990), Piga (2000, pp. 606–8) shows that it is possible to construct infinitely many nonlinear feedback strategies leading to higher steady state prices than are achieved through the open-loop one.

In the same vein, but taking an alternative route, Cellini and Lambertini (2003a,b) and Cellini *et al.* (2008) examine the possibility for firms to increase choke prices, which become the relevant state variables. In Cellini and Lambertini (2003a), the demand function is $p(t) = [a(t) - Q(t)]^{1/\beta}$, $\beta > 0$, as in Anderson and Engers (1992, 1994), and the choke price evolves according to

$$\dot{a} = \sum_{i=1}^{n} k_i(t) - \delta a(t) \tag{4.4}$$

where $\delta > 0$ is the decay rate. Advertising competition is coupled with quantity-setting behaviour. Once again, the issue underlying the game is the firms' private incentive to provide a public good, and the solution yields results in line with Piga's (2000) analysis. The appropriability of advertising effects is partially restored in Cellini and Lambertini (2003b) and Cellini *et al.* (2008), where each firm sells an imperfect substitute of its rivals' varieties, the demand function being $p_i(t) = a_i(t) - q_i(t) - \gamma \sum_{j \neq i} q_j(t)$, as in Singh and Vives (1984).[1] Here, parameter $\gamma \in (0, 1]$ measures product substitutability. Since varieties are differentiated, the model features n state variables, each following the dynamic equation

$$\dot{a}_i = k_i(t) - \beta \sum_{j \neq i} k_j(t) - \delta a_i(t) \tag{4.5}$$

in which parameter $\beta \in \left[0, 1/(n-1) \right]$ is a measure of the negative spillover effect exerted by the $n - 1$ rivals onto firm i's demand function. Although this formulation may sound intuitively acceptable, it has the undesirable shortcoming of rendering any

---

[1] Cournot competition is used in Cellini and Lambertini (2003b), while Bertrand competition appears in Cellini *et al.* (2008).

welfare analysis – and therefore also the design of policy measures – impossible, because firms' controls are endogenously affecting a magnitude appearing in the representative consumer's utility function, as we know from Dorfman and Steiner (1954).

The other approach consists in supposing that output (or sales) levels are the relevant state variables reacting to firms' advertising efforts. This is the assumption governing the Vidale and Wolfe (1957) model, its characterization as an optimal control model (Sethi, 1973), and its many follow-ups. If the industry is oligopolistic, the individual firm's sales dynamics is

$$\dot{q}_i(t) = zk_i(t)\left[1 - \frac{q_i(t)}{Q_{\max}}\right] - \delta q_i(t) \tag{4.6}$$

which, on the one hand, entails that the product life cycle is in the maturity phase and, on the other, raises two issues. The first is that (4.6) features no cross effects whatsoever between the rivals' advertising efforts and the evolution of firm i's sales, a drawback which could be easily fixed by rewriting the state equation as follows:

$$\dot{q}_i(t) = zk_i(t)\left[1 - \frac{q_i(t) + Q_{-i}(t)}{Q_{\max}}\right] - \delta q_i(t) \tag{4.7}$$

as in Deal (1979), or

$$\dot{q}_i(t) = z\left[k_i(t) - wK_{-i}(t)\right]\left[1 - \frac{q_i(t) + Q_{-i}(t)}{Q_{\max}}\right] - \delta q_i(t) \tag{4.8}$$

where $w > 0$ is a constant. In (4.7), the cross effect kicks in via the presence of rivals' collective sales $Q_{-i}(t)$; in (4.8), it is reinforced by the appearance of a negative impact of rivals' advertising efforts $K_{-i}(t)$.

The second issue is associated with the multiplicative interaction between control $k_i(t)$ and state $q_i(t)$, which makes the state dynamics nonlinear and implies that the game does not have a linear-quadratic form. This has confined the analysis of the model to open-loop strategies, as in Deal (1979), but at the same time has stimulated the search for different formulations of the game structure able to yield subgame perfection under open-loop rules, or analytically solvable under feedback rules via HJB equations.

The quest for strongly time-consistent open-loop equilibria started very early and produced notable results, starting with Leitmann and Schmitendorf (1978) and Feichtinger (1983), in which a duopoly is considered and the relevant state variable is firm i's market share $\sigma_i(t) = q_i(t)/[q_i(t) + q_j(t)] \leq 1$. Firm i's market share follows[2]

$$\dot{\sigma}_i = k_i(t) - \frac{bk_i^2(t)}{2} - ck_j(t)\sigma_i(t) - \delta\sigma_i(t) \tag{4.9}$$

in which b, c and δ are positive constants. The above dynamics contains both the effect of decreasing returns of firm i's advertising as well as the rival's negative impact and the

---

[2] This is the state dynamics used by Leitmann and Schmitendorf (1978). Feichtinger (1983) reformulates the model assuming $\dot{\sigma}_i = f(k_i(t)) - g(k_j(t))\sigma_i(t) - \delta\sigma_i(t)$, with both $f(k_i(t))$ and $g(k_j(t))$ being positive functions, increasing and concave in their respective arguments.

decay due to forgetful consumers. The mark-up is exogenously fixed at $\bar{p}$. If production takes place at constant returns to scale, posing unit production cost to zero for the sake of simplicity and defining the auxiliary variable $\mathbb{P} = \bar{p}\left[q_i(t) + q_j(t)\right]$, the instantaneous profit function is $\pi_i(t) = \mathbb{P}\sigma_i(t) - k_i(t)$. Now note that neither (4.9) nor $\pi_i(t)$ contains firm j's state. This means that the game features non-interacting dynamics and payoff functions, and this is ultimately responsible for the subgame perfection of the open-loop Nash equilibrium attained solving

$$\max_{k_i(t)} \mathcal{H}_i\left(\boldsymbol{\sigma}(t), \mathbf{k}(t), \boldsymbol{\lambda}(t)\right) = e^{-\rho t}[\mathbb{P}q_i(t) - k_i(t) + \lambda_{ii}(t)\dot{\sigma}_i + \lambda_{ij}(t)\dot{\sigma}_j] \tag{4.10}$$

over $t \in [0, T]$. Since

$$\frac{\partial \pi_i(t)}{\partial \sigma_j(t)} = \frac{\partial \dot{\sigma}_i}{\partial \sigma_j(t)} = 0 \tag{4.11}$$

at all times, $\lambda_{ij}(t) = 0$ forever. This, in turn, implies that the simplified Hamiltonian deriving from (4.10) after this piece of information has been used, satisfies the properties required for state redundancy:

$$\frac{\partial^2 \mathcal{H}_i}{\partial \sigma_i^2} = \frac{\partial^2 \mathcal{H}_i}{\partial \sigma_j^2} = \frac{\partial^2 \mathcal{H}_i}{\partial \sigma_i \partial \sigma_j} = 0$$

$$\frac{\partial^2 \mathcal{H}_i}{\partial k_i \partial \sigma_i} = \frac{\partial^2 \mathcal{H}_i}{\partial k_i \partial \sigma_j} = 0 \tag{4.12}$$

This proves:

Lemma 4.1 *The sales response advertising game in Leitmann and Schmitendorf (1978) and Feichtinger (1983) yields strong time consistency under open-loop information.*

Now note that the Hamiltonian (4.10) and, a fortiori, its simplified version incorporating $\lambda_{ij}(t) = 0$ are additively separable w.r.t. controls, making the game solvable in dominant strategies. Imposing symmetry, the resulting state-control system is

$$\dot{\sigma} = k - \frac{bk^2(t)}{2} - ck\sigma - \delta\sigma_i$$

$$\dot{k} = \frac{1}{b}[(1 - bk)(\rho + \delta + ck) - \mathbb{P}(1 - bk)^2] \tag{4.13}$$

The above dynamic system admits two steady state solutions:

$$\sigma_I^{OL} = \frac{1}{2(b\delta + k)} \; ; \; k_I^{OL} = \frac{1}{b}$$

$$\sigma_{II}^{OL} = \frac{(\mathbb{P} - \delta - \rho)[b(\mathbb{P} + \delta + \rho) + 2c]}{2(b\mathbb{P} + c)[b\delta\mathbb{P} + c(\mathbb{P} - \rho)]} \; ; \; k_{II}^{OL} = \frac{\mathbb{P} - \delta - \rho}{b\mathbb{P} + c} \tag{4.14}$$

in which pair I is the boundary solution, while pair II is the inner one. The coordinates of both points are positive provided that $\mathbb{P} > \delta + \rho$. This condition conveys a sensible message, as it implies that the markup must be larger than the implicit cost measured by the sum of depreciation and discounting. The steady state profits accruing to firms in the two equilibria are

$$\pi_I^{OL} = \frac{b\,(\mathbb{P} - 2\delta) - 2c}{2b\,(b\delta + c)} \tag{4.15}$$

$$\pi_{II}^{OL} = \frac{(\mathbb{P} - \delta - \rho)\,[b\mathbb{P}\,(\mathbb{P} - \delta + \rho) + 2c\rho]}{2\,(b\mathbb{P} + c)\,[b\delta\mathbb{P} + c\,(\mathbb{P} - \rho)]} \tag{4.16}$$

with $\mathbb{P} \geq 2\,(b\delta + c)\,/b$ ensuring $\pi_I^{OL} \geq 0$: note that this amounts to saying that $\mathbb{P}$ must be more than twice as high as the decay rate of sales (or, consumers' forgetfulness) in order for the boundary solution to be viable. The inner solution is instead viable for all $\mathbb{P} \geq \delta + \rho$, ensuring $\pi_B^* \geq 0$.[3] When both are economically admissible, which happens for all

$$\mathbb{P} \geq \max\left\{\delta + \rho, \frac{2\,(b\delta + c)}{b}\right\}, \tag{4.17}$$

the boundary equilibrium is globally asymptotically stable, while the inner solution is a saddle point (see Dragone et al., 2010).

The last exercise consists in comparing equilibrium profits in the two equilibria, to find that $\pi_{II}^{OL} > \pi_I^{OL}$ for all

$$\mathbb{P} > \frac{\sqrt{\Lambda^2 + 8bc^2\,(b\delta + c)\,\rho} - \Lambda}{2bc} \tag{4.18}$$

where $\Lambda \equiv 2c^2 + b\,(b\delta\,(\delta - \rho) + c\,(2\delta - \rho))$. In the space $(\rho, \mathbb{P})$, the above mark-up level and those identifying the viability conditions on π_I^{OL} and π_{II}^{OL} intersect each other at $\rho = (b\delta + 2c)\,/b$. The overall scenario appears in Figure 4.1, where the subset of the plane $(\rho, \mathbb{P})$ above the upper envelope of the three curves identifies the region in which $\pi_{II}^{OL} > \pi_I^{OL}$.

This boils down to the following

Proposition 4.2 *If both equilibria are viable, the mark-up above which the inner solution outperforms the boundary one is monotonically non-decreasing in time discounting.*

In other words, if the level of the discount rate is high enough, the steady state profits generated by the boundary solution will be higher then those associated with the inner solution, for any finite value of $\mathbb{P}$: as the future becomes less relevant from the firms' standpoint, they will tend to prefer the corner solution because sales expansion compensate for time discounting, this being favoured by the fact that market price is unaffected by output.

The second route consists in modifying the setup to allow for the analytical solution of the Bellman equations. This approach dates back to Sethi and Thompson (1981), Sethi (1983) and Sorger (1989), and relies on a modified version of the advertising game

---

[3] The effect of industry structure on the two steady states is characterised in Dragone et al. (2010), where it is shown that the viability condition for the boundary solution does depend on the number of firms, while that concerning the inner solution does not.

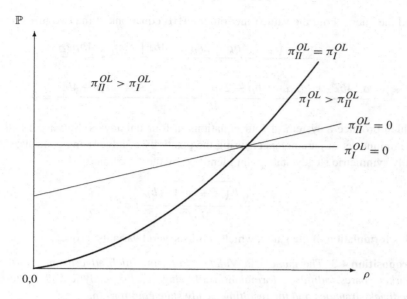

Figure 4.1 Steady state profit evaluation in the Leitmann–Schmitendorf game

proposed by Case (1979), adapting the Lanchester (1956) model, which was originally conceived as a description of military confrontations.

Once again, consider a duopoly where the mark-up $\mathbb{P}$ is constant over time. The state equation describing the evolution of firm i's market share, $\sigma(t)$, is

$$\dot{\sigma} = k_i(t)\sqrt{1 - \sigma(t)} - k_j(t)\sqrt{\sigma(t)} \qquad (4.19)$$

assuming away decay or forgetfulness. The instantaneous profits of firm i are $\pi_i(t) = \mathbb{P}\sigma(t) - bk_i^2(t)$, $b > 0$. At first sight, the shape of the game is nonlinear, but it turns out that the value function associated with the HJB equation

$$\rho V_i(\sigma(t)) = \max_{k_i(t)} \left\{ \mathbb{P}\sigma(t) - bk_i^2(t) + V_i'(\sigma(t))\left[k_i(t)\sqrt{1 - \sigma(t)} - k_j(t)\sqrt{\sigma(t)}\right] \right\}$$

$$(4.20)$$

admits a guess stipulating a linear form such as $V_i(\sigma(t)) = \varepsilon_{i1}\sigma(t) + \varepsilon_{i2}$, *even if the game is not state-linear*. Obviously, the HJB equation of firm j is

$$\rho V_j(\cdot) = \max_{k_j(t)} \left\{ \mathbb{P}[1 - \sigma(t)] - bk_j^2(t) + V_j'(\sigma(t))\left[k_i(t)\sqrt{1 - \sigma(t)} - k_j(t)\sqrt{\sigma(t)}\right] \right\}$$

$$(4.21)$$

featuring the complementary market share. Using the expressions of optimal controls solving the FOCs,

$$u_i^* = \frac{V_i'\sqrt{1 - \sigma}}{2b} \; ; \; u_j^* = \frac{V_j'\sqrt{\sigma}}{2b} \qquad (4.22)$$

and the guess about the value function, the HJB equations of the two firms become

$$\frac{\sigma\left[\varepsilon_{i1}\left(\varepsilon_{i1}+4b\rho-2\varepsilon_{j1}\right)-4b\mathbb{P}\right]-\varepsilon_{i1}^2+4b\rho\varepsilon_{i2}}{4b}=0 \qquad (4.23)$$

$$\frac{\sigma\left[4b\mathbb{P}-\varepsilon_{j1}\left(\varepsilon_{j1}-4b\rho-2\varepsilon_{i1}\right)\right]-2\varepsilon_{i1}\varepsilon_{j1}+4b\rho\varepsilon_{j2}-4b\mathbb{P}}{4b}=0 \qquad (4.24)$$

which produce a system of four equations in four unknowns. Solving it and selecting the unique set of parameters ensuring the positivity of advertising controls, we find the fully symmetric steady state point identified by the coordinates

$$k^F=\frac{\sqrt{b\left(3\mathbb{P}+b\rho^2\right)}-b\rho}{3b\sqrt{2}} \; ; \; \sigma^F=\frac{1}{2} \qquad (4.25)$$

This formulation of the game, which admits several variants, proves

Proposition 4.3 *The game à la Vidale–Wolfe, in which advertising efforts influence market shares, admits a formulation allowing for the analytical characterization of feedback strategies and the resulting steady state equilibrium.*

Three remarks are in order here. The first concerns the above specification of the game, whose solvability under feedback information still lacks a sound intuition as to why we should expect the value function to be linear in the state variable when the state equation contains the square root of the state and the payoff function is linear-quadratic. The second is more general, as it involves the entire family of games in which the mark-up is exogenously fixed. As soon as we more realistically admit that the market price should be endogenously determined along a downward-sloping demand function at every instant, we are back into a game which is formally equivalent to the capacity accumulation game investigated by Reynolds (1987, 1991) and reviewed in Chapter 3, with the difficulties this implies as for the characterisation of the feedback outcome. Otherwise, in line with Schmalensee (1976), one may argue that firms compete through non-price instruments, leaving price lists unchanged for long periods.

The third remark is more radical, if I may say so, and concerns the salvage value, time discounting and the relationship between them. In many advertising models (including games, e.g., Leitmann and Schmitendorf, 1978), the advertising campaign is realistically assumed to have a finite duration. However, discounting is either absent or is indeed used to *discount* future profits, which sounds sensible in many situations but not necessarily when the bequest function must matter, as it is, for instance, the market share in the hands of a firm at time T, which is both the terminal date of the past campaign and (possibly) the starting point of the next one – in any case, it determines the initial endowment on which that firm must build up future gains, one way or another.

Dynamic problems of this kind are common in politics, where parties care about vote shares at the end of electoral campaigns, when people vote and a candidate for some office, like premiership, wins while the others lose. Consensus during the campaign is surely important, but what determines the final outcome is its value at T, the election day. Therefore, the bequest function is of the utmost relevance. What follows is a straightforward translation of a voting game into an advertising one, in which gains are capitalised instead of being discounted, and the bequest function plays a pivotal role. The setup is based on Lambertini (2014) and relies on techniques dating back to Nordhaus (1975) and illustrated also in Chiang (1992).

The model considers a duopoly, which has in common with the previous ones the assumption of a fixed mark-ups. Here, however, it is convenient to admit the possibility for the mark-up to be firm-specific, with individual instantaneous profits $\pi_i(t) = \mathbb{P}_i\sigma_i(t) - bk_i^2(t)$. The game unravels over $t \in [0, T]$, and the state equation is

$$\dot{\sigma}_i(t) = k_i(t) - \beta k_j(t) - \delta\sigma_i \qquad (4.26)$$

where $\beta > 0$ is a constant negative spillover from candidate j's advertising effort onto candidate i's market share of votes.[4] Firm i chooses $k_i(t)$ to maximise

$$\Pi_i = \int_0^T e^{\rho t}\big[\mathbb{P}_i\sigma_i(t) - bk_i^2(t)\big]dt + e^{\rho T}\mathcal{S}\,[\sigma_i(T)] \qquad (4.27)$$

under the set of constraints (4.26). $\mathcal{S}\,[x_i(T)] \geq 0$ is the salvage value of the state at the terminal date T. The set of initial condition is $\sigma_{i0} = \sigma_i(0) \geq 0$, inherited from the previous history of the industry. From the Hamiltonian of firm i,

$$\mathcal{H}_i(\cdot) = e^{\rho t}\big[\mathbb{P}_i\sigma_i(t) - bk_i^2(t)\big] + \lambda_{ii}(t)\left[k_i(t) - sk_j(t) - \delta\sigma_i\right] \qquad (4.28)$$
$$+ \lambda_{ij}(t)\left[k_j(t) - sk_i(t) - \delta\sigma_j\right],$$

one can immediately deduce that this is a linear state game. The subgame perfect open-loop strategies correspond to

$$k_i^*(t) = \frac{\mathbb{P}_i\left(e^{(\rho-\delta)(T-t)} - 1\right)}{2b\,(\rho - \delta)} \qquad (4.29)$$

at any $t \in [0, T]$, which deliver a market share at the terminal date T equal to

$$\sigma_i^*(T) = \max\left\{0, \frac{(\mathbb{P}_i - \beta\mathbb{P}_j)\left[\delta\left(e^{(\rho-\delta)T} + e^{\delta T} - 2\right) - \rho\left(e^{\delta T} - 1\right)\right]}{e^{\delta T}\,(\rho - \delta)\,(\rho - 2\delta)} + \frac{\sigma_{i0}}{e^{\delta T}}\right\} \qquad (4.30)$$

From (4.29), we see that

$$\frac{\partial k_i^*(t)}{\partial t} = -\frac{\mathbb{P}_i e^{(\rho-\delta)(T-t)}}{2b} < 0 \qquad (4.31)$$

which proves

Lemma 4.4 *The optimal advertising effort of firm i decreases monotonically over time.*

This amounts to saying that here advertising activities have an *offensive* nature (Erickson, 1993), as part of the message conveyed during a firm's campaign is aimed at producing a business-stealing effect by attracting the rival's customers. In this case, the diminishing intensity of $k_i^*(t)$ over time indicates that the offensive effect prevails over

---

[4] Note that the spillover parameter may be greater than one, as a firm's effort might more than offset the rival's one.

the *defensive* one, aimed at retaining one's own market share intact. As is very often the case, last-minute efforts are almost worthless and the offensive scope of investment vanishes in proximity of T.

It is also true that $\mathbb{P}_i > \beta \mathbb{P}_j$ is a sufficient condition for $\sigma_i^*(T) > 0$, regardless of the initial condition σ_{i0}. Moreover,

$$\sigma_i^*(T) - \sigma_j^*(T) = \frac{1}{e^{\delta T}}\left[\sigma_{i0} - \sigma_{j0} + \Lambda\left(1 + \beta\right)\left(\mathbb{P}_i - \mathbb{P}_j\right)\right], \tag{4.32}$$

where

$$\Lambda \equiv \frac{\delta\left(e^{(\rho-\delta)T} + e^{\delta T} - 2\right) - \rho\left(e^{\delta T} - 1\right)}{2c\left(\rho - \delta\right)\left(\rho - 2\delta\right)\delta} > 0 \tag{4.33}$$

Consequently, we have

$$\sigma_i^*(T) > \sigma_j^*(T) \,\, \forall\, \sigma_{i0} > \max\left\{\sigma_{j0} - \Lambda\left(1 + \beta\right)\left(\mathbb{P}_i - \mathbb{P}_j\right), 0\right\} \tag{4.34}$$

That is,

Proposition 4.5 *If its initial share is large enough, the firm with the lower mark-up may attain a higher terminal market share than the rival's.*

It can also be verified that the offensive nature of advertising is responsible for excess investments all over the campaign. To see this, one may calculate the socially efficient strategy taking the sum of the firms' payoffs $\pi_i(t)$ as the relevant instantaneous objective.[5] This delivers the optimal advertising effort

$$k_i^{SP}(t) = \max\left\{0, \frac{\left(\mathbb{P}_i - \beta \mathbb{P}_j\right)\left(e^{\delta t + \rho T} - e^{\rho t + \delta T}\right)}{2c\left(\rho - \delta\right)e^{\rho t + \delta T}}\right\} \tag{4.35}$$

where superscript *SP* stands for *social planning*. In the parameter region where $k_i^{SP}(t) > 0$, its comparison with the privately optimal strategy reveals that

$$k_i^*(t) - k_i^{SP}(t) = \frac{\beta \mathbb{P}_j\left(e^{(\rho-\delta)(T-t)} - 1\right)}{2c\left(\rho - \delta\right)} = \frac{\beta \mathbb{P}_j k_i^*}{\mathbb{P}_i} > 0 \tag{4.36}$$

for all positive values of the spillover parameter β. I.e.,

Proposition 4.6 *Any degree of offensive advertising causes excess efforts at all times by both firms.*

This is also implicit in (4.30), where the spillover effect decreases the market share pertaining to the salvage value, and therefore also negatively affects any future history – with or without further advertising activities – of the firms' market shares and profits along paths starting at T, with $\sigma_i^*(T)$ and $\sigma_j^*(T)$ as initial conditions.

---

[5] As in games describing R&D races (see Chapter 6), consumer surplus is not considered. Its introduction, however, would reinforce the result.

4.2   Advertising for Goodwill

The first oligopolistic version of the Nerlove and Arrow (1962) model is in Fershtman (1984), where n firms operate over $t \in [0, \infty)$ in the same industry with different brands and the state equation of firm i's goodwill (or brand equity) is

$$\dot{G}_i(t) = k_i(t) - \delta G_i(t) \tag{4.37}$$

and the individual market share is determined by the function

$$\sigma_i(t) = \frac{G_i^\alpha(t)}{G_i^\alpha(t) + \sum_{j \neq i} G_j^\alpha(t)}, \quad \alpha \in [0, 1], \tag{4.38}$$

i.e., it is firm i's instantaneous *goodwill share*. If $\alpha = 0$, then $\sigma_i(t) = 1/n$ at all times, and the stock of goodwill can be neglected and consumers view all brands as net substitutes of one another. Any α lower than one implies decreasing returns to goodwill, although consumers positively respond to the creation of brand equity. In view of the dynamics of goodwill stocks, the dependence of sales on advertising efforts of all firms is obviously present, and every single firm's market share is negatively affected by the rivals' advertising investments, although these do not appear explicitly in (4.37).

At every instant, the market demand function is $Q(p)$, while marginal production cost c_i is constant. The cost of advertising is $\Gamma_i(t) = bk_i(t)$. As a result, firm i's profit function is

$$\pi_i(t) = (p - c_i) Q(p) \sigma_i(t) - bk_i(t) \tag{4.39}$$

and the advertising effort $k_i(t)$ is chosen to maximise the discounted flow of profits accruing to firm i under the constraint posed by the set of state equations (4.37) and initial conditions $G_{i0} = G_i(0) \geq 0$. Since (4.37) features only the effort of firm i, the Hamiltonian function

$$\mathcal{H}_i(\cdot) = e^{-\rho t} \{(p - c_i) Q(p) \sigma_i(t) - bk_i(t) + \lambda_i(t) [k_i(t) - \delta G_i(t)]\} \tag{4.40}$$

relies on a single costate variable, $\lambda_i(t)$. The game is solved under open-loop information, and the manipulation of necessary conditions allows one to establish that, at any time, the optimal stock of goodwill is

$$G_i^*(t) = (p - c_i) Q(p) \cdot \frac{\sigma_i(t) [1 - \sigma_i(t)]}{\rho + \delta} \tag{4.41}$$

from which we learn that $G_i^*(t) = 0$ if $\sigma_i(t) = 1$, i.e., the firm has gained monopoly power, or in the limit(s), as

$$\lim_{\delta \to \infty} G_i^*(t) = \lim_{\rho \to \infty} G_i^*(t) = 0 \tag{4.42}$$

because if either time discounting or the goodwill decay rate is infinitely high, future is altogether irrelevant and advertising becomes a totally wasteful activity. Leaving aside these extreme circumstances, the linearity of the Hamiltonian function w.r.t. the control variable, combined with the existence of a unique optimal level of goodwill, implies the following conclusion, which extends to the oligopoly case an aspect of advertising campaigns already highlighted in Nerlove and Arrow (1962):

Proposition 4.7 *At any time during the game, the optimal advertising strategy is* $k_i^* (t) = 0$ *for all* $G_i (t) > G_i^* (t)$ *, while it is the highest advertising effort compatible with the long-run survival of the firm for all* $G_i (t) < G_i^* (t)$ *.*

The optimal brand equity level in (4.41) has an additional and equally relevant implication. Since the degree of asymmetry across firms also involves marginal production costs, (4.41) tells that $G_i^* (t)$ increases monotonically as c_i decreases, and this fact, combined with the rule governing the optimal control choice, produces

Corollary 4.8 *Firms operating at lower marginal production costs will enjoy higher market shares and will advertise more than less efficient rivals.*

The intuitive explanation is that any decrease in the marginal production cost shifts $G_i^* (t)$ upwards and therefore enhances the scope of advertising by expanding the region in which any $G_i (t) < G_i^* (t)$ triggers the highest admissible advertising firm i can afford to undertake.

The last step in Fershtman's (1984) analysis is the assessment of the effect of industry structure on market shares and advertising efforts. Again on the basis of (4.41), it appears that any increase in the number of firms must be expected to decrease the individual market shares of almost all of them, except possibly that belonging to the most efficient one, provided its dominant position be so strong that it possesses at least 50% of total demand. This is mirrored by an analogous reaction of advertising efforts. Assuming for simplicity full symmetry across firms, in which case indeed all shares and advertising efforts do decrease in n, the effect of industry fragmentation on aggregate advertising investment $K^* (n) = nk^* (n)$ is captured by the sign of

$$\frac{\partial K^* (n)}{\partial n} = n \cdot \frac{\partial k^* (n)}{\partial n} + k^* (n) \gtreqless 0 \, \forall k^* (n) \gtreqless -n \cdot \frac{\partial k^* (n)}{\partial n} \qquad (4.43)$$

where the expression on the r.h.s. is positive because $\partial k^* (n) / \partial n$. Implicitly, (4.43) reveals that the relationship between aggregate expenditure and industry structure might well be non-monotone, with $K^* (n)$ reaching a maximum or a minimum in correspondence of some finite number of firms.

This possibility brings us to a hot topic in the recent debate about the impact of industry structure on aggregate investment in any direction, including R&D, installed capacity and (why not) advertising. The attention paid to the effect of variations in industry structure (and therefore in the degree of market power) on investment incentives dates back to the indirect debate between Schumpeter (1942) and Arrow (1962) on the speed and intensity of innovation, and it has been recently revived by empirical findings in Aghion et al. (2005) illustrating an inverted-U relationship between R&D industry investment and industry fragmentation. In the same paper, these authors offer the first theoretical model producing analogous predictions, to which I will come back in Chapters 6 and 7. For the moment, we may take a look at the arising of the same phenomenon in a differential oligopoly game with advertising for goodwill which appear in Lambertini and Zaccour (2015).

Suppose n *a priori* fully symmetric single-product firms supply a market over $t \in [0, \infty)$, all of them sharing an identical technology characterised by a constant marginal cost, which is normalised to zero for simplicity. Each firm sells a differentiated variety as in Singh and Vives (1984), so that, under Cournot competition, the instantaneous demand function for variety i is

$$p_i(t) = a - q_i(t) - \gamma Q_{-i}(t) \qquad (4.44)$$

where $Q_{-i}(t) = \sum_{j \neq i} q_j(t)$ is the total output of firm i's rivals and $\gamma \in [0, 1]$ is a constant measuring the degree of substitutability between any pair of varieties. In the special case $s = 0$, strategic interaction vanishes and each firm is an independent monopolist; if $\gamma = 1$, the product is homogeneous. If instead Bertrand behaviour prevails, the demand for variety i becomes

$$q_i(t) = \frac{a}{1 + \gamma(n-1)} - \frac{\left[1 + \gamma(n-2)\right] p_i(t) - \gamma \sum_{j \neq i} p_j(t)}{(1-\gamma)\left[1 + \gamma(n-1)\right]} \qquad (4.45)$$

In either case, firm i's instantaneous profits are defined as follows:

$$\pi_i(t) = G_i(t) R_i(t) = G_i(t) q_i(t) - b k_i^2(t), \qquad (4.46)$$

where $R_i(t) = p_i(t) q_i(t)$ is firm i's revenue and $G_i(t)$ is the stock of brand equity attached to variety i, whose kinematic equation is

$$\dot{G}_i \equiv \frac{dG_i(t)}{dt} = k_i(t) - \beta K_{-i}(t) - \delta G_i(t) \qquad (4.47)$$

In (4.47), parameter $\beta \in \left[0, 1/(n-1)\right]$ measures the intensity of the negative spillover effect exerted by $K_{-i}(t) = \sum_{j \neq i} k_j(t)$, the collective advertising effort of firm i's opponents. The n initial conditions are $G_{i0} = G_i(0) > 0$.

To begin with, it can be shown that this game yields subgame perfection under open-loop information, as its structure is state-separable – although, at first sight, one wouldn't instinctively draw such an implication, since the instantaneous profit function is cubic (being the product of $G_i(t)$ and a square function of either outputs or prices). The proof is extremely simple, and independent of the nature of market competition.

Without bothering about prices or quantities, think of this game as one in which firm i controls a market variable $u_i(t) = p_i(t), q_i(t)$ and a non-market variable $k_i(t)$. Its Hamiltonian function can be thus written as

$$\mathcal{H}_i(\cdot) = e^{-\rho t} \left[\pi_i(u_i(t), k_i(t), G_i(t)) + \lambda_{ii}(t) \dot{G}_i(t) + \sum_{j \neq i} \lambda_{ij}(t) \dot{G}_j(t) \right] \qquad (4.48)$$

and the resulting set of necessary conditions is

$$\frac{\partial \mathcal{H}_i}{\partial u_i} = \frac{\partial \pi_i}{\partial u_i} = G_i \cdot \frac{\partial R_i}{\partial u_i} = 0 \qquad (4.49)$$

$$\frac{\partial \mathcal{H}_i}{\partial k_i} = -2bk_i + \lambda_{ii} \cdot \frac{\partial \dot{G}_i}{\partial k_i} + \sum_{j \neq i} \lambda_{ij} \cdot \frac{\partial \dot{G}_j}{\partial k_i} = 0 \tag{4.50}$$

$$\dot{\lambda}_{ii} = -\frac{\partial \mathcal{H}_i}{\partial G_i} + \rho \lambda_{ii} \Leftrightarrow \lambda_{ii} = (\delta + \rho) \lambda_{ii} - R_i \tag{4.51}$$

$$\dot{\lambda}_{ij} = -\frac{\partial \mathcal{H}_i}{\partial G_j} + \rho \lambda_{ij} \Leftrightarrow \lambda_{ij} = (\delta + \rho) \lambda_{ij} \tag{4.52}$$

Conditions (4.49–4.52) imply

$$\left. \frac{\partial^2 \mathcal{H}_i}{\partial u_i \partial G_j} \right|_{\frac{\partial \mathcal{H}_i}{\partial u_i} = 0} = \left. \frac{\partial^2 \mathcal{H}_i}{\partial k_i \partial G_j} \right|_{\frac{\partial \mathcal{H}_i}{\partial k_i} = 0} = 0 \tag{4.53}$$

and

$$\frac{\partial^2 \mathcal{H}_i}{\partial G_j^2} = 0 \tag{4.54}$$

for all i and j. In particular, state-separability is driven by the fact that $\partial \pi_i / \partial u_i = \partial R_i / \partial u_i$, i.e., profit and revenue are simultaneously maximised by the same level of the relevant market variable. Hence, both versions of the game can be solved under open-loop information to obtain feedback strategies.

Now look at the resulting steady state advertising efforts and goodwill stocks in the two scenarios. Under quantity competition,

$$k_q^{OL} = \frac{a^2}{2b (\delta + \rho) [2 + \gamma (n - 1)]^2} \; ; \; G_q^{OL} = \frac{k_q^{OL} [1 - \beta (n - 1)]}{\delta} \tag{4.55}$$

while under price competition,

$$k_p^{OL} = \frac{a^2 (1 - \gamma) [1 + \gamma (n - 2)]}{2b (\delta + \rho) [2 + \gamma (n - 3)]^2 [1 + \gamma (n - 1)]} \; ; \; G_p^{OL} = \frac{k_p^{OL} [1 - \beta (n - 1)]}{\delta} \tag{4.56}$$

Comparing steady state magnitudes in (4.55) and (4.56), one discovers that k^{OL} and G^{OL} are both larger under Cournot than under Bertrand competition. The explanation is fully in line with the so-called *Schumpeterian hypothesis*, whereby a higher market power, all else equal, enhances firms' investment incentives. Here, market power increases switching from Bertrand to Cournot behaviour, for any given industry structure, because varieties are (imperfect) substitutes; thence this conclusion.

A totally different picture emerges if we look at the comparative statics implied by a change in n on (4.55) and (4.56). If firms compete in quantities, the following partial derivatives illustrate the impact of the numerosity of firms on the industry performance:

$$\frac{\partial K_q^{OL}}{\partial n} = \frac{a^2 [2 - \gamma (n + 1)]}{2b (\delta + \rho) [2 + \gamma (n - 1)]^3} \tag{4.57}$$

$$\frac{\partial^2 K_q^{OL}}{\partial n^2} = \frac{a^2 [\gamma (n + 2) - 4]}{b (\delta + \rho) [2 + \gamma (n - 1)]^4} \tag{4.58}$$

Since $\partial K_q^{OL}/\partial n = 0$ at $n_q = (2-\gamma)/\gamma \geq 2$ for all $\gamma \in [0, 2/3]$, and in such parameter interval $\partial^2 K_{CN}^*/\partial n^2 < 0$, we see that if product differentiation is sufficiently high, the aggregate investment in advertising has indeed an inverted-U shape and reaches its maximum level in correspondence of $n_q = (2-\gamma)/\gamma \geq 2$.

The same exercise can be carried out on (4.56), to find out that

$$\frac{\partial K_p^{OL}}{\partial n} = \Psi \cdot \frac{2 + 3\gamma(n-3) + \gamma^2(13 - 7n) - \gamma^3[n^2(n-1) - 2(2n-3)]}{2b[1 + \gamma(n-1)]^2[2 + \gamma(n-3)]^3},$$

(4.59)

where Ψ is a positive constant. Evaluating the sign and characterising the roots of the r.h.s. of (4.59) is a bit more difficult,[6] but it can be established that any $\gamma \in [0, 1/2]$ ensures $\partial K_p^{OL}/\partial n = 0$ at a unique value of $n_p \geq 2$ which identifies a maximum point. Hence,

Proposition 4.9 *Irrespective of the nature of market competition, the aggregate steady state advertising expenditure is concave and single-peaked in the number of firms. The parameter interval in which this happens under price competition is a proper subset of the interval in which the inverted-U investment curve appears under quantity competition.*

As we shall see in the remainder of the book, this is not the only setting in which this phenomenon arises at equilibrium.

The discussion on advertising for goodwill has extended itself to encompass the case of cooperative advertising. Jørgensen and Gromova (2016) adapt the capital accumulation model in Reynolds (1987, 1991) to describe a differential triopoly game where advertising effort to enhance brand equity can be undertaken either by singletons or by coalitions (a proper coalition of two firms or the grand coalition formed by the whole industry).

They assume that a firm's quantity at any time t is determined as follows:

$$q_i(t) = \left[B - \sum_{i=1}^{3} G_i(t)\right] G_i(t)$$

(4.60)

where B is a positive constant. To allow for a fully analytical solution of the feedback game, the goodwill dynamics is

$$\dot{G}_i = k_i(t)$$

(4.61)

i.e., it is unaffected by decay or forgetfulness. As in Lambertini and Zaccour (2015), the advertising activity involves convex instantaneous costs. Additionally, as in many of the aforementioned contributions, the mark-up is exogenously fixed forever.

In evaluating the feasibility of cooperative advertising in the grand coalition, Jørgensen and Gromova (2016) examine the profitability of deviations from the grand

---

[6] However, it requires no numerical calculations. A geometrical method is used in Lambertini and Zaccour (2015).

coalition by either a single firm or the only admissible sub-coalition consisting of two firms, stipulating that the firm (firms) being cheated will play a fully noncooperative game against the deviator once the initial deviation from the path prescribed by the joint profit-maximising solution for the grand coalition, which cannot be restored after any deviation. That is, deviation triggers an infinite punishment based upon the same basic idea underlying grim trigger strategies à *la* Friedman (1971). On these basis, Jørgensen and Gromova (2016) characterise the necessary conditions for the perpetual stability of the grand coalition[7] and show that (1) the cheated firms will always exert some positive advertising efforts after the deviation, while (2) deviators may or may not advertise, depending upon the values of the shadow prices (the partial derivatives of value functions) attached to their goodwill stocks.

4.3   **Durables and Product Diffusion**

Another aspect connected with advertising which has been treated using differential games is the diffusion of new products.[8] Indeed, the setup commonly used to study diffusion processes is a derivative of the Vidale and Wolfe (1957) model.

The size of potential demand for the new good may be either exogenously fixed or endogenously determined by firm's investments in marketing or pricing policies, or by growth rates of the population and/or income. Potential buyers being initially uninformed about the existence and characteristics of the good in question, word-of-mouth from consumers with a taste for trying new goods has a role in boosting product diffusion together with advertising activities.

This approach dates back to Bass (1969), where it is also assumed that the product is a durable good. In Bass (1969), it is assumed that the market is a monopoly (or, *almost* equivalently, that there are no sufficiently close substitutes for the new good to attribute a role in the model to any other firms). In this case, it is appropriate to define as $Q(t)$ the cumulative number of adopters, which evolves according to

$$\dot{Q}(t) = z[Q_{max} - Q(t)] + \frac{vQ(t)}{Q_{max}} \cdot [Q_{max} - Q(t)] \qquad (4.62)$$

where advertising plays no role. In the above state equation, parameters $z > 0$ and $v > 0$ measure, respectively, the relative weights of the *innovation effect* whereby consumers eager to try the new good buy first, and the imitation effect is generated by word-of-mouth. Note that the expression on the r.h.s. is concave in $Q(t)$. Solving (4.62), we find the size of cumulative adoptions at any instant t,

$$Q(t) = \frac{zQ_{max}\left(1 - e^{-(v+z)t}\right)}{z + ve^{-(v+z)t}} \qquad (4.63)$$

---

[7] In the jargon of cooperative game theory, Jørgensen and Gromova (2016) prove the existence of *an imputation which belongs to the core* of the game, which the grand coalition may select, thereby eliminating any incentive for a smaller coalition or a singleton to deviate at any arbitrary date during the game.

[8] These models are also labelled as *market growth* or *cumulative sales models*.

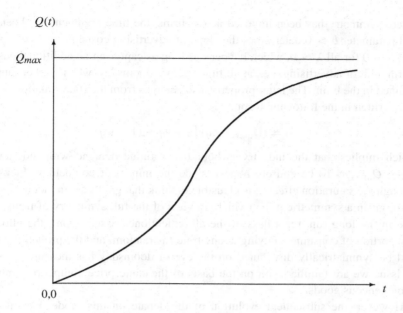

Figure 4.2 The logistic curve of cumulative sales

which delivers the familiar logistic growth curve as in the Verhulst–Lotka–Volterra model. This is illustrated in Figure 4.2, where Q_{max} is approached asymptotically. After the initial period during which innovation favours diffusion at an increasing rate, sales are sustained by imitation and then, in the limit, the market reaches saturation:

Proposition 4.10 *The diffusion of new (durable) goods mimics the growth of a natural species. Asymptotically, cumulative adoptions tend to reach the market's carrying capacity.*

Oligopolistic interaction appears in Teng and Thompson (1983), with firm i's sales following

$$\dot{q}_i(t) = [Q_{max} - Q(t)][z + vq_i(t) + (1 + wq_i(t))k_i(t)] \tag{4.64}$$

in which the presence of firm i's competitors can be detected only by their collective contribution to the saturation effect via the cumulative sales of the entire industry, $Q(t) = \sum_{j=1}^{n} q_j$. As in Vidale and Wolfe (1957), this set of state equations makes it impossible to solve the feedback game. However, the adoption of some *ad hoc* hypotheses allows one to generate the same asymptotic outcome as in Bass (1969). Suppose (1) the price p is unique and constant over time, and (2) marginal production cost is constant and common to all firms, so that it can be posed equal to zero without loss of generality. Then, the game features n controls (the advertising efforts $k_i(t)$) and n states (cumulative individual sales $q_i(t)$), and the expression of the optimal control at time t derived under open-loop information is

$$k = \frac{(Q_{max} - nq)(1 + wq)\lambda}{2b} \tag{4.65}$$

where symmetry has been imposed across firms, the time argument has been omitted and parameter $b > 0$ determines the slope of advertising costs. From (4.65), we know that $k > 0$ for all $\lambda > 0$, which happens as long as capturing an additional customer is worth a bit of advertising, i.e., at all times before doomsday, when market saturation is attained in the limit. The latter property also emerges from the state equation, which can be rewritten in the following form:

$$\dot{q} = (Q_{max} - nq)\left[z + vq + (1 + wq)k\right] \tag{4.66}$$

which implies that the industry is bound to saturate demand with individual sales $q \to Q_{max}/n$. To be entirely honest, since the impact of competitors kicks in only through the saturation effect, it is plausible to think that goods are in fact homogeneous. If so, given a symmetric price (which, in view of the full symmetry of firms, is surely true in the long run, regardless of the aforementioned assumption), the allocation of any portion of consumers buying at any time t is random, and the probability that they will be symmetrically distributed on the eve of doomsday has measure zero. This is an issue we are familiar with on the basis of the static price competition model with homogeneous goods.

However, the subsequent evolution of the debate on this model has successfully amended this problem. Fershtman et al. (1990) reformulate the model as a duopoly game with an incumbent which, at some point in time, faces the competition of a newcomer selling a substitute good. Initially, the incumbent enjoys a marginal cost advantage over the entrant (as in Schmalensee, 1982), but this advantage is eroded through spillovers or information leakages, so that firms end up symmetric in the long run. The state dynamics assumed for their sales is à la Nerlove and Arrow (1962), and looks like (4.37). This simplification notwithstanding, feedback strategies remain intractable. Hence, Fershtman et al. (1990) solve the open-loop game to characterise the conditions under which, at the steady state equilibrium, firms' market shares are unrelated to the order of entry (which, of course, matters along the path to the steady state) and the initial difference between marginal production costs. One can read the result in Fershtman et al. (1990) in terms of catching up. This property arises also elsewhere in applications of differential games to industrial organization, as we will see in Chapter 6.

Let me digress from differential games to discuss a relevant extension of the debate on industry dynamics initiated by Ericson and Pakes (1995) and discussed in Chapter 3. Using difference equations and numerical methods, Doraszelski and Markovich (2007) construct a game which has several elements in common with Friedman (1983) and Fershtman et al. (1990). Unlike the bulk of the aforementioned literature on advertising, Doraszelski and Markovich (2007) endogenise the demand function after specifying consumer preferences.

In their setup, firms may alternatively advertise to enhance brand equity (goodwill) or to inform consumers, and the related state dynamics are stochastic. Moreover, asymmetries across firms are accounted for and, contrary to what happens in Fershtman et al. (1990), do not vanish as time goes by. On the contrary, asymmetries not only arise and persist but may also generate asymmetric equilibria, to the effect that initial incumbents may quit while newcomers may enter the industry.

While these general features of the model are independent of the exact nature of advertising, the sources of asymmetries are indeed sensible to it. Under goodwill advertising, the relative size of firms interact with market size and advertising cost in such a way that the incentive to invest in a campaign is increasing in firm size, opening up to the possibility for large firms to adopt a sort of limit strategy whereby small rivals do not advertise at all. These effects are mitigated or altogether absent if the market is large or advertising costs are small, in which case a symmetric equilibrium outcome as in Fershtman et al. (1990) arises. If instead advertising is informative, asymmetries depend on the intensity of market competition, whereby tough competition makes the model reproduce something closely resembling a preemption race. The game investigated by Doraszelski and Markovich (2007) has the additional property of delivering relevant implications as far as the regulation of advertising activities is concerned: regulating or prohibiting advertising campaigns (as it has happened for tobacco) makes it more difficult for small firms to reach consumers, a fact which may indirectly facilitate the acquisition of a dominant position by a large one.

These considerations lead us to the empirical side of the research strand on advertising competition, which is as lively as the theoretical one since the very beginning of this literature. In fact, the point of departure of both Vidale and Wolfe (1957) and Bass (1969) is empirical evidence, which prompted for the formulation of theoretical models fitting the data. Subsequently, the Lanchester-Case model – unlike the other variations on the basic theme of the dynamic advertising game – has been extensively used to carry out empirical tests confirming the basic assumption concerning decreasing returns to advertising, the persistence of the effects of advertising on sales and even the implications of alternative information structures on the evolution of either sales or market shares. In particular, evidence confirming the adoption of feedback strategies can be found in Chintagunta and Vilcassim (1992, 1994), Erickson (1992), Fruchter and Kalish (1997), Breton et al. (2006) and Wang and Wu (2007), among others. Conjectural variations are estimated by Erickson (1997). Moreover, a particularly important aspect of empirical analysis based upon the prescriptions produced by dynamic games is that one should use data to verify whether firms in the real world operate along equilibrium paths or not. Confirmations to this regard can be found in Chintagunta and Jain (1995). Of particular interest is the uncommon but very relevant aspect considered by Chintagunta (1993), who investigates the so-called *flat maximum principle*, whereby firms' profits are insensitive to changes in optimal advertising effort levels. This piece of both theoretical and empirical analysis is carried out under open- and closed-loop strategies, using data coming from the pharmaceutical industry and the soft-drink sector (indeed, Coke vs. Pepsi). If attained, as in these cases, the confirmation of the flat maximum principle suggests that firms could equally well hold the same market shares by never investing a single penny in advertising activities. This not only testifies the presence of excess investment but also indicates the prisoners' dilemma structure underlying advertising competition.

Further Reading

For comprehensive surveys of differential games of advertising, see Sethi (1977), Little (1979), Jørgensen (1982), Feichtinger et al. (1994), Erickson (1995, 2003), Jørgensen and Zaccour (2004, 2007) and Huang et al. (2012). Generic and brand-specific advertising is in Bass et al. (2005). For further insights about defensive vs. offensive advertising in the Lanchester model, see Jørgensen and Sigué (2015). For more on the Leitmann–Schmitendorf game, see Wang and Wu (2001) and Jørgensen et al. (2010). Oligopolistic models of advertising are in Tapiero (1979), Rao (1985), Erickson (1985, 2009), Mesak (1999), Fruchter (1999) and Fruchter et al. (2001). Additional elements about goodwill advertising, including the presence of adverse exogenous effects, are in Wernerfelt (1991), Grosset and Viscolani (2009), Viscolani and Zaccour (2009) and Grosset et al. (2011), among many others. Cooperative advertising to increase the choke price is characterised in Cellini and Lambertini (2003a,b) and Lambertini and Palestini (2009), where coalition theory tools are used to determine the optimal size of the advertising cartel. A survey of cooperative advertising games is in Jørgensen and Zaccour (2014). On product diffusion and market saturation, see Wernerfelt (1985), Fornell et al. (1985), Dockner and Jørgensen (1988), Dockner and Gaunersdorfer (1996) and Krishnamoorthy et al. (2010). Connected with the debate on product diffusion is the model by Xie and Sirbu (1995), studying the interplay between optimal intertemporal pricing, network externalities and compatibility. Their model adapts the setup in Bass (1969), with a given market potential. Among the many papers seeking empirical evidence, see Mesak and Calloway (1995a,b), constructing and testing a pulsing model of advertising competition (i.e., a model in which the advertising spending is not constant) nested in the Lanchester tradition.

Bibliography

Aghion, P., N. Bloom, R. Blundell, R. Griffith and P. Howitt (2005), "Competition and Innovation: An Inverted-U Relationship", *Quarterly Journal of Economics*, **120**, 701–28.

Anderson, S. and M. Engers (1992), "Stackelberg vs Cournot Oligopoly Equilibrium", *International Journal of Industrial Organization*, **10**, 127–35.

Anderson, S. and M. Engers (1994), "Strategic Investment and Timing of Entry", *International Economic Review*, **35**, 833–53.

Arrow, K. (1962), "Economic Welfare and the Allocation of Resources for Invention", in R. Nelson (ed.), *The Rate and Direction of Industrial Activity*, Princeton, NJ, Princeton University Press.

Bagwell, K. (2007), "The Economic Analysis of Advertising", in M. Armstrong and R. Porter (eds), *Hanbdook of Industrial Organization*, vol. 3, Amsterdam, North-Nolland.

Bass, F.M. (1969), "New Product Growth Model for Consumer Durables", *Management Science*, **15**, 215–27.

Bass, F.M., A. Krishnamoorthy, A. Prasad and S. Sethi (2005), "Generic and Brand Advertising Strategies in a Dynamic Duopoly", *Marketing Science*, **24**, 556–68.

Becker, G. and K. Murphy (1993), "Simple Theory of Advertising as a Good or Bad", *Quarterly Journal of Economics*, **108**, 941–64.

Braithwate, D. (1928), "The Economic Effects of Advertising", *Economic Journal*, **38**, 16–37.

Breton, M., R. Jarrar and G. Zaccour (2006), "A Note on Feedback Sequential Equilibria in a Lanchester Model with Empirical Application", *Management Science*, **52**, 804–11.

Case, J. (1979), *Economics and the Competitive Process*, New York, New York University Press.

Cellini, R. and L. Lambertini (2003a), "Advertising in a Differential Oligopoly Game", *Journal of Optimization Theory and Applications*, **116**, 61–81.

Cellini, R. and L. Lambertini (2003b), "Advertising with Spillover Effects in a Differential Oligopoly Game with Differentiated Goods", *Central European Journal of Operations Research*, **11**, 409–23.

Cellini, R., L. Lambertini and A. Mantovani (2008), "Persuasive Advertising under Bertrand Competition: A Differential Game", *Operations Research Letters*, **36**, 381–14.

Chiang, A.C. (1992), *Elements of Dynamic Optimization*, New York, McGraw-Hill.

Chintagunta, P.K. (1993), "Investigating the Sensibility of Equilibrium Profits to Advertising Dynamics and Competitive Effects", *Management Science*, **39**, 1146–62.

Chintagunta, P.K. and D. Jain (1995), "Empirical Analysis of a Dynamic Duopoly Model of Competition", *Journal of Economics and Management Strategy*, **4**, 109–31.

Chintagunta, P.K. and N.J. Vilcassim (1992), "An Empirical Investigation of Advertising Strategies in a Dynamic Duopoly", *Management Science*, **38**, 1230–44.

Chintagunta, P.K. and N.J. Vilcassim (1994), "Marketing Investment Decisions in a Dynamic Duopoly: A Model and Empirical Analysis", *International Journal of Research in Marketing*, **11**, 287–306.

Clemhout, S., G. Leitmann and H.Y. Wan, Jr. (1971), "A Differential Game Model of Duopoly", *Econometrica*, **39**, 911–38.

Deal, K. (1979), "Optimizing Advertising Expenditure in a Dynamic Duopoly", *Operations Research*, **27**, 682–92.

Dhrymes, P.J. (1962), "On Optimal Advertising Capital and Research Expenditure under Dynamic Conditions", *Economica*, **29**, 275–79.

Dixit, A.K. and V. Norman (1978), "Advertising and Welfare", *Bell Journal of Economics*, **9**, 1–17.

Dockner, E. and A. Gaunersdorfer (1996), "Strategic New Product Pricing when Demand Obeys Saturation Effects", *European Journal of Operational Research*, **90**, 589–98.

Dockner, E. and S. Jørgensen (1988), "Optimal Pricing Strategies for New Products in Dynamic Oligopolies", *Marketing Science*, **7**, 315–34.

Doraszelski, U. and S. Markovich (2007), "Advertising Dynamics and Competitive Advantage", *RAND Journal of Economics*, **38**, 557–92.

Dorfman, R. and P. Steiner (1954), "Optimal Advertising and Optimal Quality", *American Economic Review*, **44**, 826–36.

Dragone, D., L. Lambertini and A. Palestini (2010), "The Leitmann-Schmitendorf Advertising Game with n Players and Time Discounting", *Applied Mathematics and Computation*, **217**, 1010–16.

Erickson, G. (1985), "A Model of Advertising Competition", *Journal of Marketing Research*, **22**, 297–304.

Erickson, G. (1992), "Empirical Analysis of Closed-Loop Duopoly Advertising Strategies", *Management Science*, **38**, 1732–49.

Erickson, G. (1993), "Offensive and Defensive Marketing: Closed-Loop Duopoly Strategies", *Marketing Letters*, **4**, 285–95.

Erickson, G. (1995), "Differential Game Models of Advertising Competition", *European Journal of Operational Research*, **83**, 431–38.

Erickson, G. (1997), "Dynamic Conjectural Variations in a Lanchester Duopoly", *Management Science*, **43**, 1603–08.

Erickson, G. (2003), *Dynamic Models of Advertising Competition. Second Edition*, Dordrecht, Kluwer.

Erickson, G. (2009), "An Oligopoly Model of Dynamic Advertising Competition", *European Journal of Operational Research*, **197**, 374–88.

Ericson, R. and A. Pakes (1995), "Markov-Perfect Industry Dynamics: A Framework for Empirical Work", *Review of Economic Studies*, **62**, 53–82.

Feichtinger, G. (1983), "The Nash Solution of an Advertising Differential Game: Generalization of a Model by Leitmann and Schmitendorf", *IEEE Transactions on Automatic Control*, **28**, pp. 1044–48.

Feichtinger, G., R. Hartl and P. Sethi (1994), "Dynamic Optimal Control Models in Advertising: Recent Developments", *Management Science*, **40**, 195–226.

Fershtman, C. (1984), "Goodwill and Market Shares in Oligopoly", *Economica*, **51**, 271–81.

Fershtman, C. and M. Kamien (1987), "Dynamic Duopolistic Competition with Sticky Prices", *Econometrica*, **55**, 1151–64.

Fershtman, C., V. Mahajan and E. Muller (1990), "Market Share Pioneering Advantage: A Theoretical Approach", *Management Science*, **36**, 900–18.

Fershtman, C. and S. Nitzan (1991), "Dynamic Voluntary Provision of Public Goods", *European Economic Review*, **35**, 1057–67.

Fornell, C., W.T. Robinson and B. Wernerfelt (1985), "Consumption Experience and Sales Promotion Expenditures", *Management Science*, **31**, 1084–105.

Friedman, J.W. (1971), "A Non-Cooperative Equilibrium for Supergames", *Review of Economic Studies*, **28**, 1–12.

Friedman, J.W. (1983), "Advertising and Oligopolistic Equilibrium", *Bell Journal of Economics*, **14**, 464–73.

Friedman, L. (1958), "Game-Theory Models in the Allocation of Advertising Expenditures", *Operations Research*, **6**, 699–709.

Fruchter, G.E. (1999), "The Many-Player Advertising Game", *Management Science*, **45**, 1609–11.

Fruchter, G.E., G. Erickson and S. Kalish (2001), "Feedback Competitive Advertising Strategies with a General Objective Function", *Journal of Optimization Theory and Applications*, **109**, 601–13.

Fruchter, G.E. and S. Kalish (1997), "Closed-Loop Advertising Strategies in a Duopoly", *Management Science*, **43**, 54–63.

Grosset, L., P. Roberti and B. Viscolani (2011), "A Goodwill Model with Predatory Advertising", *Operations Research Letters*, **39**, 419–22.

Grosset, L. and B. Viscolani (2009), "Optimal Dynamic Advertising with an Adverse Exogenous Effect on Brand Goodwill", *Automatica*, **45**, 863–70.

Huang, J., M. Leng and L. Liang (2012), "Recent Developments in Dynamic Advertising Research", *European Journal of Operational Research*, **220**, 591–609.

Jørgensen, S. (1982), "A Survey of Some Differential Games in Advertising", *Journal of Economic Dynamics and Control*, **4**, 341–69.

Jørgensen, S. and E. Gromova (2016), "Sustaining Cooperation in a Differential Game of Advertising Goodwill Accumulation", *European Journal of Operational Research*, **254**, 294–303.

Jørgensen, S., G. Martín-Herrán and G. Zaccour (2010), "The Leitmann-Schmitendorf Advertising Differential Game", *Applied Mathematics and Computation*, **217**, 1110–16.

Jørgensen, S. and S.-P. Sigué (2015), "Defensive, Offensive, and Generic Advertising in a Lanchester Model with Market Growth", *Dynamic Games and Applications*, **5**, 523–39.

Jørgensen, S. and G. Zaccour (2004), *Differential Games in Marketing*, Kluwer, Dordrecht.

Jørgensen, S. and G. Zaccour (2007), "Developments in Differential Game Theory and Numerical Methods: Economic and Management Applications", *Computational Management Science*, **4**, 159–82.

Jørgensen, S. and G. Zaccour (2014), "A Survey of Game-Theoretic Models of Cooperative Advertising", *European Journal of Operational Research*, **237**, 1–14.

Kaldor, N. (1950), "The Economic Aspects of Advertising", *Review of Economic Studies*, **18**, 1–27.

Krishnamoorthy, A., A. Prasad and S. Sethi (2010), "Optimal Pricing and Advertising in a Durable-Good Duopoly", *European Journal of Operational Research*, **200**, 486–97.

Lambertini, L. (2014), "Dynamic Analysis of an Electoral Campaign", in J. Haunschmied, V. Veliov and S. Wrzaczek (eds), *Dynamic Games in Economics*, Heidelberg, Springer, 187–204.

Lambertini, L. and A. Palestini (2009), "Dynamic Advertising with Spillovers: Cartel vs Competitive Fringe", *Optimal Control, Applications and Methods*, **30**, 562–72.

Lambertini, L. and G. Zaccour (2015), "Inverted-U Aggregate Investment Curves in a Dynamic Game of Advertising", *Economics Letters*, **132**, 34–38.

Lanchester F.W. (1956) "Mathematics in Warfare", in J.R. Newman (ed.), *The World of Mathematics*, New York, Simon and Schuster, pp. 2138–57.

Leitmann, G. and W.E. Schmitendorf (1978), "Profit Maximization Through Advertising: A Nonzero Sum Differential Game Approach", *IEEE Transactions on Automatic Control*, **23**, pp. 646–50.

Little, J.D.C. (1979), "Aggregate Advertising Models: The State of the Art", *Operations Research*, **27**, 629–67.

Mesak, H.I. (1999), "On the Generalizability of Advertising Pulsation Monopoly Results to an Oligopoly", *European Journal of Operational Research*, **117**, 429–49.

Mesak, H.I. and J.A. Calloway (1995a), "A Pulsing Model of Advertising Competition: A Game Theoretic Approach, Part A – Theoretical Foundation", *European Journal of Operational Research*, **86**, 231–48.

Mesak, H.I. and J.A. Calloway (1995b), "A Pulsing Model of Advertising Competition: A Game Theoretic Approach, Part B – Empirical Application and Findings", *European Journal of Operational Research*, **86**, 422–33.

Nordhaus, W.D. (1975), "The Political Business Cycle", *Review of Economic Studies*, **42**, 169–90.

Nerlove, M. and K. Arrow (1962), "Optimal Advertising Policy under Dynamic Conditions", *Economica*, **29**, 129–42.

Pauwels, W. (1977), "Optimal Dynamic Advertising Policies in the Presence of Continuously Distributed Time Lags", *Journal of Optimization Theory and Applications*, **22**, 79–89.

Piga, C. (2000), "Competition in a Duopoly with Sticky Price and Advertising", *International Journal of Industrial Organization*, **18**, 595–614.

Rao, R. (1985), "Advertising Decisions in Oligopoly: An Industry Equilibrium Analysis", *Optimal Control Applications and Methods*, **5**, 331–44.

Reynolds, S. (1987), "Capacity Investment, Preemption and Commitment in an Infinite Horizon Model", *International Economic Review*, **28**, 69–88.

Reynolds, S. (1991), "Dynamic Oligopoly with Capacity Adjustment Costs", *Journal of Economic Dynamics and Control*, **15**, 491–514.

Schmalensee, R. (1976), "A Model of Promotional Competition in Oligopoly", *Review of Economic Studies*, **43**, 493–507.

Schmalensee, R. (1982), "Product Differentiation Advantages of Pioneering Brands", *American Economic Review*, **72**, 349–65.

Schumpeter, J.A. (1942), *Capitalism, Socialism and Democracy*, New York, Harper.

Sethi, S. (1973), "Optimal Control of the Vidale-Wolfe Advertising Model", *Operations Research*, **21**, 998–1013.

Sethi, S. (1977), "Dynamic Optimal Control Models in Advertising: A Survey", *SIAM Review*, **19**, 685–725.

Sethi, S. (1983), "Deterministic and Stochastic Optimization of a Dynamic Advertising Model", *Optimal Control Applications and Methods*, **4**, 179–84.

Sethi, S. and G. Thompson (1981), *Optimal Control Theory: Applications to Management Science*, Boston, Nijhoff.

Simaan, M. and T. Takayama (1978), "Game Theory Applied to Dynamic Duopoly Problems with Production Constraints", *Automatica*, **14**, 161–66.

Singh, N. and X. Vives (1984), "Price and Quantity Competition in a Differentiated Duopoly", *RAND Journal of Economics*, **15**, 546–54.

Sorger, G. (1989), "Competitive Dynamic Advertising: A Modification of the Case Game", *Journal of Economic Dynamics and Control*, **13**, 55–80.

Stigler, G. and G. Becker (1977), "De Gustibus non Est Disputandum", *American Economic Review*, **67**, 7–90.

Tapiero, C. (1979), "A Generalization of the Nerlove-Arrow Model to Multi-Firms Advertising under Uncertainty", *Management Science*, **25**, 907–15.

Teng, J.T. and G. Thompson (1983), "Oligopoly Models for Optimal Advertising When Production Costs Obey a Learning Curve", *Management Science*, **12**, 1087–101.

Tirole, J. (1988), *The Theory of Industrial Organization*, Cambridge, MA, MIT Press.

Tsutsui, S. and K. Mino (1990), "Nonlinear Strategies in Dynamic Duopolistic Competition with Sticky Prices", *Journal of Economic Theory*, **52**, 136–61.

Vidale, M. and H. Wolfe (1957), "An Operations Research Study of Sales Response to Advertising", *Operations Research*, **5**, 370–81.

Viscolani, B. and G. Zaccour (2009), "Advertising Strategies in a Differential Game with Negative Competitor's Interference", *Journal of Optimization Theory and Applications*, **140**, 153–70.

Wang, Q. and Z. Wu (2001), "A Duopolistic Model of Dynamic Competitive Advertising", *European Journal of Operational Research*, **128**, 213–26.

Wang, Q. and Z. Wu (2007), "An Empirical Study on the Lanchester model of Combat for Competitive Advertising Decisions", *European Journal of Operational Research*, **183**, 871–81.

Wernerfelt, B. (1985), "The Dynamics of Prices and Market Shares over the Product's Life Cycle", *Management Science*, **31**, 928–39.

Wernerfelt, B. (1991), "Brand Loyalty and Market Equilibrium", *Marketing Science*, **10**, 229–45.

Xie, J. and M. Sirbu (1995), "Price Competition and Compatibility in the Presence of Positive Demand Externalities", *Management Science*, **41**, 909–26.

5   Product Differentiation

The DNA helix of the material discussed in this chapter has a lot in common with the contents of Chapters 4 and 6, as it deals with competition based on non-price tools. Indeed, the effects of product differentiation on consumer behaviour are largely analogous to those exerted by advertising campaigns, and product differentiation is usually the outcome of firms' investment in R&D.

However, this component of firms' strategies deserves a place of its own, as is the case in the tradition of the theory of industrial organization, for (at least) two relevant reasons. The first is that it has spurred a large and productive stream of research on discrete choice theory, where it is explicitly admitted that there may not exist a representative consumer buying a basket including all goods supplied by any given industry. In fact, this subject is replaced by another with preferences focussed upon a detailed list of characteristics defining her/his preferred variety, and the resulting consumption choice is determined by a compromise between pure preferences, the actual varieties supplied by firms, market prices and consumer income. In the early stages of the construction of this part of IO theory, the discrete choice approach was often labelled as the *address approach* (Archibald et al., 1986), where the 'address' is the vector of coordinates identifying the position of any given product variety in the space of relevant characteristics. The alternative view connected with the figure of a representative consumer was accordingly defined as the non-address approach. In the latter framework, the typical modelization of product differentiation takes the form of a parametric preference for variety, dating back to Bowley (1924) and then revived by the modern version of monopolistic competition (Dixit and Stiglitz, 1977), the *new trade theory* (Helpman and Krugman, 1985, 1989), as well as IO (Singh and Vives, 1984). The second reason is that the discrete choice theory of product differentiation has produced new insights on the entry process and the evolution and long-run equilibrium configuration of industry structure. More explicitly, while under horizontal differentiation, in the vein of the Hotelling (1929) model, free entry drives prices to marginal cost and the degree of differentiation between adjacent varieties to zero, under vertical differentiation this outcome is impossible if quality improvements hinge upon fixed costs which can be likened to R&D costs (Gabszewicz and Thisse, 1980; Shaked and Sutton, 1983).

The small literature covered by this chapter illustrates two main issues. The first is that modelling horizontal differentiation (or, location choice) in a differential game is a delicate task, as minimum differentiation is bound to emerge if firms costlessly adjust locations at every instant, irrespective of the shape of consumer preferences.

The second consists in reconstructing the limit properties of the entry process under vertical differentiation, replicating a result holding in static games. Not surprisingly, both setups allow advertising activities to play a role. The chapter is concluded by a brief discussion of multidimensional differentiation models.

To complement the material illustrated in the remainder, one must mention the large literature dealing with dynamic advertising problems where product quality has a role, but consumer preferences are not usually modelled in a hedonic form. This stream of research, an excellent survey of which is in Feichtinger et al. (1994), is connected with pioneering contributions (Nelson, 1974; Schmalensee, 1978; Kotowitz and Mathewson, 1979a,b), where products are experience goods, information is incomplete and advertising is of mixed nature (i.e., also informative). Moreover, this same literature uses elements borrowed by diffusion models (Bass, 1969; Gould, 1970), including word-of-mouth effects, both positive and negative (see El Ouardighi et al., 2016), or, alternatively, has nested product quality into goodwill advertising models (see Conrad, 1985; El Ouardighi and Pasin, 2006) or in setups based upon the Lanchester (1956) – Case (1979) game or the Vidale and Wolfe (1957) one (see Ringbeck, 1985; Feichtinger et al., 1988). The relevance of the quality dimension in the diffusion of an experience good is modelled by Spremann (1985). All of these contributions, also covering the interplay between product quality and network externalities (Lambertini and Orsini, 2010), are, however, optimal control models with a single agent, as they consider monopolistic industries only. The same holds for the analysis of advertising campaigns and R&D for product innovation in the Hotelling setup (Lambertini, 2005, 2007). The lack of contributions in this field, compared to others, has already been stressed by Jørgensen and Zaccour (2004, pp. 153–54). One plausible explanation is that the formal structure of discrete choice models is somewhat cumbersome and does not lend itself to a simple and intuitive treatment in a differential game framework. Nonetheless, this evidently remains an area open to and asking for further developments in virtually any directions.

5.1   Horizontal Differentiation

A *leitmotiv* of the discrete choice theory of product differentiation is the existence of a pure-strategy Nash equilibrium in the price space. This is the backbone of the debate connecting the pioneering model by Hotelling (1929) to the evolution of the theory of horizontal differentiation based upon d'Aspremont et al. (1979).[1] Closely connected with equilibrium existence is the discussion about the extent of differentiation characterising products at the subgame perfect equilibrium.[2] This is the balance of two

---

[1] The problem with the existence of equilibrium in the spatial product differentiation model is a topic extensively treated in Shaked (1975, 1982), de Palma et al. (1985), Dasgupta and Maskin (1986) and Osborne and Pitchick (1987), among others.

[2] Economides (1986), using the original linear model with a uniform consumer distribution, augmented by a variable degree of convexity of the transportation cost function, shows that the degree of differentiation increases in the aforementioned convexity. Lambertini (1994, 1997a) and Tabuchi and Thisse (1995) show that differentiation can be *more than maximal* if firms are allowed to exit the linear city boundaries. A general model encompassing non-uniform distributions is in Anderson et al. (1997).

opposite forces: one is the *strategic effect*, whereby firms should use as much product differentiation as possible to soften price competition in the market stage; the other is the *demand effect*, whereby firms are attracted by the average or median consumer (the same person, if the distribution of consumers is uniform). In Hotelling (1929), the second effect prevails on the first because of the linearity of transportation costs, which is also responsible for the undercutting incentive jeopardising equilibrium existence in pure strategies. In d'Aspremont *et al.* (1979), the introduction of quadratic transportation costs eliminates the undercutting incentive, thereby ensuring the existence of a unique pure-strategy equilibrium, and flips over the balance between the two effects, in favour of the strategic effect which drives firms towards maximum differentiation.

It is easily understood that differential game theory has a say in this area of IO, for two related reasons, which can be spelled out as follows.

- The first, apparently, has nothing to do with dynamics; indeed, it emerges in well-known static games based on spatial competition *à la* Hotelling (1929). Imagine a model without prices (or, where prices are exogenously fixed). In this case, one is left with a pure location problem, and this is precisely what happens in the stream of literature based on Downs' (1957) analysis of *political competition* for votes. The spectrum of constitutional political platforms is a unit segment, along which voters are distributed uniformly. Each voter has a net surplus from patronising one party or the other, equal to $U = s - f(d_i)$, where (1) s is the gross satisfaction generated by voting, and (2) $f(d_i)$ is the disutility associated to the distance d_i between the voter's ideal political platform (or location) and the actual platform (or location) of party i; $f(d_i)$ is positive, increasing and at least quasi-convex in d_i. Provided $s > f(d_i)$, everybody votes (which is the equivalent of the full coverage assumption so common in spatial models of product differentiation). Irrespective of the specific form of the disutility function, the absence of prices eliminates the strategic effect and leaves only the gravitational attraction exerted by the median voter onto parties, who flock toward the middle of the unit segment. This generates minimum differentiation between electoral programmes, which is quite common a phenomenon, at least on very relevant aspects connected with internal affairs.
- The second reason relies on a well-known point made by Novshek (1980), according to whom there does not exists a pure strategy Nash equilibrium in prices if firms set prices and locations in the same stage. More explicitly, (1) the price equilibrium does not exist with firms at different locations, since in that situation each firm has an incentive to relocate towards the rival and then go for undercutting to steal the rival's customers; consequently, (2) *a fortiori* the price equilibrium fails to exist in pure strategies if firms are located at the same point, for this triggers a price war leading to marginal cost pricing annihilating profits. This of course holds if firms are identical and use exactly the same technology. If they have different marginal cost, then the price war creates a monopoly for the most efficient firm. All of this applies irrespective of the exact shape of consumer distributions and transportation costs.

The consequences of the above arguments become evident when it comes to treating horizontal differentiation in dynamic games, where firms take all FOCs simultaneously at every time, the multistage structure we are familiar with from the literature on static games being absent. Hence, keeping location costless is bound to make the dynamic analysis of horizontal differentiation either trivial or impossible. To get around this difficulty and restore the spatial model to make it treatable and potentially capable of producing new results, one has to assume explicitly that the choice of location or differentiation is a costly one. Borrowing from Lambertini (1997b), Bertuzzi and Lambertini (2010) and Lambertini (2012) use the linear transportation cost version of the Hotelling model to investigate informative advertising and product innovation, respectively.

5.1.1 Informative Advertising

The game takes place over an infinite horizon. Two single-product firms, located at $x_1(t)$ and $x_2(t)$, supply a linear city of unit length, under full market coverage. Let the transportation cost function be

$$f(d_i(t)) = \tau |d_i(t)| = \tau |x_i(t) - x| \qquad (5.1)$$

where $|d_i(t)| = |x_i(t) - x|$ is the distance between firm i's location and a generic consumer at x (which of course is time-invariant); and τ is a positive constant. At any time t, the same consumer enjoys a net utility equal to

$$U(t) = s - p_i(t) - \tau |x_i(t) - x| \qquad (5.2)$$

As usual, full market coverage is assumed to prevail.[3] Using (5.2) and assuming a uniform consumer distribution with density $D(t)$ (so that $D(t)$ also measures total demand) the position of the indifferent consumer is

$$\bar{x}(t) = \frac{p_2(t) - p_1(t) + \tau [x_1(t) + x_2(t)]}{2\tau} \qquad (5.3)$$

and the market demand functions are

$$q_1(t) = D(t)\bar{x}(t) = \frac{D(t) [p_2(t) - p_1(t) + \tau (x_1(t) + x_2(t))]}{2\tau} \qquad (5.4)$$

$$q_2(t) = D(t) - q_1(t)$$

Firms invest in an informative advertising campaign, whereby the density of consumer changes over time according to the following state equation:

$$\dot{D}(t) = \alpha [k_1(t) + k_2(t)] - \delta D(t) \qquad (5.5)$$

---

[3] A few contributions in the Hotelling (1929) vein contemplate partial market coverage, with full coverage emerging as a special case. Static duopoly games with this feature can be found in Hinloopen and van Marrewijk (1999) and Chirco et al. (2003). Dynamic monopoly with either advertising investment or capital accumulation is considered in Lambertini (2005, 2009).

in which $k_i(t)$ is the instantaneous advertising effort of the individual firm, and α and δ are positive parameters with an intuitive meaning. The instantaneous cost of advertising is $C_i(k_i(t)) = bk_i^2(t)$, with $b > 0$.[4]

To cope with the problem of location choice, Bertuzzi and Lambertini (2010) assume that firms bear the following convex costs of location,

$$\Gamma_1(x_1(t)) = c[\eta_1 - x_1(t)]^2 \; ; \; \Gamma_2[x_2(t)] = c[\eta_2 - x_2(t)]^2, \; c > 0 \qquad (5.6)$$

at any time t. Note that the cost function $\Gamma_i(x_i(t))$ contemplates a single free location, η_i, for each firm. Assuming production costs away for simplicity, firm i's instantaneous profits are

$$\pi_i(t) = p_i(t)q_i(t) - c[\eta_i - x_i(t)]^2 - bk_i^2(t) \qquad (5.7)$$

Each firms control three variables: price $p_i(t)$, advertising effort $k_i(t)$ and location $x_i(t)$; the only state variable is consumer density $D(t)$. The game has a linear quadratic shape, and therefore the equilibrium can be characterised under feedback rules, solving the pair of Bellman equations:

$$\rho V_i(D(t)) = \max_{p_i(t), k_i(t), x_i(t)} \left\{ p_i(t)q_i(t) - c[\eta_i - x_i(t)]^2 - bk_i^2(t) \right.$$

$$\left. + V_i'(D(t))[\alpha[k_1(t) + k_2(t)] - \delta D(t)] \right\} \qquad (5.8)$$

where $V_i'(D(t)) = \partial V_i(D(t))/\partial D(t)$. Guessing a linear-quadratic form for the value function, Bertuzzi and Lambertini use $V_i(N(t)) = \varepsilon_1 D^2(t)/2 + \varepsilon_2 D(t) + \varepsilon_3$, and consequently $V_i'(D(t)) = \varepsilon_1 D(t) + \varepsilon_2$. Full symmetry is completed by posing $\eta_1 = \eta \in [0, 1/2)$ and $\eta_2 = 1 - \eta \in (1/2, 1]$. The resulting feedback strategies give rise to a unique subgame perfect equilibrium, at which optimal prices

$$p_1^F = \frac{\tau(2 + x_1 + x_2)}{3} \; ; \; p_2^F = \frac{\tau(4 - x_1 - x_2)}{3} \qquad (5.9)$$

obviously have the same form as in the original static formulation appearing in Hotelling (1929), but locations are

$$x_1^F = \eta + \frac{\tau D}{4c} \; ; \; x_2^F = 1 - \eta - \frac{\tau D}{4c} \qquad (5.10)$$

whereby $c > \tau D/(1 - 4\eta)$ is necessary and sufficient for the strategic effect, complemented by the cost of location, to prevent the disruptive consequences of the demand effect, i.e., to ensure $x_1^* < 1/4$ and $x_2^* > 3/4$ at all times. Finally, feedback advertising efforts are

$$k^F = \frac{\alpha(\varepsilon_1 D + \varepsilon_2)}{2b}, \; i = 1, 2, \qquad (5.11)$$

---

[4] The state dynamics in (5.5) has the same flavour as in Nerlove and Arrow (1962) and Fershtman (1984). However, since the distribution of consumers remains uniform irrespective of the relative intensity of firms' efforts, the state variable is a public good from the firms' standpoint, as in Fershtman and Nitzan (1991).

with

$$\varepsilon_2 = \frac{b\tau}{2b(\delta + \rho) - 3\alpha^2\varepsilon_1}$$

$$\varepsilon_1 = \frac{2bc(2\delta + \rho) - \sqrt{bc[3\alpha^2\tau^2 + 4bc(2\delta + \rho)^2]}}{6\alpha^2 c}$$

(5.12)

The steady state density and profits are

$$D^F = \frac{2\alpha k^*}{\delta} ; \ \pi^* = \frac{\tau D^F (8c - \tau D^F)}{16c} - \frac{\alpha^2 (D^F \varepsilon_1 + \varepsilon_2)^2}{4c}$$

(5.13)

Moreover, it is easily established that

$$\frac{\partial \left(x_2^F - x_1^F \right)}{\partial \delta} > 0 ; \ \frac{\partial \left(x_2^F - x_1^F \right)}{\partial \rho} > 0$$

$$\frac{\partial k^F}{\partial \delta} < 0 ; \ \frac{\partial k^F}{\partial \rho} < 0 ; \ \frac{\partial D^F}{\partial \rho} < 0$$

(5.14)

The model thus delivers

Proposition 5.1 *If location costs are sufficiently steep, a unique price equilibrium in pure strategies exists at all times, sustained by a degree of horizontal product differentiation equal to at least 1/2. As decay and time discounting increase, product differentiation increases while advertising efforts and consumer density decrease monotonically.*

Hence, it appears that, in the space of parameters defining the intertemporal values of all endogenous variables, advertising and product differentiation behave in opposite way, one balancing off the other as forgetfulness and discounting are modified. The game in Bertuzzi and Lambertini (2010) generalises the model proposed by Piga (1998), adopting the assumption that firms locate at the opposite extremes of the linear city at all times. The setup is the same under all other respects. Under this hypothesis, Piga (1998) proves that the open-loop equilibrium and the feedback equilibrium of the game with price competition and informative advertising coincide. However, the discussion that has opened this section puts in evidence the delicate aspects of modelling location choices in dynamic games. Hence, assuming maximum differentiation, while serving the purpose of simplifying calculations, imposes a price in terms of the robustness of results. I will come back to this issue in the last section of the chapter.

5.1.2   Locations as State Variables

In Lambertini (2012), the idea that the choice of location is costly becomes more explicit by turning locations into the state variables of the duopoly game, which, once again, lasts forever. Transportation costs being linear, the system of market demand functions is the same as in (5.4), except that consumer density is $D = 1$ at all times, with firms controlling prices and the costly effort to modify locations. The instantaneous individual profit is therefore $\pi_i(t) = p_i(t)q_i(t) - bk_i(t)$, where $k_i(t) \geq 0$ is the amount of resources invested by firm i at time t, and b is a positive constant. The kinematic equations governing the evolution of firms' locations are

$$\dot{x}_1(t) = \frac{k_1(t)}{1 + k_1(t)} \cdot \left[\frac{1}{2} - x_1(t)\right] \tag{5.15}$$

$$\dot{x}_2(t) = -\frac{k_2(t)}{1 + k_2(t)} \cdot \left[x_2(t) - \frac{1}{2}\right] \tag{5.16}$$

Initial conditions are $x_1(0) < 1/2$ and $x_2(0) > 1/2$. Equations (5.15–5.16) describe activities which can be labelled as R&D for product innovation or just investments in product design, and, unlike most models describing R&D, advertising, or capacity accumulation, incorporate decreasing intertemporal returns to scale via the concave function $k_i(t)/[1 + k_i(t)]$, while the instantaneous cost appearing in profits is linear in the effort.[5] Also note that the dynamics of locations in (5.15–5.16) reflect the presence of the demand effect, attracting firms towards the median and average consumer.

The game is noncooperative and takes place under simultaneous play. Given that is form is not linear-quadratic, it is solved under open-loop and closed-loop memoryless information. Under open-loop rules, Nash equilibrium prices coincide with (5.9), while the expressions of the optimal costate and investment are

$$\lambda_i(t) = \frac{2b\left[1 + k_i(t)\right]^2}{1 - 2x_i(t)} \tag{5.17}$$

and

$$k_i^{OL}(t) = \sqrt{\frac{\lambda_i(t)\left[1 - 2x_i(t)\right]}{2b}} - 1 \tag{5.18}$$

which produces the following control equation (omitting the time argument for brevity):

$$\dot{k}_i = -\frac{2\lambda_i \dot{x}_i + \lambda_i\left[2x_i(t) - 1\right]}{2\sqrt{2b\lambda_i\left(1 - 2x_i\right)}} \tag{5.19}$$

In absence of any decay of product design, in steady state we must have $\dot{k}_i^{OL} = 0$. Indeed, the open-loop steady state equilibrium – which is a saddle point – has the following coordinates:

$$k_i^{OL} = 0 \; ; \; x_1^{OL} = \frac{1}{2} - \frac{2\rho b}{\tau} < \frac{1}{4} \; ; \; x_2^{OL} = 1 - x_1^{OL} > \frac{3}{4} \tag{5.20}$$

for all $\rho > \tau/(8b)$. This condition, ensuring that firms will locate outside the second and third quartiles of the unit segment at the steady state, says that the price war engendered by undercutting incentives can be avoided if firms are sufficiently discounting future gains (which sounds the opposite of the wisdom acquired from the theory of repeated games), or, equivalently, if the unit transportation cost rate τ is low enough.

---

[5] The same feature characterises the advertising game in Leitmann and Schmitendorf (1978) illustrated in Chapter 4, and will appear again in Chapter 6.

Qualitatively speaking, the same applies under closed-loop information, as firms reach the steady state point

$$k_i^{CL} = 0 \; ; \; x_1^{CL} = \frac{1}{2} - \frac{3\rho b}{\tau} \; ; \; x_2^{CL} = 1 - x_1^{CL} \tag{5.21}$$

Here, the parametric condition for locations to lie outside the interval $[1/4, 3/4]$ is $\rho > \tau/(12b)$. This is less demanding than the previous one, and reflects the fact that $x_1^{CL} < x_1^{OL}$ and $x_2^{CL} > x_2^{OL}$. Under closed-loop information, firms become more aware of strategic interaction and therefore also of the relevance of preserving prices, and consequently invest less than in the open-loop setting. That is, the strategic effect is reinforced by feedbacks appearing in the adjoint equations, and the resulting amount of product differentiation at equilibrium is larger.

In both cases, the analysis reveals the following:

Proposition 5.2 *If location choices are costly and their dynamics accounts for the demand effect, there exists an admissible region of parameters wherein a unique price equilibrium does exist in pure strategies, sustained by a positive amount of product differentiation, which is augmented by closed-loop information.*

5.1.3   Club Goods and Externalities

The spatial differentiation model has also been used to analyse competition among *profit-maximising clubs*, i.e., collective entities gathering people who want to share the benefits of a public good (a golf green or a swimming pool) and are willing to pay to be admitted. The earliest analysis of this problem is in Scotchmer (1985), and the theme is connected with the presence of demand externalities which depend negatively on the size of the club (whereby we talk about congestion effects) or positively on the number of individuals which are left out of the club's door (in which case we talk about positional effects).

Laussel *et al.* (2004) explore the first route, combining network externalities, congestion effects and durability, which we have already examined in Chapter 2 in Driskill's (2001) model. The two clubs are located at the endpoints of the unit segment, and a unit mass of individuals is uniformly distributed over the same interval.

Membership lasts forever, and to keep the population constant while at the same time adding a pinch of realism, it is assumed that a fraction $\delta \in (0, 1)$ of people die at any point in time, being replaced by an analogous number of individuals. A quadratic disutility of transportation is assumed, and the lifetime gross satisfaction from membership enjoyed by anyone located at $x \in [0, 1]$ and admitted at time $\tilde{t}$ is

$$w(x, x_i) = \int_{\tilde{t}}^{\infty} \left[s - \tau(x - x_i)^2 - a_i \sigma_i(t) \right] e^{-(\delta + \rho)(t - \tilde{t})} dt \tag{5.22}$$

where $x_i \in \{0, 1\}$ is the location of club i, $\sigma_i(t)$ is its instantaneous market share and $\delta + \rho$ is the effective discount rate, and $a_i = A/k_i$ measures the congestion effect. $A > 0$ is a parameter, and k_i is club i's capacity, exogenously fixed. The lifetime net utility of the same individual is $U(x, x_i) = w(x, x_i) - p_i(\tilde{t})$, where $p_i(\tilde{t})$ is the price paid to acquire the membership at $\tilde{t}$. This individual compares $U(x, 0)$ and $U(x, 1)$ and subscribes to the club offering the highest net lifetime utility. Identifying the indifferent consumer at $\bar{x}(t)$ solving $U(x, 0) = U(x, 1)$ yields the two clubs' memberships (or demands) $q_i(t)$ at every instant.

Laussel *et al.* (2004) solve the game under linear feedback strategies, imposing rational expectations on the lifetime congestion associated with the negative externality produced by the accumulation of memberships in each club. This congestion is measured by

$$\Lambda_i(t) = \int_{\tilde{t}}^{\infty} \sigma_i(t) e^{-(\delta+\rho)(t-\tilde{t})} dt \tag{5.23}$$

and therefore congestion appears in the demand function of each club at all times:

$$q_i(t) = \delta \left[\frac{1}{2} + \frac{(p_j(t) - p_i(t) + (a_i + a_j)\Lambda_i(t))(\delta + \rho) - a_j}{2\tau} \right] \tag{5.24}$$

In this game, market shares are state variables following

$$\dot{\sigma}_i = q_i(t) - \delta\sigma_i(t) \tag{5.25}$$

while firms control prices $p_i(t)$ to maximise their respective discounted profit flows noncooperatively. The instantaneous profit function is $\pi_i(t) = p_i(t)q_i(t) - c_i\sigma_i(t)$, where c_i is a time-invariant marginal cost, possibly asymmetric.

The main findings can be summarised as follows. At equilibrium, if a firm has a larger market share than does its rival, then it also charges a lower price than the rival does, as a result of the associated higher congestion rate affecting its club members. Otherwise, if firms are identical and therefore the equilibrium is symmetric in all respects, steady state equilibrium prices are higher than they would be in absence of congestion. An explanation could be that if both clubs have the same size, then consumers cannot 'run away' to the other firm, and the outcome is that a negative demand externality has a quasi-collusive effect which has the same flavour as switching costs increasing brand loyalty (cf. Klemperer, 1995).

5.2   Vertical Differentiation

The reference models treating quality competition in oligopoly deal with the idea that vertical differentiation has asymmetric effects on equilibrium prices (because vertical differentiation, unlike the horizontal one, is inherently asymmetric in nature), and therefore, while serving the purpose of softening competition (Gabszewicz and Thisse, 1979; Shaked and Sutton, 1982), it also drives the entry process towards the attainment of a completely different outcome, as a vertically differentiated industry in which quality improvements do not affect variable costs[6] will sustain a limited number of

---

[6] If instead they do, because, e.g., skilled labour matters, then spatial and vertical differentiation models are isomorphic. The formal proof is in Cremer and Thisse (1991), but a simple model illustrating the same property can be found in Tirole (1988, chapter 7).

firms enjoying prices above marginal costs and positive market share at the long-run equilibrium (Gabszewicz and Thisse, 1980; Shaked and Sutton, 1983).

5.2.1   The Finiteness Property

To begin with, I will briefly reconstruct the finiteness property (Shaked and Sutton, 1983), using a simple static duopoly model with no costs at all, as in Choi and Shin (1992), where hedonic consumer preferences are specified as in Mussa and Rosen (1978). Two single-product firms, H and L, supply qualities $\Theta \geq \theta_H \geq \theta_L > 0$, and compete à la Bertrand in the marketplace. Θ is the highest technologically feasible quality level. Consumers are uniformly distributed, with unit density, over the interval $[0, \overline{m}]$, with $\overline{m} > 1$. Therefore, the total mass of consumers is $\overline{m}$.[7] Each consumer is indexed by a marginal willingness to pay for quality $m \in [0, \overline{m}]$, and buys at most one unit of the vertically differentiated good, in such a way that her/his net utility from consumption is:

$$U = \begin{cases} m\theta_i - p_i \geq 0 \text{ if she/he buys} \\ 0 \text{ otherwise} \end{cases} \tag{5.26}$$

where p_i is the price of variety i. Admitting the possibility that consumers with low income levels – and therefore low m's – may not be able to buy either variety, the demand functions for generic quality and price vectors are

$$q_H = \overline{m} - \frac{p_H - p_L}{\theta_H - \theta_L} \; ; \; q_L = \frac{p_H - p_L}{\theta_H - \theta_L} - \frac{p_L}{\theta_L} \tag{5.27}$$

and firms' revenues (or profits) are

$$\pi_H = p_H \left(\overline{m} - \frac{p_H - p_L}{\theta_H - \theta_L} \right) \; ; \; \pi_L = p_L \left(\frac{p_H - p_L}{\theta_H - \theta_L} - \frac{p_L}{\theta_L} \right) \tag{5.28}$$

Proceeding by backward induction, the Nash equilibrium prices at the market stage are

$$p_H^N = \frac{2\overline{m}\theta_H (\theta_H - \theta_L)}{4\theta_H - \theta_L} \; ; \; p_L^N = \frac{\overline{m}\theta_L (\theta_H - \theta_L)}{4\theta_H - \theta_L} \tag{5.29}$$

for any quality pair. Then, at the first stage, $\partial \pi_H / \partial \theta_H > 0$ everywhere, so that $\theta_H^N = \Theta$, while $\partial \pi_L / \partial \theta_L = 0$ at $\theta_L^N = 4\theta_H^N / 7 = 4\Theta / 7$. This result, of course, is sensitive to the model specification and is modified as soon as a cost function describing the R&D costs of quality improvement is added up; for instance, $\Gamma_i = cq_H^2$, as in Motta (1993) and Lehmann-Grube (1997), among others.

Yet, the toy model we are examining allows us to single out the extreme form of the aforementioned finiteness property in the Mussa and Rosen (1978) formulation. Since, at the subgame perfect equilibrium, firms' outputs are $q_H = 7\overline{m}/12$ and $q_L = 7\overline{m}/24$, we see not only that the high-quality product outsells the rival (in this case, by 100%) but also, which is more important, that $q_L > 0$ provided that $\overline{m} \in (0, 12/7)$. The

---

[7] One could assume a density equal to $1/\overline{m}$ in order to have a unit mass of consumers, but it doesn't make so much of a difference concerning the predictive power of the model.

reason is that the consumer indifferent between buying the high- or low-quality good is indexed by

$$\frac{p_H^N - p_L^N}{\theta_H^N - \theta_L^N} = \frac{5\overline{m}}{12} \tag{5.30}$$

and this value of the marginal willingness to pay must be higher than $\overline{m} - 1$ in order for the low-quality firm to have a positive market share. Obviously, this reveals that, for all $\overline{m} \geq 12/7$, the market is a *natural monopoly* in which the high-quality firm has no rivals.

Including explicitly some positive fixed costs $k_H \geq k_L$ associated with product quality does not change the picture, except that it adds up an additional non-negativity requirement on equilibrium profits. The differential game version of this model (Lambertini, 2006) shows that Choi and Shin's (1992) 4/7 rule is something more than a mere theoretical curiosum, as it is reproduced at the steady state equilibrium of the dynamic model under closed-loop rules.

5.2.2 Dynamic Quality Competition

The time horizon of the duopoly game is infinite, and the basic assumptions about the demand side are the same as above. In particular, the generic consumer's surplus function is (5.26), giving rise to the demand system (5.27) at any point in time. So, what matters is the appearance of the time argument in all endogenous variables. Now qualities are state variables, evolving over time according to

$$\dot{\theta}_H = ak_H(t) - \delta\theta_H(t) \tag{5.31}$$

$$\dot{\theta}_L = ak_L(t) \tag{5.32}$$

in which a is a positive parameter measuring the effectiveness of R&D for quality improvement, and $k_i(t)$ is the instantaneous R&D effort of firm i, entailing a cost $\Gamma_i(k_i(t)) = bk_i^2(t)$, $b > 0$. Ruling out decay for the low-quality good may seem a bit ad hoc, although one could, conversely, justify the high-quality good invoking a more demanding nature on the part of rich consumers. However, let's keep $\delta > 0$ in (5.31), for the moment. Initial conditions are $q_i(0) = q_{i0} \geq 0$. As above, production costs are nil. Hence, as long as demand functions (5.26) are indeed admissible, the instantaneous profit functions are

$$\pi_H(t) = p_H(t)\left(\overline{m} - \frac{p_H(t) - p_L(t)}{\theta_H(t) - \theta_L(t)}\right) - bk_H^2(t) \tag{5.33}$$

$$\pi_L(t) = p_L(t)\left(\frac{p_H(t) - p_L(t)}{\theta_H(t) - \theta_L(t)} - \frac{p_L(t)}{\theta_L(t)}\right) - bk_L^2(t) \tag{5.34}$$

Firms control prices investment efforts, playing simultaneously and noncooperatively at all times. Firms play simultaneously and noncooperatively. Since the game is not linear-quadratic and states appear at the denominator in both objective functions, (1) the open-loop solution is only weakly time consistent, and (2) the lack of a sensible conjecture for the value function prevents the attainment of the feedback solution, the game is solved under closed-loop memoryless information by inserting the effects of states on controls into the costate equations derived from the firms' Hamiltonians.

5.2.3   Closed-Loop Memoryless Strategies

Firm i's Hamiltonian function is:

$$\mathcal{H}_i(t) = e^{-\rho t} \cdot \left[\pi_i(t) + \lambda_{ii}(t) \frac{dq_i(t)}{dt} + \lambda_{ij}(t) \frac{dq_j(t)}{dt} \right] \tag{5.35}$$

where $i,j = H, L; \ i \neq j$. It is evident from the definition of instantaneous profits that the FOCs w.r.t. prices are quasi-static, optimal instantaneous prices coinciding with (5.29). The FOC on the investment effort is

$$\frac{\partial \mathcal{H}_i}{\partial k_i} = -2bk_i + a\lambda_{ii} = 0 \Leftrightarrow k_i^N = \frac{a\lambda_{ii}}{2b} \ , \ i = H, L \tag{5.36}$$

while the costate equations, augmented by the loops, are

$$-\frac{\partial \mathcal{H}_H}{\partial \theta_H} - \frac{\partial \mathcal{H}_H}{\partial p_L} \cdot \frac{\partial p_L^N}{\partial \theta_H} - \frac{\partial \mathcal{H}_H}{\partial k_L} \cdot \frac{\partial k_L^N}{\partial \theta_H} = \dot{\lambda}_{HH} - \rho \lambda_{HH} \Rightarrow \tag{5.37}$$

$$\dot{\lambda}_{HH} = (\rho + \delta) \lambda_{HH} - \frac{p_H (p_H - p_L)}{(\theta_H - \theta_L)^2} - \frac{3\overline{m} p_H \theta_L^2}{(\theta_H - \theta_L)(4\theta_H - \theta_L)^2}$$

$$-\frac{\partial \mathcal{H}_H}{\partial \theta_L} - \frac{\partial \mathcal{H}_H}{\partial p_L} \cdot \frac{\partial p_L^N}{\partial \theta_L} - \frac{\partial \mathcal{H}_H}{\partial k_L} \cdot \frac{\partial k_L^N}{\partial \theta_L} = \dot{\lambda}_{HL} - \rho \lambda_{HL} \tag{5.38}$$

$$-\frac{\partial \mathcal{H}_L}{\partial \theta_L} - \frac{\partial \mathcal{H}_L}{\partial p_H} \cdot \frac{\partial p_H^N}{\partial \theta_L} - \frac{\partial \mathcal{H}_L}{\partial k_H} \cdot \frac{\partial k_H^N}{\partial \theta_L} = \dot{\lambda}_{LL} - \rho \lambda_{LL} \Rightarrow \tag{5.39}$$

$$\dot{\lambda}_{LL} = \rho \lambda_{LL} - \frac{p_L \left(p_H \theta_L^2 - 2p_L \theta_H \theta_L + p_L \theta_H^2 \right)}{[\theta_L (\theta_H - \theta_L)]^2} + \frac{6\overline{m} p_L \theta_H^2}{(\theta_H - \theta_L)(4\theta_H - \theta_L)^2}$$

$$-\frac{\partial \mathcal{H}_L}{\partial \theta_H} - \frac{\partial \mathcal{H}_L}{\partial p_H} \cdot \frac{\partial p_H^N}{\partial \theta_H} - \frac{\partial \mathcal{H}_L}{\partial k_H} \cdot \frac{\partial k_H^N}{\partial \theta_H} = \dot{\lambda}_{LH} - \rho \lambda_{LH} \tag{5.40}$$

and the set of transversality conditions is defined as $\lim_{t \to \infty} e^{-\rho t} \lambda_{ij}(t) \theta_i(t) = 0$, $i, j = H, L$. Observe, from (5.36), that the loops between states and controls are limited to prices because $\partial k_i^N / \partial \theta_j = 0$, and adjoint equations (5.38) and (5.40) are redundant due to the degree of additive separability of the model (in particular, the fact that $\partial \dot{\theta}_i / \partial \theta_j = 0$). Again from (5.36), the dynamics of investment is

$$\dot{k}_i = \frac{a\dot{\lambda}_{ii}}{2b} \tag{5.41}$$

and using (5.36), (5.37) and (5.39), one obtains

$$\text{sign}\left\{\dot{k}_H\right\} = \text{sign}\left\{b\left(\rho+\delta\right)\left(4\theta_H-\theta_L\right)^3 k_H - 2a\bar{m}^2\theta_H\left(4\theta_H^2 - 3\theta_H\theta_L + 2\theta_L^2\right)\right\}$$

(5.42)

$$\text{sign}\left\{\dot{k}_L\right\} = \text{sign}\left\{2b\rho\left(4\theta_H-\theta_L\right)^3 k_L - a\bar{m}^2\theta_H^2\left(4\theta_H - 7\theta_L\right)\right\}$$

(5.43)

At the unique steady state equilibrium, which is a saddle point, the optimal closed-loop investment efforts are

$$k_H^{CL} = \frac{2a\bar{m}^2\theta_H\left(4\theta_H^2 - 3\theta_H\theta_L + 2\theta_L^2\right)}{b\left(\rho+\delta\right)\left(4\theta_H-\theta_L\right)^3}$$

(5.44)

$$k_L^{CL} = \frac{a\bar{m}^2\theta_H^2\left(4\theta_H - 7\theta_L\right)}{2b\rho\left(4\theta_H-\theta_L\right)^3}$$

(5.45)

Substituting the pair $\left(k_H^{CL}, k_L^{CL}\right)$ into the state dynamics, and recalling that $\dot{\theta}_L = ak_L \geq 0$ for all $k_L \geq 0$, one sees that the 4/7 rule is implied by (5.45), as $\dot{\theta}_L = ak_L = 0$ at $\theta_L^{CL} = 4\theta_H^{CL}/7$, with

$$\theta_H^{CL} = \frac{7a^2\bar{m}^2}{48b\delta\left(\rho+\delta\right)}$$

(5.46)

which, in turn, entails that the steady state effort of firm H is $k_H^{CL} = 7a\bar{m}^2/$ $[48b\delta\left(\rho+\delta\right)] > k_L^{CL} = 0$. This applies for all $\delta > 0$. If the high quality does not depreciate, then $\dot{\theta}_H \geq 0$ for all $k_H \geq 0$, and θ_H^{CL} reaches the sup of the range of technologically feasible quality levels Θ, as in the static game. In both cases, steady state outputs are the same as in Choi and Shin (1992), with identical implications. All of this boils down to

Proposition 5.3 *The 4/7 rule is replicated by the closed-loop memoryless solution of the differential game with quality dynamics. If neither quality depreciates, the high quality shoots all the way up to the upper bound of feasible qualities. The finiteness property is exactly the same as in the static model.*

It is worth stressing that here the Markovian (but not properly feedback) solution reproduces the subgame perfect equilibrium attained through the static analysis of the same basic model, unlike what happens in the sticky price model (Fershtman and Kamien, 1987) illustrated in Chapter 2, where the static Cournot–Nash equilibrium is the limit of the open-loop solution, which is not subgame perfect.

This model lends itself to extensions in several directions, all of them equally relevant and explored in the literature using a static approach, but still unreplicated in dynamic settings. One is the discussion about the incentive to undersupply product quality (some preliminary hints about this issue are in Lambertini, 2006), a topic investigated by Spence (1975), Mussa and Rosen (1978), Itoh (1983), Maskin and Riley (1984), Besanko *et al.* (1987, 1988) and Champsaur and Rochet (1989), among others.

Another is intraindustry trade under vertical differentiation (Shaked and Sutton, 1984; Motta, 1992; Motta et al., 1997). Finally, an obvious terrain where dynamic analysis could produce relevant insights is the regulation of quality supply via minimum quality standards (Ronnen, 1991; Crampes and Hollander, 1995; Ecchia and Lambertini, 1997).

5.2.4   Advertising under Vertical Differentiation

As mentioned at the outset of the chapter, product quality has entered dynamic advertising models (most of them optimal control models) in several ways. However, the intersection between the dynamic analysis of advertising and the literature on vertical differentiation based on hedonic consumer preferences is quite small. Here, I will briefly review the examples of what can be done in this respect.

The first one (Colombo and Lambertini, 2006) is based on much the same structure as above, except that Cournot competition is used. Hence, the instantaneous market demands of the two firms are

$$p_H(t) = \theta_H(t)\left[\overline{m}(t) - q_H(t)\right] - \theta_L(t) q_L(t) \tag{5.47}$$

$$p_L(t) = \theta_L(t)\left[\overline{m}(t) - q_H(t) - q_L(t)\right] \tag{5.48}$$

Firms' profit functions are

$$\pi_i(t) = p_i(t)q_i(t) - y_i^2(t) - k_i^2(t) , \; i = H, L \tag{5.49}$$

where $y_i(t)$ and $k_i(t)$ are firm i's instantaneous investments in persuasive advertising and product quality improvements, respectively. Quality i evolves according to

$$\dot{\theta}_i = k_i(t) - \delta\theta_i(t) \tag{5.50}$$

while advertising is aimed at increasing the sup of the marginal willingness to pay for quality:

$$\dot{\overline{m}} = y_H(t) + y_L(t) - \delta\overline{m}(t) \tag{5.51}$$

whereby advertising, as in Piga (1998), models the private provision of a public good. Hence, the present setup features six controls (outputs and investments) and three states (qualities and willingness to pay). To make the solution of the game more reader-friendly, the decay rate is the same for all state variables.

Colombo and Lambertini (2006) solve the game under both open-loop and closed-loop memoryless information, the resulting predictions being qualitatively the same in both cases. For illustrative purposes, a short summary of the open-loop case is sufficient. The steady state reached under open-loop information has the following coordinates:

$$q_H^{OL} = \overline{m}\left(1 - \frac{2\theta_H}{4\theta_H - \theta_L}\right) \; ; \; q_L^{OL} = \frac{\overline{m}\theta_H}{4\theta_H - \theta_L} \tag{5.52}$$

$$k_H^{OL} = \frac{\overline{m}^2\theta_H(2\theta_H - \theta_L)}{(\delta + \rho)(4\theta_H - \theta_L)^2} \; ; \; k_L^{OL} = \frac{\overline{m}^2\theta_H^2}{2(\delta + \rho)(4\theta_H - \theta_L)^2} \tag{5.53}$$

$$y_H^{OL} + \frac{\overline{m}\theta_H \left(2\theta_H - \theta_L\right)}{2\left(\delta + \rho\right)\left(4\theta_H - \theta_L\right)} \; ; \; y_L^{OL} = \frac{\overline{m}\theta_H \theta_L}{2\left(\delta + \rho\right)\left(4\theta_H - \theta_L\right)} \tag{5.54}$$

while the equilibrium levels of the states are $\overline{m}^{OL} = \left(y_H^{OL} + y_L^{OL}\right)/\delta$ and $\theta_i^{OL} = k_i^{OL}/\delta$. First of all, note that the R&D efforts in (5.53) show that the 4/7 rule is not emerging under open-loop information.[8] Secondly, (5.53–5.54) imply

Proposition 5.4 *Under open-loop rules, the high-quality firm invests more than does the low-quality rival in both directions.*

A remark is in order concerning relative advertising intensity. Note that the game takes place under full information, any informative role for advertising being ruled out by assumption. This means that the common wisdom holding that high-quality firms advertise less than their competitors do seems not so robust when advertising campaigns are meant to convince consumers to pay more for *a priori observable* superior-quality levels.

A direct consequence of the above is that the high-quality firm outsells the low-quality one, $q_H^{OL} > q_L^{OL}$. Yet, it does not systematically outperform its low-quality opponent, because of the higher investment costs curtailing profits.

Similar, although not entirely analogous, properties also emerge in a different context in which advertising expand sales, as in Leitmann and Schmitendorf (1978) and Reynolds (1987). This case is in Colombo and Lambertini (2003), where the utility function, although still modelling discrete choices under hedonic tastes, takes a different form:

$$U_H = m + \theta_H\left(t\right) - p_H\left(t\right) \tag{5.55}$$

if the consumer buys the high-quality good,

$$U_L = \gamma m + \theta_L\left(t\right) - p_L\left(t\right) \tag{5.56}$$

if she/he buys the low-quality alternative, and zero otherwise. In (5.56), parameter $\gamma \in (0, 1)$ measures the consumer's awareness that purchasing a low-quality variety involves some degree of dissatisfaction. The model is constructed under partial market coverage, with inverse demand functions

$$\begin{aligned} p_H\left(t\right) &= \overline{m} + \theta_H\left(t\right) - q_H\left(t\right) - \gamma q_L\left(t\right) \\ p_L\left(t\right) &= \theta_L\left(t\right) + \gamma\left[\overline{m} - q_H\left(t\right) - q_L\left(t\right)\right] \end{aligned} \tag{5.57}$$

Advertising has again a persuasive nature, and individual sales follow the kinematic equation

$$\dot{q}_i = k_i\left(t\right) - \delta q_i\left(t\right) \tag{5.58}$$

and the total instantaneous costs borne by firm i amount to $C_i\left(t\right) = c\theta_i^2\left(t\right)q_i\left(t\right) + b_i k_i^2\left(t\right)$. The nature of technology described by this cost function is such that the quality level is determined at every instant by the craftsmanship of skilled labour, rather than

---

[8] Except for the presence of depreciation in both state equations of product qualities, and the normalization $a = 1$ in (5.50), the present framework is the same as in Lambertini (2006).

evolving over time thanks to R&D. Moreover, the curvature of the advertising is firm-specific.

The game features four controls (qualities and advertising expenditures) and two states (sales), while prices are endogenously determined by inverse demands (5.57) at all times. Thanks to the additive separability of consumer preferences, its open-loop solution is strongly time consistent. At the steady state, the ranking of advertising efforts, sales and profits depends on the steepness of the advertising cost, measured by parameter b, as follows. There exists a sequence $\tilde{b}_H > \bar{b}_H > 0$, such that

- for all $b_H \in (0, \bar{b}_H)$, $k_H^{OL} > k_L^{OL}$; $q_H^{OL} > q_L^{OL}$; and $\pi_H^{OL} > \pi_L^{OL}$;
- for all $b_H \in (\bar{b}_H, \tilde{b}_H)$, $k_H^{OL} < k_L^{OL}$; $q_H^{OL} < q_L^{OL}$; and $\pi_H^{OL} > \pi_L^{OL}$;
- for all $b_H > \tilde{b}_H$, $k_H^{OL} < k_L^{OL}$; $q_H^{OL} < q_L^{OL}$; and $\pi_H^{OL} < \pi_L^{OL}$.

Hence,

Proposition 5.5 *If the advertising activity of the high-quality firm is sufficiently efficient, this firm's investment, sales and profits are higher then the rival's. The ranking of these magnitudes gradually changes as the high-quality firm's cost function becomes steeper, until all inequalities flip over in favour of the low-quality firm.*

These results are in sharp contrast to those emerging from the static literature on vertically differentiated industries, where the high-quality product produces a premium over inferior varieties in terms of equilibrium price and output, and therefore systematically gains higher profits. Note that the commonly adopted assumption of a rectangular consumer distribution, inherited by the bulk of the literature on spatial (or horizontal) differentiation, might be considered as responsible for this type of outcome, but this implication is not necessarily reliable, as the same assumption also characterises the differential games reviewed in this section.

5.3   Bidimensional Differentiation

Casual observation suggests that products are differentiated along several dimensions, some having to do with consumer income, others not. Although research on bidimensional differentiation started quite early (Economides, 1986), the paper by Neven and Thisse (1990) is one out of very few contributions illustrating the interplay between horizontal and vertical product differentiation.[9] The difficulties of modelling spatial and hedonic preferences are already evident in the pioneering work, and, indeed, in their main finding, whereby, depending upon some specific conditions, one can characterise two pure strategy equilibria with maximum differentiation along one dimension and minimum differentiation along the other. The properties of any other possible equilibria with intermediate differentiation along either dimension remain out of reach.

A brief recollection of the static model introduced by Neven and Thisse (1990) is useful to grasp the nature of the problem as well as its potential, still largely unexplored.

---

[9] Another relevant contribution in the same fields is that of Dos Santos Ferreira and Thisse (1996).

Two single-product firms, 1 and 2, supply the market with products which are differentiated along two dimensions, a vertical one and a horizontal one. The generic consumer
has a net surplus from consumption equal to

$$U = s + m\theta_i - p_i - \tau (x - x_i)^2 \tag{5.59}$$

where $m \in [\underline{m}, \overline{m}]$, $\underline{m} = \overline{m} - 1$ and each firm is located at $x_2 \geq x_1$, $x_i \in [0, 1]$. Qualities
are $\theta_2 \geq \theta_1$, $\theta_i \in [0, \Theta]$; note that the normalization of the minimum quality to zero
is a problem of measure only. Full market coverage is assumed (i.e., total demand is
$(\overline{\theta} - \underline{\theta}) \cdot 1 = 1$). There exists an indifferent consumer, given firms' prices, qualities and
locations, that can be identified by solving the following condition:

$$s + \tilde{m}\theta_1 - p_1 - \tau (x - x_1)^2 = s + \tilde{m}\theta_2 - p_2 - \tau (x - x_2)^2 \tag{5.60}$$

yielding:

$$\tilde{m} = \frac{p_2 - p_1 + \tau \left[x_2^2 - x_1^2 - 2x (x_2 - x_2)\right]}{\theta_2 - \theta_1} \tag{5.61}$$

which is depicted in Figure 5.1. This is the case of *vertical dominance*, in which $\tilde{m} \in$
$[\underline{m}, \overline{m}]$ and consumers in the left neighbourhood of $\overline{m}$ patronise firm 2. There are other
possible configurations where $\tilde{\theta}$ does not intersect the vertical axes on both sides. In
particular, if the indifference locus does intersect both horizontal axes (which happens
for $\tilde{m} > \overline{m}$), we are then in the case of *horizontal dominance*.

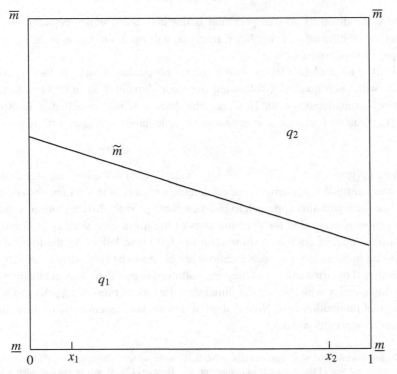

Figure 5.1 Bidimensional differentiation, vertical dominance

As a result, the market demand for product 1 at any time during the game is:

$$q_1(t) = \int_0^1 \tilde{m}dx = \frac{p_2 - p_1 + \tau(x_1 - x_2)(1 - x_1 - x_2)}{q_2 - q_1} \tag{5.62}$$

while the remaining demand, $y_2(t) = 1 - y_1(t)$, accrues to product 2. Neven and Thisse (1990) consider the case in which quality improvements impact variable costs only. An evident issue, bound to make the equilibrium analysis cumbersome, is the presence of the generic consumer's location x in the demand system, and this is the reason why the authors confine their attention to the opposite scenarios in which, respectively, (i) $x_1 = 0$ and $x_2 = 1$, and therefore also $q_1 = q_2$, and (ii) $x_1 = x_2 = 1/2$, and therefore firms fully exploit vertical differentiation to soften price competition.

Tractability problems notwithstanding, the simultaneous presence of vertical and horizontal (or spatial) differentiation is being treated in very recent applications of differential games (Brekke et al., 2010, 2012). While Brekke et al. (2010) use the bidimensional model to describe the regulated provision of health care services, Brekke et al. (2012) introduce sluggish demand dynamics à la Wirl (2010) to investigate the interplay between consumers' evolving beliefs (underlying the sluggishness of instantaneous demand), quality supply and the regulator's intervention on market price. While in the first paper quality levels are states, in the second they are controls. In both, consumer preferences are modelled as follows:

$$U(t) = s + m\theta_i(t) - p_i(t) - \tau |x_i(t) - x| \tag{5.63}$$

where the disutility of transportation is linear in the distance between consumer and firm and, for the sake of simplicity, marginal willingness to pay m is the same across the population of consumers.

In Brekke et al. (2010), the two firms are hospitals investing in the quality of health care, with each quality θ_i following the same dynamics as in (5.31) and involving a convex instantaneous cost. However, the disease is not modelled.[10] In Brekke et al. (2012), quality is chosen at every instant and demand evolves according to

$$\dot{q}_i = \hat{q}_i(\theta_i(t), \theta_j(t)) - q_i(t) \tag{5.64}$$

where $\hat{q}_i(\theta_i(t), \theta_j(t)) = 1/2 + (\theta_i(t) - \theta_j(t))/(2\tau)$ is the notional demand for firm i. Consequently, that for firm j is the complement to one, as in the Lanchester-Case model.

The issue with this approach to bidimensional product differentiation is that firms are exogenously located at the opposite ends of the linear city, with $x_1 = 0$ and $x_2 = 1$ at all times (and, of course, location costs are left unmodelled). In the light of the model exposed in Section 5.1.2, such locations are bound to be suboptimal, and they would be abandoned by firms as soon as they were allowed to move towards the median consumer, leaving entirely with the vertical dimension the task of preserving prices to fall down to marginal production cost. Note that all of this holds independently of the assumption of linear transportation costs.

---

[10] A differential game with unidimensional (vertical) differentiation describing the dynamics of health care quality and that of the disease is in Lambertini and Tampieri (2015), where price regulation can be finely tuned to ensure (1) universal access to the health system and (2) the eradication of the disease, under feedback rules.

Needless to say, this is an area demanding for more efforts to improve our understanding of firms' strategies and their policy implications. In particular, the issue of location choice should be carefully investigated in order to amend the aforementioned difficulties, which have been discussed throughout the chapter. The exogeneity of locations leaves an essential feature of any spatial model aside, as Laussel *et al.* (2004, p. 658) are well aware:

An alternative specification, linear travel cost, is also tractable, but computation would be more awkward. We conjecture that the results would be much similar. (If we were to allow firms to choose locations in the interior of the interval [0, 1], some serious problems would arise with linear travel cost; see d'Aspremont *et al.*, 1979.)

Additionally, modelling costly locations as in Bertuzzi and Lambertini (2010) and Lambertini (2012) is only a partial and not fully satisfactory remedy, since it remains true that model-specific restrictions on the admissible intervals of parameters are needed to prevent firms from triggering the price undercutting process which disrupts the pure strategy equilibrium. And this is bound to hold true irrespective of the specific controls or states complementing a spatial differentiation setting, as several other models mentioned in this chapter clearly show.

In more general terms, a resurgence of interest in the dynamic modelization of both horizontal and vertical differentiation and its interaction with other strategic variables belonging to the *panoplia* in the hands of entrepreneurs and managers is highly desirable. In the meantime, however, be aware that we will encounter again horizontal and bidimensional differentiation in Chapter 6, concerning the firms' incentives to carry out product and process innovation.

Further Reading

An exhaustive exposition of the discrete choice theory of product differentiation is in Beath and Katsoulacos (1991) and Anderson *et al.* (1997). The equilibrium analysis of spatial models with non-convex disutility of transportation is in Stahl (1982). For electoral competition models, see Ordeshook (1986, 1992). For a comprehensive illustration of network externalities, see Shy (2000). Static games of R&D for quality improvement are in Beath and Katsoulacos (1987), Dutta *et al.* (1995), Rosenkranz (1997) and Lambertini *et al.* (2002). The simultaneous arising of minimum and maximum differentiation in a multidimensional Hotelling model is illustrated in Irmen and Thisse (2001). Vertical differentiation along two dimensions (not necessarily both hedonic or desirable) is the topic tackled by Vandenbosch and Weinberg (1995), Johnson and Myatt (2003) and Garella and Lambertini (1999, 2014). Another model dealing with dynamic quality supply in presence of price regulation and semi-altruistic firms is in Siciliani *et al.* (2013).

Bibliography

Anderson, S., A. de Palma and J.-F. Thisse (1992), *Discrete Choice Theory of Product Differentiation*, Cambridge, MA, MIT Press.

Anderson, S., J. Goeree and R. Ramer (1997), "Location, Location, Location", *Journal of Economic Theory*, **77**, 102–27.

Archibald, G.C., B. Eaton and R.G. Lipsey (1986), "Address Models of Value Theory", in J. Stiglitz and G.F. Mathewson (eds), *New Developments in the Analysis of Industry Structure*, London, Macmillan.

Bass, F.M. (1969), "New Product Growth Model for Consumer Durables", *Management Science*, **15**, 215–27.

Beath, J., Y. Katsoulacos and D. Ulph (1987), "Sequential Product Innovation and Industry Evolution", *Economic Journal*, **97**, 32–43.

Beath, J. and Y. Katsoulacos (1991), *The Economic Theory of Product Differentiation*, Cambridge, Cambridge University Press.

Bertuzzi, G. and L. Lambertini (2010), "Existence of Equilibrium in a Differential Game of Spatial Competition with Advertising", *Regional Science and Urban Economics*, **40**, 155–60.

Besanko, D., S. Donnenfeld and L. White (1987), "Monopoly and Quality Distortion: Effects and Remedies", *Quarterly Journal of Economics*, **102**, 743–68.

Besanko, D., S. Donnenfeld and L. White (1988), "The Multiproduct Firm, Quality Choice, and Regulation", *Journal of Industrial Economics*, **36**, 411–29.

Bowley, A.L. (1924), *The Mathematical Groundwork of Economics*, Oxford, Oxford University Press.

Brekke, K., R. Cellini, L. Siciliani and O.R. Straume (2010), "Competition and Quality in Health Care Markets: A Differential Game Approach", *Journal of Health Economics*, **29**, 508–23.

Brekke, K., R. Cellini, L. Siciliani and O.R. Straume (2012), "Competition in Regulated Markets with Sluggish Beliefs about Quality", *Journal of Economics and Management Strategy*, **21**, 131–78.

Case, J. (1979), *Economics and the Competitive Process*, New York, New York University Press.

Champsaur, P. and J.-C. Rochet (1989), "Multiproduct Duopolists", *Econometrica*, **57**, 533–57.

Chirco, A., L. Lambertini and F. Zagonari (2003), "How Demand Affects Optimal Prices and Product Differentiation", *Papers in Regional Science*, **82**, 555–68.

Choi, J. and H. Shin (1992), "A Comment on a Model of Vertical Product Differentiation", *Journal of Industrial Economics*, **40**, 229–31.

Colombo, L. and L. Lambertini (2003), "Dynamic Advertising under Vertical Product Differentiation", *Journal of Optimization Theory and Applications*, **119**, 261–80.

Colombo, L. and L. Lambertini (2006), "A Differential Game of Advertising under Vertical Differentiation", in L. Lambertini, *The Economics of Vertically Differentiated Markets*, Cheltenham, Edward Elgar.

Conrad, K. (1985), "Quality, Advertising, and the Formation of Goodwill under Dynamic Conditions", in G. Feichtinger (ed.), *Optimal Control Theory and Economic Analysis*, vol. 2, Amsterdam, North-Holland.

Crampes, C. and A. Hollander (1995), "Duopoly and Quality Standards", *European Economic Review*, **39**, 71–82.

Cremer, H. and J.-F. Thisse (1991), "Location Models of Horizontal Differentiation: A Special Case of Vertical Differentiation Models", *Journal of Industrial Economics*, **39**, 383–90.

Dasgupta, P. and E. Maskin (1986), "The Existence of Equilibrium in Discontinuous Economic Games, II: Applications", *Review of Economic Studies*, **53**, 27–42.

d'Aspremont, C., J.J. Gabszewicz and J.-F. Thisse (1979), "On Hotelling's 'Stability in Competition'", *Econometrica*, **47**, 1045–50.

de Palma, A., V. Ginsburgh, Y. Papageorgiou and J.-F. Thisse (1985) "The Principle of Minimum Differentiation Holds under Sufficient Heterogeneity", *Econometrica*, **53**, 767–82.

Dixit, A. and J. Stiglitz (1977), "Monopolistic Competition and Optimum Product Diversity", *American Economic Review*, **67**, 297–308.

Dos Santos Ferreira, R. and J.-F. Thisse (1996), "Horizontal and Vertical Differentiation: The Launhardt Model", *International Journal of Industrial Organization*, **14**, 485–506.

Downs, A. (1957), *An Economic Theory of Democracy*, New York, Harper & Row.

Driskill, R. (2001), "Durable Goods Oligopoly", *International Journal of Industrial Organization*, **19**, 391–413.

Dutta, P.K., S. Lach and A. Rustichini (1995), "Better Late than Early: Vertical Differentiation in the Adoption of a New Technology", *Journal of Economics and Management Strategy*, **4**, 563–89.

Ecchia, G. and L. Lambertini (1997), "Minimum Quality Standards and Collusion", *Journal of Industrial Economics*, **45**, 101–14.

Economides, N. (1986), "Nash Equilibrium in Duopoly with Products Defined by Two Characteristics", *RAND Journal of Economics*, **17**, 431–39.

El Ouardighi, F., G. Feichtinger, D. Grass, R. Hartl and P. Kort (2016), "Advertising and Quality-Dependent Word of Mouth in a Contagion Sales Model", *Journal of Optimization Theory and Applications*, **170**, 323–42.

El Ouardighi, F. and F. Pasin (2006), "Quality Improvement and Goodwill Accumulation in a Dynamic Duopoly", *European Journal of Operational Research*, **175**, 1021–32.

Gabszewicz, J.J. and J.-F. Thisse (1979), "Price Competition, Quality, and Income Disparities, *Journal of Economic Theory*, **20**, 340–59.

Gabszewicz, J.J. and J.-F. Thisse (1980), "Entry (and Exit) in a Differentiated Industry", *Journal of Economic Theory*, **22**, 327–38.

Garella, P. and L. Lambertini (1999), "Good vs Bad Characteristics in Vertical Differentiation", *Economics Letters*, **65**, 245–48.

Garella, P. and L. Lambertini (2014), "Bidimensional Vertical Differentiation", *International Journal of Industrial Organization*, **32**, 1–10.

Gould, J.P. (1970), "Diffusion Processes and Optimal Advertising Policy", in E. Phelps (ed.), *Microeconomic Foundations of Employment and Inflation Theory*, New York, Norton.

Feichtinger, G., R. Hartl and S. Sethi (1994), "Dynamic Optimal Control Models in Advertising: Recent Developments", *Management Science*, **40**, 195–226.

Feichtinger, G., A. Luhmer and G. Sorger (1988), "Optimal Price and Advertising Policy for a Convenience Good Retailer", *Marketing Science*, **7**, 187–201.

Fershtman, C. (1984), "Goodwill and Market Shares in Oligopoly", *Economica*, **51**, 271–82.

Fershtman, C. and M. Kamien (1987), "Dynamic Duopolistic Competition with Sticky Prices", *Econometrica*, **55**, 1151–64.

Fershtman, C. and S. Nitzan (1991), "Dynamic Voluntary Provision of Public Goods", *European Economic Review*, **35**, 1057–67.

Helpman, E. and P. Krugman (1985), *Market Structure and Foreign Trade: Increasing Returns, Imperfect Competition, and the International Economy*, Cambridge, MA, MIT Press.

Helpman, E. and P. Krugman (1989), *Trade Policy and Market Structure*, Cambridge, MA, MIT Press.

Hinloopen, J. and C. van Marrewijk (1999), "On the Limits and Possibilities of the Principle of Minimum Differentiation", *International Journal of Industrial Organization*, **17**, 735–50.

Hotelling, H. (1929), "Stability in Competition", *Economic Journal*, **39**, 41–57.

Irmen, A. and J.-F. Thisse (1998), "Competition in Multi-Characteristics Space: Was Hotelling Almost Right?", *Journal of Economic Theory*, **78**, 76–102.

Itoh, M. (1983), "Monopoly, Product Differentiation and Economic Welfare", *Journal of Economic Theory*, **31**, 88–104.

Johnson, J.P. and D.P. Myatt (2003), "Multiproduct Quality Competition: Fighting Brands and Product Line Pruning", *American Economic Review*, **93**, 748–74.

Jørgensen, S. and G. Zaccour (2004), *Differential Games in Marketing*, Kluwer, Dordrecht.

Klemperer, P. (1995), "Competition When Consumers Have Switching Costs: An Overview with Applications to Industrial Organization, Macroeconomics, and International Trade", *Review of Economic Studies*, **62**, 515–39.

Kotowitz, Y., and F. Mathewson (1979a), "Advertising, Consumer Information, and Product Quality", *Bell Journal of Economics*, **10**, 566–88.

Kotowitz, Y., and F. Mathewson (1979b), "Informative Advertising and Welfare", *American Economic Review*, **128**, 284–94.

Lambertini, L. (1997a), "Unicity of the Equilibrium in the Unconstrained Hotelling Model", *Regional Science and Urban Economics*, **27**, 785–98.

Lambertini, L. (1997b), "Optimal Fiscal Regime in a Spatial Duopoly", *Journal of Urban Economics*, **41**, 407–20.

Lambertini, L. (2005), "Advertising in a Dynamic Spatial Monopoly", *European Journal of Operational Research*, **166**, 547–56.

Lambertini, L. (2006), "A Differential Game with Quality Improvement", in L. Lambertini, *The Economics of Vertically Differentiated Markets*, Cheltenham, Edward Elgar.

Lambertini, L. (2007), "Dynamic Spatial Monopoly with Product Development", *Spatial Economic Analysis*, **2**, 157–66.

Lambertini, L. (2009), "Capital Accumulation for Production in a Dynamic Spatial Monopoly", *Journal of Mathematical Sciences*, **161**, 226–34.

Lambertini, L. (2012), "Dynamic Hotelling Duopoly with Linear Transportation Costs", *Optimal Control, Applications and Methods*, **33**, 114–26.

Lambertini, L. and R. Orsini (2010), "R&D for Quality Improvement and Network Externalities", *Networks and Spatial Economics*, **10**, 113–24.

Lambertini, L. and A. Tampieri (2015), "Price Regulation and Health Care with Disease Dynamics", *Review of Economic Analysis*, **7**, 157–73.

Lambertini, L., S. Poddar and D. Sasaki (2002), "Research Joint Ventures, Product Differentiation and Price Collusion", *International Journal of Industrial Organization*, **20**, 829–54.

Lanchester F.W. (1956) "Mathematics in Warfare", in J.R. Newman (ed.), *The World of Mathematics*, New York, Simon and Schuster.

Laussel, D., M. de Montmarin and N.V. Long (2004), "Dynamic Duopoly with Congestion Effects", *International Journal of Industrial Organization*, **22**, 655–77.

Lehmann-Grube, U. (1997), "Strategic Choice of Quality when Quality is Costly: The Persistence of the High-Quality Advantage", *RAND Journal of Economics*, **28**, 372–84.

Leitmann, G. and W.E. Schmitendorf (1978), "Profit Maximization Through Advertising: A Nonzero Sum Differential Game Approach", *IEEE Transactions on Automatic Control*, **23**, 646–50.

Maskin, E. and J. Riley (1984), "Monopoly with Incomplete Information", *RAND Journal of Economics*, **15**, 171–96.

Motta, M. (1992), "Sunk Costs and Trade Liberalization", *Economic Journal*, **102**, 578–87.

Motta, M. (1993), "Endogenous Quality Choice: Price vs Quantity Competition", *Journal of Industrial Economics*, **41**, 113–31.

Motta, M, Thisse J.-F. and A. Cabrales (1997), "On the Persistence of Leadership or Leapfrogging in International Trade", *International Economic Review*, **38**, 809–24.

Mussa, M. and S. Rosen (1978), "Monopoly and Product Quality", *Journal of Economic Theory*, **18**, 301–17.

Nelson, P. (1974), Advertising as Information, *Journal of Political Economy*, **82**, 729–54.

Neven, D. and J.F. Thisse (1990), "Quality and Variety Competition", in J.J. Gabszewicz, J.-F. Richard and L. Wolsey (eds), *Economic Decision Making: Games, Econometrics, and Optimization. Contributions in Honour of Jacques Drèze*, Amsterdam, North-Holland.

Nerlove, M. and K.J. Arrow (1962), "Optimal Advertising Policy under Dynamic Conditions", *Economica*, **29**, 129–42.

Novshek, W. (1980), "Equilibrium in Simple Spatial (or Differentiated Product) Models", *Journal of Economic Theory*, **22**, 313–26.

Ordeshook, P. (1986), *Game Theory and Political Theory*, Cambridge, Cambridge University Press.

Ordeshook, P. (1992), *A Political Theory Primer*, London, Routledge.

Osborne, M. and C. Pitchik (1987), "Equilibrium in Hotelling's Model of Spatial Competition", *Econometrica*, **55**, 911–22.

Piga, C. (1998), "A Dynamic Model of Advertising and Product Differentiation", *Review of Industrial Organization*, **13**, 509–22.

Reynolds, S. (1987), "Capacity Investment, Preemption and Commitment in an Infinite Horizon Model", *International Economic Review*, **28**, 69–88.

Ringbeck, J. (1985), "Mixed Quality and Advertising Strategies under Asymmetric Information", in G. Feichtinger (ed.), *Optimal Control Theory and Economic Analysis*, vol. 2, Amsterdam, North-Holland.

Ronnen, U. (1991), "Minimum Quality Standards, Fixed Costs, and Competition", *RAND Journal of Economics*, **22**, 490–504.

Rosenkranz, S. (1997), "Quality Improvements and the Incentive to Leapfrog", *International Journal of Industrial Organization*, **15**, 243–61.

Schmalensee, R. (1978), "A Model of Advertising and Product Quality", *Journal of Political Economy*, **86**, 1213–25.

Scotchmer, S. (1985), "Profit-Maximizing Clubs", *Journal of Public Economics*, **27**, 25–45.

Shaked, A. (1975), "Non-Existence of Equilibrium for the Two-dimensional Three-Firms Location Problem", *Review of Economic Studies*, **42**, 51–56.

Shaked, A. (1982), "Existence and Computation of Mixed Strategy Nash Equilibrium for 3-Firms Location Problem", *Journal of Industrial Economics*, **31**, 93–96.

Shaked, A. and J. Sutton (1982), "Relaxing Price Competition through Product Differentiation", *Review of Economic Studies*, **69**, 3–13.

Shaked, A. and J. Sutton (1983), "Natural Oligopolies", *Econometrica*, **51**, 1469–83.

Shaked, A. and J. Sutton (1984), "Natural Oligopolies and International Trade", in H. Kierzkowski (ed.), *Monopolistic Competition and International Trade*, Oxford, Clarendon Press.

Shy, O. (2000), *The Economics of Networks Industries*, Cambridge, Cambridge University Press.

Siciliani, L., O.R. Straume and R. Cellini (2013),"Quality Competition with Motivated Providers", *Journal of Economic Dynamics and Control*, **37**, 2041–61.

Singh, N. and X. Vives (1984), "Price and Quantity Competition in a Differentiated Duopoly", *RAND Journal of Economics*, **15**, 546–54.

Spence, A.M. (1975), "Monopoly, Quality and Regulation", *Bell Journal of Economics*, **6**, 417–29.

Spremann, K. (1985), "The Signalling of Quality by Reputation", in G. Feichtinger (ed.), *Optimal Control Theory and Economic Analysis*, vol. 2, Amsterdam, North-Holland.

Stahl, K. (1982), "Location and Spatial Pricing Theory with Nonconvex Transportation Cost Schedules", *Bell Journal of Economics*, **13**, 575–82.

Tabuchi, T. and J.-F. Thisse (1995), "Asymmetric Equilibria in Spatial Competition", *International Journal of Industrial Organization*, **13**, 213–27.

Tirole, J. (1988), *The Theory of Industrial Organization*, Cambridge, MA, MIT Press.

Vandenbosch, M. and C. Weinberg (1995), "Product and Price Competition in a Two-Dimensional Vertical Differentiation Model", *Marketing Science*, **14**, 224–49.

Vidale, M. and H. Wolfe (1957), "An Operations Research Study of Sales Response to Advertising", *Operations Research*, **5**, 370–81.

Wirl, F. (2010), "Dynamic Demand and Noncompetitive Intertemporal Output Adjustments", *International Journal of Industrial Organization*, **28**, 220–29.

6   Innovation

This is an area in which a lot has been achieved, but also a lot is still left for future research. The reason, of course, is the dynamic nature of innovation processes, together with their manifold linkages with related disciplines in economics, like the theory of growth and, of course, environmental and resource economics (some models belonging to this field and contemplating R&D investment are reviewed in the next chapter).

The material appearing in this chapter summarises the extant debate and its evolution, in two related but inherently different subfields. In the first, attention is drawn by uncertainty affecting innovative industries, and the resulting models describe the properties of stochastic R&D races. In the second, uncertainty is commonly assumed away, and the research questions being addressed focus on the private and social convenience of cooperative vs. noncooperative R&D projects, technological spillovers and learning by doing.

Section 6.1 briefly reconstructs the difference between classical studies of R&D races with stochastic innovation dates and exogenous R&D efforts and the transformation of this literature in the form of differential games where R&D efforts are strategic instruments controlled by firms.

Section 6.2 contains an exposition on deterministic models examining either process or product innovation in isolation or the combination of both, then learning by doing and the role of technological leadership as a barrier to entry, and finally returns to race models where the race takes place in the space of innovation portfolios.

The reader will note the higher degree of homogeneity characterising the literature compacted in Section 6.1 as compared to that grouped in Section 6.2. This is the consequence of the higher degree of maturity reached by the discussion on patent races, while the debate concerning deterministic R&D appears more like a scatter diagram. This, which might sound as a negative appraisal, in fact implies the opposite. A positive interpretation is that the second literature still offers considerable room for productive research in several directions which have been intensively and extensively explored using static games.

6.1   Stochastic Innovation Races

A large stream of literature starting with Kamien and Schwartz (1972; 1976) and then taking a well-defined shape with Loury (1979), Dasgupta and Stiglitz (1980) and Lee and Wilde (1980) investigates R&D races under uncertainty. The number of contributions enriching our understanding of this matter is so high that it would be simply impossible to list all of them. For illuminating accounts of the early debate and its main achievements, see Kamien and Schwartz (1980), Tirole (1988) and Reinganum (1989), among others.

Here, it will suffice to mention that the bulk of the pioneering papers couples uncertainty with exogenous R&D efforts, with a view to characterise the relationship between industry structure and the pace of technical progress, discussing the so-called Schumpeterian hypothesis (Schumpeter, 1942) and the Arrovian objection (Arrow, 1962). Reinganum (1982a) steers in a totally new direction, in several respects.

The initial debate not only assumes exogenous instantaneous R&D efforts but also stipulates that the price to the winner of a race is independent of the date of discovery time, and therefore its present value shrinks in the date of discovery (see Lee and Wilde, 1980). Reinganum (1981a, 1982a) drops both of these assumptions, treating efforts as control variables in a proper differential game whose structure is exponential (Reinganum, 1982b) and therefore state redundant, ensuring the attainment of subgame perfection under open-loop information (see Chapter 1). Moreover, she allows for the prize to grow at a rate which coincides with the rate of time discounting. This entails that R&D efforts are solely driven by rivalry, being unaffected by changes in the prize.

The game in Reinganum (1982a) can be summarised as follows. Consider an innovation race played by n firms competing over $t \in [0, T]$ for a technological innovation, whose exact nature is immaterial.[1] It may be either a process or a product innovation which, being patentable forever, in absence of further technological breakthrough, will grant the winner a prize whose present value is W, but imperfect patent protection allows the $n - 1$ losers of the race for the first innovation to remain in the industry using either the old technology or imitating the winner. Hence, the model contemplates the case of a *non-drastic innovation*, in which the winner does not take all, so to speak.[2]

The innovation date for firm i – call it τ_i – is a random variable whose cumulative distribution is $F_i(t) = \Pr\{\tau_i \leq t\}$. Also assume innovation dates τ_i are i.i.d.. If the innovation occurs at $\tau = \min_i \tau_i$, the innovator is another firm, say, firm j, whose $\tau_j = \tau$. By the independency assumption, we have that

$$F(t) = \Pr\{\tau \leq t\} = 1 - \Pi_{i=1}^{n} [1 - F_i(t)] \tag{6.1}$$

Let $k_i(t)$ be the instantaneous R&D effort rate chosen by firm i. The associated cost of R&D activities is $C_i(t) = k_i^2(t)/2$. One last element of the model to be defined is firm i's conditional probability of innovation at date t, or, the *hazard rate*:

$$\dot{F}_i = \varphi k_i(t) [1 - F_i(t)] \tag{6.2}$$

where φ is a positive constant and $F_i(0) = 0$.

---

[1] The irrelevance of the precise nature of the innovation at stake can be easily justified by thinking that a product incorporating a new productive technology is also *different* from existing ones. Hence, as also casual observation consistently suggests, process and product innovation very often go hand in hand. On this issue, see, e.g., Futia (1980) and Spence (1984).

[2] The alternative scenario created by the race for a *drastic innovation* is in Reinganum (1981a). The properties of its open-loop solution are unaffected by the nature of the innovation.

Along with the present value of the innovation to the winner, W, there exists also a present value of an alternative technology, L, to any of the losers. Since losers may either imitate the innovation or keep using the old technology, W is strictly larger than L. The expected profit flow of firm i is then:

$$E\left(\Pi_i\right) = \int_0^T \left\{ WF_i(t) \prod_{j\neq i} [1 - F_j(t)] + L \sum_{j\neq i} \dot{F}_j(t) \prod_{m\neq j} [1 - F_j(t)] \right.$$

$$\left. - \frac{k_i^2(t)}{2e^{\rho t}} \prod_{\ell=1}^n [1 - F_\ell(t)] \right\} dt \tag{6.3}$$

To simplify exposition, one can define $\ln[1 - F_i(t)] = -\varphi x_i(t)$, so that it is possible to write the expression appearing on the r.h.s. of (6.3) as follows:

$$E\left(\Pi_i\right) = \int_0^T \exp\left\{ -\varphi \sum_{j=1}^n x_j(t) \right\} \cdot \left[\varphi W k_i(t) + \varphi L \sum_{j\neq i} k_j(t) - \frac{k_i^2(t)}{2e^{\rho t}} \right] dt \tag{6.4}$$

subject to

$$\dot{x} = k_i(t); \ x_i(0) = 0 \tag{6.5}$$

As anticipated above, the exponential structure of the present game makes it equivalent to a linear state game. Therefore, its strongly time-consistent equilibrium can indeed be characterised under open-loop rules. To this purpose, Reinganum (1982a) uses one last transformation which introduces a new state variable,

$$\eta(t) = \exp\left\{ -\alpha\varphi \sum_{j=1}^n x_j(t) \right\} \tag{6.6}$$

whereby, provided α is not identically equal to zero, one can write the Hamiltonian function of firm i as follows:

$$\mathcal{H}_i(t) = \eta^{\frac{1}{\alpha}} \cdot \left[\varphi W k_i(t) + \varphi L \sum_{j\neq i} k_j(t) - \frac{k_i^2(t)}{2e^{\rho t}} \right] - \mu_i(t)\alpha\varphi\eta(t) - \sum_{\ell=1}^n k_\ell(t) \tag{6.7}$$

in which $\mu_i(t) = \lambda_i(t) e^{-\rho t}$. From the FOC taken w.r.t. the R&D control $k_i(t)$, we obtain the open-loop (but subgame perfect) R&D strategy

$$k_i^{OL}(t) = \left[W - \alpha\lambda_i(t)\eta^{\frac{\alpha-1}{\alpha}} \right] \varphi e^{\rho t} \tag{6.8}$$

where the costate variable $\lambda_i(t)$ (which, in this case, is a proper shadow value) must satisfy, together with its adjoint equation, the terminal condition $\lambda_i(T) = 0$ (because the salvage value is nil). The expression in (6.8) illustrates that any increase in the winner's prize W induces all firms to increase their optimal efforts $k_i^{OL}(t)$ at any time during the game.

In summary, one can formulate

Proposition 6.1 *The exponential structure of the stochastic innovation race ensures subgame perfection under open-loop information. If the innovation is non-drastic, exogenously increasing the award granted to invention increases the R&D efforts of the entire industry over the whole time horizon.*

That is, if a higher reward is looming on the horizon, this stimulates the appetite of firms, which react by investing larger amounts of resources – which means, in general, bad news on the efficiency front. In this respect, some cooperative solution – either R&D cartelization or a research joint venture (RJV) – could be adopted to reduce overinvestment. This is the route taken by Reinganum (1981a). This case envisages the winner-take-all scenario, but its predictions as to the effect of cooperation are relevant in general. Indeed, Reinganum (1981a) proves that cooperating on R&D allows firms to attain a reduction in wasteful effort duplication. Of course, this has a price, as it implies that cooperative R&D delays the expected date of the technological innovation. The underlying trade-off between saving on R&D costs and innovating as soon as possible remains therefore an elusive problem.

Moreover, as a last remark on the stream of research initiated by Loury (1979), Dasgupta and Stiglitz (1980) and Lee and Wilde (1980), let me recall that one of its main objectives was to shed light upon the impact of industry structure on individual and aggregate R&D investment, in connection with the opposite positions taken by Schumpeter (1942) and Arrow (1962).[3] This has remained a focal point in the literature based on these tradition (see, e.g., Delbono and Denicolò, 1991), while it has been largely neglected in the alternative bulk of contributions using stochastic differential games on R&D races, which could instead be tuned to produce interesting and robust results in this direction, responding to the stimulus coming from the pathbreaking contribution of Aghion *et al.* (2005) about the existence of inverted U-shaped R&D curves at the industry level.

Extensions of the models in Reinganum (1981a, 1982a) – recall that in the first the innovation in sight is assumed to be drastic – have modified a few aspects. The viewpoint chosen by Choi (1991) rests on the relaxation of the usual assumption on the hazard rate. In Choi (1991), the firms involved in the race have imperfect information about the true hazard function characterising R&D activities. This more realistic assumption, however, is coupled with constant R&D efforts, as in the early literature. Malueg and Tsutsui (1997) also raise this point concerning the hazard rate, and construct their game on the basis of a distribution of priors about this key feature of the R&D race, with firms revising these priors as the game unravels, through a form of learning by doing. The model in Malueg and Tsutsui (1997), however, cannot be solved analytically.[4]

---

[3] Another extension, where the use of differential games has not taken root, deals with the analysis of industry evolution. In this regard, see Reinganum (1985), Vickers (1986) and Beath *et al.* (1987).

[4] A few words are necessary to mention another stream of literature dealing with a specific feature of the dynamics of technical progress, i.e., innovation adoption. This important aspect of the evolution of an industry has been treated using dynamic games which are not proper differential games because the state is the number or the identity of those firms that have adopted the new technology at a given time, and the model hosts no state equation. See Reinganum (1981b, 1985), Fudenberg and Tirole (1985), Katz and Shapiro (1987) and Dutta *et al.* (1995), among others. These models are illustrated in Long (2010, chapter 5).

One feature characterising the early debate on R&D incentives in stochastic innovation races is the fact that they are *memoryless*, in the sense that firms' acquired knowledge through their past efforts – irrespective of whether these are endogenous or not – exerts no impact on their current strategies. This fact hinges upon the Poisson distribution governing the innovation date in all of those models. This, in turn, prevents the treatment of history dependence, which is intuitively an important issue. To characterise history dependence, knowledge accumulation must play a role in shaping firms' R&D investment plans.

This challenge has been taken up by multistage race models, which contemplate the presence of several steps in the R&D process and therefore also the possibility for one firm to be ahead of rivals. The winner needs to carry out successfully every step to get the prize. A subset of the contributions taking this angle to look at races uses deterministic models (in which transition across stages is deterministic), whose main outcome is the so called ϵ-preemption result. This label describes situation in which the smallest technological gap induces all laggards to quit the race once and for all (see Fudenberg *et al.*, 1983; Harris and Vickers, 1985; Vickers, 1986; Lippman and McCardle, 1988; Delbono, 1989, *inter alia*). The introduction of uncertainty affecting transition mitigates this sharp conclusion, through a reformulation of the model which recovers the flavour of memoryless races, as the exponential distribution determines the completion of each step of the process. In memoryless multistage race models, the laggards invest systematically less than the leader; as a consequence, the technological gap increases monotonically throughout the race (see Grossman and Shapiro, 1987; Harris and Vickers, 1987; Lippman and McCardle, 1987).

Doraszelski (2003) builds up a differential game modelling a stochastic R&D race where the bearings of accumulated knowledge stocks on firms' strategies become evident, thereby neatly illustrating the limitations of multistage races in which the leader needs to create a technological gap as soon as possible to enjoy a quiet life thereafter and complete the project without worrying about rivals, as they have already abandoned the race.

Suppose two firms are involved in the race. Denote as $x_i(t)$ the knowledge stock possessed by firm $i = 1, 2$ at time t. This stock accumulates according to

$$\dot{x}_i = k_i(t) - \delta x_i(t) \tag{6.9}$$

The same firm's hazard rate is $h_i(t) = \varpi k_i(t) + \varrho x_i^\alpha(t)$, with parameters $\varpi, \varrho \geq 0$ and $\alpha > 0$. Depending on the value of ϱ, $h_i(t)$ can be concave, linear or convex in $x_i(t)$. If $\varrho = 0$, Doraszelski's (2003) model reproduces Reinganum's (1981a, 1982a) as a special case. For any $\varrho > 0$, the model features instead learning by doing and therefore also history dependence.

As in the previous setting, the winner receives a patent whose total value is embodied in the prize W, while losers receive $L \in [0, W)$, the lower bound being relevant only under perfect patent protection. The instantaneous cost of investing is $C_i(k_i(t)) = bk_i^{1/b}(t)$, where b is positive and lower than one; $1/b$ measures the elasticity of the cost function to the effort produced by firm i. The HJB equation of firm i is

$$\rho V_i \left(x_i \left(t \right), x_j \left(t \right) \right) = \max_{k_i(t)} \left\{ h_i \left(t \right) \left[W - V_i \left(\cdot \right) \right] + h_j \left(t \right) \left[L - V_j \left(\cdot \right) \right] \right. \tag{6.10}$$

$$\left. - C_i \left(k_i \left(t \right) \right) + V_i' \left(\cdot \right) \left[k_i \left(t \right) - \delta x_i \left(t \right) \right] + V_j' \left(\cdot \right) \left[k_j \left(t \right) - \delta x_j \left(t \right) \right] \right]$$

Since $b \in (0, 1)$, the FOC suffices to identify the interior equilibrium, where the feedback R&D control is

$$k_i^{LF} = \left[\varpi \left(W - V_i \left(\cdot \right) \right) + V_i' \left(\cdot \right) \right]^{\frac{b}{1-b}} \tag{6.11}$$

The game cannot be solved analytically, and Doraszelski (2003) resorts to collocation techniques (Judd, 1992, 1998) to perform computational analysis. However, the core of the model is entirely captured by (6.11), which reveals the following properties of the feedback strategy:

Proposition 6.2 k_i^{LF} *is increasing in* W, ω *and* $V_i' \left(\cdot \right)$.

The first property has already emerged in memoryless models. The fact that k_i^{LF} reacts positively to an increase in ω means that the difference $W - V_i \left(\cdot \right)$ also matters. More important is the third factor, whereby the R&D incentive is augmented by any increase in the slope of the value function of firm i w.r.t. its own knowledge stock $x_i \left(t \right)$, showing that learning over time matters, and therefore that the development and outcome of this race are indeed history dependent.

6.2   Deterministic R&D Games

This section offers a selective survey of a variety of innovation games sharing the property of featuring no stochastic component. All models are proper differential games investigating open-loop equilibria and, sometimes, closed-loop or feedback ones as well.

6.2.1   Process Innovation

This section relies on Cellini and Lambertini (2005, 2009) and Smrkolj and Wagener (2016).[5] These contributions revisit the relevant debate about the role of spillovers and the possibility for firms to adopt a cooperative stance as far as investments in process innovation are concerned.

The theoretical debate was spurred by the adoption of the National Research Cooperation Act in the United States in 1984. After Katz (1986), a number of static multistage models flourished, all of them investigating the efficiency properties of either R&D cartels or research joint ventures (RJVs) in settings envisaging R&D projects aimed at

---

[5] Cellini and Lambertini (2005) solve the oligopoly game with n firms to find the Arrovian result whereby aggregate R&D is increasing in the number of firms. The same structure, rewritten to accomodate Bertrand competition in differentiated products, is used in Cellini and Lambertini (2011).

reducing marginal production costs, mainly accompanied by Cournot competition at the market stage (see d'Aspremont and Jacquemin, 1988; Katz and Ordover, 1990; Kamien et al., 1992; Suzumura, 1992; Amir, 2000, among many others).

For illustrative purposes, let me focus upon the duopolistic differential game in Cellini and Lambertini (2009). Firms are Cournot agents interacting over an infinite horizon and selling a homogeneous good whose demand function is $p(t) = a - q_i(t) - q_j(t)$ at all times. Firms' marginal costs are constant w.r.t to the scale of production but vary over time, obeying the following state equation,[6]

$$\dot{c}_i = c_i(t)\left[-k_i(t) - \beta k_j(t) + \delta\right] \tag{6.12}$$

in which $k_i(t)$ is the instantaneous R&D effort of firm i, while parameter $\beta \in [0, 1]$ measures the technological spillover received from the R&D activity of its rival. The cost function associated with the R&D division of firm i is $C_i(k_i(t)) = bk_i^2(t)$.

The Fully Noncooperative Game

Suppose firms don't cooperate at all. The instantaneous profit function of firm i is therefore $\pi_i(t) = \left[p(t) - c_i(t)\right]q_i(t) - bk_i^2(t)$, and the Hamiltonian function is

$$\mathcal{H}_i(t) = e^{-\rho t}\Big\{\left[a - q_i(t) - q_j(t) - c_i(t)\right]q_i(t) - b\left[k_i(t)\right]^2 \tag{6.13}$$

$$- \lambda_{ii}(t)c_i(t)\left[k_i(t) + \beta k_j(t) - \delta\right] - \lambda_{ij}(t)c_j(t)\left[k_j(t) + \beta k_\ell(t) - \delta\right]\Big\}$$

The relevant FOCs on controls are:

$$\frac{\partial \mathcal{H}_i(\cdot)}{\partial q_i(t)} = a - 2q_i(t) - q_j(t) - c_i(t) = 0 \tag{6.14}$$

$$\frac{\partial \mathcal{H}_i(\cdot)}{\partial k_i(t)} = -2bk_i(t) - \lambda_{ii}(t)c_i(t) - \beta\lambda_{ij}(t)c_j(t) = 0 \tag{6.15}$$

while the costate equations are:

$$\dot{\lambda}_{ii} = \rho\lambda_{ii}(t) - \frac{\partial \mathcal{H}_i(\cdot)}{\partial c_i(t)} \tag{6.16}$$

$$\dot{\lambda}_{ij} = \rho\lambda_{ij}(t) - \frac{\partial \mathcal{H}_i(\cdot)}{\partial c_j(t)} \tag{6.17}$$

The costate equation (6.17) is a differential equation in separable variables and admits the solution $\lambda_{ij}(t) = 0$ at any time t. Moreover, the FOC () looks quasi-static. These two elements induce Cellini and Lambertini (2005, 2009) to focus on the open-loop solution, considered as subgame perfect. By doing so, they overlook the fact, correctly noted instead by Smrkolj and Wagener (2016), that the instantaneous Cournot–Nash solution is identified by an output level equal to $q_i^{CN}(t) = \left[a - 2c_i(t) + c_j(t)\right]/3$,

---

[6] This is also used in a monopoly model (which requires dropping indeces and setting $\beta = 0$) by Hinloopen et al. (2013), who admit the possibility that the initial marginal cost exceeds the choke price a. This enables these authors to investigate process innovation for products which may or may not be marketable.

showing that state-control loops do matter, and therefore one should solve the related HJB equations. This is a subject for future research, as the subject matter is so relevant in terms of its policy implications that the characterization of feedback strategies is extremely desirable. In any case, a few interesting implications can be drawn from the open-loop game as well.

Taking this route, FOC (6.15) on the R&D control yields (dropping the time argument)

$$k_i^N = -\frac{\lambda_{ii} c_i}{2b} \tag{6.18}$$

and the resulting control equation is

$$\dot{k}_i = -\frac{1}{2b}\left(c_i \dot{\lambda}_{ii} + \lambda_{ii}\dot{c}_i\right)$$

whose final form under full symmetry is

$$\dot{k} = \rho k - \frac{c(a-c)}{6b} \tag{6.19}$$

The above control equation, together with the state equation also rewritten under symmetry,

$$\dot{c} = c\left[-k(1+\beta)+\delta\right] \tag{6.20}$$

forms the state-control system of this game under open-loop information. It stationary points – excluding the pair $(0,0)$, which is clearly unstable for the presence of the decay rate δ, and the larger root of (6.20) – are identified by the following coordinates:

$$k^{OL} = \frac{\delta}{1+\beta}$$
$$c^{OL} = \frac{a(1+\beta)-\sqrt{(1+\beta)\left[a^2(1+\beta)-24b\delta\rho\right]}}{2(1+\beta)} \tag{6.21}$$

provided that $a^2 > 24b\delta\rho/(1+\beta)$.

R&D Cartel

Here it is assumed that firms build up an R&D cartel. Hence, the related controls and states are symmetric from the outset, with $k_1(t) = k_2(t) = k(t)$ and $c_1(t) = c_2(t) = c(t)$ at $t = 0$, while firms still choose output levels noncooperatively. The single state equation is

$$\dot{c} = c(t)\left[-(1+\beta)k(t)+\delta\right] \tag{6.22}$$

and the Hamiltonian function of firm i is

$$\mathcal{H}_i(t) = e^{-\rho t}\Big\{\left[a - q_i(t) - q_j(t) - c(t)\right]q_i(t)$$
$$-bk^2(t) + \lambda_i(t)c(t)\left[-(1+\beta)k(t)+\delta\right]\Big\} \tag{6.23}$$

The solution of the cartel game (indeed, it remains a *game* because quantity competition accompanies R&D cooperation) yields the following kinematic equation for the R&D control:[7]

$$\dot{k} = \rho k - \frac{c(a-c)(1+\beta)}{6b} \tag{6.24}$$

The above expression can be compared with (6.19) to verify that, all else equal, the performance of the R&D cartel is enhanced by virtue of the internalisation of the spillover effect, which is a typical feature of R&D cooperation. The ultimate consequence of this property is that the (stable) steady state marginal cost reached under the cartelised R&D activity is

$$c^{\mathcal{C}} = \frac{a(1+\beta) - \sqrt{a^2(1+\beta)^2 - 24b\delta\rho}}{2(1+\beta)} \tag{6.25}$$

which is lower than the corresponding level appearing in (6.21), reached at the equilibrium of the fully noncooperative game. Also note that the steady state individual R&D investment is exactly the same as in (6.21), because at the steady state the effort must only account for decay and spillover parameters.

The comparison of firms' profits and consumer surplus across regimes reveals that, in the parameter range in which both R&D arrangements are admissible and yield the internal equilibria outlined above, R&D cooperation is both privately and socially preferable to independent ventures for all levels of the technological spillover parameter β.

Some additional considerations are necessary to fully grasp the analogies and differences from this setup and the static two-stage game in d'Aspremont and Jacquemin (1988). First, the limit levels of states and controls for $\rho \to 0$ do not coincide with those emerging at the subgame perfect equilibrium of the static model. Second, firms always invest more and, as a result, reach a lower marginal production cost under cartelization than under independent venture. That is, no cutoff level of β emerges in the differential game, unlike what happens in the static game, where the relative magnitudes of these variables, as well as social welfare, changes depending on β being higher or lower than one. Hence, the third property to be stressed is that in the differential game there is no conflict between social and private incentives towards R&D cooperation. The fourth is, however, that R&D cooperation does not appear to be a solution to the problem of effort duplication, i.e., the cost-saving instrument invoked by the advocates of cooperative arrangements – although indeed it appears that cooperative R&D improves welfare.

All of this, *a fortiori*, prompts for the solution of the feedback game, which in this case is complicated by the fact that the state equation, be that (6.12) or (6.22), is not linear, and therefore the game, as it stands, is not defined in a linear quadratic form.

In the meantime, however, a very interesting advancement in this direction has emerged thanks to Kobayashi (2015), where the layout of the model differs from the above one in two equally important respects. The first is that the current level of marginal cost is $c_i(t) = c_0 - \alpha x_i(t)$, where α is a positive parameter and $x_i(t)$ is firm

---

[7] It is worth stressing that also in this case feedback controls via the HJB equations should be derived.

i's stock of knowledge, which is the relevant state variable in this model. The second is that the state equation is linear:

$$\dot{x}_i = k_i(t) + \beta k_j(t) + \delta x_i(t) \tag{6.26}$$

The remaining features of the model are the same as in Cellini and Lambertini (2005, 2008), with a linear demand for a homogeneous good sold under Cournot competition, and instantaneous costs $C_i(k_i(t)) = bk_i^2(t)$. Kobayashi solves the game under both open-loop and feedback information. At the steady state of the open-loop game, the equilibrium expressions of state and control are, respectively,

$$x^{OL} = \frac{4\alpha(1+\beta)(2-\beta)(a-c_0)}{9b\delta(\delta+\rho) - 4\alpha^2(1+\beta)(2-\beta)} \tag{6.27}$$

$$k^{OL} = \frac{4\alpha\delta(2-\beta)(a-c_0)}{9b\delta(\delta+\rho) - 4\alpha^2(1+\beta)(2-\beta)} \tag{6.28}$$

and therefore marginal cost is $c^{OL} = c_0 - \alpha x^{OL}$.

Then, the solution generated by the R&D cartel is

$$x^C = \frac{4\alpha(1+\beta)^2(a-c_0)}{9b\delta(\delta+\rho) - 4\alpha^2(1+\beta)^2} \tag{6.29}$$

$$k^C = \frac{4\alpha\delta(1+\beta)(a-c_0)}{9b\delta(\delta+\rho) - 4\alpha^2(1+\beta)^2} \tag{6.30}$$

and it is immediate to verify that $k^{OL} \gtreqless k^C$ for all $\beta \lesseqgtr 1/2$, as in the original d'Aspremont and Jacquemin (1988). Moreover, if $\rho \to 0$ and $\alpha = 1$, the steady state of this open-loop game coincides with the subgame perfect equilibrium in d'Aspremont and Jacquemin (1988). Once again (cf. Chapter 3), we have an open-loop equilibrium whose limit reproduces the outcome of the corresponding static model. However, in my view, the most interesting interpretation of Kobayashi's (2015) result can be spelled out as follows:

Proposition 6.3 *The subgame perfect equilibrium of the static game with Cournot competition and process R&D with spillovers is the limit for $\rho \to \infty$ of the steady state of a differential game where, all else equal, the reduction of marginal production costs is determined by the accumulated stock of technological knowledge.*

As expected, solving the game under feedback rules yields optimal R&D efforts in excess of the open-loop ones, demonstrating once again (1) the amplifying effect of feedback information on firms' perception of strategic interplay and (2) the lack of correspondence between subgame perfect outcomes in static and dynamic games apparently based on the same elements.

Moreover, the interpretation of the nature of technical progress formalised in Kobayashi (2015), by the very fact that it relies on accumulated knowledge, is suggestive of yet another form of learning by doing. We will see more about this phenomenon in the remainder, where it is explicitly evoked.

On the Role of Completion Dates in RJVs

The foregoing models compare fully noncooperative solutions to R&D *cartels*, but disregard the concrete possibility for firms to form RJVs to reduce the individual cost of a given innovation. This organizational design is quite common in the real world, especially when it comes to extremely costly projects as those concerning the design of, e.g., large civil aircraft. Indeed, the two largest industrial groups in this sector – Airbus Group (formerly EADS) and BMD (Boeing McDonnell Douglas) – are the outcomes of a gigantic R&D consortium (Airbus) and two horizontal mergers (first between McDonnell and Douglas and then between MD and Boeing).

This issue is examined by Navas and Kort (2007), where n Cournot firms sell a homogeneous good and join an RJV for a process innovation. The common state variable is the residual knowledge to be acquired, $\chi(t)$, which follows

$$\dot{\chi} = -\sum_{i=1}^{n} k_i(t) \tag{6.31}$$

where depreciation is ruled out. Each member of the RJV bears an instantaneous cost function $C_i(t) = k_i(t)[h + bk_i(t)]$ for its own research effort, with parameters $b, h > 0$, and the demand function is $p(t) = a - \sum_{i=1}^{n} q_i(t)$.

The RJV elapses at time T. At that date, $\chi(T) = 0$, the project is completed and marginal production cost drops from $\bar{c}$ to $\underline{c} < \bar{c}$ for each firm alike. For each of them, the discounted gain from innovation, gross of the individual R&D cost, is measured by

$$\Delta\Pi^{CN} = \frac{1}{\rho}\left[\frac{(a - \underline{c})^2}{(n+1)^2} - \frac{(a - \bar{c})^2}{(n+1)^2}\right] \tag{6.32}$$

if Cournot–Nash behaviour prevails on the market. If instead firms join an industry-wide cartel, the discounted gain is

$$\Delta\Pi^{C} = \frac{1}{\rho}\left[\frac{(a - \underline{c})^2}{4n} - \frac{(a - \bar{c})^2}{4n}\right] \tag{6.33}$$

In line with Kamien *et al.* (1992), Navas and Kort (2007) consider two different regimes:

- RJV competition, under which firms share the outcome of the RJV *but* choose efforts $k_i(t)$ noncooperatively, to maximise individual profits;
- RJV cartelization, which means that firms share the outcome of the RJV *and* choose efforts $k_i(t)$ cooperatively, to maximise collective profits.

Both scenarios are solved under feedback information. In the first case, the relevant problem for firm i is

$$V_i^{comp}(\chi(0)) = \max_{k_i(t)}\left\{-\int_0^T e^{-\rho t}k_i(t)[h + bk_i(t)]\,dt + \Delta\Pi^I e^{-\rho T}\right\} \tag{6.34}$$

while in the second they have to choose the n investment strategies solving the following problem:

$$V_i^{cart}(\chi(0)) = \max_{k_1(t)...k_n(t)} \left\{ -\int_0^T e^{-\rho t} \sum_{i=1}^n k_i(t)[h + bk_i(t)]dt + n\Delta\Pi^I e^{-\rho T} \right\} \quad (6.35)$$

In both cases, $I = CN, C$.

Navas and Kort (2007) solve three cases, i.e., (1) the fully cooperative game in which firms adopt cartel behaviour in both phases, $(cartC)$; (2) the 'hybrid' game in which RJV cartelization is followed by Cournot–Nash behaviour, $(cartCN)$; (3) and the fully noncooperative game, $(compCN)$. They leave aside the admittedly unrealistic case $(compC)$, with firms forming a cartel in output levels after RJV competition.[8] The manifold findings produced by this setup can be summarised as follows.

Define as $\overline{\chi}_\ell$, with $\ell = cartC, cartCN, compC$, the highest level of χ for which the RJV is profitable in each of the three scenarios. Accordingly, we know that the optimal R&D effort under feedback information will be

$$k_\ell^F > 0 \text{ for all } \chi < \overline{\chi}_\ell \quad (6.36)$$

and nil otherwise. The equilibrium levels of state and controls imply the following:

Proposition 6.4 *For any number of firms involved in the RJV,*

$$\overline{\chi}_{cartC} > \overline{\chi}_{cartCN} > \overline{\chi}_{compCN}$$

and therefore also

$$k_{cartC}^F(\overline{\chi}_{cartC}) > k_{cartCN}^F(\overline{\chi}_{cartCN}) > k_{compCN}^F(\overline{\chi}_{compCN})$$

This means that increasing the extent of cooperation expands the set of feasible projects by increasing the maximum amount of accumulated knowledge to which the RJV may aspire. This clearly reflects the fruitful bearings of cooperating inside the project by sharing information across members. Moreover, the second chain of inequalities in the above proposition has another relevant implication. Let $\tilde{\chi}_\ell < \overline{\chi}_\ell$ be the amount of pending work (i.e., the portion of the R&D project still to be performed) in scenario ℓ. Then, the following holds:

Corollary 6.5 *For any number of firms involved in the RJV,*

$$k_{cartC}^F(\tilde{\chi}_{cartC}) > k_{cartCN}^F(\tilde{\chi}_{cartCN}) > k_{compCN}^F(\tilde{\chi}_{compCN})$$

This amounts to saying that full cooperation also intensifies the effort on the part of each member of the RJV to bring the project to completion. Put differently, under cooperation, firms hasten to complete the project. This property derives from the fact that

$$\frac{\partial k_\ell^F}{\partial t} > 0; \quad \frac{\partial^2 k_\ell^F}{\partial t^2} > 0 \quad (6.37)$$

implying that the optimal instantaneous k_ℓ^F is increasing and convex w.r.t. time in all regimes.[9] This produces a synergy with the stimulus produced by cooperation in any phase.

---

[8] This case would also justly attract the attention of the antitrust agency, and represents exactly the opposite of what legislators have in mind when they design laws promoting R&D cooperation.

[9] In this model, firms hasten to complete the R&D project, with the highest efforts being observed at the last intants. Much the same as it happens when writing a book, I would say.

These findings, in turn, have another essential implication which sheds light on the endogenous effects which the organizational design of R&D may exert on the completion date. This is the subject of the following

Proposition 6.6 *For any $\overline{\chi}_\ell$ and any $\chi(0)$,*

$$T_{cartC}\left(\overline{\chi}_{cartC}\right) < T_{cartCN}\left(\overline{\chi}_{cartCN}\right) > T_{compCN}\left(\overline{\chi}_{compCN}\right)$$

and

$$T_{cartC}\left(\chi(0)\right) < T_{cartCN}\left(\chi(0)\right) > T_{compCN}\left(\chi(0)\right)$$

In words, this result tells that (1) the higher is the maximum amount of attainable knowledge, the sooner the RJV is brought to completion and (2) for any anticipated total R&D improvement, increasing cooperation among firms at all stages reduces the terminal time.

Navas and Kort (2007) complement the main body of their analysis by examining other issues which have received attention in the IO literature in this area. They show that the optimal size of the RJV, i.e., the number of its members, increases from 2 to plus infinity switching from *compCN* to *cartC*. Moreover, they single out the beneficial effects of product differentiation in shortening the completion time and expanding the range of feasible R&D programmes.

6.2.2 Product Innovation

Now we may turn to product innovation, or, more precisely, to firms' investment in product differentiation. This problem is analysed by Cellini and Lambertini (2002, 2004) using the demand structure of Singh and Vives (1984) under quantity-setting behaviour.

Consider a market where n single-product firms sell differentiated varieties of the same product over $t \in [0, \infty)$. The individual demand function is

$$p_i(t) = a - q_i(t) - \gamma(t) \sum_{j \neq i} q_j(t) \tag{6.38}$$

where substitutability $\gamma(t) \in [0, 1]$ changes over time according to the following differential equation:

$$\dot{\gamma} = -\frac{K(t)\gamma(t)}{1 + K(t)} = -\frac{\left[k_i(t) + \sum_{j \neq i} k_j(t)\right] \gamma(t)}{1 + k_i(t) + \sum_{j \neq i} k_j(t)} \tag{6.39}$$

which describes a situation where product differentiation is a sort of public good, as its beneficial effects spill over to the whole population of firms, irrespective of the relative intensity of their individual R&D efforts $k_i(t)$, whose outcome is known to all players via the demand function. Differentiation does not depreciate (i.e., consumers are not 'forgetful') and decreases monotonically as time goes by, if at least one firm does invest a positive amount of resources in this activity.

The production of the final good takes place at constant returns to scale, and the marginal cost of all firms is set to zero for simplicity. Moreover, since (6.39) features decreasing returns to R&D efforts, the cost of the R&D division is linear in the effort, $C_i(t) = k_i(t)$, so that instantaneous profits are $\pi_i(t) = p_i(t)q_i(t) - k_i(t)$. As usual, the discount rate is the same for all firms, and constant. Each firm controls two variables, $q_i(t)$ and $k_i(t)$.

The form of the state dynamics in (6.39) does not allow for the characterisation of feedback strategies.[10] Cellini and Lambertini (2002) solve the fully noncooperative game and that where firms cooperate in product innovation, under open-loop rules. The closed-loop memoryless game is in Cellini and Lambertini (2004).

Noncooperative R&D

If firms choose both controls noncooperatively, the relevant Hamiltonian function for the individual firm is

$$\mathcal{H}_i(t) = e^{-\rho t}\left\{\left[a - q_i(t) - \gamma(t)\sum_{j\neq i}q_j(t)\right]q_i(t) - k_i(t)\right.$$

$$\left. -\lambda_i(t)\gamma(t)\left[\frac{k_i(t) + \sum_{j\neq i}k_j(t)}{1 + k_i(t) + \sum_{j\neq i}k_j(t)}\right]\right\}$$
(6.40)

Omitting overlong calculations, it suffices to note that (1) the individual equilibrium output is the same as in the static game,

$$q(t) = \frac{a}{2 + (n-1)\gamma(t)}$$
(6.41)

except for the presence of the time argument characterising the state variable, and (2) the dynamics of individual R&D is

$$\dot{k} = \frac{\rho[1 + nk(t)]^2 - \gamma s(t)(n-1)q^2(t)}{2\gamma(t)n(1 + nk(t))}$$
(6.42)

Noting that the denominator of the expression on the r.h.s. of () is positive for all $\gamma(t) \in (0, 1]$, and using (6.41), we see that

$$\dot{k} > 0 \text{ for all } k(t) > \frac{1}{n}\left[\frac{a\sqrt{(n-1)\gamma(t)}}{[2 + (n-1)\gamma(t)]\sqrt{\rho}} - 1\right]$$
(6.43)

The resulting phase diagram in the positive quadrant of the space $\{\gamma, k\}$ appears in Figure 6.1, where locus $\dot{k} = 0$ (labelled as k^{OL}) is a concave curve. The graph portrays a scenario in which the constellation of parameters ensure the existence of an internal steady state solution, which, if it exists, is identified by the following expression:

$$\gamma^{OL} = \frac{a^2 - 4\rho - A\sqrt{A^2 - 8\rho}}{2(n-1)\rho}$$
(6.44)

The R&D Cartel

If instead Cournot competition goes along with an R&D cartel, $k_i(t) = k(t)$ for all $i = 1, 2, ...n$, and firm i chooses $q_i(t)$ and $k(t)$ to maximise the discounted profit flow

---

[10] Observe that the product $p_i(t)q_i(t)$ defining revenues contains the product $\gamma(t)\sum_{i\neq j}q_j(t)$ appearing in the inverse demand function. Hence, even adopting a linear version of (6.39), the game would not take a linear quadratic form.

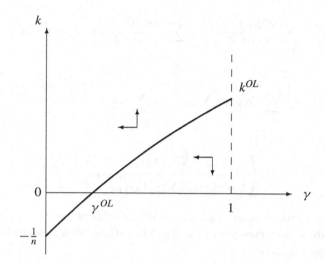

Figure 6.1 Phase diagram in the space (σ, k) under open-loop rules

$$\Pi_i = \int_0^\infty \left\{ q_i(t) \left[a - q_i(t) - \gamma(t) \sum_{j \neq i} q_j(t) \right] - k(t) \right\} e^{-\rho t} dt \qquad (6.45)$$

subject to the state equation

$$\dot{\gamma} = -\frac{nk(t)\gamma(t)}{1 + nk(t)} \qquad (6.46)$$

The resulting candidate steady state level of product substitutability (if admissible) is

$$\gamma^C = \frac{na^2 - 4\rho - a\sqrt{n(nA^2 - 8\rho)}}{2(n-1)\rho} \qquad (6.47)$$

and, comparing γ^{OL} and γ^C in the parameter region where both are real and acceptable, one finds $\gamma^C < \gamma^{OL}$. This reveals that the steady state level of product differentiation is higher under the R&D cartel than under strictly noncooperative behaviour. Now note that γ^{OL} and γ^C obtain by solving $k^{OL} = 0$ or $k^C = 0$ (because of the definition of the state equation), and therefore in steady state individual and aggregate R&D efforts are necessarily nil in both regimes. Hence, the inequality $\gamma^C < \gamma^{OL}$ is necessarily the outcome of the paths followed by firms on the way to the steady state points. That is, this is yet another game in which cooperation does not deliver a cost reduction:

Proposition 6.7 *By internalising the externality exerted by product differentiation via the demand functions, firms involved in an R&D cartel invest globally more than they would do along the equilibrium path of a fully noncooperative game (except on doomsday).*

The Close-Loop Memoryless Game
State-control loops are inserted into the adjoint equations of the fully noncooperative game in Cellini and Lambertini (2004):

$$\dot{\lambda}_i = -\frac{\partial \mathcal{H}_i(t)}{\partial \gamma(t)} - \sum_{j \neq i} \frac{\partial \mathcal{H}_i(t)}{\partial q_j(t)} \frac{\partial q_j^*(t)}{\partial \gamma(t)} - \sum_{j \neq i} \frac{\partial \mathcal{H}_i(t)}{\partial k_j(t)} \frac{\partial k_j^*(t)}{\partial \gamma(t)} + \rho \lambda_i(t) \Rightarrow \quad (6.48)$$

$$\dot{\lambda}_i = q_i(t) \sum_{j \neq i} q_j(t) - \left[\sum_{j \neq i} \gamma(t) q_j(t) \sum_{\ell \neq j} \frac{q_\ell(t)}{2} + \sum_{j \neq i} \frac{\lambda_i(t)\sqrt{\lambda_i(t)\gamma(t)}}{2\left[1 + k_i(t) + \sum_{j \neq i} k_j(t)\right]^2} \right]$$

$$+ \lambda_i(t) \left(\frac{k_i(t) + \sum_{j \neq i} k_j(t)}{1 + \left[k_i(t) + \sum_{j \neq i} k_j(t)\right]} + \rho \right)$$

Adopting the usual procedure to characterise the dynamics of the R&D control, one finds that the steady state expression of the R&D investment under closed-loop rules k^{CL} is nil in correspondence of

$$\gamma_{\pm}^{CL} = \frac{a\left[a - 2(2\rho + n - 1) \pm \sqrt{a^2 - 8(2\rho + n - 1)}\right]}{(n - 1)(a^2 + 2\rho + n - 1)} \quad (6.49)$$

This generates two cases. The first, in which only the smaller solution belongs to the unit interval, produces a phase diagram analogous to Figure 6.1. In the second case, both γ_-^{CL} and γ_+^{CL} belong to the unit interval, with slight modifications to the phase diagram. In both cases, however, the dynamic properties of the resulting state-control system closely replicate those of the open-loop solution. In particular, the stability analysis shows that only γ_-^{CL} is stable in the saddle point sense.

The main conclusion is that the Arrovian flavour of the model is more than confirmed under closed-loop information. Additionally, for obvious reasons, one discovers that $\gamma^{OL} > \gamma_-^{CL}$ in the parameter range where both magnitudes are correctly defined.

6.2.3   Process and Product Innovation

Intuitively, the separate analysis of product and process innovation is a choice dictated by the necessity of keeping models tractable. This is not true not only of dynamic models but also of static ones, judging from the scant number of contributions dealing with the simultaneous presence of both types of innovation. A few treat this issue in monopoly settings (see Athey and Schmutzler, 1995; Lambertini, 2003; Mantovani, 2006), others in oligopoly games (Bonanno and Haworth 1998; Lin and Saggi 2002; Rosenkranz, 2003). Be that as it may, it is obvious that, more often than one would think, process and product R&D coexist. In many cases, they do simply because a new product incorporates a new technology with its own marginal cost (think of laser discs and DVD or CD players). All of this is also strongly related to the extant theory on product life cycle (Abernathy and Utterback, 1975, 1982; Klepper, 1996; Adner and Levinthal, 2001).

A few applications of optimal control and differential game theory in this area have recently emerged. What follows is a summary of the models in Lambertini and Mantovani (2009, 2010) and Chenavaz (2012).

In particular, Lambertini and Mantovani (2009) and Chenavaz (2012) deal with monopoly (optimal control) models where cost reductions are accompanied by either product differentiation or proliferation (Lambertini and Mantovani, 2009) or quality improvements (Chenavaz, 2012). Both papers contain a close inspection of the arising of either complementarity or substitutability between the two R&D dimensions.

This exercise can be quickly carried out through a linear quadratic version of the model considered by Chevanaz (2012). Examine a monopolistic industry in which the market demand function for the single good supplied by the firm is

$$Q(t) = a - p(t) + v\theta(t) \tag{6.50}$$

where $\theta(t)$ is product quality and v is a positive parameter. The firm's marginal cost $c(t)$ follows

$$\dot{c} = -k(t) + \delta c(t) \tag{6.51}$$

while the dynamics of quality is

$$\dot{\theta} = y(t) - \eta\theta(t) \tag{6.52}$$

and the overall instantaneous costs associated with the R&D portfolio is $C(t) = bk^2(t) + hy^2(t)$, with parameters $b, h > 0$ admitting asymmetric marginal innovation costs in the two directions. The firm has three controls (market price and the two R&D efforts) and faces two states (marginal production cost and product quality). Its current value Hamiltonian function is

$$\mathcal{H}(t) = e^{-\rho t}\left\{\left[p(t) - c(t)\right]Q(t) - C(t) + \lambda_c\dot{c} + \lambda_\theta\dot{\theta}\right\} \tag{6.53}$$

From the necessary conditions, one finds that the optimal price is $p^*(t) = [a + c(t) + v\theta(t)]/2$, which is increasing in marginal cost and quality, while output $Q^*(t) = [a - c(t) + v\theta(t)]/2$ is decreasing in marginal cost and increasing in quality. Consequently, whether the monopolist considers the two R&D instruments as complements or substitutes is not clear, *a priori*.

Manipulating the set of necessary conditions, we obtain the following pair of control equations:

$$\dot{k} = -\frac{a - c(t) + v\theta(t) + 4b(\delta - \rho)k(t)}{4b} \tag{6.54}$$

$$\dot{y} = -\frac{[a - c(t) + v\theta(t)]v - 4h(\eta + \rho)y(t)}{4h} \tag{6.55}$$

Now, considering that we can think of marginal cost and quality as $c(k(t))$ and $\theta(y(t))$, the above expressions imply

$$\frac{\partial\dot{k}}{\partial y(t)} = -\frac{v}{4b}\cdot\frac{\partial\theta(y(t))}{\partial y(t)} \tag{6.56}$$

and

$$\frac{\partial\dot{y}}{\partial k(t)} = \frac{v}{4h}\cdot\frac{\partial c(k(t))}{\partial k(t)} \tag{6.57}$$

both of which are negative whenever each R&D effort exceeds the depreciation of its respective state variable. The partial derivatives in (6.56–6.57) indicate that one should expect an increase in the R&D intensity in one direction to induce a decrease in the other, as long as R&D makes up for decay in both dimensions.

Another way of looking at the cross effects taking place inside the research portfolio of the firm requires using the so-called time elimination method. This consists in observing that

$$\frac{\dot{k}}{\dot{y}} = \frac{dk\,(t)}{dt} \cdot \frac{dt}{dy\,(t)} = \frac{dk\,(t)}{dy\,(t)} \tag{6.58}$$

which, using (6.54–6.55), produces

$$\frac{dk\,(t)}{dy\,(t)} = \frac{h\,[a - c + v\theta\,(t) + 4b\,(\delta - \rho)\,k]}{b\,[[a - c\,(t) + v\theta\,(t)]\,v - 4h\,(\eta + \rho)\,y\,(t)]} \tag{6.59}$$

which can take either sign and proves

Proposition 6.8 *At an arbitrary instant, R&D efforts for cost reduction and quality improvement can be either complements (if $\dot{k}$ and $\dot{y}$ have the same sign) or substitutes (if $\dot{k}$ and $\dot{y}$ have opposite signs).*

Analogous properties can be singled out in Lambertini and Mantovani (2009), where the model describing the activities of the monopolist is largely different from Chenavaz (2012). Their model proposes a differential game approach to the economic theory of research portfolios (Bhattacharya and Mookherjee, 1986; Dasgupta and Maskin, 1987).

The firm may activate R&D projects for (1) marginal cost reduction, (2) product differentiation and (3) expansion of the product range. It offers $n\,(t)$ differentiated varieties, each of which has the following market demand function:

$$p_i(t) = a - q_i(t) - \gamma\,(t) \sum_{j \neq i} q_j(t) \tag{6.60}$$

where $\gamma\,(t) \in [0, 1]$. Production takes place at constant returns to scale, with the same marginal cots $c\,(t)$ for all varieties, in such a way that total production costs are $C\,(\mathbf{q}\,(t)) = c\,(t) \sum_{i=1}^{n(t)} q_i\,(t)$.

Marginal production cost, product substitutability and the number of varieties change according to the following state equations:

$$\dot{c} = c(t)\,[-k(t) + \delta] \tag{6.61}$$

$$\dot{\gamma} = \gamma(t)\,[-y(t) + \eta] \tag{6.62}$$

$$\dot{n} = n(t)\,[z(t) - \psi] \tag{6.63}$$

where $\{k\,(t), y\,(t), z(t)\}$ is the set of R&D controls. The instantaneous cost of investing along each dimension is $C\,(k\,(t)) = bk^2\,(t)$, $C\,(y\,(t)) = hy^2\,(t)$ and $C\,(z\,(t)) = rz^2\,(t)$; parameters b, h and r are positive. The monopolist is assumed to activate a portfolio including at least any two projects, if not all of them.

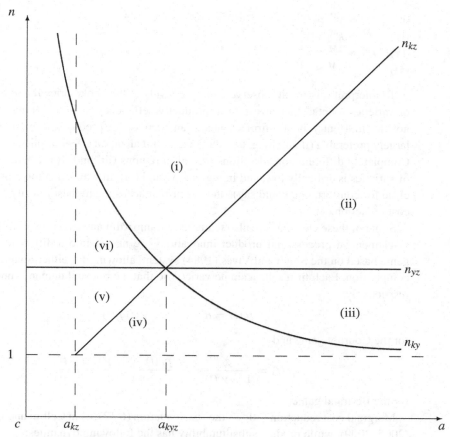

Figure 6.2 The threefold R&D portfolio in the space (a, n)

If the firm invests to (1) reduce $c(t)$ and $s(t)$ for a given number of varieties or (2) reduce $c(t)$ and increase $n(t)$ for a given degree of substitutability, the predictions of the model – in particular those concerning the arising of either complementarity or substitutability between R&D efforts – are qualitatively analogous to those emerging from Chevenaz (2012).

The third case, in which the monopolist activates three R&D projects, is obviously richer and permits a geometrical illustration of the properties of the optimal portfolio, which appears in Figure 6.2 (which replicates figure 1 in Lambertini and Mantovani, 2009, p. 516). Since the portfolio is three-dimensional, the choice of magnitudes defining the bidimensional graph contains a pinch of arbitrariness, but the space (a, n) gives a rough idea of the combination between market size and the crowding effect associated with any expansion of the product range.

The figure serves the purpose of comparing the steady state levels of the three R&D efforts. Six regions, denoted by (i)–(vi), are identified, with the following properties:

(i) $y^M > k^M > z^M$
(ii) $y^M > z^M > k^M$

(iii) $z^M > y^M > k^M$
(iv) $z^M > k^M > y^M$
(v) $k^M > z^M > y^M$
(vi) $k^M > y^M > z^M$

To interpret this result, observe that high levels of the choke price a and the number of varieties n entail that investing in productive efficiency or in additional varieties is not the first entry in the firm's agenda, an increase in product differentiation being largely preferable (if anything, to reduce the cannibalization effect implied by a large n). Completely different considerations prevail in regions (iii) and (iv), where the number of varieties is critically low, and in regions (v) and (vi), in which a is too close to c (too close for comfort, one could say), and the firm attaches the highest priority to marginal cost reduction.

Some of these elements are also featured in Lambertini and Mantovani (2010), where investment in process and product innovations are nested into a differential duopoly game based on the Singh and Vives (1984) system, allowing for either quantity or price competition. Each firm sells a single variety, so that the relevant demand functions are, respectively,

$$p_i(t) = a - q_i(t) - \gamma(t)q_j(t) \tag{6.64}$$

for the Cournot game and

$$q_i(t) = \frac{a}{1 + \gamma(t)} - \frac{p_i(t)}{1 - \gamma^2(t)} + \frac{\gamma(t)p_j(t)}{1 - \gamma^2(t)} \tag{6.65}$$

for the Bertrand game.

Marginal cost reduction follows the state equation (6.12), as in Cellini and Lambertini (2005, 2009), while product substitutability has the following dynamics:

$$\dot{\gamma} = \gamma(t)\left[-y_i(t) - y_j(t) + \eta\right] \tag{6.66}$$

where spillovers do not appear, since differentiation is in fact a public good. Quadratic costs are involved in both dimensions, as above.

Six games are investigated, covering the presence of a single type of innovation or both under either Cournot or Bertrand behaviour. The most interesting picture emerges when firms hold a bidimensional research portfolio.

The essence of bidimensional R&D competition is portrayed in Figure 6.3, which is a simplified version of figure 3 in Lambertini and Mantovani (2010, p. 244). The graph is qualitatively the same irrespective of the market variable being controlled by firms.

The two curves labelled as $c^N(\gamma)$ and $\gamma^N(c)$ are the steady state loci which can be analytically characterised after substituting the equilibrium R&D efforts in equations (6.65–6.66). The system whose graphical representation is given by $c^N(\gamma)$ and $\gamma^N(c)$ identifies two steady states at the intersections between the curves, points A and B. Intuition suggests that B cannot be an equilibrium, as its coordinates imply too high levels of marginal cost and substitutability. This is indeed confirmed by the stability properties of the system, represented by the arrows which indicate convergence towards point A along a saddle path.

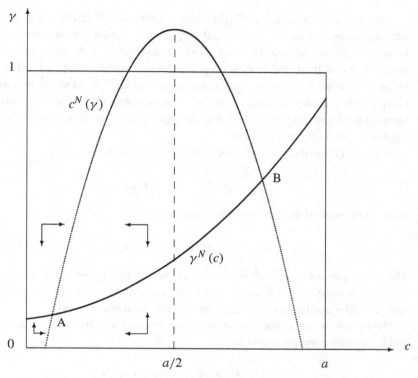

Figure 6.3 The optimal R&D portfolio in the state space

Having said that, there remains to say that the comparative evaluation between the Cournot and Bertrand frameworks reveals what follows:

Proposition 6.9 *The saddle point equilibrium attained under Bertrand competition lies to the south-west of the analogous saddle point equilibrium engendered by Cournot competition.*

That is, technological efficiency and product differentiation are both lower under price competition. This conclusion is decidedly Arrovian, being generated by the higher pressure which firms are subject to, all else equal, when Bertrand behaviour takes place.

6.2.4 Learning by Doing

Now we get back to a theme which has popped up a few times in the previous section and revisit it in more explicit terms. On the role of learning processes in the evolution of an industry, a lot has been said using discrete time models with finite horizon (Spence, 1981; Fudenberg and Tirole; 1983; Ghemawat and Spence, 1985; Dasgupta and Stiglitz, 1988; Jovanovic and MacDonald; 1994a,b; Cabral and Riordan, 1994; 1997, among others). Here, I will expose two dynamic models where the focus is on knowledge acquisition and technical progress for a given industry structure.

Colombo and Labrecciosa (2012) study a Cournot differential duopoly game with learning spillovers and organizational forgetting to investigate the evolution of both know-how and productive efficiency, as well as the impact of the diffusion of knowledge across firms on their ability to keep prices above marginal cost as much as possible, i.e., market power and its bearings upon social welfare. To do so, these authors admit two possible diffusion processes. One involves passive learning (an alternative label for learning by doing) and active learning, whereby it is meant that firms invest to acquire knowledge from the environment.

In the first case, the stock of knowledge of firm i follows

$$\dot{x}_i = q_i(t) - \delta x_i(t) \tag{6.67}$$

while in the second the relevant state equation is

$$\dot{x}_i = k_i(t) - \delta x_i(t) \tag{6.68}$$

The decay parameter $\delta > 0$ measuring organizational forgetting is common to both settings. In (6.68), $k_i(t)$ is some type of investment, for instance in human capital – which, unlike passive learning, does involve the usual convex cost.

The instantaneous demand is for a homogeneous good, $p(t) = a - q_1(t) - q_2(t)$, and the constant marginal cost is

$$c_i(t) = c_0 - x_i(t) - \beta x_j(t) \tag{6.69}$$

which has more than something in common with the assumption made by Kobayashi (2015). Obviously, $\beta \in [0, 1]$ measures the intensity of technological spillovers in the industry.

Colombo and Labrecciosa solve both games under closed-loop memoryless information, demonstrating the uniqueness of the saddle point equilibrium. More importantly, they show the following results:

Proposition 6.10 *Under passive learning, information diffusion through β is anti-competitive, but its effect on industry output more than compensates consumers for the increase in prices.*

That is, learning by doing is welfare enhancing, and thus gives rise to a win-win solutions. In the alternative case, we have:

Proposition 6.11 *Under active learning, information diffusion through β is anti-competitive and increases consumer surplus only if technological spillovers are low enough.*

Consequently, the Paretian result whereby information diffusion has a positive impact on social welfare only arises for sufficiently low values of parameter β, a conclusion which conveys the message that promoting the diffusion of know-how is not necessarily a wise policy. The intuition is that if firms actively engage themselves in the acquisition of knowledge, they end up investing more to know more and overinvest, thereby driving market price so high that the resulting impact on output causes a reversal of fortunes for all agents involved.

Li and Ni (2016) focus instead on a completely different formalisation of learning by doing, and do so using a monopoly model. They modify a model used in Lambertini and Orsini (2015) and Kogan *et al.* (2016) to accomodate learning by doing in the research portfolio of a firm which invests in cost-reducing and quality-enhancing activities:

$$\dot{c} = -k(t) + \delta c(t) \tag{6.70}$$

$$\dot{\theta} = y(t) - \eta \theta(t) \tag{6.71}$$

with quadratic costs in both directions, combining with production costs and the instantaneous costs of quality in such a way that the total cost function is

$$C(t) = c(t) q(t) + bk^2(t) - \ell_c l_c(t) + hy^2(t) - \ell_\theta l_\theta(t) + v\theta^2(t) \tag{6.72}$$

in which ℓ_c and ℓ_θ are positive weights attached to endogenous variables $l_c(t)$ and $l_\theta(t)$. These are the gains from learning by doing, abating the costs of process and product innovation:

$$l_c(t) = \int_0^t k(s)\, ds \,;\, l_\theta(t) = \int_0^t y(s)\, ds \tag{6.73}$$

This in turn implies the presence of two additional state equations,

$$\dot{l}_c = k(t) \,;\, \dot{l}_\theta = y(t) \tag{6.74}$$

To complete the model, Li and Ni (2016) use the same demand function as in Chenavaz (2012). All in all, the model features three controls (market price and two R&D efforts) and four states (marginal production cost, product quality and the two learning effects).

Solving the monopolist's optimal control problem, Li and Ni (2016) reproduce the properties already identified in Lambertini and Mantovani (2009) and Chenavaz (2012) and the focus on learning by doing, demonstrating that, along the path leading to the monopoly equilibrium, the instantaneous optimal investments in the two types of innovation decrease monotonically in the learning weights, ℓ_c and ℓ_θ. This finding implies that learning processes allow for cost abatements in correspondence of any targeted levels of $c(t)$ and $\theta(t)$. Even more interesting is their conclusion about the social (in)efficiency of the monopoly solution, as there exists an admissible range of ℓ_c and ℓ_θ wherein the monopoly equilibrium (in particular, its performance in terms of quality level and productive efficiency) is not characterised by the usual underinvestment associated with monopoly power.

6.2.5   Technological Leadership and Entry Barriers

A recent revival of the debate on entry barriers has been complemented by the dynamic version (Kováč *et al.*, 2010) of the original static model (Etro, 2004, 2006, 2007) where technological leadership can be used by the incumbent as an instrument to preserve its monopoly power. Note that this can also be considered as a revisitation of the classical discussion on innovation, entry and the persistence of monopoly (Gilbert and Newbery, 1982; Reinganum, 1983; Krishna, 1993, *inter alia*).

The model features a differential game over an infinite horizon played by an incumbent, firm 1 (at the outset, a monopolist), and a set of $\mathcal{N} = 2, 3, ...n + 1$ identical outsiders. Consumers demand a homogeneous good whose demand is $p(t) = a - Q(t)$. If at least one outsider enters, Cournot–Nash competition takes place. Initially, marginal cost is the same for all firms alike, c_0, but the leader may activate an R&D project for process innovation to get a lower marginal cost $c_1(t)$, while all of its potential rivals keep using the initial technology.

At any t, market interaction can be solved in a static way, optimal output levels being

$$q_1^{CN}(t) = \frac{a - c_0 + (n+1)\Delta c}{n+2} ; q_i^{CN}(t) = \frac{a - c_0 - \Delta c}{n+2}, j = 1, 2, \ldots n+1 \quad (6.75)$$

where $\Delta c = c_0 - c_1(t) > 0$. The above expressions, in particular the output level of a generic entrant, reveal that there exists a cutoff level of $c_1(t)$, say, $\widehat{c}$, ensuring monopoly power to the incumbent for all $c_1(t) \in [0, \widehat{c}]$. Thence the stimulus for the incumbent to invest in R&D to reduce its own marginal cost:

$$\dot{c} = s\left[c_0 - c_1(t) - \phi k_1^2(t)\right] \quad (6.76)$$

where parameter $s > 0$ determines the speed of the R&D process and parameter ϕ determines the instantaneous returns to R&D effort $k_1(t)$. Firm 1's instantaneous profits are $\pi_1(t) = \left[q_1^{CN}(t)\right]^2 - k_1^2(t)$. Hence, the incumbents' problem consists in choosing control $k_i(t)$ so as to maximise its discounted profit flow under the constraint posed by the state equation (6.76) and the initial condition $c(0) = c_0$.

Here, the only effective player is the incumbent. Kováč et al. (2010) solve this optimal control problem identifying two distinct regimes, which depend on whether the monopoly does or does not persist:

Accomodation: In this case, the incumbent's R&D is low and its marginal cost never reaches the cutoff price $\widehat{c}$. As a consequence, the industry is at least a duopoly at all times.

Predation: In this regime, the incumbents R&D is so intense that, eventually, all competitors are thrown out of business (or simply can never enter the market), so that the incumbent acquires a definitive monopolistic position at a finite date T.

This setup is not only interesting but also open to plausibly very productive extensions, the first of which is probably admitting the possibility that a similar behaviour is also adopted by outsiders, which here are, *a prori*, supposed to be unable to carry out any innovative activities. This could be done granting some advantage to the incumbent, perhaps a more efficient R&D instrument, to keep the model asymmetric but not too strongly so. A second extension would consist in including the outputs of all firms in the set of controls at all times, thereby giving rise to a proper differential game in which market competition is not blackboxed.

6.2.6   More on Portfolio Races

Back to races: Denicolò and Zanchettin (2012) use a bidimensional differentiation model to contribute to a currently developing discussion about research portfolios, or better, a paradox whereby firms are driven by strategic incentives to expand their portfolio by adding several patents which they will, most probably, never use.

The resulting literature pivots around the existence of complementarity among innovations, giving rise to hold-up problems. Hence, the idea is that the task of (possibly huge) patent portfolios is to create reciprocal hold-up positions which constitute a shield against the threat of blocking patents. Then, mutual hold-ups are cleared through cross-licensing instead of enforcing patents (see Kortum and Lerner, 1998; Hall and Ziedonis, 2001; Ziedonis, 2004; Siebert and von Graevenitz, 2010, *inter alia*).

Denicolò and Zanchettin (2012) take a different route to investigate this issue, as they leave complementarity aside and instead stipulate that the key element is the incremental knowledge acquired by firms over time, modelling the level of technological advancement embodied in a firm's research portfolio as a quality level, very much like that considered in discrete choice models of vertical differentiation. This is combined with horizontal differentiation with a rectangular distribution of consumers along a linear city of unit length, and linear transportation costs as in the original Hotelling (1929) model.

Firms 1 and 2 are located at $x_1 = 0$ and $x_2 = 1$ forever. Full market coverage prevails at all times, and the utility function of a consumer located at $x \in [0, 1]$ is

$$U(t) = \begin{cases} \theta_1(t) - p_1(t) - \tau x \text{ if buying variety 1} \\ \theta_2(t) - p_2(t) - \tau(1-x) \text{ if buying variety 2} \end{cases} \tag{6.77}$$

where $\theta_i(t)$ is the 'quality level' characterising variety i.

Firms seek a very large number of innovations through efforts $k_i(t)$. Taken together, the firms' efforts determine the evolution of the state-of-the-art technology of the industry, $\chi(t)$, which changes over time according to

$$\dot{\chi} = k_1(t) + k_2(t) \tag{6.78}$$

If firm i holds a patent portfolio of size $n_i(t)$ at any time t, the highest quality that firm j can supply at the same instant is $\theta_j(t) = \chi(t) - n_i(t)$. Differentiating w.r.t. time both sides and using (6.78), we can write $\dot{n}_i = k_i(t) - \delta n_i(t)$, in which the decay rate $\delta > 0$ is an inverse indicator of the duration of patent protection. As a result, the game can be specified in terms of a single state variable, $\theta(t) = \theta_1(t) - \theta_2(t)$, whose dynamics is

$$\dot{\theta} = \dot{\theta}_1 - \dot{\theta}_2 = k_1(t) - k_2(t) - \delta\theta(t) \tag{6.79}$$

At a generic instant during the game, the indifferent consumer is located at $\tilde{x}(t) = [p_2(t) - p_1(t) + \theta_2(t) - \theta_1(t) + \tau] / (2\tau)$, so that instantaneous market demands are $q_1(t) = \tilde{x}(t)$ and $q_2(t) = 1 - \tilde{x}(t)$, respectively. Hence, setting to zero the marginal production cost of both firms and assuming quadratic costs of research and development, firm i's profit function is $\pi_i(t) = p_i(t) q_i(t) - bk_i^2(t)/2$. Each firm chooses price and R&D effort to noncooperatively maximise its discounted profit flow over $t \in [0, \infty)$, under feedback information.

By construction, the game describes a story in which firm 1 is the quality leader and invests to keep its position, while firm 2 is the follower and tries to catch up, as in Harris and Vickers (1987), Serrano and Zapater (1998) and Aghion *et al.* (2001).

Guessing a linear quadratic form for the value function and confining their attention to symmetric equilibrium solutions, Denicolò and Zanchettin (2012) show the existence of a linear feedback equilibrium with $k_1^{LF}(\theta) = k_2^{LF}(\theta)$, which implies that the state equation may reduce to $\dot{\theta} = -\delta\theta(t)$, which drives the quality gap to zero. This equilibrium is stable, given the sign of the product appearing on the r.h.s. of the state equation under symmetry.

In this equilibrium, firms keep investing positive (symmetric) amounts of resources in R&D and hold equivalent research portfolios. This, from their point of view, is the inefficient outcome of a prisoners' dilemma: each would like to take the lead, and neither would be happy being the laggard. Note the common DNA with some of the literature discussed in Section 6.1.

Further Reading

Further extensions on innovation races can be found in Doraszelski (2004, 2008). For more on innovation adoption, see Jensen (1982), Balcer and Lippman (1984) and Quirmbach (1986). For multistage patent races, see Park (1987). A more recent revisitation of adoption timing is in Farzin *et al.* (1998); see also Doraszelski (2001). A unified view of the literature on industry evolution is in Budd *et al.* (1993). Dynamic games of R&D competition versus cooperation defined in discrete time are in Petit and Tolwinski (1996, 1999). A feedback differential game of R&D competition versus cooperation with numerical analysis is in Dawid *et al.* (2013). Further extensions of the differential game with process R&D and spillovers are in Li and Zhang (2013) and Bramati *et al.* (2016). Open innovation has been treated in differential games by Caulkins *et al.* (2013) and Hasnash *et al.* (2014). A dynamic game of innovation, imitation and fashion cycles is in Caulkins *et al.* (2007). R&D for transportation technologies is investigated in a differential game by Colombo *et al.* (2009). For more on product innovation in dynamic games, see Dawid *et al.* (2013b, 2015). A discrete time monopoly model analysing process and product innovation in a vertically differentiated monopoly is in Saha (2007), while a differential game with stock-dependent spillovers is in El Ouardighi *et al.* (2014). Quality improvements and cost-reducing investments are also modelled in J. Vörös (2006). For additional insights on learning by doing, see Teng and Thompson (1996); for a comprehensive overview, see Tompson (2010). Besanko *et al.* (2010) perform a discrete time analysis of learning by doing and organizational forgetting.

Bibliography

Abernathy, W.J. and J.M. Utterback (1975), "A Dynamic Model of Product and Process Innovation", *Omega*, **3**, 639–56.

Abernathy, W.J. and J.M. Utterback (1982), "Patterns of Industrial Innovation", in M.L. Tushman and W.L. Moore (eds), *Readings in the Management of Innovation,* Boston, Pitman8.

Adner R. and D. Levinthal (2001), "Demand Heterogeneity and Technology Evolution: Implications for Product and Process Innovation", *Management Science, 47*, 611–28.

Aghion, P., N. Bloom, R. Blundell, R. Griffith and P. Howitt (2005), "Competition and Innovation: An Inverted-U Relationship", *Quarterly Journal of Economics, 120*, 701–28.

Aghion, P., C. Harris, P. Howitt and J. Vickers (2001), "Competition and Growth with Step-by-Step Innovation", *Review of Economic Studies, 68*, 467–92.

Amir, R. (2000), "Modelling Imperfectly Appropriable R&D via Spillovers", *International Journal of Industrial Organization, 18*, 1013–32.

Arrow, K.J. (1962), "Economic Welfare and the Allocation of Resources for Invention", in R. Nelson (ed.), *The Rate and Direction of Industrial Activity*, Princeton, NJ, Princeton University Press.

Athey, S. and A. Schmutzler (1995), "Product and Process Flexibility in an Innovative Environment", *Rand Journal of Economics, 26*, 557–74.

Balcer, Y. and S. Lippman (1984), "Technological Expectations and Adoption of Improved Technology", *Journal of Economic Theory, 34*, 292–318.

Bhattacharya, S. and D. Mookherjee (1986), "Portfolio Choice in Research and Development", *RAND Journal of Economics, 17*, 594–605.

Beath, J., Y. Katsoulacos and D. Ulph (1987), "Sequential Product Innovation and Industry Evolution", *Economic Journal* (Conference Papers), *97*, 32–43.

Besanko, D., U. Doraszelski, Y. Kryukov and M. Satterthwaite (2010), "Learning by Doing, Organizational Forgetting, and Industry Dynamics", *Econometrica, 78*, 453–508.

Bonanno, G. and B. Haworth (1998), "Intensity of Competition and the Choice between Product and Process Innovation", *International Journal of Industrial Organization, 16*, 495–510.

Bramati, M.C., A. Palestini and M. Rota (2016), "Effects of Law-Enforcement Efficiency and Duration of Trials in an Oligopolistic Competition among Fair and Unfair Firms", *Journal of Optimization Theory and Applications, 170*, 650–69.

Budd, C., C. Harris and J. Vickers (1993), "A Model of the Evolution of Duopoly: Does the Asymmetry between Firms Tend to Increase or Decrease?", *Review of Economic Studies, 60*, 543–73.

Cabral, L. and M. Riordan (1994), "The Learning Curve, Market Dominance, and Predatory Pricing", *Econometrica, 62*, 1115–40.

Cabral, L. and M. Riordan (1997), "The Learning Curve, Predation, Antitrust, and Welfare", *Journal of Industrial Economics, 2*, 155–69.

Caulkins, J., G. Feichtinger, D. Grass, R. Hartl, P. Kort and A. Seidl (2013), "When to Make Proprietary Software Open Source", *Journal of Economic Dynamics and Control, 37*, 1182–94.

Caulkins, J., R. Hartl, P. Kort and G. Feichtinger (2007), "Explaining Fashion Cycles: Imitators Chasing Innovators in Product Space", *Journal of Economic Dynamics and Control, 31*, 1535–56.

Cellini, R., and L. Lambertini (2002), "A Differential Game Approach to Investment in Product Differentiation", *Journal of Economic Dynamics and Control, 27*, 51–62.

Cellini, R. and L. Lambertini (2004), "Private and Social Incentives Towards Investment in Product Differentiation", *International Game Theory Review, 6*, 493–508.

Cellini, R. and L. Lambertini (2005), "R&D Incentives and Market Structure: A Dynamic Analysis", *Journal of Optimization Theory and Applications, 126*, 85–96.

Cellini, R. and L. Lambertini (2009), "Dynamic R&D with Spillovers: Competition vs Cooperation", *Journal of Economic Dynamics and Control, 33*, 568–82.

Cellini, R. and L. Lambertini (2011), "R&D Incentives under Bertrand Competition: A Differential Game", *Japanese Economic Review*, **62**, 387–400.

Chenavaz, R. (2012), "Dynamic Pricing, Product and Process Innovation", *European Journal of Operations Research*, **222**, 553–57.

Choi, J.P (1991), "Dynamic R&D Competition under 'Hazard Rate' Uncertainty", *RAND Journal of Economics*, **22**, 596–610.

Colombo, L. and P. Labrecciosa (2012), "Inter-Firm Knowledge Diffusion, Market Power, and Welfare", *Journal of Evolutionary Economics*, **22**, 1009–27.

Colombo, L., L. Lambertini and A. Mantovani (2009), "Endogenous Transportation Technology in a Cournot Differential Game with Intraindustry Trade", *Japan and the World Economy*, **21**, 133–39.

Dasgupta, P. and E. Maskin (1987), "The Simple Economics of Research Portfolios", *Economic Journal*, **97**, 581–95.

Dasgupta, P. and J. Stiglitz (1980), "Uncertainty, Industrial Structure, and the Speed of R&D", *Bell Journal of Economics*, **11**, 1–28.

Dasgupta, P. and J. Stiglitz (1988), "Learning-by-Doing, Market Structure and Industrial and Trade Policy", *Oxford Economic Papers*, **40**, 246–68.

d'Aspremont, C. and A. Jacquemin (1988), "Cooperative and Noncooperative R&D in Duopoly with Spillovers", *American Economic Review*, **78**, 1133–37.

Dawid, H., M. Keoula, M. Kopel and P.M. Kort (2015), "Product Innovation Incentives by an Incumbent Firm: A Dynamic Analysis", *Journal of Economic Behavior and Organization*, **117**, 411–38.

Dawid, H., M. Kopel and P.M. Kort (2013a), "R&D Competition versus R&D Cooperation in Oligopolistic Markets with Evolving Structure", *International Journal of Industrial Organization*, **31**, 527–37.

Dawid, H., M. Kopel and P.M. Kort (2013b), "New Product Introduction and Capacity Investment by Incumbents: Effects of Size on Strategy", *European Journal of Operational Research*, **230**, 133–42.

Delbono, F. (1989), "Market Leadership with a Sequence of History Dependent Patent Races", *Journal of Industrial Economics*, **38**, 95–101.

Delbono, F. and V. Denicolò (1991), "Incentives to Innovate in a Cournot Oligopoly", *Quarterly Journal of Economics*, **106**, 951–61.

Denicolò, V. and P. Zanchettin (2012), "A Dynamic Model of Patent Portfolio Races", *Economics Letters*, **117**, 924–27.

Doraszelski, U. (2001), "The Net Present Value Method versus the Option Value of Waiting: A Note on Farzin, Huisman, and Kort (1998)", *Journal of Economic Dynamics and Control*, **25**, 1109–15.

Doraszelski, U. (2003), "An R&D Race with Knowledge Accumulation", *RAND Journal of Economics*, **34**, 20–42.

Doraszelski, U. (2004), "Innovations, Improvements, and the Optimal Adoption of New Technologies", *Journal of Economic Dynamics and Control*, **28**, 1461–80.

Doraszelski, U. (2008), "Rent Dissipation in R&D Races", in R. Cellini and L. Lambertini (eds), *The Economics of Innovation. Incentives, Cooperation, and R&D Policy*, Bingley, Emerald.

Dutta, P.K., S. Lach and A. Rustichini (1995), "Better Late than Early: Vertical Differentiation in the Adoption of a New Technology", *Journal of Economics and Management Strategy*, **4**, 563–89.

El Ouardighi, F., M. Shnaiderman and F. Pasin (2014), "Research and Development with Stock-Dependent Spillovers and Price Competition in a Duopoly", *Journal of Optimization Theory and Applications*, **161**, 626–47.

Etro, F. (2004), "Innovation by Leaders", *Economic Journal*, **114**, 281–303.

Etro, F. (2006), Aggressive Leaders", *RAND Journal of Economics*, **37**, 1–10.

Etro, F. (2007), *Competition, Innovation, and Antitrust: A Theory of Market Leaders and its Policy Implications*, Berlin, Springer.

Farzin, Y.H., K. Huisman and P. Kort (1998), "Optimal Timing of Technology Adoption", *Journal of Economic Dynamics and Control*, **228**, 779–99.

Fudenberg, D., R. Gilbert, J. Stiglitz and J. Tirole (1983), "Preemption, Leapfrogging and Competition in Patent Races", *European Economic Review*, **22**, 3–31.

Fudenberg, D. and J. Tirole (1983), "Learning-by-Doing and Market Performance", *Bell Journal of Economics*, **14**, 522–30.

Fudenberg, D. and J. Tirole (1985), "Preemption and Rent Equalization in the Adoption of New Technology", *Review of Economic Studies*, **52**, 383–401.

Futia, C. (1980), "Schumpeterian Competition", *Quarterly Journal of Economics*, **94**, 675–95.

Ghemawat, P. and M. Spence (1985), "Learning Curve Spillovers and Market Performance", *Quarterly Journal of Economics*, **100**, 839–52.

Gilbert, R. and D. Newbery (1982), "Preemptive Patenting and the Persistence of Monopoly", *American Economic Review*, **72**, 514–26.

Grossman, G.M. and C. Shapiro (1987), "Dynamic R&D Competition", *Economic Journal*, **97**, 372–87.

Hall, B. and R. Ziedonis (2001), "The Patent Paradox Revisited: An Empirical Study of Patenting in the US Semiconductor Industry, 1979–1995", *RAND Journal of Economics*, **32**, 101–28.

Harris, C. and J. Vickers (1985), "Perfect Equilibrium in a Model of a Race", *Review of Economic Studies*, **52**, 193–209.

Harris, C. and J. Vickers (1987), "Racing with Uncertainty", *Review of Economic Studies*, **54**, 1–21.

Hasnas, I., L. Lambertini and A. Palestini (2014), "Open Innovation in a Dynamic Cournot Duopoly", *Economic Modelling*, **36**, 79–87.

Hinloopen, J., G. Smrkolj and F. Wagener (2013), "From Mind to Market: A Global, Dynamic Analysis of R&D", *Journal of Economic Dynamics and Control*, **37**, 2729–54.

Hotelling, H. (1929), "Stability in Competition", *Economic Journal*, **39**, 41–57.

Jensen, R. (1982), "Adoption and Diffusion of an Innovation of Uncertain Profitability", *Journal of Economic Theory*, **27**, 182–92.

Jovanovic, B. and G.M. MacDonald (1994a), "Competitive Diffusion", *Journal of Political Economy*, **102**, 24–56.

Jovanovic, B. and G.M. MacDonald (1994b), "The Life Cycle of a Competitive Industry", *Journal of Political Economy*, 102, 322–47.

Judd, K. (1992), "Projection Methods for Solving Aggregate Growth Models", *Journal of Economic Theory*, **58**, 410–52.

Judd, K. (1998), *Numerical Methods in Economics*, Cambridge, MA, MIT Press.

Kamien, M.I., and N. Schwartz (1972), "Timing of Innovations under Rivalry", *Econometrica*, **40**, 43–60.

Kamien, M.I., and N. Schwartz (1976), "On the Degree of Rivalry for Maximum Innovation Activity", *Quarterly Journal of Economics*, **90**, 245–60.

Kamien, M. and N. Schwartz (1980), *Market Structure and Innovation*, Cambridge, Cambridge University Press.

Kamien, M.I., E. Muller and I. Zang (1992), "Cooperative Joint Ventures and R&D Cartels", *American Economic Review*, **82**, 1293–1306.

Katz, M. (1986), "An Analysis of Cooperative Research and Development", *RAND Journal of Economics*, **17**, 527–43.

Katz, M. and J. Ordover (1990), "R&D Cooperation and Competition", *Brookings Papers, Microeconomics*, 137–203.

Katz, M. and C. Shapiro (1987), "R&D Rivalry with Licensing or Imitation", *American Economic Review*, **77**, 402–20.

Klepper, S. (1996), "Entry, Exit and Innovation over the Product Life Cycle", *American Economic Review*, **86**, 562–83.

Kobayashi, S. (2015), "On a Dynamic Model of Cooperative and Noncooperative R and D in Oligopoly with Spillovers", *Dynamic Games and Applications*, **5**, 599–619.

Kogan, K., F. El Ouardighi and T. Chernonog (2016), "Learning by Doing with Spillovers: Strategic Complementarity versus Strategic Substitutability", *Automatica*, **67**, 282–94.

Kortum, S. and J. Lerner (1998), "Stronger Protection or Technological Revolution: What Is behind the Recent Surge in Patenting?", *Carnegie-Rochester Conference Series Public Policy*, **48**, 247–304.

Kováč, E., V. Vinogradov and K. Zigic (2010), "Technological Leadership and Persistence of Monopoly under Endogenous Entry: Static versus Dynamic Analysis", *Journal of Economic Dynamics and Control*, **34**, 1421–41.

Krishna, K. (1993), "Auctions with Endogenous Valuations: The Persistence of Monopoly Revisited", *American Economic Review*, **83**, 147–60.

Lambertini, L. (2003), "The Monopolist's Optimal R&D Portfolio", *Oxford Economic Papers*, **55**, 561–78.

Lambertini, L. (2012), "Dynamic Hotelling Duopoly with Linear Transportation Costs", *Optimal Control, Applications and Methods*, **33**, 114–26.

Lambertini, L. and A. Mantovani (2009), "Process and Product Innovation by a Multiproduct Monopolist: A Dynamic Approach", *International Journal of Industrial Organization*, **27**, 508–18.

Lambertini, L. and A. Mantovani (2010), "Process and Product Innovation: A Differential Game Approach to Product Life Cycle", *International Journal of Economic Theory*, **6**, 227–52.

Lambertini, L. and R. Orsini (2015), "Quality Improvement and Process Innovation in Monopoly: A Dynamic Analysis", *Operations Research Letters*, **43**, 370–73.

Lee, T. and L. Wilde (1980), "Market Structure and Innovation: A Reformulation", *Quarterly Journal of Economics*, **94**, 429–36.

Li, C. and J. Zhang (2013), "Dynamic Games of R&D Competition in a Differentiated Duopoly", *Journal of Institutional and Theoretical Economics*, **169**, 660–79.

Li, S. and J. Ni (2016), "A Dynamic Analysis of Investment in Process and Product Innovation with Learning-by-Doing", *Economics Letters*, **145**, 104–08.

Lin, P. and K. Saggi (2002), "Product Differentiation, Process R&D, and the Nature of Market Competition", *European Economic Review*, **46**, 201–11.

Lippman, S. and K. McCardle (1987), "Dropout Behaviour in R&D Races with Learning", *RAND Journal of Economics*, **18**, 287–95.

Lippman, S. and K. McCardle (1988), "Preemption in R&D Races", *European Economic Review*, **32**, 1661–69.

Long, N.V. (2010), *A Survey of Dynamic Games in Economics*, Singapore, World Scientific.

Loury, G. (1979), "Market Structure and Innovation", *Quarterly Journal of Economics*, **93**, 395–410.

Malueg, D. and S. Tsutsui (1997), "Dynamic R&D Competition with Learning", *RAND Journal of Economics*, **28**, 751–72.

Mantovani, A. (2006), "Complementarity between Product and Process Innovation in a Monopoly Setting", *Economics of Innovation and New Technology*, **15**, 219–34.

Navas, J. and P. Kort (2007), "Time to Complete and Research Joint Ventures: A Differential Game Approach", *Journal of Economic Dynamics and Control*, **31**, 1672–96.

Park, J. (1987), "Dynamic Patent Races with Risky Choices", *Management Science*, **33**, 1563–71.

Petit, M.L. and B. Tolwinski (1996), "Technology Sharing Cartels and Industrial Structure", *International Journal of Industrial Organization*, **15**, 77–101.

Petit, M.L. and B. Tolwinski (1999), "R&D Cooperation or Competition?", *European Economic Review*, **43**, 185–208.

Quirmbach, H.C. (1986), "The Diffusion of New Technology and the Market for an Innovation", *RAND Journal of Economics*, **17**, 33–47.

Reinganum, J. (1981a) "Dynamic Games of Innovation", *Journal of Economic Theory*, **25**, 21–41.

Reinganum, J. (1981b) "On the Diffusion of New Technology: A Game Theoretic Approach", *Review of Economic Studies*, **48**, 385–405.

Reinganum, J. (1982a) "A Dynamic Game of R&D: Patent Protection and Competitive Behavior", *Econometrica*, **50**, 671–88.

Reinganum, J. (1982b), "A Class of Differential Games for Which the Closed Loop and Open Loop Nash Equilibria Coincide", *Journal of Optimization Theory and Applications*, **36**, 253–62.

Reinganum, J. (1983), "Uncertain Innovation and the Persistence of Monopoly", *American Economic Review*, **73**, 741–48.

Reinganum, J. (1985), "Innovation and Industry Evolution", *Quarterly Journal of Economics*, **100**, 81–99.

Reinganum, J. (1989), "The Timing of Innovation: Research, Development and Diffusion", in R. Schmalensee and R. Willig (eds.), *Handbook of Industrial Organization*, vol. 1, Amsterdam, North-Holland.

Rosenkranz, S. (2003), "Simultaneous Choice of Process and Product Innovation", *Journal of Economic Behavior and Organization*, **50**, 183–201.

Saha, S. (2007), "Consumer Preferences and Product and Process R&D", *RAND Journal of Economics*, **38**, 250–68.

Schumpeter, J.A. (1942), *Capitalism, Socialism and Democracy*, London, Allen & Unwin.

Serrano, R. and I. Zapater (1998), "The Three-Legged Race: Cooperating to Compete", *Games and Economic Behavior*, **22**, 343–63.

Siebert, R. and G. von Graevenitz (2010), "Jostling for Advantage or Not: Choosing between Patent Portfolio Races and ex-ante Licensing", *Journal of Economic Behavior and Organization*, **73**, 225–45.

Singh, N. and X. Vives (1984), "Price and Quantity Competition in a Differentiated Duopoly", *RAND Journal of Economics*, **15**, 546–54.

Smrkolj, G. and F. Wagener (2016), "Dynamic R&D with Spillovers: A Comment", *Journal of Economic Dynamics and Control*, **73**, 453–57.

Spence, M. (1981), "The Learning Curve and Competition", *Bell Journal of Economics*, **12**, 49–70.

Spence, M. (1984), "Cost Reduction, Competition and Industry Performance", *Econometrica*, **52**, 101–21.

Suzumura, K. (1992), "Cooperative and Noncooperative R&D in an Oligopoly with Spillovers", *American Economic Review*, **82**, 1307–20.

Teng, J. and G. Thompson (1996), "Optimal Strategies for General Price-Quality Decision Models of New Products with Learning Production Costs", *European Journal of Operational Research*, **93**, 476–89.

Thompson, P. (2010), "Learning by Doing", in B. Hall and N. Rosenberg (eds), *Handbook of the Economics of Innovation*, vol. 1, Amsterdam, North-Holland.

Tirole, J. (1988), *The Theory of Industrial Organization*, Cambridge, MA, MIT Press.

Vickers, J. (1986), "The Evolution of Industry Structure When There Is a Sequence of Innovations", *Journal of Industrial Economics*, **35**, 1–12.

Vörös, J. (2006), "The Dynamics of Price, Quality and Productivity Improvement Decisions", *European Journal of Operational Research*, **170**, 809–23.

Ziedonis, R. (2004), "Don't Fence Me In: Fragmented Market for Technology and Patent Acquisition Strategies of Firms", *Management Science*, **50**, 804–20.

7 The Environment and Natural Resources

This is one of the areas in which the use of differential games has been more intense and the use of feedback structure more frequent. The first fact is driven by both the relevance and the intrinsically dynamic nature of the subject matter, which hardly lends itself to be treated through static models; the second, in itself highly desirable, has been facilitated by the almost systematic construction of linear quadratic games, very often with a single state variable. In turn, these features have also allowed researchers to draw a few solid policy prescriptions from the subgame perfect equilibrium features of analytically solvable theoretical models.

The structure of the chapter can be outlined as follows. Section 7.1 contains the layout of the basic oligopoly models with either polluting emissions or resource extraction, and their open-loop solutions. Section 7.2 illustrates the subgame perfect equilibria of pollution games with emission taxation and green R&D investments. In Section 7.3, the backbone of the large literature on resource extraction is reviewed, considering both renewables and nonrenewables. Here, as anticipated in Chapter 3, I also illustrate in detail an alternative approach to the full characterisation of nonlinear strategies in the oligopolistic model illustrating the tragedy of commons. Several relevant extensions of the main models appear in Section 7.4.

7.1 Unregulated Open-Loop Games

Our departure point is the same as in Chapter 2, except for the presence of n Cournot firms selling a homogeneous good, instead of a single monopolist. The market exists forever with an instantaneous inverse demand function $p(t) = a - Q(t)$, where $Q(t) = \sum_{i=1}^{n} q_i(t)$ is the sum of individual outputs $q_i(t)$. The same technology, characterised by a constant marginal cost $c \in (0, a)$, is common to all firms. Our aim here is to describe their behaviour in two different scenarios, assuming both regulation and consumer environmental awareness away for the moment.

The first in one in which pollution matters. As in Chapter 2, the stock of emissions $S(t)$ evolves according to the following dynamics:

$$\dot{S} = \sum_{i=1}^{n} q_i(t) - \delta S(t) \tag{7.1}$$

In the second scenario, the relevant variable is the stock of a renewable natural resource or species, whose kinematic equation is

$$\dot{X} = \eta X(t) - \sum_{i=1}^{n} q_i(t) \tag{7.2}$$

In both cases, we may suppose that firms (1) do not internalise the externalities implied by their strategies, and therefore (2) choose their respective output à la Cournot–Nash to maximise individual discounted profit flows

$$\Pi_i = \int_0^\infty \left[p(t) - c \right] q_i(t) e^{-\rho t} dt, \tag{7.3}$$

under (7.1) or (7.2) and the relevant initial condition, $S(0) = S_0 \geq 0$ or $X(0) = X_0 > 0$. The resulting Hamiltonian is

$$\mathcal{H}_i(t) = e^{-\rho t} \left\{ \left[a - q_i(t) - \sum_{j \neq i} q_j(t) - c \right] q_i(t) + \lambda_i(t) \dot{O} \right\} \tag{7.4}$$

where $O = S, X$. It is easily checked that, irrespective of the nature of the state variable, this is a linear state game, and therefore its open-loop solution is strongly time consistent, or subgame perfect. In both games, firms play in a quasi-static way at all times, adopting the Cournot–Nash strategy $q^{OL} = (a - c)/(n + 1)$, so that the steady state level of the relevant stock is either $S^{OL} = nq^{OL}/\delta$ or $X^{OL} = nq^{OL}/\eta$.

What makes a difference, as in the monopoly case, is the stability (or lack thereof) of this solution. Indeed, the stability properties of the two games can be fully grasped by looking back at Figures 2.3–2.4, to see that the open-loop equilibrium is stable when the state variable is the stock of pollutants, while it is unstable when the state is a natural resource. Hence, one may confidently rely (so to speak) upon the open-loop model when pollution is at stake, but not when natural resources are, because in the latter case one should imagine that firms, being aware of instability and its possible consequences on their rent from extraction, will look for a stable solution under feedback rules.

7.2   Emissions Taxation and Green R&D

The subgame perfect solution of the differential Cournot oligopoly game with emission taxation is in Benchekroun and Long (1998). Their aim is demonstrating that there exists a tax inducing profit-maximising firms to reproduce both the socially efficient outcome and the path leading to it. This amounts to saying that the regulator avails of an optimal policy which leads private firms to fully replicate the behaviour of a public monopolist maximising social welfare.[1] Benchekroun and Long (1998) prove this result in a general

---

[1] The same problem has been extensively treated in the monopoly case. See Bergstrom *et al.* (1981), Karp and Livernois (1992) and Benchekroun and Long (2002). In the latter contribution, a multiplicity of efficient tax rules has been characterised. A brief illustration of the model in Benchekroun and Long (2002) is in Chapter 9.

setting. Here I will confine the exposition to the state-linear (unregulated) model and the linear-quadratic game (which is relevant if the tax policy is introduced).

The benchmark consists in characterising the command optimum. This requires defining the instantaneous social welfare function as $SW(t) = \pi(t) + CS(t) - D(S(t))$, where (1) $\pi(t)$ is the profit of a single firm (under constant returns to scale, n is irrelevant); (2) $CS(t)$ is consumer surplus; and $D(t) = \varsigma S^2(t)/2$ is the environmental damage caused by polluting emissions, with ς strictly positive and constant. Here, obviously, profits are not curtailed by any tax rate, as a benevolent planner controls production. The command optimum is attained by choosing $Q(t)$ to maximise

$$\mathcal{H}(t) = e^{-\rho t}\left\{[a - Q(t) - c]Q(t) + \frac{Q^2(t)}{2} - \frac{\varsigma S^2(t)}{2} + \lambda(t)[Q(t) - \delta S(t)]\right\} \quad (7.5)$$

From the necessary conditions

$$\frac{\partial \mathcal{H}}{\partial Q} = a - Q - c + \lambda = 0 \quad (7.6)$$

$$\dot{\lambda} = -\frac{\partial \mathcal{H}}{\partial S} + \rho\lambda \Leftrightarrow \dot{\lambda} = (\delta + \rho)\lambda + \varsigma S \quad (7.7)$$

one obtains

$$\lambda = Q - a + c \quad (7.8)$$

which tells that the socially optimal shadow price is negative for all $Q < a - c$, i.e., for all levels of the industry output lower than the perfectly competitive one, and the control equation $\dot{Q} = \dot{\lambda}$. Using (7.7–7.8), it can be written as

$$\dot{Q} = \varsigma S - (a - c - Q)(\delta + \rho) \quad (7.9)$$

The unique socially efficient steady state, which identifies a saddle point, is reached in correspondence of

$$Q^{SP} = \frac{(a - c)(\delta + \rho) - \varsigma S^{SP}}{\delta + \rho}; \ S^{SP} = \frac{(a - c)(\delta + \rho)}{\varsigma + \delta(\delta + \rho)} \quad (7.10)$$

where superscript SP stands for *social planning*.

What Benchekroun and Long (1998) show is the following:

Proposition 7.1 *There exists a time-invariant subgame perfect tax policy driving the profit-maximising Cournot industry to achieve the socially efficient output path and therefore also the socially efficient steady state outcome, under both open-loop and feedback rules.*

To prove this claim, Benchekroun and Long (1998) stipulate that the regulator adopts a linear tax policy $\tau(S) = \alpha + \beta S$ whose intercept α and slope β will be finely tuned to achieve the policy maker's goal declared in the above proposition. Note that, anticipating the contents of Chapter 9, this is an example of a Stackelberg game with the policy maker taking the lead and the firms following. The design of the emission tax as a linear function of the emission volume has a twofold scope: the first is that such a policy allows for the replication of the first best; the second is that, being state-dependent, this policy instrument and the firms' production plans are indeed Markovian.

From the firms' standpoint, this tax is equivalent to an increase in average and marginal production cost, as the total cost function of firm i becomes $C_i(S) = [c + \tau(S)] q_i$. It is worth stressing that this implies that the cost function becomes state-dependent.

Obviously, the most interesting case is the feedback game, where firms, being aware of the impact of polluting emissions on their profits, adopt Markovian strategies $q_i(S)$ throughout. Given the linear shape of the tax rule, this amounts to saying that the feedback output can be defined as $q_i(\alpha, \beta, S)$, i.e., as a function of current emissions and the actual policy instruments α and β.

As a result, the Hamiltonian of firm i is

$$\mathcal{H}_i = e^{-\rho t} \left\{ \left(a - q_i(\alpha, \beta, S) - \sum_{j \neq i} q_j(\alpha, \beta, S) - c - \alpha - \beta S \right) q_i(\alpha, \beta, S) \right.$$

$$\left. + \lambda_i \left[q_i(\alpha, \beta, S) + \sum_{j \neq i} q_j(\alpha, \beta, S) - \delta S \right] \right\} \tag{7.11}$$

Once necessary conditions and the control equation have been derived, the problem of the regulator is choosing α and β in such a way that

$$\dot{q}(\alpha, \beta, S) = \frac{\dot{Q}}{n} = \frac{\varsigma S - (a - c - Q)(\delta + \rho)}{n} \tag{7.12}$$

and

$$q^{CN}(\alpha, \beta, S) = \frac{Q^{SP}}{n} = \frac{(a - c)(\delta + \rho) - \varsigma S^{SP}}{2(\delta + \rho)} \tag{7.13}$$

so that $S^{CN} = S^{SP}$. The unique pair solving the policy maker's problem (7.12–7.13) is

$$\alpha^{SP} = \frac{\varsigma}{\delta + \rho} - \frac{\delta(\delta + \rho) + [\delta - \omega + n(\rho + \rho + \omega)] S^{SP}}{n(\delta + \rho) - (n - 1)\omega} \tag{7.14}$$

$$\beta^{SP} = \frac{(n + 1)\varsigma + (n - 1)\omega^2}{n(2\delta + \rho) - 2(n - 1)\omega} \tag{7.15}$$

where $\omega = \left[2\delta + \rho - \sqrt{(2\delta + \rho)^2 + 4\varsigma} \right] / 2 < 0$.[2]

---

[2] Reproducing the social optimum may not be possible, in view of the amount of information required to design the emission tax appropriately. Since, under noncooperative behaviour, pollution increases monotonically in industry output and the number of firms, collusive behaviour might be acceptable with a view to reducing emissions. Benchekroun and Chaudhury (2011) show this assuming an explicit cartel stabilised as in d'Aspremont et al. (1983), also proving that emission taxation helps cartel members in their attempt to stick together.

As is well known, carbon taxes are very rarely adopted and, if so, are also usually abandoned quite quickly, the reasons being that determining optimal (i.e., Pigouvian) tax rates is a very demanding task in terms of the information required, and, even in the most optimistic perspective in which this difficulty can be overcome, they are bound to be considered as unfair because firms reproducing the socially optimal outcome may ask for the removal of the regulatory policy, in absence of which they would go back to a 'business as usual' strategy, which in turn would trigger the reintroduction of the same policy. A way out of this problem is envisaged in Dragone *et al.* (2014), where regulation is implemented directly through the presence of a single public firm in the industry, conditioning the behaviour of the entire population of firms in such a way as to attain the same aggregate output and emission stock as in the public monopoly case. Intuitively, the source of this result is that the public firm pursues welfare maximization, thereby forcing profit-seeking firms (regardless of their number) to internalise the external effect and modify their production plans accordingly. All of this holds notwithstanding the realistic assumption concerning the presence of X-inefficiency (Leibenstein, 1966) raising the marginal production cost of the public entity.

All of the aforementioned contributions model the interplay between output controls, polluting emissions and, possibly, emission taxes. However, what is most interesting is the possibility for regulation to trigger investments in green technologies. While this scenario has been extensively explored in static games (for an overview, see Lambertini, 2013, 2017a), it has received little attention thus far in differential games, possibly because the addition of R&D controls implies that the game itself becomes more involved, to such an extent that feedback strategies may in fact be very difficult if not even impossible to characterise analytically. However, the basic elements of this 'augmented' game are easily laid out, and do deliver interesting results.

Unlike the previous game, here we will suppose for simplicity that τ is a constant. Firms, reacting to taxation, may invest in green innovation in two different ways, taking the form of either *replacement* or *abatement* technologies. A replacement technology is intrinsically characterised by lower emissions (this is the case, for example, of windmills, fuel cells, hybrid engines and photovoltaic panels); an abatement technology, on the contrary, usually consists of a device applied to existing machines, cars or plant whose nature remains brown (for example, catalytic exhaust pipes).

In Dragone *et al.* (2013), a replacement technology is envisaged, whereby the state equation becomes

$$\dot{S} = \sum_{i=1}^{n} r_i(t) q_i(t) - \delta S(t) \qquad (7.16)$$

where the coefficient $r_i(t) \geq 0$ determines the amount of CO_2-equivalent particles emitted by each unit of output. With no consequences on the nature of the game and its predictions, the above state equation can be decomposed into n firm-specific equations with the following form:

$$\dot{s}_i = r_i(t) q_i(t) - \delta s_i(t) \qquad (7.17)$$

where $s_i(t)$ is firm i's contribution to aggregate pollution.

Each technological coefficient $r_i(t)$ represents an additional state variable, evolving over time according to the following dynamics:

$$\dot{r}_i = r_i(t)\left[\upsilon - k_i(t)\right], \upsilon > 0. \tag{7.18}$$

Whenever until $k_i(t) \in [0, \upsilon)$, r_i increases. The instantaneous cost of green R&D activities is $C_i(t) = bk_i^2(t)$, $b > 0$. As a result, firm i's instantaneous profit function is $\pi_i(t) = \left[p(t) - c\right]q_i(t) - bk_i^2(t)$, and firm i chooses $q_i(t)$ and $k_i(t)$ to maximise the flow of its discounted profits under the set of state dynamics (7.17–7.18) and initial conditions $r_i(0) = r_{i0} \geq 0$, $S(0) = S_0 \geq 0$.

If the tax is levied on the individual amount of emissions, the relevant Hamiltonian is

$$\mathcal{H}_i = e^{-\rho t}\left\{\left[a - q_i(t) - \sum_{j \neq i} q_j(t) - c\right]q_i(t) - \tau s_i(t) - bk_i^2(t) + \lambda_{is}\dot{s}_i + \lambda_{ir}\dot{r}_i\right\} \tag{7.19}$$

where the remaining $2(n-1)$ state equations do not appear due to the additive separability between them and those pertaining to firm i. Now, it is not obvious that the presence of a tax triggers green R&D efforts at any time, since the FOC w.r.t. the R&D control

$$\frac{\partial \mathcal{H}_i}{\partial k_i} = -2bk_i - r_i\lambda_{ir} = 0 \tag{7.20}$$

does not contain either s_i or τ. That is, (7.20) seemingly tells that, if a replacement technology is at stake, then taxing pollution may not be a good idea. This is a *negative* interpretation of the above FOC. However, its *positive* interpretation is that emission taxation is not needed for firms to undertake investments in green replacement technologies, for if they do invest in this direction, the source of their incentives is unrelated to tax policy. Indeed, the source is to be found in the costate equation

$$\dot{\lambda}_{ir} = \left[\rho - \upsilon + k_i\right]\lambda_{ir} - \lambda_{is}q_i \tag{7.21}$$

which does not admit the nil solution for λ_{ir} at any time t.

Moreover, the FOC on output yields the following best reply

$$q_i^* = \frac{a - c - \sum_{j \neq i} q_j + \lambda_{is}r_i}{2} \tag{7.22}$$

for any costate vector $\lambda_{-i}(t)$, including (but not necessarily in correspondence of) the nil solution for λ_{is}. Since $\partial q_i^*/\partial \lambda_{is} > 0$ and

$$\lambda_{is} = -\frac{a - c - 2q_i - \sum_{j \neq i} q_j}{r_i} \tag{7.23}$$

is negative whenever $Q < n(a-c)/(n+1)$, which is the industry output at the static Cournot–Nash equilibrium, then any output reduction below the Cournot–Nash level creates a scenario where firms may find it convenient to invest resources in replacement technologies accompanied by a quasi-collusive behaviour on the production side, even in absence of emission taxation or any other environmental policy, for that matter.

This reformulates as the outcome of a differential game framework, a result already highlighted through the use of a repeated game by Damania (1996). More explicitly, the existence of green R&D incentives when $\lambda_{ts} < 0$ can be intuitively grasped observing that

$$\pi^{CN} = \frac{(a-c)^2}{(n+1)^2} < (a - nq - c)\, q - bk^2 \tag{7.24}$$

for infinitely many $k > 0$ and $q \in (0, (a-c)/(n+1))$. Also note that the model rules out the role of consumers' environmental awareness, which might replace, at least to some extent, environmental policy. All of this leads to

Proposition 7.2 *Cournot oligopolists may autonomously (i.e., without being spurred by any regulation or green consumerism) decide to invest in replacement technology, sustaining green R&D via output contractions.*

Of course, consumers pay a price (literally) for a cleaner environment, but still there exist infinitely many combinations of the control paths ensuring higher industry profits and welfare than in the alternative case in which firms do not carry out any innovation effort, and then the income from corporate taxation could be redistributed like manna from heaven onto consumers to compensate the decrease in consumer surplus.

An alternative route is pursued in Feichtinger *et al.* (2016), where market price is not determined along a market demand function, being instead regulated by a public authority. In this respect, the model has much in common with several others reviewed in Chapter 4, and can be considered as an extension of the setup in Leitmann and Schmitendorf (1978) and Feichtinger (1983), with a different interpretation. A market is supplied by *n a priori* symmetric firms with individual capacity $x_i(t)$ over $t \in [0, \infty)$. Assuming all firms always operate at full capacity, the instantaneous profit of firm i is

$$\pi_i(t) = \mathbb{P}x_i(t) - \frac{I_i^2(t)}{2} - ck_i(t) - \frac{k_i^2(t)}{2} - \tau s_i, \tag{7.25}$$

where $k_i(t)$ is the firm's instantaneous green R&D effort and c is a positive constant. The firm invests resources $I_i(t)$ at every instant, to increase capacity $x_i(t)$, whose dynamics is

$$\dot{x}_i(t) = I_i(t) - \delta x_i(t) \tag{7.26}$$

The volume of individual emissions evolves according to

$$\dot{s}_i(t) = x_i(t) - zk_i - h \sum_{j \neq i} k_j - \eta s_i(t) \tag{7.27}$$

where z and η are positive and $h \in [0, z)$ measures the technological externality (if any) from the rivals' R&D investments.

Hence, the game features $2n$ controls in the hands of firms and $2n$ states, while the regulator has to instruments, the market price (determining the mark-up $\mathbb{P}$) and the emission tax τ. Moreover, the game is state-redundant as long as the policy instruments are constant throughout, so that the open-loop solution is strongly time consistent. Firms play simultaneously and noncooperatively at all times.

The current-value Hamiltonian is

$$\mathcal{H}_i(s, x, I, k) = \pi_i + \lambda_{ii}\dot{x}_i + \sum_{j \neq i} \lambda_{ij}\dot{x}_j + \mu_{ii}\dot{s}_i + \sum_{j \neq i} \mu_{ij}\dot{s}_j \tag{7.28}$$

From FOCs, one obtains the Nash equilibrium controls of firm i:

$$I_i^N = \lambda_{ii}$$
$$k_i^N = -c - z\mu_{ii} - h \sum_{j \neq i} \mu_{ij} \tag{7.29}$$

while the set of adjoint equations yields a unique set of solutions,

$$\lambda_{ii} = \frac{1}{\rho + \delta}\left(p - \frac{\tau}{\rho + \eta}\right)$$
$$\lambda_{ij} = 0$$
$$\mu_{ii} = \frac{-\tau}{\rho + \eta} \tag{7.30}$$
$$\mu_{ij} = 0$$

whereby (7.29) delivers the symmetric steady state equilibrium controls corresponding to

$$I^{OL} = \frac{1}{\rho + \delta}\left(p - \frac{\tau}{\rho + \eta}\right)$$
$$k^N = \frac{z\tau}{\rho + \eta} - \gamma \tag{7.31}$$

The regulator can use its toolkit to maximise the levels of social welfare and minimise the volume of industry emissions. Hence, the green R&D investment of the industry at equilibrium is:

$$K^N(\tau(\mathbb{P})) = \frac{n[z\tau(\mathbb{P}) - \gamma(\rho + \eta)]}{\rho + \eta} \tag{7.32}$$

where $\tau(\mathbb{P})$ testifies the interplay between the optimal tax rate solving $\partial SW^N/\partial \tau = 0$ and the optimal mark-up solving $\partial S^N/\partial \mathbb{P} = 0$, which must be accompanied by $\partial^2 SW^N/\partial \tau^2 \leq 0$ and $\partial^2 S^N/\partial \mathbb{P}^2 \geq 0$. Solving this problem, which identifies a unique pair of regulatory instruments $(\mathbb{P}^*, \tau^*)$ meeting second-order conditions for welfare maximization and emission minimization, Feichtinger *et al.* (2016) prove

Proposition 7.3 *In correspondence of the social optimum, where $P^* = \arg\min S^N$ and $\tau^* = \arg\max SW^*$, aggregate R&D in green technology K^N is concave and single-peaked in the number of firms.*

That is, Feichtinger *et al.* (2016) reveal the presence of an inverted U-shaped R&D investment at the industry level, reflecting the findings of Aghion *et al.* (2005) along the current frontier of the Arrow (1962) vs. Schumpeter (1942) debate. The standpoint of the model constructed by Feichtinger *et al.* (2016) suggests that concave R&D curves might be engendered by some forms of regulation rather than by firms' pure incentives (observe that, if $\mathbb{P}$ and τ were truly exogenous, K^N would be increasing in n, delivering thus an Arrovian conclusion).

7.3   Resource Extraction

Also in this case, the use of feedback information extends the analysis illustrated in Chapter 1 to oligopoly. This allows us to understand oligopoly games of resource exploitation as a branch of the literature on the *tragedy of commons* (Gordon, 1954; Hardin, 1968), which we have already encountered in Chapter 2. The background consists in the Verhulst–Lotka–Volterra model (Verhulst, 1838; Lotka, 1925; Volterra, 1931), based on the logistic growth of a natural resource or species, also known as the *prey*:

$$\dot{X} = zX(t)[1 - bX(t)] - Q(t) \tag{7.33}$$

where $X(t)$ is the existing stock and $b, z > 0$ are constants. The dynamics of the prey population is 'disturbed' by the *predator*, harvesting at the instantaneous rate $Q(t)$. This is the essential element of the model we find in the debate on fish wars (Clark and Munro, 1975; Levhari and Mirman, 1980), where $Q(t) = \sum_{i=1}^{n} q_i(t)$ is the collective harvest carried out by n fishermen exploiting the same fishing grounds. Given the quadratic nature of (7.33), the analytic solution of Bellman equations which would deliver the feedback equilibrium remains out of reach, and therefore the current literature makes use of the linear approximation $\dot{X} = \eta X(t) - Q(t)$.

What follows is a synthetic overview of the main results produced by Benchekroun (2003, 2008), Fujiwara (2008), Colombo and Labrecciosa (2013a,b, 2015), Lambertini and Mantovani (2014, 2016) and Lambertini (2016a). In particular, the following exposition pays particular attention to the characterization of the *continuum* of nonlinear feedback equilibria based upon Rowat's (2007) method, instead of Tsutsui and Mino's (1990), which is used in Colombo and Labrecciosa (2015).

7.3.1   The Tragedy in Nonlinear Strategies

The first step consists in characterising the linear feedback strategies in two different ways. To ease the exposition, I will drop the time argument. Under feedback rules, firm i chooses q_i to maximise the following HJB equation:

$$\rho V_i(X) = \max_{q_i} \left[(a - c - Q) q_i + V_i'(X) \dot{X} \right] \tag{7.34}$$

where parameters a and c have the usual meaning. The game takes place under full information and simultaneous play over an infinite horizon (the possibility of resource exhaustion is considered below). Now take a look at the FOC w.r.t. the individual control,

$$a - c - 2q_i - \sum_{j \neq i} q_j - V_i'(X) = 0 \tag{7.35}$$

The imposition of symmetry delivers $q = \max\{0, [a - c - V'(X)]/(n+1)\}$. Provided $a - c > V'(X)$, substituting $q = [a - c - V'(X)]/(n+1)$ into the Bellman equation and conjecturing the form $V(X) = \varepsilon_1 X^2 + \varepsilon_2 X + \varepsilon_3$ for the value function, one may solve (7.34) in the way we have by now seen several times, to obtain two

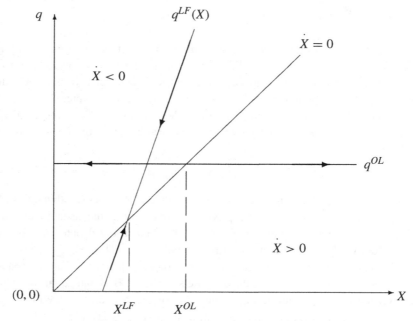

Figure 7.1 Open-loop and linear feedback solutions in the (X, q) space

strategies: one is the quasi-static Cournot open-loop quantity, independent of X and unstable, while the other is a proper linear feedback output policy:

$$q^{LF}(X) = \max\left\{0, \frac{\eta(2\eta - \rho)(n+1)^2 X - (a-c)\left[2\eta - \rho(n^2+1)\right]}{2\eta(n+1)n^2}\right\} \quad (7.36)$$

which implies that the residual stock in steady state is

$$X^{LF} = \frac{nq^{LF}}{\eta} = \max\left\{0, \frac{(a-c)\left[2\eta - \rho(n^2+1)\right]}{\delta[2\eta - \rho(n+1)](n+1)}\right\} > 0 \,\forall\, \eta > \frac{\rho(n^2+1)}{2} \quad (7.37)$$

provided that $q^{LF}(X)$ in (7.36) is positive. Note that the expression appearing in curly brackets in (7.37) is indeed positive for all $\eta > \rho(n^2+1)/2$.

Both linear feedback strategies are drawn, together with the steady state locus $\dot{X} = 0$, in Figure 7.1, where the arrows have the usual task of illustrating stability (or instability). Going back to Figure 2.6, one immediately notes that, when at least two firms operate in the industry, the intersections between quantity strategies and the steady state locus identify a segment which is a portion of the line $\dot{X} = 0$. This will be of special interest in what follows.

Now observe that in order to characterise nonlinear feedback strategies, we can treat the problem in a reverse perspective, starting from (7.35) and reading it as an equilibrium relationship between the optimal control and the partial derivative of the value function w.r.t. the state. This alternative method consists in posing $q = q(X)$ and then solving (7.35) w.r.t. the partial derivative of the value function, whereby we have $V'(X) = a - c - (n+1)q(X)$. This can be substituted back into (7.34), thus yielding an identity in X. The HJB equation can then be differentiated w.r.t. the state variable and rearranged so as to obtain the following differential equation

$$q'(X) = \frac{(\eta - \rho)\left[(n+1)q(X) - a + c\right]}{2n^2 q(X) - \eta(n+1)X - (n-1)(a-c)}, \tag{7.38}$$

which identifies every single feedback strategy, linear and nonlinear alike. Let's focus for the moment on the linear solutions, to be obtained anew from (7.38).

If the control is linear in X, we may stipulate that $q(X) = \phi X + \varrho$ to rewrite (7.38) as

$$\phi = \frac{(\eta - \rho)\left[(n+1)(\phi X + \varrho) - a + c\right]}{2n^2(\phi X + \varrho) - \eta(n+1)X - (n-1)(a-c)} \tag{7.39}$$

which is equivalent to

$$(\eta - \rho)\left[a - c - \varrho(n+1)\right] + \phi\left[2\varrho n^2 - (a-c)(n-1)\right]$$

$$+ \phi\left[\rho(n+1) - 2\left(\eta(n+1) - (a-c)n^2\right)\right]X = 0 \tag{7.40}$$

Hence, solving the above equation entails solving the following system:

$$\phi\left[\rho(n+1) - 2\left(\eta(n+1) - \phi n^2\right)\right] = 0$$
$$(\eta - \rho)\left[a - c - \varrho(n+1)\right] + \phi\left[2\varrho n^2 - (a-c)(n-1)\right] = 0 \tag{7.41}$$

w.r.t. the unknown parameters $\{\phi, \varrho\}$. Since (7.41) is quadratic in ϕ, it produces two solutions. The first,

$$\phi = 0; \varrho = \frac{a-c}{n+1} \tag{7.42}$$

generates the open-loop control $q = (a-c)/(n+1)$; the second,

$$\phi = \frac{(n+1)(2\eta - \rho)}{2n^2}; \varrho = \frac{(a-c)\left[\rho(n^2+1) - 2\eta\right]}{2\eta(n+1)n^2} \tag{7.43}$$

delivers the non-degenerate linear feedback control appearing in (7.36).

Enough about the alternative derivation of linear feedback strategies. Now we may turn to nonlinear ones. The following exposition uses the method of Rowat (2007) – as anticipated above – and summarises the analysis carried out in Lambertini (2016a).

To begin with, look at (7.38) to note that $q'(X) = 0$ in correspondence of

$$q_0(X) = \frac{a-c}{n+1} = q^{OL} \tag{7.44}$$

and $q'(X) \to \pm\infty$ at

$$q_\infty(X) = \frac{(a-c)(n-1) + \eta(n+1)X}{2n^2} \tag{7.45}$$

which identifies the so-called *non invertibility* line. Then, observe that the Bellman equation is

$$\rho V(S) - \delta S V'(S) = 0 \tag{7.46}$$

if $V'(X) \geq a - c$, and therefore $q = [a - c - V'(X)] / (n + 1)$. In such a case, the solution of (7.46) is $V(X) = S^{\rho/\eta} C$, provided $C > \left[\eta (a - c) X^{\frac{\eta - \rho}{\eta}} \right] / \rho$.

A completely different scenario appears for all $V'(X) < a - c$, with the Bellman equation taking the following form:

$$\rho V(X) = \frac{n^2 [V'(X)]^2 + (a - c)^2 + V'(X) [\eta (n + 1)^2 X - (a - c) (n^2 + 1)]}{(n + 1)^2} \tag{7.47}$$

For all $\sigma > V'(S)$, differentiating (7.47) one obtains

$$V''(X) = \frac{(\eta - \rho) (n + 1)^2 V'(X)}{(a - c) (n^2 + 1) - \eta (n + 1)^2 X - 2nV'(X)} \tag{7.48}$$

provided $a \neq c + [\eta (n + 1)^2 X + 2nV'(X)] / (n^2 + 1)$. To solve (7.48), we may use the auxiliary variable $V'(X) = x + \mathbb{A}$ and $X = \psi + \mathbb{B}$, with $\mathbb{A} = 0$ and $\mathbb{B} = (n^2 + 1) (a - c) / [\eta (n + 1)^2]$ to obtain

$$\frac{dx}{d\psi} = \frac{(n^2 + 1) (\rho - \eta) x}{\eta (n + 1)^2 \psi + 2n^2 x} \tag{7.49}$$

which is homogeneous of degree zero. This can be further rewritten, using $\varpi \equiv x / \psi$, whereby $x = \psi \varpi$ and $\partial x / \partial \psi = \varpi + \psi \cdot \partial \varpi / \partial \psi$, into

$$\varpi + \psi \frac{\partial \varpi}{\partial \psi} = \frac{(n^2 + 1) (\rho - \eta) \varpi}{\eta (n + 1)^2 + 2n^2 \varpi} \tag{7.50}$$

whose solutions are $\varpi^{OL} = 0$ and $\varpi^{LF} = (n + 1)^2 (\rho - 2\eta) / (2n^2)$, whereby, reverting to the output strategies, we obtain the linear feedback solutions once again:

$$q(\varpi^{OL}) = \frac{a - c}{n + 1} = q^{OL}$$

$$q(\varpi^{LF}) = \frac{\eta (2\eta - \rho) (n + 1)^2 X - (a - c) [2\eta - \rho (n^2 + 1)]}{2\eta (n + 1) n^2} = q^{LF} \tag{7.51}$$

To conclude the procedure, solve

$$\frac{d\psi}{\psi} = \frac{[\eta (n + 1)^2 / (2n^2) + \varpi] d\varpi}{(\varpi - \varpi^{OL}) (\varpi - \varpi^{LF})} = \frac{\overline{\varphi} d\varpi}{(\varpi - \varpi^{OL})} + \frac{\underline{\varphi} d\varpi}{(\varpi - \varpi^{LF})} \tag{7.52}$$

w.r.t. coefficients $\overline{\varphi}$ and $\underline{\varphi}$,[3] which brings us to the following equation,

$$M = [V'(X) - \mathbb{A} - X^{OL} (X - \mathbb{B})]^{\overline{\varphi}} \cdot [V'(X) - \mathbb{A} - X^{LF} (X - \mathbb{B})]^{\underline{\varphi}} \tag{7.53}$$

where X^{OL} and X^{LF} are the solutions of $X = 0$ at $q = q(\varpi^{OL})$ and $q = q(\varpi^{LF})$, respectively. In fact, this is the same equation which would emerge from the method used by Tsutsui and Mino (1990) for the case in which $V'(X) < a - c$. The present procedure follows Rowat (2007), where the adoption of the *catching-up optimality*

---

[3] This can be done by using the method of partial fractions, yielding $\overline{\varphi} = \eta (2\eta - \rho)$ and $\underline{\varphi} = (\eta - \rho) / (2\eta - \rho)$, which sum up to one.

criterion allows one to address the possibility of infinitely valued value functions without imposing restrictions on the state space, a procedure which endogenises the domain over which strategies are defined.

A degenerate solution to Equation (7.53) is the tangency one, which can be easily characterised by identifying the coordinates of the tangency point between the highest isocline to the south-east of the steady state locus, and the steady state locus itself. The tangency condition requires $q'(X) = \eta/n$ and $q(X) = \eta X/n$. Consequently, (7.38) takes the following shape

$$\frac{\eta}{n} = \frac{(\eta - \rho)\,[n(a - c) - \eta(n + 1)X]}{n\,(n - 1)\,(a - c - \eta X)} \tag{7.54}$$

which implies

$$q^{T} = \frac{(a - c)\,(\eta - n\rho)}{n\,[2\eta - \rho\,(n + 1)]} \tag{7.55}$$

and $X^{T} = nq^{T}/\eta$. The interpretation of superscript T is intuitive. However, the interesting result can be formulated in these terms:

Proposition 7.4 *The adoption of feedback rules generates uncountably many nonlinear feedback equilibria, all of which are stable.*

This *continuum* of nonlinear feedback solutions is engendered by the infinitely many values of the constant M. Its graphical representation is in Figure 7.2, which replicates Figure 7.1 with the *addendum* of the tangency solution (point T), which is the first

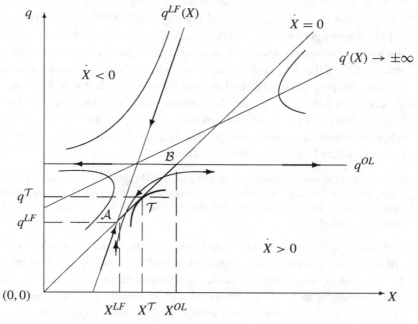

Figure 7.2 The *continuum* of nonlinear feedback solutions

unstable nonlinear feedback solution. In particular, every intersection between an iso-cline and the steady state locus, from $\mathcal{T}$ to $\mathcal{B}$ (the open-loop equilibrium), is indeed unstable. Conversely, any intersection from $\mathcal{A}$ (the feedback equilibrium associated with the linear feedback strategy) to $\mathcal{T}$ is a stable steady state equilibrium. The thick linear segment $\mathcal{AB}$ measures the whole set of nonlinear feedback solutions.

The scenario emerging under feedback information is extremely suggestive and deserves a few comments. The first thing to note is

Proposition 7.5 *Any (stable) feedback steady state equilibrium is characterised by a lower individual and aggregate harvest than that associated with open-loop rules.*

Also note that the lowest steady state harvest is generated by the linear feedback solution. Relatedly, the second point worth stressing is that, as already highlighted in Tsutsui and Mino (1990) concerning the sticky price model, stable feedback solutions have a quasi-collusive flavour, but given the positive slope of the steady state locus, any reduction in the steady state harvest goes along with a proportional reduction, whose extent depends on the ratio n/η, in the residual resource stock. I will come back to these issues in the next section.

7.3.2   Efficiency Issues

The solution of the feedback oligopoly game of resource extraction brings us back to recurrent issue in IO, which pops up again in connection with the tragedy of the commons: Is there an optimal industry structure? Or, is there an optimal number of firms in the commons? This is the subject of a subset of this literature (Cornes *et al.*, 1986; Mason *et al.*, 1988; Mason and Polasky, 1997, 2002). Its main finding is twofold: (1) one cannot get two eggs in one basket, i.e., there is no industry structure striking the balance between welfare maximisation and the parallel objective of maximising the preservation of the stock; and (2) the compromise between the natural resource's growth rate and the pressure exerted by time discounting is such that it is socially efficient to have at least a duopoly, for any level of the stock and time discounting (Mason and Polasky, 1997). This second conclusion is not only at odds with the *a priori* intuition whereby one would expect monopoly to exert the lowest pressure on the stock, but it also contradicts Hotelling (1931, p. 138):

In contrast to the conservationist belief that a too rapid exploitation of natural resources is taking place, we have the retarding influence of monopolies ... the tendency of monopoly and partial monopoly is to keep production below the optimum rate and to exact excessive prices from consumers.

While indeed we are unable to find a single industry structure which can be deemed efficient under all respects, it is nonetheless true that a public authority interested in the preservation of the resource or species may want to regulate the access to the commons. This problem is tackled by Lambertini and Mantovani (2014), where the possibility of resource depletion is explicitly admitted. They find simple conditions involving n, η and ρ such that the residual stock in steady state is positive. Keeping in mind that the steady state condition is $X = nq/\eta$ under any information structure (which implies that if $X = 0$, then also $q = 0$) and using the expressions of q^{LF} and q^{T}, one can establish that $q^{T}, X^{T} > 0$ for all $n < \max\{\eta/\rho, 1\}$ and $q^{LF}, X^{LF} > 0$ for all $n < \max\{\sqrt{(2\eta - \rho)/\rho}, 1\}$, with $\eta/\rho > \sqrt{(2\eta - \rho)/\rho}$ always. This proves

Proposition 7.6 *If $\sqrt{(2\eta - \rho)/\rho} \geq 2$, then there exists an industry structure (possibly oligopolistic) ensuring the survival of a positive resource stock at any stable (linear and nonlinear) feedback steady state equilibrium. If $\sqrt{(2\eta - \rho)/\rho} \leq 1$, then the stock is bound to fully deplete for any industry structure.*

And there is more to it. Ever since Fershtman and Kamien (1987) and Reynolds (1987), we are accustomed to the idea that feedback information enhances strategic interaction, driving firms to expand output (in this case, harvest) to outsell each other. Here, a mixed picture seems to emerge at equilibrium, with progressively lower outputs and stocks as we move to the south-west of the tangency point along the locus $\dot{X} = 0$. This is the consequence of the so-called voracity effect, first defined by Lane and Tornell (1996) and Tornell and Lane (1999) in another context and then outlined in the present model by Benchekroun (2008).

For a moment, forget about the specific nature of the game and consider a state variable growing at an instantaneous rate $\eta > 0$. A priori, one would expect the steady state stock to be increasing in η. If this does not happen, we are observing the consequences of voracity, for the following reason. Any increase in the growth rate induces players to increase their pressure on the state accordingly, whereby voracity couples with feedback information along the path to the steady state, compromising the survival of the stock in steady state. This is the case of the resource extraction game, in any of its stable feedback equilibria, as can be easily checked by verifying that $\partial X^{T}/\partial \eta < 0$ and $\partial X^{LF}/\partial \eta < 0$.

Adding up a parametric formulation of strategic delegation à la Vickers (1985), Lambertini (2016a) shows that the presence of managers mitigates the voracity effect under feedback rules, thereby favouring the preservation of the resource stock. A similar effect is exerted by the emergence of social status concerns in the minds of oligopolists exploiting a common-pool renewable resource, as illustrated in Benchekroun and Long (2016).

Colombo and Labrecciosa (2015) further extend the model by including product differentiation as in Singh and Vives (1984), to investigate also price-setting behaviour. This allows them to prove that, again in contrast with acquired wisdom, there exist plausible conditions ensuring that Cournot behaviour outperforms Bertrand behaviour in terms of welfare, profits and consumer surplus both during the game and in steady state, because in the Bertrand setting firms are more sensitive to the consequences of price cuts associated with output expansion at any time, being aware that such price cuts are endogenously punished, as they diminish all firms' harvesting possibilities in the future.

Another relevant extension, also due to Colombo and Labrecciosa (2013a), considers the initial parcelization of a common pool across a population of Cournot oligopolists, leading to several entirely new conclusions in terms of exploitation rates and their welfare consequence, both in the short and in the long run. The impact effect of parcelization is that extraction rates are higher (resp., lower) than those adopted by the same number of firms exploiting a common pool, if the asset stock is sufficiently larger (resp., small). This is in sharp contrast with the acquired wisdom concerning free-riding incentives in the tragedy of the commons. A related consequence is that, in a range of resource stocks, common property is socially preferable to private access to a single pool. The long-run repercussions of private property are positive, as this allocation welfare-dominates common property.[4]

Using the duopolistic version of the same model, Colombo and Labrecciosa (2013b) show that if the growth rate of the resource is sufficiently high, then there exists a unique globally asymptotically stable steady state of the differential game which indeed reproduces the static Cournot–Nash solution. Moreover, the limit game which generates if ρ approaches zero yields multiple linear feedback strategies whose associated price trajectory asymptotically converges to a level higher than the static Cournot–Nash price.

7.3.3   Nonrenewable Resources and Cartel Behaviour

The analysis of the dynamic behaviour of an industry exploiting nonrenewable resources, like fossil fuels, requires $\eta = 0$, so that the state equation is simply $\dot{X} = -Q$. The starting point of the related literature is the Hotelling (1931) model, which sets out by describing the free access case and then also describes the optimal extraction strategy of a monopolist (and therefore also a cartel made up by identical firms using the same technology and not threatened by any competitors) via the Hotelling rule defining the optimal path of the price:

$$\frac{\dot{p}}{p(t) - c(X(t))} = \rho \qquad (7.56)$$

which, if extraction is costless, states that the instantaneous growth rate of the price at which the resource is sold on the final market must coincide with the discount rate used by the firms. Otherwise, $p(t) - c(X(t))$ is the *royalty*.

If these firms expect a replacement technology to become operational at a finite date T (for instance, some green technology using renewable resources), then the rent must be fully exploited before the resource becomes altogether worthless. This yields the price curve in Figure 7.3, where (1) p_0 is the initial price, (2) p_R is the market price of the replacement technology, and (3) the extraction cost is constant (so that the royalty increases monotonically over time).

Manipulating Figure 7.3, one can intuitively predict the consequences of any change in relevant parameters, like the price p_R of the replacement technology or the discount rate ρ. The first scenario appears in Figure 7.4, where a reduction of p_R brings about a reduction of the horizon for the exploitation of the resource being extracted.

Figure 7.5 portrays the case in which the firms become more impatient, whereby the increase in ρ also shrinks the terminal time to T' and, to allow for the full extraction

---

[4] Colombo and Labrecciosa (2013a) also prove that, beyond a well-defined threshold of the stock, the exact definition of property rights over the asset has no impact on welfare, since the two regimes yield the same welfare level.

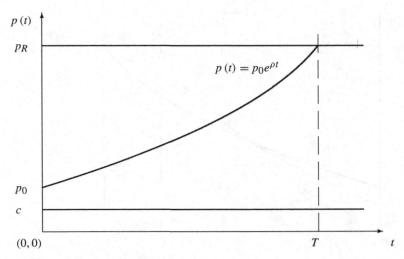

Figure 7.3 The optimal path of price and royalty

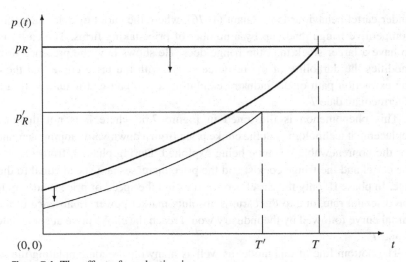

Figure 7.4 The effect of a reduction in p_R

of the rent, the initial price must also diminish. Reversing the perspective, the same graph also illustrate the scenario created by a decrease in T. By the way, this is related to the green paradox (Sinn, 2012), according to which an earlier adoption of a substitute technology causes a faster accumulation of emissions and consequently a higher environmental damage.[5]

Indeed, Hotelling (1931) obtains his intertemporal pricing rule under the assumption of a perfectly competitive industry. Probably the earliest analysis of the same problem

---

[5] The discussion about the green paradox is expanding. See Grafton *et al.* (2012), Smulders *et al.* (2012), van der Ploeg and Withagen (2012) and Pittel *et al.* (2014).

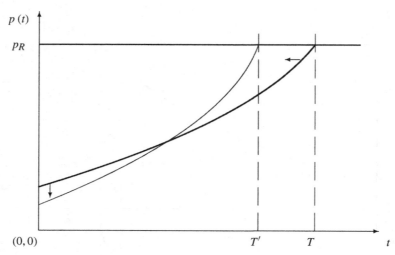

Figure 7.5 The effect of an increase in ρ or a decrease in T

under cartel behaviour is in Salant (1976), where the cartel or a dominant firm faces a competitive fringe made up by a number of price-taking firms. The cartel is assumed to have a larger stock than the fringe does. He shows how the presence of this fringe modifies the durability of the resource stock, with the price curve and therefore also the extraction path of the industry exhibiting a two-phase structure, with a kink at an intermediate date $\widehat{T}$.[6]

This phenomenon is illustrated in Figure 7.6, where $\bar{p}$ is not the price of the replacement technology, but the choke price from a downward-sloping demand function for the nonrenewable resource being exploited. During phase I, from $t = 0$ to $t = \widehat{T}$, the cartel and the fringe coexist and the price increases at a speed equal to the discount rate. In phase II, only the cartel is operation and the speed of price is strictly lower than the discount rate, due to the cartel's absolute market power. In absence of a cartel, the initial curve followed by the industry would reach the choke price at some date between $\widehat{T}$ and T.

The bottom line of this model as well as many others contemplating the same landscape is

Proposition 7.7 *A competitive fringe erodes part of the cartel rent. However, the presence of the cartel extends the time horizon along which a positive stock exists.*

It is also worth noting that the essence of the cartel vs. fringe game is already contained in Hotelling (1931), where the price curves of a pure monopoly and a perfectly competitive industry are derived, yielding the picture in Figure 7.7. The thick curve describes the intertemporal evolution of the price if the industry is controlled by a single

---

[6] This literature leaves cartel stability aside, as cartels exploiting nonrenewables are, more often than not, explicit (OPEC is the most evident example). The issue of stability is instead considered in relation to cartels extracting renewable resources. In such cases, stability criteria rely either on threats to enforce bargaining solutions, as in Hämäläinen *et al.* (1985), or on trigger strategies, as in Kaitala and Pohjola (1988).

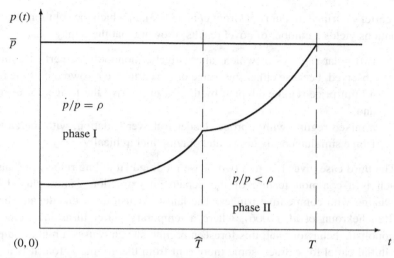

Figure 7.6 Cartel vs. fringe: The modified Hotelling rule

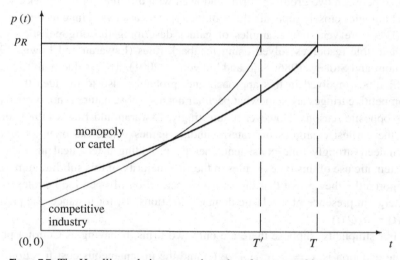

Figure 7.7 The Hotelling rule in monopoly and perfect competition

firm or a cartel. Intuitively, the lower envelope of the two curves in Figure 7.7 has the same qualitative properties of the modified Hotelling rule appearing in Figure 7.6; in fact, a similar graph appears in Salant (1976, figure 2, p. 1087).

Salant's (1976) analysis relies on open-loop information, with the cartel taking the fringe 's collective extraction rate as given and all firms' activities being costless. Later extensions remove the last two assumptions to assign a realistic dominant position to the cartel and to encompass the case of positive (and sometimes increasing and asymmetric) marginal extraction costs.[7] Probably the only case of a feedback Stackelberg solution to

---

[7] See Gilbert (1978), Pindyck (1978), Lewis and Schmalensee (1980), Ulph and Folie (1980), Newbery (1981), Loury (1986), Groot et al. (1992) and Gaudet and Long (1994), *inter alia*.

the cartel vs. fringe model is in Groot *et al.* (2003), in which the solution of the Bellman equations yields a number of novel results, showing that there may exist

- two polar regimes in which, alternatively, monopoly or perfect competition is observed, because either the fringe or the cartel are thrown out of the industry;
- a limit price regime adopted by the cartel to drive the fringe out of the market; and
- a mixed regime with a proper leader-follower situation, with the cartel and the fringe simultaneously active and playing hierarchically.

The third case gives rise to a two-phase modified Hotelling rule as in Salant (1976), which is a common feature of the debate on extraction games played by cartels coexisting with competitive fringes. The latest extensions of this debate can be found in Benchekroun *et al.* (2006), where a temporary cartel turns into noncooperative oligopolistic behaviour and this foreseen regime switch causes a higher output rate by the initial cartel to 'extract' some more rent from the ground before it is too late; and in Benchekroun *et al.* (2009, 2010), where the limit properties of a noncooperative game between two groups of firms endowed with different reserve stock and extraction technologies closely replicate those of the typical cartel vs. fringe model.

There are very few examples of games describing the oligopolistic extraction of exhaustible resources solved using feedback rules (Eswaran and Lewis, 1985; Reinganum and Stokey, 1986; Salo and Tahvonen, 2001). This is due both to the technical difficulties involved in this approach and, probably, also to the idea that cartels and competitive fringes are somewhat *peculiar* agents whose nature is not properly strategic, for opposite reasons. However, interestingly, Eswaran and Lewis (1985) provide one of the earliest examples of state-redundant games where the open-loop equilibrium is indeed strongly time consistent, thereby providing a technical justification to the systematic use of this type of rules in the vast majority of this sub-literature. Even more importantly, they prove that the subgame perfection of open-loop strategies may also emerge in presence of isoelastic demand functions, as, for instance, the parabolic one, $p(t) = a/Q(t)$.

For simplicity, suppose there are only two firms, behaving as Cournot players. The state equation is $\dot{X} = -q_1(t) - q_2(t)$ and the instantaneous cost function is $C_i(t) = cq_i(t)$ (while in Eswaran and Lewis, 1985, extraction costs are nil). Instead of using the method illustrated in Chapter 1, here I will show that the open-loop solution is strongly time consistent because the Bellman equation of each player can be solved by guessing a linear form for the value function, such as $V_i(X) = \varepsilon_1 X(t) + \varepsilon_2$. The HJB equation of firm i is

$$\rho V_i(X(t)) = \max_{q_i(t)} \left\{ \frac{aq_i(t)}{q_i(t) + q_j(t)} - cq_i(t) - V_i'(X(t))\left[q_1(t) + q_2(t)\right] \right\} \quad (7.57)$$

and the resulting FOC, after imposing symmetry, is

$$\frac{a}{4q} - c - V'(X) = 0 \quad (7.58)$$

Then, plugging the Nash instantaneous control $q^N = a/\left[4\left(c + V'\left(X\right)\right)\right]$ back into (7.57) and relying on the aforementioned guess about the shape of the value function, the symmetric Bellman equation becomes

$$\frac{4\rho\left(c + \varepsilon_1\right)\left(\varepsilon_2 + \varepsilon_1 X\right) - ac}{4\left(c + \varepsilon_1\right)} = 0 \tag{7.59}$$

which gives rise to the following system:

$$\begin{aligned} 4\rho\left(c + \varepsilon_1\right)\varepsilon_2 - ac &= 0 \\ 4\rho\varepsilon_1\left(c + \varepsilon_1\right)X &= 0 \end{aligned} \tag{7.60}$$

The first equation is solved by $\varepsilon_2 = ac/\left[4\rho\left(c + \varepsilon_1\right)\right]$, while the second clearly admits the solutions $\varepsilon_1 = 0$ and $\varepsilon_1 = -c$. Note that the absence of a quadratic term in (7.59) indicates that the initial guess is correct, and therefore open-loop information grants subgame perfection. Regrettably, this promising line of research has been left aside for a long time. It should be revived, also, in view of the discussion contained in Chapter 3 about the need to extend existing models to nonlinear demand functions.

7.4 Extensions

This section offers a compact overview of further applications of the basic setups to account for auxiliary but still extremely relevant issues concerning both renewable and nonrenewable resource exploitation. As we will see, the following examples, on the one hand, offer a confirmation of the potential of the basic model and, on the other, accomplish the task of stimulating further efforts to enhance our comprehension of the general picture.

7.4.1 Renewables

The resource extraction model initially conceived to describe the tragedy of the commons leaves the problem of capacity aside. Take the fish war just to fix ideas: installed capacity is determined by the number and size of fishing vessels owned by firms, and this needs investment in capacity as in Reynolds (1987). The first work in this direction is in Clark et al. (1979), subsequently generalised by Jørgensen and Kort (1997) where the matter is treated using a general equilibrium approach.

They consider a single firm holding exclusive fishing rights. The stock growth rate is the same as in Chapter 1,

$$F\left(X\left(t\right)\right) = \begin{cases} \eta X\left(t\right) & \forall X\left(t\right) \in \left(0, X_y\right] \\ \eta X_y\left(\dfrac{X_{\max} - X\left(t\right)}{X_{\max} - X_y}\right) & \forall X\left(t\right) \in \left(X_y, X_{\max}\right] \end{cases} \tag{7.61}$$

but the state equation is now

$$\dot{X} = F\left(X\left(t\right)\right) - vh\left(t\right)X\left(t\right) \tag{7.62}$$

where $h(t)$ is the effort put by the firm in harvesting and v is a positive parameter measuring *catchability*. This reformulation of the evolution of the stock amounts to saying that $vh(t)X(t) = Q(t)$. At the same time, the firm invest in capacity, with the same dynamics as in Reynolds (1987):

$$\dot{k} = I(t) - \delta k(t) \tag{7.63}$$

and the installed capacity poses an upper bound to the harvesting effort $h(t)$ at every instant. This rules out any equilibria with harvesting volumes exceeding capacity. Moreover, holding idle capacity is irrational; hence, the reversibility of investment has the relevant implication of making $h(t) = k(t)$ at every instant, which has the advantage of eliminating a variable.

Once again, the market price is assumed to be constant at p.[8] Accordingly, instantaneous revenues are $R(t) = pQ(t) = pvh(t)X(t)$. The cost function is linear in the harvesting effort, $C(t) = ch(t)$. As a result, instantaneous gross profits from harvesting are $\pi(t) = [pvX(t) - c]h(t)$.

The firm may finance its investment either by using internal funds (retained profits) or by borrowing resources on to the financial market. Defining $B(t)$ its debt/lending position and $\mathcal{E}(t)$ its stock of equities, the balance sheet implies the identity $k(t) = B(t) + \mathcal{E}(t)$ at all times. Finally, if $d(t)$ is the rate of dividend payout and $C(B(t))$ is the cost of borrowing, we have that net profits are either distributed as dividends or retained as internal funds:

$$[pvX(t) - c]h(t) - \delta k(t) - C(B(t)) = d(t) + \dot{\mathcal{E}}(t) \tag{7.64}$$

and the associated cash account identity is

$$[pvX(t) - c]h(t) = d(t) + C(B(t)) + I(t) - \dot{B}(t) \tag{7.65}$$

The firm chooses controls $h(t)$ and $d(t)$ to maximise its present value

$$\mathbf{d} = \int d(t) e^{-\rho t} dt \tag{7.66}$$

where the expression for $d(t)$ obtains from (7.65), and the discount rate ρ is higher than the rate paid to lenders, ρ_B. The dynamic constraints (7.62–7.64). Candidate paths are characterised by the following features:

Path I: $h = d = 0$, and therefore the firm is lending ($B < 0$) but is also out of business, as capacity and investment are also nil.

Path II: $h, d > 0$, and therefore the firm is indebted at a constant level.

Path III $h \geq 0, d = 0$. In this case, either (a) $B \leq 0$, which is equivalent to saying $h = 0$, or (b) $B > 0$, which is equivalent to saying that $h > \mathcal{E}$. The first subcase admits a constant resource stock. In the second subcase, the evolution of the stock depends on the evolution of the firm's debt/lending position B.

---

[8] This assumption is common to the original Verhulst–Lotka–Volterra model which can be found in any textbook on resource economics (see Dasgupta and Heal, 1979; Pearce and Turner, 1989). The present model can indeed be seen as a general reformulation of that model to account for capital accumulation and financial issues.

Jørgensen and Kort (1997) solve the model proving that the shape of the optimal harvesting strategy is captured by the following

Proposition 7.8 *Consider dates* $0 < \widetilde{T} < \overline{T} < \infty$. *Then, (1) if* X_0 *is low enough, optimal harvesting follows Path I from* $t = 0$ *to* $\widetilde{T}$, *Path IIIa/b from* $\widetilde{T}$ *to* $\overline{T}$, *and Path II onwards; (2) if* X_0 *is high enough, Path I is not adopted (*$\widetilde{T}$ *collapses to zero), and optimal harvesting follows Path IIIb from* $\widetilde{T}$ *to* $\overline{T}$, *and Path II onwards.*

This result has two relevant implications. The first is that the model actually predicts that if the initial stock is small, the firm exploits the reversibility of investment to shrink its capacity and harvesting effort to zero in order to leave the resource into the sea or ground and grow up undisturbed. As soon as it is convenient (at $\widetilde{T}$), harvesting activity starts at an increasing rate and then becomes flat at $\overline{T}$. The second is that as soon as the harvest rate becomes flat w.r.t. time, the same happens to the equity stock $\mathcal{E}$, the debt position $\mathcal{B}$ and the resource stock X. The latter finding mirrors the classical result of optimal harvesting under monopoly we are accustomed to from the Verhulst–Lotka–Volterra model.

7.4.2 Nonrenewables

The main model examining the optimal extraction of nonrenewable resources relies on the assumption of a given initial stock and treats the problem of the replacement technology as a boundary condition. Both assumptions facilitate the analysis, and this explains their adoption in the early debate. However, they are quite unrealistic, and casual observation suggests that firms carry out costly exploration activities trying to enlarge the exploitable stock, while other agents (but sometimes also the same extracting firms) invest considerable amounts of resources in search of replacement or *backstop* technologies.

Research in the first direction justifies the efforts to enlarge the stock on several grounds, including uncertainty about its exact size, extraction cost abatement or the by now familiar motive to preempt or just outsell rivals (see Peterson, 1978; Arrow and Chang, 1982; Mohr, 1988; Quyen, 1988, 1991). Indeed, strategic interaction may drive firms to overinvest in exploration, as shown by Boyce and Vojtassak (2008). This also suggests the possible existence of an endogenous effect of industry structure on aggregate exploration investment, as in Lambertini (2014), where n Cournot single-product firms selling differentiated goods as in Singh and Vives (1984), with individual demand functions $p_i(t) = a - q_i(t) - \gamma \sum_{j \neq i} q_j(t)$, invest in drilling while exploiting either n private pools or a single common pool. In the first case, the i-th state equation is

$$\dot{x}_i = v x_i(t) k_i(t) - q_i(t) \tag{7.67}$$

where $x_i(t)$ is the stock contained in firm i's pool, $k_i(t)$ is the instantaneous drilling effort and $v > 0$ is a constant. In the second case, the unique state equations is

$$\dot{X} = v X(t) \sum_{i=1}^{n} k_i(t) - \sum_{i=1}^{n} q_i(t) \tag{7.68}$$

whereby the model has much the same flavour as that in Fershtman and Nitzan (1991). In both scenarios, the total cost function of firm i is $C_i(t) = cq_i^2(t) + bk_i^2(t)$ at every instant. Due to the presence of a multiplicative effect in the state dynamics, the game is solved under open-loop information and yields the following results.

If private pools are exploited, the model reaches a unique stable steady state at

$$x_{pp}^{OL} = \frac{av + \sqrt{a^2v^2 - 8\beta\rho^2\left[2(1+c) + \gamma(n-1)\right]}}{2v\left[2(1+c) + \gamma(n-1)\right]\rho} \; ; \; k_{pp}^{OL} = \frac{\rho}{v} \; ; \; q_{pp}^{OL} = \rho x_{pp}^{OL} \quad (7.69)$$

where subscript pp mnemonics for *private pools*. The expressions in (7.69) imply the following:

Proposition 7.9 *If each firm has private access to a pool, the industry investment in exploration is monotonically increasing in the number of firms, and the proportion between equilibrium extraction and stock is measured by the discount rate.*

If instead all firms exploit the commons, the system reaches the following saddle point equilibrium:

$$X_{cp}^{OL} = \frac{anv + \sqrt{a^2n^2v^2 - 8\beta\rho^2\left[2(1+c) + \gamma(n-1)\right]}}{2v\left[2(1+c) + \gamma(n-1)\right]\rho} \; ; \; k_{cp}^{OL} = \frac{\rho}{nv}; \; q_{cp}^{OL} = \frac{\rho X_{cp}^{OL}}{n}$$

$$(7.70)$$

where subscript cp stands for *common pool*. Hence,

Proposition 7.10 *Under free access to a common pool resource, aggregate drilling investment is independent of industry structure, and the proportion between per-firm equilibrium extraction and common stock is measured by the ratio between the discount rate and the number of firms.*

Jointly, these two propositions says that, in presence of private pools, the behaviour of aggregate investment is Arrovian, while if a common pool is jointly exploited, it is neither Arrovian nor Schumpeterian. Indeed, as firms are aware of the problems connected with the private provision of a public good, aggregate investment in expanding the common stock is actually equal to the equilibrium amount of resources invested by each firm in the alternative model. That is, the tragedy of commons literally sweeps $n - 1$ efforts away. This problem is also mirrored by the contraction of the extraction rate, q_{cp}^{OL}.

The second strand on research, studying the endogenous investments in replacement technologies, dates back at least to Hoel (1978) and includes Dasgupta *et al.* (1983), Gallini *et al.* (1983) and Olsen (1988). The full-fledged illustration of the problem is in Harris and Vickers (1995), where the game – which does not exactly fit the IO literature but has a lot in common with the workhorse model of R&D races mentioned in Chapter 6 – takes place between two countries, 1 and 2. Country 1 has monopoly power over nonrenewable resource consumed in country 2, which is investing under uncertainty to find and adopt a backstop technology. Uncertainty is modelled using the hazard rate approach, so that the arrival time T at which the substitute technology is expected to become operational is stochastic. Were it not so, the monopoly problem would closely replicate what we know from Hotelling (1931).

The inverse demand function in country 2 is $p\,(q\,(t))$, and the state equation is $\dot{X} = -q\,(t)$. The monopolist's marginal extraction cost is constant at c_1, while the marginal cost of the backstop technology is $c_2 < c_1$, so that as soon as the innovation is marketed, the old technology does not sell any more. Let $k_2\,(t)$ identify the instantaneous research effort, whereby this magnitude also defines the hazard rate,

$$k_i\,(t) = \frac{\dot{F}}{1 - F\,(t)} \tag{7.71}$$

where $F\,(t) = 1 - e^{-\kappa(t)}$, $\kappa\,(t)$ being country 2's accumulated knowledge, which evolves according to $\dot{\kappa} = k_2\,(t)$. The instantaneous research cost is $C_2\,(t) = f\,(k_2\,(t))$, increasing in $k_2\,(t)$.

Hence, the relevant objective functions are discounted profits

$$\Pi_1\,(t) = \int_0^T \left[p\,(q\,(t)) - c_1\right] q\,(t)\,e^{-\rho t}dt \tag{7.72}$$

for the monopolist and social welfare

$$SW\,(t) = \int_0^T \left[CS_2\,(q\,(t)) - f\,(k_2\,(t))\right]e^{-\rho t}dt + \int_0^T CS_2^{BT}\,(q\,(t))\,e^{-\rho t}dt \tag{7.73}$$

for country 2. In the above expression, the superscript BT characterising consumer surplus from T to doomsday stands for *backstop technology*.

Harris and Vickers (1995) solve the feedback Nash equilibrium, by characterising the properties of optimal controls (the R&D investment k_2 and extraction rate q) as a function of the two states (the resource stock X in use and the accumulated knowledge κ), to single out the conditions under which the monopolist's reaction to the importing country's investment causes the extraction path of the nonrenewable resource in use to be non-monotone in the residual stock. This illustrates how the exporting monopolist is trying to delay the attainment of the substitute technology which will make the existing one worthless. This of course also affects the intertemporal price behaviour of the optimal price, which does not replicate the original Hotelling (1931) rule.

In this respect, it is also worth mentioning that the search for a backstop technology has a strong connection with the aforementioned green paradox as well as the so-called Porter hypothesis (Porter, 1991; Porter and van der Linde, 1995a,b), according to which firms may pursue green innovations to circumvent and possibly eliminate the burden of environmental regulation, and discover that this engenders a win-win solution in the form of higher profits and social welfare. To the best of my knowledge, at the moment the only piece of research illustrating this possibility using the instruments of dynamic analysis in continuous time can be found in Xepapadeas and de Zeeuw (1999).

Further Reading
Comprehensive surveys of differential games in environmental and resource economics, also covering the details of models I haven't treated in this chapter, can be found in

Jørgensen *et al.* (2010), Long (2010, 2011) and Lambertini (2013, 2017b). Endogenous growth à *la* Ramsey is combined with Cournot behaviour and polluting emissions in Dragone *et al.* (2010), showing that the presence of emission dynamics may prevent the economic system to reach the golden rule. The impact of corporate social responsibility on the dynamic behaviour of a polluting industry is characterised in Wirl *et al.* (2013) and Lambertini *et al.* (2016). For more on the dynamic analysis of natural resource exploitation, see Clark (1973, 1990), Clemhout and Wan (1985a,b), Fischer and Mirman (1986), Cave (1987), Benhabib and Radner (1992), Karp (1992a,b), Dockner and Sorger (1996), Dawid and Kopel (1997) and Sorger (1998), among many others. The small literature on the interplay between polluting emissions and natural resource exploitation is reviewed in Lambertini and Leitmann (2013) and Lambertini (2016b); in this regard, see also Wirl (1994, 1995, 2007), Wirl and Dockner (1995), Tahvonen (1996), Rubio and Escriche (2001) and Prieur *et al.* (2013). In particular, Wirl's (1994) model is briefly illustrated at the end of the next chapter. For an exhaustive assessment of the extant research on the Porter hypothesis, see Ambec *et al.* (2013) and Lambertini (2017a).

Bibliography

Aghion, P., N. Bloom, R. Blundell, R. Griffith and P. Howitt (2005), "Competition and Innovation: An Inverted-U Relationship", *Quarterly Journal of Economics*, **120**, 701–28.

Ambec, S., M.A. Cohen, S. Elgie and P. Lanoie (2013), "The Porter Hypothesis at 20: Can Environmental Regulation Enhance Innovation and Competitiveness?", *Review of Environmental Economics and Policy*, **7**, 2–22.

Arrow, K. (1962), "Economic Welfare and the Allocation of Resources for Invention", in R. Nelson (ed.), *The Rate and Direction of Industrial Activity*, Princeton, NJ, Princeton University Press.

Arrow, K.J. and S. Chang (1982), "Optimal Pricing, Use, and Exploration of Uncertain Resource Stocks", *Journal of Environmental Economics and Management*, **9**, 1–10.

Benchekroun, H. (2003), "Unilateral Production Restrictions in a Dynamic Duopoly", *Journal of Economic Theory*, **111**, 214–39.

Benchekroun, H. (2008), "Comparative Dynamics in a Productive Asset Oligopoly", *Journal of Economic Theory*, **138**, 237–61.

Benchekroun, H. and A.R. Chaudhury (2011), "Environmental Policy and Stable Collusion: The Case of a Dynamic Polluting Oligopoly", *Journal of Economic Dynamics and Control*, **35**, 479–90.

Benchekroun, H., G. Gaudet and N.V. Long (2006), "Temporary Natural Resource Cartels", *Journal of Environmental Economics and Management*, **52**, 663–74.

Benchekroun, H., A. Halsema and C. Withagen (2009), "On Nonrenewable Resource Oligopolies: The Asymmetric Case", *Journal of Economic Dynamics and Control*, **33**, 1867–79.

Benchekroun, H., A. Halsema and C. Withagen (2010), "When Additional Resource Stocks Reduce Welfare", *Journal of Environmental Economics and Management*, **59**, 109–14.

Benchekroun, H. and N.V. Long (1998), "Efficiency Inducing Taxation for Polluting Oligopolists", *Journal of Public Economics*, **70**, 325–42.

Benchekroun, H. and N.V. Long (2002), "On the Multiplicity of Efficiency-Inducing Tax Rules", *Economics Letters*, **76**, 331–36.

Benchekroun, H. and N.V. Long (2016), "Status Concern and the Exploitation of Common Pool Renewable Resources", *Ecological Economics*, **125**, 70–82.

Benhabib, J. and R. Radner (1992), "The Joint Exploitation of Productive Asset: A Game-Theoretic Approach", *Economic Theory*, **2**, 155–90.

Bergstrom, T., J. Cross and R. Porter (1981), "Efficiency-Inducing Taxation for a Monopolistically Supplied Depletable Resource", *Journal of Public Economics*, **15**, 23–32.

Boyce, J. and L. Vojtassak (2008), "An 'Oil'igopoly Theory of Exploration", *Resource and Energy Economics*, **30**, 428–54.

Cave, J. (1987), "Long-Term Competition in a Dynamic Game: The Cold Fish War", *RAND Journal of Economics*, **18**, 596-610.

Chiarella, C., M. Kemp, N.V. Long and K. Okuguchi (1984), "On the Economics of International Fisheries", *International Economic Review*, **25**, 85–92.

Clark, C.W. (1973), "Profit Maximization and the Extinction of Animal Species", *Journal of Political Economy*, **81**, 950–60.

Clark, C.W. (1990). *Mathematical Bioeconomics: The Optimal Management of Renewable Resources*, New York, Wiley.

Clark, C.W., F.H. Clarke and G.R. Munro (1979), "The Optimal Exploitation of Renewable Resource Stocks: Problems of Irreversible Investment", *Econometrica*, **47**, 25–47.

Clark, C.W. and G.R. Munro (1975), "The Economics of Fishing and Modern Capital Theory", *Journal of Environmental Econonomics and Management*, **2**, 92–106.

Clemhout, S. and H. Wan, Jr. (1985a), "Dynamic Common Property Resources and Environmental Problems", *Journal of Optimization Theory and Applications*, **46**, 471–81.

Clemhout, S. and H.Y. Wan, Jr. (1985b), "Cartelization Conserves Endangered Species", in G. Feichtinger (ed.), *Optimal Control Theory and Economic Analysis*, vol. 2, Amsterdam, North-Holland.

Colombo, L. and P. Labrecciosa (2013a), "Oligopoly Exploitation of a Private Property Productive Asset", *Journal of Economic Dynamics and Control*, **37**, 838–53.

Colombo, L. and P. Labrecciosa (2013b), "On the Convergence to the Cournot Equilibrium in a Productive Asset Oligopoly", *Journal of Mathematical Economics*, **49**, 441–45.

Colombo, L., and P. Labrecciosa (2015), "On the Markovian Efficiency of Bertrand and Cournot Equilibria", *Journal of Economic Theory*, **155**, 332–58.

Cornes, R., C.F. Mason and T. Sandler (1986), "The Commons and the Optimal Number of Firms", *Quarterly Journal of Economics*, **101**, 641–46.

d'Aspremont, C., A. Jacquemin, J.J. Gabszewicz and J.A. Weymark (1983), "On the Stability of Collusive Price Leadership", *Canadian Journal of Economics*, **16**, 17–25.

Damania, R. (1996), "Pollution Taxes and Pollution Abatement in an Oligopoly Supergame", *Journal of Environmental Economics and Management*, **30**, 323–36.

Dasgupta, P., R. Gilbert and J. Stiglitz (1983), "Strategic Considerations in Invention and Innovation: The Case of Natural Resources", *Econometrica*, **51**, 1439–48.

Dasgupta, P.S. and G.M. Heal (1979), *Economic Theory and Exhaustible Resources*, Cambridge, Cambridge University Press.

Dawid, H. and M. Kopel (1997), "On the Economically Optimal Exploitation of a Renewable Resource: The Case of a Convex Environment and a Convex Return Function", *Journal of Economic Theory*, **76**, 272–97.

Dockner, E.J. and G. Sorger (1996), "Existence and Properties of Equilibria for a Dynamic Game on Productive Assets", *Journal of Economic Theory*, **171**, 201–27.

Dragone, D., L. Lambertini and A. Palestini (2010), "Dynamic Oligopoly with Capital Accumulation and Environmental Externality", in J. Crespo Cuaresma, T. Palokangas and A. Tarasjev (eds), *Dynamic Systems, Economic Growth, and the Environment*, Heidelberg, Springer.

Dragone, D., L. Lambertini and A. Palestini (2013), "The Incentive to Invest in Environmental-Friendly Technologies: Dynamics Makes a Difference", in J. Crespo Cuaresma, T. Palokangas and A. Tarasjev (eds), *Green Growth and Sustainable Development*, Heidelberg, Springer.

Dragone, D., L. Lambertini and A. Palestini (2014), "Regulating Environmental Externalities through Public Firms: A Differential Game", *Strategic Behavior and the Environment*, **4**, 15–40.

Eswaran, M. and T. Lewis (1985), "Exhaustible Resources and Alternative Equilibrium Concepts", *Canadian Journal of Economics*, **18**, 459–73.

Feichtinger, G. (1983), "The Nash Solution of an Advertising Differential Game: Generalization of a Model by Leitmann and Schmitendorf", *IEEE Transactions on Automatic Control*, **28**, 1044–48.

Feichtinger, G., L. Lambertini, G. Leitmann and S. Wrzaczek (2016), "R&D for Green Technologies in a Dynamic Oligopoly: Schumpeter, Arrow and Inverted U's", *European Journal of Operational Research*, **249**, 1131–38.

Fershtman, C. and M. Kamien (1987), "Dynamic Duopolistic Competition with Sticky Prices", *Econometrica*, **55**, 1151–64.

Fershtman, C. and S. Nitzan (1991), "Dynamic Voluntary Provision of Public Goods", *European Economic Review*, **35**, 1057–67.

Fischer, R.D. and L. Mirman (1986), "The Compleat Fish Wars: Biological and Dynamic Interactions", *Journal of Environmental Economics and Management*, **30**, 34–42.

Fujiwara, K. (2008), "Duopoly Can Be More Anti-Competitive than Monopoly", *Economics Letters*, **101**, 217–19.

Gallini, N., T. Lewis and R. Ware (1983), "Strategic Timing and Pricing of a Substitute in a Cartelized Resource Market", *Canadian Journal of Economics*, **16**, 429–46.

Gaudet, G. and N.V. Long (1994), "On the Effects of the Distribution of Initial Endowments in a Non-Renewable Resource Duopoly", *Journal of Economic Dynamics and Control*, **18**, 1189–98.

Gilbert, R. (1978), "Dominant Firm Pricing Policy in a Market for an Exhaustible Resource", *Bell Journal of Economics*, **9**, 385–95.

Gordon, H.S. (1954), "The Economic Theory of a Common-Property Resource: The Fishery", *Journal of Political Economy*, **62**, 124–42.

Grafton, R.Q., T. Kompas and N.V. Long (2012), "Substitution between Biofuels and Fossil Fuels: Is There a Green Paradox?", *Journal of Environmental Economics and Management*, **64**, 328–41.

Groot, F., C. Withagen and A. de Zeeuw (1992), "Note on the Open-Loop von Stackelberg Equilibrium in the Cartel-versus-Fringe Model", *Economic Journal*, **102**, 1478–84.

Groot, F., C. Withagen and A. de Zeeuw (2003), "Strong Time-Consistency in the Cartel-versus-FringeModel", *Journal of Economic Dynamics and Control*, **28**, 287–306.

Hämäläinen, R.P., A. Haurie and V. Kaitala (1985), "Equilibria and Threats in a Fishery Management Game", *Optimal Control Applications and Methods*, **6**, 315–33.

Hardin, G. (1968), "The Tragedy of the Commons", *Science* **162**, 1243–48.

Harris, C. and J. Vickers (1995), "Innovation and Natural Resources: A Dynamic Game with Uncertainty", *RAND Journal of Economics*, **26**, 418–30.

Hoel, M. (1978), "Resource Extraction, Substitute Production, and Monopoly", *Journal of Economic Theory*, **19**, 28–77.

Hotelling, H. (1931), "The Economics of Exhaustible Resources", *Journal of Political Economy*, **39**, 137–75.

Jørgensen, S. and P. Kort (1997), "Optimal Investment and Finance in Renewable Resource Harvesting", *Journal of Economic Dynamics and Control*, **21**, 603–30.

Jørgensen, S., G. Martín-Herrán and G. Zaccour (2010), "Dynamic Games in the Economics and Management of Pollution", *Environmental Modelling and Assessment*, **15**, 433–67.

Kaitala, V. and M. Pohjola (1988), "Optimal Recovery of a Shared Resource Stock: A Differential Game Model with Efficient Memory Equilibria", *Natural Resource Modelling*, **3**, 91–119.

Karp, L. (1992a), "Efficiency Inducing Tax for a Common Property Oligopoly", *Economic Journal*, **102**, 321–32.

Karp, L. (1992b), "Social Welfare in a Common Property Oligopoly", *International Economic Review*, **33**, 353–72.

Karp, L. and J. Livernois (1992), "On Efficiency-Inducing Taxation for a Non-Renewable Resource Monopolist", *Journal of Public Economics*, **49**, 219–39.

Karp, L. and J. Livernois (1994), "Using Automatic Tax Changes to Control Pollution Emissions", *Journal of Environmental Economics and Management*, **27**, 38–48.

Lambertini, L. (2013), *Oligopoly, the Environment and Natural Resources*, London, Routledge.

Lambertini, L. (2014), "Exploration for Nonrenewable Resources in a Dynamic Oligopoly: An Arrovian Result", *International Game Theory Review*, **16**, DOI: 10.1142/S0219198914400118.

Lambertini, L. (2016a), "Managerial Delegation in a Dynamic Renewable Resource Oligopoly", in H. Dawid, K. Doerner, G. Feichtinger, P. Kort and A. Seidl (eds), *Dynamic Perspectives on Managerial Decision Making: Essays in Honor of Richard F. Hartl*, Heidelberg, Springer.

Lambertini, L. (2016b), "On the Interplay between Resource Extraction and Polluting Emissions in Oligopoly", in A. Espinola-Arredondo and F. Munoz-Garcia (eds), *Game Theory Applications to Environmental Economics*, Singapore and New York, World Scientific.

Lambertini, L. (2017a), "Green Innovation and Market Power", *Annual Review of Resource Economics*, **9**, 231–52.

Lambertini, L. (2017b), "Differential Oligopoly Games in Environmental and Resource Economics", in L. Corchòn and M. Marini (eds), *Handbook of Game Theory and Industrial Organization*, Cheltenham, Edward Elgar, forthcoming.

Lambertini, L. and G. Leitmann (2013), "Market Power, Resource Extraction and Pollution: Some Paradoxes and a Unified View", in J. Crespo Cuaresma, T. Palokangas and A. Tarasjev (eds), *Green Growth and Sustainable Development*, Heidelberg, Springer, forthcoming.

Lambertini, L. and Mantovani, A. (2014), "Feedback Equilibria in a Dynamic Renewable Resource Oligopoly: Pre-emption, Voracity and Exhaustion", *Journal of Economic Dynamics and Control*, **47**, 115–22.

Lambertini, L. and A. Mantovani (2016), "On the (In)stability of Nonlinear Feedback Solutions in a Dynamic Duopoly with Renewable Resource Exploitation", *Economics Letters*, **143**, 9–12.

Lambertini, L., A. Palestini and A. Tampieri (2016), "CSR in Asymmetric Duopoly with Environmental Externality", *Southern Economic Journal*, **83**, 236–52.

Lane, P.R. and A. Tornell (1996), "Power, Growth, and the Voracity Effect", *Journal of Economic Growth*, **1**, 213–41.

Leinbenstein, H. (1966), "Allocative Efficiency versus X-efficiency", *American Economic Review*, **56**, 392–415.

Leitmann, G. and W.E. Schmitendorf (1978), "Profit Maximization through Advertising: A Nonzero Sum Differential Game Approach", *IEEE Transactions on Automatic Control*, **23**, 646–50.

Levhari, D. and L. Mirman (1980), "The Great Fish War: An Example Using a Dynamic Cournot-Nash Solution", *Bell Journal of Economics*, **11**, 322–34.

Lewis, T. and R. Schmalensee (1980), "Cartel and Oligopoly Pricing of Non-Replenishable Natural Resources", in P. Liu (ed.), *Dynamic Optimization and Application to Economics*, New York, Plenum Press.

Long, N.V. (2010), *A Survey of Dynamic Games in Economics*, Singapore, World Scientific.

Long, N.V. (2011), "Dynamic Games in the Economics of Natural Resources: A Survey", *Dynamic Games ands Applications*, **1**, 115–48.

Lotka, A.J. (1925), *Elements of Physical Biology*, Philadelphia, Williams and Wilkins.

Loury, G. (1986), "A Theory of 'Oil'igopoly: Cournot Equilibrium in Exhaustible Resource Market with Fixed Supplies", *International Economic Review*, **27**, 285–301.

Mason, C.F. and S. Polasky (1997), "The Optimal Number of Firms in the Commons: A Dynamic Approach", *Canadian Journal of Economics*, **30**, 1143–60.

Mason, C. and S. Polasky (2002), "Strategic Preemption in a Common Property Resource: A Continuous Time Approach", *Environmental and Resource Economics*, **23**, 255–78.

Mason, C., T. Sandler and R. Cornes (1988), "Expectations, the Commons, and Optimal Group Size", *Journal of Environmental Economics and Management*, **15**, 99–110.

Mohr, E. (1988), "Appropriation of Common Access Natural Resources Through Exploration: The Relevance of the Open-Loop Concept", *International Economic Review*, **29**, 307–20.

Newbery, D. (1981), "Oil Prices, Cartels, and the Problem of Dynamic Inconsistency", *Economic Journal*, **91**, 617–46.

Olsen, T.E. (1988), "Strategic Considerations in Invention and Innovation: The Case of Natural Resources Revisited", *Econometrica*, **56**, 841–49.

Pearce, D.W. and R.K. Turner (1989), *Economics of Natural Resources and the Environment*, Hemel Hempstead, Harvester-Wheatsheaf.

Peterson, F.M. (1978), "A Model of Mining and Exploration for Exhaustible Resources", *Journal of Environmental Studies and Management*, **5**, 236–51.

Pindyck, R. (1978), "Gains to Producers from the Cartelization of Exhaustible Resources", *Review of Economics and Statistics*, **60**, 238–51.

Pittel, K., F. van der Ploeg and C. Withagen (2014), *Climate Policy and Nonrenewable Resources: The Green Paradox and Beyond*, Cambridge, MA, MIT Press.

Porter, M. (1991), "America's Green Strategy", *Scientific American*, **264**, 96.

Porter, M. and C. van der Linde (1995a), "Toward a New Conception of the Environment-Competitiveness Relationship", *Journal of Econonomic Perspectives*, **9**, 97–118.

Porter, M. and C. van der Linde (1995b), "Green and Competitive: Ending the Stalemate", *Harvard Business Review* (September-October), 120–34.

Prieur, F., M. Tidball and C. Withagen (2013), "Optimal Emission-Extraction Policy in a World of Scarcity and Irreversibility", *Resource and Energy Economics*, **35**, 637–58.

Quyen, N.V. (1988), "The Optimal Depletion and Exploration of a Non-Renewable Resource", *Econometrica*, **56**, 1467–71.

Quyen, N.V. (1991), "Exhaustible Resources: A Theory of Exploration", *Review of Economic Studies*, **58**, 777–89.

Reinganum, J. and N. Stokey (1985), "Oligopoly Extraction of a Common Property Resource: The Importance of the Period of Committment in Dynamic Games", *International Economic Review*, **26**, 161–73.

Reynolds, S. (1987), "Preemption and Commitment in an Infinite Horizon Model", *International Economic Review*, **28**, 69–88.

Rowat, C. (2007), "Non-Linear Strategies in a Linear Quadratic Differential Game", *Journal of Economic Dynamics and Control*, **31**, 3179–202.

Rubio, S. and L. Escriche (2001), "Strategic Pigouvian Taxation, Stock Externalities and Non-Renewable Resources", *Journal of Public Economics*, **79**, 297–313.

Salant, S.W. (1976), "Exhaustible Resources and Industrial Structure: A Nash-Cournot Approach to the World Oil Market", *Journal of Political Economy*, **84**, 1079–94.

Salo, S. and O. Tahvonen (2001), "Oligopoly Equilibria in Nonrenewable Resource Markets", *Journal of Economic Dynamics and Control*, **25**, 671–702.

Schumpeter, J.A. (1942), *Capitalism, Socialism and Democracy*, New York, Harper.

Singh, N. and X. Vives (1984), "Price and Quantity Competition in a Differentiated Duopoly", *RAND Journal of Economics*, **15**, 546–54.

Sinn, H.W. (2012), *The Green Paradox*, Cambridge, MA, MIT Press.

Smulders, S., Y. Tsur and A. Zemel (2012), "Announcing Climate Policy: Can a Green Paradox Arise without Scarcity?", *Journal of Environmental Economics and Management*, **64**, 364–76.

Sorger, G. (1998), "Markov-Perfect Nash Equilibria in a Class of Resource Games", *Economic Theory*, **11**, 79–100.

Tahvonen, O. (1996), "Trade with Polluting Non-Renewable Resources", *Journal of Environmental Economics and Management*, **30**, 1–17.

Tornell, A. and P.R. Lane (1999), "The Voracity Effect", *American Economic Review*, **89**, 22–46.

Tsutsui, S. and K. Mino (1990), "Nonlinear Strategies in Dynamic Duopolistic Competition with Sticky Prices", *Journal of Economic Theory* **52**, 136–61.

Ulph, A. and G.M. Folie (1980), "Exhaustible Resources and Cartels: An Intertemporal Nash-Cournot Model", *Canadian Journal of Economics*, **13**, 645–58.

van der Ploeg, F. and C. Withagen (2012), "Is There Really a Green Paradox?", *Journal of Environmental Economics and Management*, **64**, 342–63.

Verhulst, P.H. (1838), "Notice sur la loi que la population poursuit dans son accroissement", *Correspondance mathématique et physique*, **10**, 113–21.

Vickers, J. (1985), "Delegation and the Theory of the Firm", *Economic Journal*, **95** (Conference Papers), 138–47.

Volterra, V. (1931), "Variations and Fluctuations of the Number of Individuals in Animal Species Living Together", in R.N. Chapman (ed.), *Animal Ecology*, New York, McGraw-Hill.

Wirl, F. (1994), "Pigouvian Taxation of Energy for Flow and Stock Externalities and Strategic, Noncompetitive Energy Pricing", *Journal of Environmental Economics and Management*, **26**, 1–18.

Wirl, F. (1995), "The Exploitation of Fossil Fuels under the Threat of Global Warming and Carbon Taxes: A Dynamic Game Approach", *Environmental and Resource Economics*, **5**, 333–52.

Wirl, F. (2007), "Energy Prices and Carbon Taxes under Uncertainty about Global Warming", *Environmental and Resource Economics*, **36**, 313–40.

Wirl, F. and E. Dockner (1995), "Leviathan Governments and Carbon Taxes: Costs and Potential Benefits", *European Economic Review*, **39**, 1215–36.

Wirl, F., G. Feichtinger and P. Kort (2013), "Individual Firm and Market Dynamics of CSR Activities", *Journal of Economic Behavior and Organization*, **86**, 169–82.

Xepapadeas, A. and A. de Zeeuw (1999), "Environmental Policy and Competitiveness: The Porter Hypothesis and the Composition of Capital", *Journal of Environmental Economics and Management*, **37**, 165–82.

8 International Trade

The economic theory of international trade has taken a well-defined strategic flavour in its modern version, which is known as the *new trade theory*. Its building blocks are monopolistic competition, consumers' preference for variety and increasing returns to scale, but also the strategic behaviour characteristic of oligopoly theory has acquired almost immediately a considerable role in it, as testified by the volumes of Helpman and Krugman (1985, 1989), Grossman (1992), and the survey in Brander (1995), to mention only a few reference works.

This chapter offers a compact overview of relevant contributions applying differential game theory to the analysis of problems either directly connected with the dynamic translations of classical themes in trade theory, such as the optimal design of trade policies including tariffs and voluntary restraints (Section 8.1), or to issues falling in the area of environmental and resource economics with an eye to capture the impact of trade strategies and policies on the quality of the environment and the preservations of resource stocks, as well as a synthetic portray of the interaction between trade, resource exploitation and global warming (Section 8.2).

8.1 Trade and Trade Policies

This section is a survey of differential games in which the subject is the design and impact of different trade policies either in three-country models where firms export towards a third market or in two-country models where intraindustry trade takes place between them. The basic layout used in the ensuing models can be seen as a differential game version of the Cournot models with trade dating back to Brander (1981) and Brander and Krugman (1983).

8.1.1 Sticky Prices, Once Again

The differential game literature on the choice between import tariffs and export subsidies revisits a discussion whose building blocks are in Brander and Spencer (1985) and Eaton and Grossman (1986). Not surprisingly, all of the initial debate (Dockner and Haug, 1990,1991; Driskill and McCafferty, 1996) relies on modified versions of the Cournot sticky price oligopoly game of Simaan and Takayama (1978) and Fershtman and Kamien (1987).

Without following the chronological order of appearance, I will set out with the summary of the analysis carried out by Driskill and McCafferty (1996), who use the sticky price game to describe a classical situation in international trade theory.

The scenario contemplates a three-country world, in which firms 1 and 2, each located in a country identified by the same index as the firm, export a homogeneous good towards country 3, where the good is consumed but not produced. In the third country, the price follows the kinematic equation

$$\dot{p} = s\left[\widehat{p} - p(t)\right] \tag{8.1}$$

where the linear 'notional' inverse demand is $\widehat{p} = a - q_1(t) - q_2(t)$ and the constant $s \in [0, \infty)$ is a measure of the speed at which price instantaneously adjusts. As in the original model, firms have the same production costs $C_i(t) = q_i(t)\left[c + q_i(t)/2\right]$ and are supposed to maximise their respective profit flows, discounted at the same rate $\rho > 0$.

However, the total costs borne by firm i is modified by a tax or subsidy on exports introduced by the government of its country of origin, so that the net instantaneous profits of firm i is

$$\pi_i(t) = p(t)q_i(t)(1 - t_i) - (c - t_i)q_i - \frac{q_i^2(t)}{2} \tag{8.2}$$

in which t_i is an *ad valorem* tax and t_i is an export subsidy (if t_i is positive). The absence of a time argument accompanying the two policy instruments signals that the governments are able to precommit themselves to a specific policy at the initial time $t = 0$ (before firms take any decisions about their production plans) and stick to it forever.

Driskill and McCafferty (1996) solve the game for the closed-loop memoryless equilibrium,[1] given the vector of policy instruments, and then characterise the policy game between the two governments tuning their respective tools t_i and t_i to maximise noncooperatively welfare functions, which, in view of the way the model has been constructed, coincide with each firm's profits net of any taxes or subsidies, since tax incomes of either sign are redistributed upon (or paid by) citizens of the same country as the firm and government.

To perform this task, Driskill and McCafferty (1996) focus in particular on the limit game generated by either $s \to \infty$ or $\rho \to 0$. Even in this case, the initial game between governments in the space of policy instruments does not lend itself to an analytical solutions, and the authors have to perform numerical simulations by calibrating model parameters to find that the optimal trade policy (which is *both* welfare *and* profit maximising) consists in adopting a specific tax on output $t_i > 0$. Their explanation of this apparently counterintuive result hinges upon a discussion of the dynamic conjectural variations involved in the limit differential game, in relation to the dominant view about consistent conjectures at the time (Bresnahan, 1981; Perry, 1982; Kamien and Schwartz, 1983; Klemperer and Meyer, 1988).

---

[1] Driskill and McCafferty (1996) refer to either feedback or closed-loop memoryless strategies throughout the paper (see, e.g., their Definitions 1 and 2, p. 359), but what they actually solve is the closed-loop memoryless game based on the Hamiltonian functions, with state-control loops appearing in the adjoint equations (see Driskill and McCafferty, Appendix A, p. 368).

A simpler explanation comes from the fact that increasing production costs through an export tax brings about a contraction in output levels which in turns causes a price increase, much the same as in a collusive situation. Here, however, those bearing the consequences of such a behaviour are consumers in the third country, whose surplus is irrelevant from the standpoint of the public authorities placed in the exporting countries.[2]

The same structure, although reconfigured to host a single country, is used by Dockner and Haug (1990, 1991) to discuss the equivalence between tariffs and quotas (in the first of their companion papers) and the adoption of voluntary export restraints, or VERs (in the second).

International trade theory has dwelled upon the choice between alternative trade policies such as tariffs or subsidies acting on costs (and therefore affecting prices) or restrictions on output levels, in the form of either quotas or voluntary export restraints (VER) for a long time.

The discussion has focussed on a comparative evaluation of their relative effectiveness, and the equivalence between import tariffs and quotas emerged almost immediately, from models assuming perfectly competitive markets (Bhagwati, 1965, 1968; Shibata, 1968). Conversely, this equivalence mail fail to exist when firms do have some degree of market power. Its emergence has been confirmed by Eaton and Grossman (1986) and Hwang and Mai (1988), and confuted by others, e.g., Itoh and Ono (1982, 1984), Harris (1985) and Krishna (1989).

As stressed by Dockner and Haug (1990, pp. 147-48), the early comparative evaluation of tariffs and quotas does not capture their dynamic implications. This argument holds true, of course, also for VERs, and is the primary source of the use of differential games in this area.

The model in Dockner and Haug (1990) describes the market of the home country, where firm 1 is based and faces the competition of firm 2, based in the foreign country. The essential elements of the setup (the demand function for a homogeneous good and sticky price dynamics) are the same as above, except that the foreign firm is subject either to a tariff $\tau \in (0, a - c)$ or to an equivalent quota $\bar{q}_2$ alternatively introduced by the government of country 1.

Examine first the relative effects of tariffs and quotas under feedback rules. Its adoption implies that the total cost function of firm 2 (omitting the time argument hereinafter) becomes $C_2 = (c + \tau + q_2/2) q_2$. If the tariff policy is adopted, the firms' HJB equations are

$$\rho V_1 = \max_{q_1} \left\{ \left(p - c - \frac{q_1}{2} \right) q_1 + V_1's (a - q_1 - q_2 - p) \right\}$$

$$\rho V_2 = \max_{q_2} \left\{ \left(p - c - \tau - \frac{q_2}{2} \right) q_2 + V_2's (a - q_1 - q_2 - p) \right\}$$

(8.3)

---

[2] Driskill and Horowitz (1996) adopt the durable good oligopoly model in Driskill (2001) to investigate the implications of durability on the choice of trade policy in the three-country setting. They find that, if firms sell the durable, the optimal policy for their home governments is a tax on output; if instead firms lease, the optimal policy is a subsidy.

Guessing linear quadratic forms for the value functions and solving for linear feed-back strategies, one finds that the following relationship between outputs must hold at equilibrium:

$$\left(2 + \frac{s}{s\,(2 - s\varepsilon_1) + \rho}\right) q_1^{LF}\,(\tau) = a - c - q_2^{LF}\,(\tau) \tag{8.4}$$

in which

$$\varepsilon_1 = \frac{\rho + 6s - \sqrt{(\rho + 6s)^2 - 12s^2}}{6s^2} \tag{8.5}$$

is the coefficient of the quadratic term in the value function of firm $i = 1, 2$, $V_i = \varepsilon_1 p^2 + \varepsilon_{2i} p + \varepsilon_{3i}$.[3]

Now suppose a tariff-equivalent quota is adopted, $\bar{q}_2 = q_2^*$. As the volume of imports is fixed, the matter boils down to solving the HJB equation of the home firm:

$$\rho V_1 = \max_{q_1} \left\{ \left(p - c - \frac{q_1}{2}\right) q_1 + V_1' s\,(a - q_1 - \bar{q}_2 - p) \right\} \tag{8.6}$$

This yields the equilibrium relation

$$\left(2 + \frac{s}{s + \rho}\right) q_1^{LF}\,(\bar{q}_2) = a - c - \bar{q}_2 \tag{8.7}$$

which differs from (8.4) and, accounting for the stability requirement, implies $q_1^{LF}\,(\tau) > q_1^{LF}\,(\bar{q}_2)$ and therefore also $p^{LF}\,(\bar{q}_2) > p^{LF}\,(\tau)$.

It is a matter of simple calculations to verify that, instead, the equivalence between tariff and quota holds under open-loop strategies which, however, are not strongly time consistent. This discussion proves

Proposition 8.1 *At the subgame perfect equilibrium of a sticky price game with intraindustry trade, tariffs and quotas are not equivalent: the tariff generates a higher output and a lower price than the quota in the domestic market.*

By the way, the confirmation of the equivalence under open-loop information comes as no surprise, since the limit of the open-loop game coincides with the static Cournot equilibrium under the same demand and cost conditions, as we know from Fershtman and Kamien (1987) and the recollection of their seminal results in Chapter 3.

The theory of voluntary export restraints sees them, most often, as coordinating or quasi-collusive devices (see, e.g., Harris, 1985; Krishna, 1989) to be adopted under Bertrand competition as a means of preventing the market price to fall onto marginal cost (under product homogeneity) or too close to it (under product differentiation). And, of course, this should explain why such restrictions might be voluntarily adopted by firms.

An exception is the paper by Mai and Hwang (1988), using an approach based on conjectural variations to model VERs under quantity-setting behaviour. Their main findings are that if the free trade equilibrium replicates the Cournot one, then VERs do not affect profits. Conversely, if the free trade equilibrium quantity is lower than the Cournot one,

---

[3] The first coefficient is the same in both value functions because the tariff only affects the linear component, and therefore ε_{2i} and ε_{3i} must be expected to differ across firms, as is indeed the case.

the adoption of a VER corresponding to the free trade output reduces the profits accruing to the foreign firm while at the same time increasing those of the domestic firm. Hence, Mai and Hwang (1988) deduce that in this case the VER is *involuntary*. In the residual case where conjectures reflect a more competitive scenario than the Cournot one, both firms' profits are increased by the adoption of a VER.[4]

Dockner and Haug (1991) use the sticky price game to illustrate the arising of voluntary restraints, restricting their attention to the limit properties of the feedback solution.

The departure point is the same as above, without the tariff, which means that the initial model replicates the duopoly game appearing in Chapter 3, which, if the speed of price adjustment is infinitely high, yields (here I'm using the same expressions as in Dockner and Haug, 1991, p. 682):

$$\lim_{s \to \infty} p^{LF} = \frac{a + 2(c - \varpi)}{3 - 2\varphi} \equiv \tilde{p} \tag{8.8}$$

$$q_1^{LF} = q_2^{LF} = \sqrt{\frac{2}{3}\tilde{p}} + \varpi - c \tag{8.9}$$

where

$$\varpi = \frac{c - \varphi(a + 2c)}{3(1 - \varphi)}; \varphi = 1 - \sqrt{\frac{2}{3}} \tag{8.10}$$

If the foreign firm adopts (or is forced to adopt) a VER corresponding to $q_2^{VER} = q_2^{LF}$, the problem of the domestic firm reduces to an optimal control model as the other output is exogenously fixed. This problem can be solved by

$$\max_{q_1} \mathcal{H}_1 = e^{-\rho t} \left\{ \left(p - c - \frac{q_1}{2} \right) q_1 + \lambda_1 s \left(a - q_1 - q_2^{VER} - p \right) \right\} \tag{8.11}$$

which, through the standard procedure, leads to

$$q_1^{VER} = \frac{a - c - q_2^{VER}}{3} \tag{8.12}$$

This expression can be easily compared to the output of the home firm under free trade, conveniently rewritten as

$$q_1^{LF} = \frac{(1 + \sqrt{2/3})(a - c - q_2^{VER})}{2(1 + \sqrt{2/3}) + 1} > q_1^{VER} \tag{8.13}$$

The implications of the last inequality are spelled out in

Proposition 8.2 *The adoption of a VER by the foreign firm (1) decreases industry output and the production of the home firm and increases price, and consequently (2) increases the foreign firm's profits.*

Accordingly, sticky price dynamics indeed reconstruct a picture corresponding to the scenario identified by both Harris (1985) and Mai and Hwang (1988) under negative conjecture, implying harsher competition than in the Cournot model.

[4] More on the involuntary adoption of a VER is in Suzumura and Ishikawa (1997).

To conclude the treatment of trade under sticky prices, it is worth stressing that the feedback solution of a two-country free trade model with different populations of firms in each country yields a very powerful intuition as to the relevance of feedback effects. This is a point raised by Fujiwara (2009a), which will emerge again later in the chapter, in a model where the exploitation of natural resources is considered.

Suppose n_1 and n_2 firms are located in countries 1 and 2, respectively. All of them produce a homogeneous good with the usual linear-quadratic cost function, and the free trade regime prevails on the world market. Look, for instance, at country 1, where market price follows the differential equation:

$$\dot{p}_1 = s \left[a - \sum_{i=1}^{n_1} q_i(t) - \sum_{j=1}^{n_2} q_j(t) - p_1(t) \right] \tag{8.14}$$

Except for the presence of n_1 and n_2, this is the usual Cournot game under price stickiness, whose feedback solution yields the equilibrium price $p^{LF} = (a - n_1\beta_1 - n_2\beta_2) / [1 + (n_1 + n_2)\alpha]$, where α and β_i are the intercept and slope of the linear feedback output $q_i^{LF} = \alpha + \beta_i p_1$.

As in Dockner and Haug (1991), Fujiwara (2009a) considers the limit game which obtains under instantaneous price adjustment (or no discounting), to find that there exist parameter constellations wherein the home country's welfare is higher in autarky than under free trade. This happens, for instance, if $n_2 \geq n_1 = 1$ and $c = 0$. More explicitly, if the linear part of the cost function disappears and there is a single firm in each country, free trade hinders welfare in the home country, and this consequence is reinforced if the single home firm faces at least two competitors. Note that this cannot happen in the limit of the open-loop game (which, as we know, is the static Cournot game) and is to be imputed to the feedback effect, insofar as this causes a price drop so large that the profit loss for the home firm outweighs the increase in consumer surplus.

8.1.2 Trade in the Ramsey Model

The same topic is taken up again in Calzolari and Lambertini (2006, 2007) in an adaptation of the Ramsey oligopoly game introduced by Cellini and Lambertini (1998) to accomodate intraindustry trade. The presence of product differentiation à la Singh and Vives (1984) makes it possible to treat the adoption of the VER under both Cournot and Bertrand competition.

The game lasts forever. The instantaneous inverse demand function of firm $i = 1, 2$ is:

$$p_i(t) = a - q_i(t) - \gamma q_j(t) \tag{8.15}$$

under Cournot competition, and

$$q_i(t) = \frac{a}{1+\gamma} - \frac{p_i(t)}{1-\gamma^2} + \frac{\gamma p_j}{1-\gamma^2} \tag{8.16}$$

under Bertrand competition, with $\gamma \in [-1, 1]$. Firms accumulate physical capital $k_i(t)$ à *la* Ramsey (1928),

$$\dot{k_i} = f(k_i(t)) - q_i(t) - \delta k_i(t) \qquad (8.17)$$

with initial conditions $k_i(0) = k_{0i} > 0$.

The evaluation of quotas and import tariffs is carried in Calzolari and Lambertini (2006) out under quantity-setting behaviour, in the special case where the good is homogeneous ($\gamma = 1$).

Under an import tariff, the model is largely analogous to the duopolistic setting illustrated in Chapter 3. Since the game is state-redundant, open-loop rules yields subgame perfect strategies leading either to the quasi-static Cournot–Nash equilibrium driven by demand and cost conditions, with the time-invariant tariff τ producing an asymmetry in effective marginal costs:

$$q_1^{OL} = \frac{a - c + \tau}{3} \; ; \; q_2^{OL} = \frac{a - c - 2\tau}{3} \qquad (8.18)$$

or to those associated with the Ramsey golden rule:

$$f'(k_D(t)) = f'(k_F(t)) = f'(k_P) \equiv \rho + \delta \qquad (8.19)$$

The phase diagram illustrating the dynamics of the system and the steady state solutions is in Figure 8.1, portraying a situation in which $0 < q_2^{OL} < q_1^{OL} < q_{GR}$, where subscript *GR* stands for golden rule. As we already know, if parameter values lead to a situation like this, the market-driven equilibrium is a saddle point while the Ramsey golden rule equilibrium is not reachable (and is also unstable).

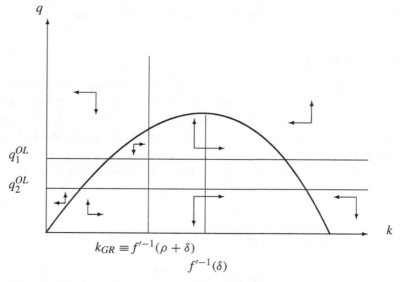

Figure 8.1 The phase diagram generated by an import tariff

Suppose for the moment that the scenario described by Figure 8.1 is the relevant one. If the government of country 1 imposes an equivalent import quota, the quantity of firm 2 is fixed at $\bar{q}_2 = q_2^{OL}$. The consequences of this trade policy can be immediately appreciated by taking a look at the instantaneous best reply of the home firm:

$$q_1^*(t) = \frac{a - c - \bar{q}_2 - \lambda_{11}(t)}{2} \tag{8.20}$$

This implies that, while under the tariff the control equation of firm 1 is

$$\dot{q}_1 = -\frac{\dot{q}_2 + \lambda_{11}}{2} \tag{8.21}$$

under the quota (not necessarily set at the tariff-equivalent level), it becomes

$$\dot{q}_1 = -\frac{\dot{\lambda}_{11}}{2} = \frac{\left[f'(k_1(t)) - \rho - \delta \right] \lambda_{11}(t)}{2} \tag{8.22}$$

i.e., it depends only on the dynamic properties of firm 1's own shadow price, precisely because the quota of the rival is fixed *at some level*. Imposing stationarity on $q_1(t)$ shows that the steady state production of firm 1 is either q_{GR} or $q_1^*(\bar{q}_2) = (a - \bar{q}_2)/2$, depending on the initial condition $k_1(0)$. What really matters is that the adoption of any quota may drive the home firm into the golden rule. In particular, if the quota is set at the tariff-equivalent volume, we have:

Proposition 8.3 *Suppose that (1)* $0 < q_2^{OL} < q_1^{OL} < q_{GR}$, *and (2) the government of country 1 introduces the quota* $\bar{q}_2 = q_2^{OL}$. *This causes a unilateral expansion of the domestic firm's production (possibly to the golden-rule level) and drives market price down, thereby increasing social welfare in country 1 as compared to the market driven equilibrium under an import tariff.*

Additionally, it is also easily shown that all of this goes along with an increase in the domestic firm's profits (irrespective of the exact output it produces), with a rare alignment between private and collective incentives of all agents in the home country. The lack of equivalence here speaks neatly in favour of quotas, and this conclusion is entirely to be imputed to the Ramsey accumulation dynamics and the possibility for the home producer of unilaterally reaching the golden rule with the assistance of the home government.

Now note that this result also emerges – for the very same reasons – if instead the foreign firm adopts a VER by fixing its exports to country 1 at the free trade level of the market-driven equilibrium generated if the demand system is defined as in (8.15). The proof of this result is in Calzolari and Lambertini (2007) and is omitted, being based on a straightforward reformulation of (8.20–8.22) in which $\bar{q}_2 = q_2^{OL}$ is replaced by $q_2^{VER} = q_2^{OL}$. Hence, given that the adoption of a VER has negative consequences on the foreign firm's profits, this simple argument proves

Proposition 8.4 *In the Cournot–Ramsey game, it is never optimal for the foreign firm to adopt a voluntary export restraint.*

The problem is slightly more involved – and also very different in nature, as we are about to see – under Bertrand competition, where the Hamiltonian of firm i is

$$
\mathcal{H}_i(t) = e^{-\rho t} \left\{ \left[\frac{a}{1+\gamma} - \frac{p_i(t)}{1-\gamma^2} + \frac{\gamma p_j(t)}{1-\gamma^2} \right] p_i(t) + \right.
$$
$$
\lambda_{ii}(t) \left[f(k_i(t)) - \frac{a}{1+\gamma} + \frac{p_i(t)}{1-\gamma^2} - \frac{\gamma p_j(t)}{1-\gamma^2} - \delta k_i(t) \right] + \quad (8.23)
$$
$$
\left. \lambda_{ij}(t) \left[f(k_j(t)) - \frac{a}{1+\gamma} + \frac{p_j(t)}{1-\gamma^2} - \frac{\gamma p_i(t)}{1-\gamma^2} - \delta k_j(t) \right] \right\}
$$

Obviously, the game remains state-redundant, the objects of interest being the instantaneous best reply in the price space,

$$
p_i^*(t) = \frac{a(1-\gamma) + \gamma p_j(t) + \lambda_{ii}(t)}{2} \quad (8.24)
$$

and the consequent control dynamics

$$
\dot{p}_i = \frac{\gamma \dot{p}_j + \dot{\lambda}_{ii}}{2} \quad (8.25)
$$

which, using the set of necessary conditions, can be rewritten under full symmetry as

$$
\dot{p} = \frac{1}{2-\gamma} \left[(2-\gamma)p - a(1-\gamma) \right] \left[\rho + \delta - f'(k(t)) \right] \quad (8.26)
$$

to ascertain that the stationary points are $q_{GR} = f(k_{GR}) - \delta k_{GR}$ and $p^{OL} = a(1-\gamma)/(2-\gamma)$. In correspondence of the market-driven solution, the individual steady state equilibrium output is

$$
q^{OL} = \frac{a}{(1+\gamma)(2-\gamma)} \quad (8.27)
$$

If firm 2 adopts an export restraint q_2^{VER}, one has to rewrite the Hamiltonian function of the domestic firm as follows:

$$
\mathcal{H}_1(t) = e^{-\rho t} \left\{ \left[a - p_1(t) - \gamma q_2^{VER} \right] p_i(t) + \right.
$$
$$
\lambda_{ii}(t) \left[f(k_i(t)) - a + p_1(t) + \gamma q_2^{VER} - \delta k_i(t) \right] + \quad (8.28)
$$
$$
\left. \lambda_{ij}(t) \left[f(k_j(t)) - q_2^{VER} - \delta k_j(t) \right] \right\}
$$

since the relevant demand function for firm 1 is now $q_1(t) = a - p_1(t) - \gamma q_2^{VER}$. As a result, the instantaneous reaction function of the home is

$$
p_1^*(t) = \frac{a - \gamma q_F^{VER} + \lambda_{ii}(t)}{2} \quad (8.29)
$$

which implies the control equation $\dot{p}_1 = \dot{\lambda}_{ii}/2$, i.e., after a simple manipulation,

$$
\dot{p}_1 = \frac{(2p_1 - a + \gamma \bar{q}_F) \left[\rho + \delta - f'(k_1) \right]}{2} \quad (8.30)
$$

The two stationary points of the state-control dynamic system are identified by

$$f'(k_{GR}) = \rho + \delta$$

$$p_1^* \left(q_2^{VER} \right) = q_1^* \left(q_2^{VER} \right) = \frac{a - \gamma q_2^{VER}}{2} \tag{8.31}$$

The second solution coincides with the expression obtained in the Cournot game, because the domestic firm is a monopolist on the residual demand function by virtue of the restriction adopted by its competitor. As for the attitude of the latter towards the adoption of a VER, what matters is the presence of complementarity or substitutability between the two varieties, i.e., the sign of parameter γ:

Proposition 8.5 *Consider the market-driven solution under Bertrand competition. The adoption of any VER*

$$q_2^{VER} \in \left(\widehat{q}_2, q^{OL} \right)$$
$$\widehat{q}_2 = \arg\max_{q_2} \pi_2 \left(p_1^* \left(q_2^{VER} \right) \right)$$

increases both firms's profits, with $\pi_2^{VER} > \pi_1^{VER}$ for all $\gamma \in (0, 1]$. Otherwise, if either $q^{OL} \geq q_{GR}$ or $s \in [-1, 0)$, then π_2^{VER} is lower than under free trade, and the foreign firm has no incentive to adopt it.

The above proposition says that an output restriction may be voluntarily chosen by the foreign firm as long as the free trade equilibrium is dictated by demand and cost conditions alone and goods are substitutes. Its nature is indeed anti-competitive because it enhances both firms' performance (being thus welcomed by the home firm as well) and of course hinders consumer surplus and profits. Additionally, the foregoing analysis contains a clear-cut message which cannot be delivered by static models. In plain words, the positive side of the story is that the golden rule, whenever it prevails as the saddle point equilibrium of the industry, is a safeguard against this type of behaviour, and cannot be disrupted by any output restriction whatsoever.

8.1.3 Habit Formation

An interesting and quite original application of differential game theory to intraindustry trade in a two-country world is in Yin (2004), where habit formation à la Pollack (1970) determines the dynamics of market demand, and the trade policy instrument being considered is a *voluntary import expansion* (VIE).

The literature on VIEs departs from Bhagwati (1987) and is extended by Bjorksten (1990) and Greaney (1996, 1999) using several oligopoly models under price or quantity competition and even capacity constraints as in Kreps and Scheinkman (1983), while Dinopoulos and Kreinin (1990) consider the effects of VIEs in perfectly competitive markets.

Yin (2004) illustrates what happens in one of the two countries as markets are separated, and shows that habit formation can induce the voluntary adoption of an import expansion as it is welfare improving for the home country, where market demand is

$$p_1(t) = vh(t) + a - b[q_1(t) + q_2(t)] \tag{8.32}$$

In (8.32), a, b and v are positive constants, and $h(t)$ is habit, which here is the relevant state variable whose dynamics is described by

$$\dot{h} = q_1(t) + q_2(t) - \delta h(t) \tag{8.33}$$

saying that habit fades away in absence of consumption. For the model to make sense and solutions to be viable, assume $\delta > v/b$. Note the pronounced analogy between habit formation and the goodwill or brand equity effect illustrated in Chapter 4 (but see also Chapter 9).

Firms operate with a common technology characterised by a constant marginal cost c and tariffs and subsidies are assumed away. Hence, the profit function of firm i is $\pi_i(t) = [p(t) - c]q_i(t)$. Under free trade, feedback strategies solve the following HJB equation:

$$\rho V_i(h(t)) = \max_{q_i(t)} \left\{ [p(t) - c]q_i(t) + V_i'(h(t))[q_1(t) + q_2(t) - \delta h(t)] \right\} \tag{8.34}$$

The resulting symmetric linear feedback strategies are $q^{LF} = \alpha + \beta h$, with

$$\alpha = \frac{a - c + \varepsilon_2}{3}; \beta = \frac{v + 2\varepsilon_1}{3} \tag{8.35}$$

where ε_1 and ε_2 are two of the three coefficients of the symmetric value function $V = \varepsilon_1 h^2 + \varepsilon_2 h + \varepsilon_3$. The resulting steady state level of habit, h^{LF}, may then be easily computed.

Now suppose the government of country 1 implements a VIE policy by requiring its firm to shrink output as compared to the free trade equilibrium just sketched. This amounts to saying that firm 1 produces

$$\alpha + \beta h^{LF} - \xi \equiv q_1^{VIE} \in \left(0, \alpha + \beta h^{LF}\right) \tag{8.36}$$

Note that q_1^{VIE} is a pure number, as is the case with VERs and quotas in the previous models. Consequently, the problem of the foreign firm in presence of the VIE is represented by

$$\rho V_2(h(t)) = \max_{q_2(t)} \left\{ [vh(t) + a - b(q_1^{VIE} + q_2(t)) - c]q_2(t) \right. \tag{8.37}$$

$$\left. + V_2'(h(t))[q_1^{VIE} + q_2(t) - \delta h(t)] \right\}$$

Now pause for a moment to recall that, in a static Cournot game without habit effects, the linearity of demand and technology would yield a linear best reply $q_i^* = (a - c - q_j)/2$, with $\partial q_i^*/\partial q_j = -1/2$: any given reduction in firm j's output induces an optimal increase in firm i's output, which amounts to 50% of the reduction practiced by the rival.

As it turns out, the solution of (8.37) reveals that the output expansion by firm 2 along the residual demand function is always larger than $\xi/2$ and, under admissible and plausible parametric conditions, can be even larger than ξ. The driving force is the feedback effect through the state variable, inducing excess reaction on the part of the foreign firm. For this reason, industry output and the habit stock under the VIE exceed those determined by free trade, and the following holds:

Proposition 8.6 *The adoption of a VIE, via the induced increase in the equilibrium level of habit stock, may increase both profits and consumer surplus in the home country.*

The profit increase for the home country is due to habit compensating the negative effect on market price, evidently. The overall effect on welfare being positive, we observe a coincidence between social and private preferences in the home country concerning the introduction of VIEs.

8.2 Trade, the Environment and Natural Resources

Intuitively, there exists a very strong connection between trade, the environment and economic growth. The huge literature examining the endogenous linkages between them is thoroughly assessed in Copeland and Taylor (2003, 2004, 2009). Quite naturally, several efforts have been produced to understand the impact of market power on trade *and* the environment in differential game models. Most of the resulting contributions rely on models we have encountered in Chapter 7. Here I will summarise the contents of a few papers connecting either polluting emissions or the extraction of renewables or both to intraindustry trade in differential games solved under feedback information.

8.2.1 Trade and Pollution

The first game has a well-defined IO flavour. Feenstra *et al.* (2001) use a model of capacity accumulation which shares some features with Reynolds (1987) to illustrate intraindustry trade in a homogeneous good, taking place between two countries, 1 and 2, each hosting a single firm. The game revisits the *vexata quaestio* of the relative performance of environmental standards and emission taxation (see Ulph, 1992; Requate and Unold, 2003; Requate, 2005; Lambertini, 2017).

Technology is represented by a Cobb–Douglas production function $q_i(t) = \sqrt{k_i(t) z_i(t)}$ using physical capital $k_i(t)$ and a polluting input (a fossil fuel) $z_i(t)$, $i = 1, 2$. Firms invest to accumulate capacity, according to

$$\dot{k}_i = I_i(t) - \delta k_i(t) \tag{8.38}$$

while instantaneous emissions are linear in $z_i(t)$. The cost of investment is $C_i(t) = b I_i^2(t)$, while the polluting input is bought at price p_z. On the common market (which may be placed in a third country), demand is linear and accomodates for some degree of product differentiation, with $p_i(t) = a - q_i(t) - \gamma q_j(t)$, as in Singh and Vives (1984).

Two alternative scenarios are accounted for. If both governments adopt an emission tax τ_i, the problem of firm i is

$$\max_{I_i} \Pi_i = \int_0^\infty \left[\left(a - \sqrt{k_i z_i} - \gamma \sqrt{k_j z_j} \right) \sqrt{k_i z_i} - b I_i^2 - (\tau_i + p_z) z_i \right] e^{-\rho t} dt \tag{8.39}$$

subject to (8.40). If instead an environmental standard $\bar{z}_i$ is bilaterally adopted, firm i has to

$$\max_{I_i} \Pi_i = \int_0^\infty \left[\left(a - \sqrt{k_i z_i} - \gamma \sqrt{k_j z_j} \right) \sqrt{k_i z_i} - b I_i^2 - p_z z_i \right] e^{-\rho t} dt \qquad (8.40)$$

subject to (8.40) and $z_i \le \bar{z}_i$.

Given the difficulties in solving the feedback game without policy instruments and pollution (which would be much the same as in Reynolds, 1987), a fortiori this setup requires numerical simulations. However, a relevant result emerges neatly:

Proposition 8.7 *Firms' investments are higher under the environmental standard than under emission taxation iff $\partial z_i / \partial k_i < 0$.*

This proposition says that if the two inputs are substitutes, then (1) the adoption of a standard leads to higher investments and higher equilibrium capacities, and this, by virtue of $\partial z_i / \partial k_i < 0$, (2) also implies that firms use lower volumes of the polluting input, partially replacing it with productive capacity. Hence, ultimately, (3) equilibrium emissions are also reduced in presence of a standard.

The second game directly sprouts from the benchmark model in Benchekroun and Long (1998). Fujiwara (2009b) extends it to explain why environmentalists oppose trade liberalisation, using a two-country model with transboundary pollution.

Consider first the autarky case. In each country, a monopolist $i = 1, 2$ faces a linear demand $p_i(t) = a - q_i(t)$. Production costs are linear and marginal cost c is time-invariant, so that the instantaneous profit function is

$$\pi_i(t) = \left[a - q_i(t) - c \right] q_i(t) - \upsilon S^2(t) \qquad (8.41)$$

where υ is a positive parameter and the state variable $S(t)$, measuring global emissions, follows

$$\dot{S} = q_1(t) + q_2(t) - \delta S(t) \qquad (8.42)$$

the presence of the term $\upsilon S^2(t)$ in (8.41) may represent either a taxation levied upon the environmental damage or environmental concern. The autarkic problem can be solved using both open-loop and feedback information, due to the presence of $q_j(t)$ in the monopoly problem of firm i.[5]

If trade opens, and no policy is adopted by the governments of the two countries, the common market expresses a demand function $p(t) = a - \left[q_1(t) + q_2(t) \right]/2$, which replaces the autarkic one in the definition of instantaneous profits, while the relevant dynamic constraint remains (8.42).

Solving both the autarkic model and the free trade game under open-loop and linear feedback information, Fujiwara finds out that, for obvious reasons, the steady state stock of pollutants produced under feedback strategies, S^{LF}, exceeds that reached under open-loop strategies in both regimes, as firms overproduced being stimulated by feedback information. Then, comparing pollution before and after the opening of trade, one obtains

---

[5] Indeed, Fujiwara (2009b) also identifies the tangency point between the highest isocline of firm i and the steady state locus under nonlinear feedback strategies, under both autarky and free trade.

Proposition 8.8 *Free trade expands the stock of pollutants as compared to autarky, irrespective of the information structure.*

In itself, this result would be sufficient to explain why a considerable portion of the public opinion, being concerned about global warming, has a negative view of trade liberalisation. The perspective becomes even gloomier if one considers that the desirable price effect generated by competition under free trade can be more than offset by the increase in pollution – which happens if the efficiency of natural carbon sinks is too low – causing a decrease in total welfare under free trade.

Note that, although the model in Fujiwara (2009b) admits the presence of environmental damages in the firms' objective functions, it does not envisage their possible reaction in the form of investments in clean technologies. These are instead considered in a literature based on perfect competition (Dutta and Radner, 2006; Benchekroun and Chauduri, 2014), where, under certain conditions, a rebound effect emerges: countries may react to investments in green technologies by increasing emissions and therefore also the stock of pollution, thereby lowering welfare. This is a direction that also the literature dealing with strategic trade should take.

Using a variation of the same model, Yanase (2007) carries out a comparative evaluation of the performance of emission taxes and emission quotas under feedback rules. The main finding is that the adoption of a tax on polluting emissions is more distortionary than emission quotas, for the indirect effect on prices, and therefore the resulting level of pollution, is higher than that associated with quotas.

8.2.2 Globalization and Resource Extraction

One of the most productive lines of research focusses upon access to the commons and, more specifically, on the extraction of renewable resources (Clark and Munro, 1975). Often, this is labelled as the *international fishery model* (Khalitbari, 1977; Levhari and Mirman, 1980; Chiarella *et al.*, 1984). This literature is a natural extension of the discussion about the pressure exerted on natural resources by free access to the commons to a setup where, in general, players are countries rather than oligopolistic firms, and the matter is to find a socially optimal extraction path at a global level. This also allows for the adoption of open-loop rules, as the related command optimum is the outcome of an optimal control problem rather than a proper game (on this aspect, see, in particular, Chiarella *et al.*, 1984).

What I want to illustrate here in some detail is instead a quite direct implication of globalization on the tragedy of commons produced by a differential game (Fujiwara, 2011) in which the presence of different countries is, paradoxically, not entirely explicit but rather obvious.

The setup is a straightforward extension of the baseline Cournot game of renewable resource extraction analysed by Benchekroun (2003, 2008), Fujiwara (2008) and Lambertini and Mantovani (2016), except that it is assumed that the population of firms is made up by $n_1 + n_2$ firms with different technologies. So, think of the following scenario: $n_1 \geq 1$ firms are based in country 1 and use an efficient technology with (for simplicity) zero costs, while the other $n_2 \geq 1$ firms are based in country 2 and their marginal cost is $c > 0$.

All of them exploit a common pool renewable resource whose state equation is

$$\dot{X} = \eta X(t) - \sum_{i=1}^{n_1} q_i(t) - \sum_{j=1}^{n_2} q_j(t) \qquad (8.43)$$

and sell the final good to consumers on the global market, whose demand function is $p(t) = a - \sum_{i=1}^{n_1} q_i(t) - \sum_{j=1}^{n_2} q_j(t)$. Hence, the instantaneous profit function of a firm based in country 1 is $\pi_i(t) = p(t) q_i(t)$, while that of a firm located in country 2 is $\pi_j(t) = [p(t) - c] q_j(t)$. The game lasts forever, and all firms noncooperatively maximise their individual profit flow using the same discount rate $\rho > 0$, under the constraint (8.43).

The linear feedback strategies $q_i(X) = \phi X + \varrho_i$ for all $i = 1, 2, ...n_1$ and $q_j(X) = \phi X + \varrho_j$ for all $j = 1, 2, ...n_2$ solving the asymmetric system of HJB equations can be written as follows:

$$q_i(X) = \begin{cases} 0 \text{ for all } X \leq \dfrac{\varrho_j}{\phi} \\[2mm] \phi X + \varrho_i \text{ for all } X \in \left(\dfrac{\varrho_j}{\phi}, \widetilde{X}_j \right) \\[2mm] \dfrac{a + cn_2}{n_1 + n_2 + 1} \text{ for all } X \geq \widetilde{X}_j \end{cases} \qquad (8.44)$$

$$q_i(X) = \begin{cases} 0 \text{ if } X \leq \dfrac{\varrho_j}{\phi} \\[2mm] \phi X + \varrho_j \text{ for all } X \in \left(\dfrac{\varrho_j}{\phi}, \widetilde{X}_j \right) \\[2mm] \dfrac{a - c(n_1 + 1)}{n_1 + n_2 + 1} \text{ for all } X \geq \widetilde{X}_j \end{cases} \qquad (8.45)$$

in which ϱ_j/ϕ and $\widetilde{X}_j$ identify the kinks in an inefficient firm's strategy; moreover, $\widetilde{X}_j$ is the level of the resource stock at which *all* firms start adopting the static Cournot–Nash strategies, which depend only on demand and cost parameters. Given the asymmetry in marginal costs, (8.44) tells that the efficient firms' output strategies are discontinuous in correspondence of resource volumes ϱ_j/ϕ and $\widetilde{X}_j$, while those of inefficient firms are continuous but not differentiable everywhere.

On the basis of (8.44–8.45), Fujiwara (2011) discovers that, as long as the proper linear feedback strategies identify the inner solution, the following holds:

Proposition 8.9 *Steady state social welfare (in the present interpretation of the model, global welfare) monotonically decreases in the number of efficient firms.*

The intuition is straightforward: the difference in marginal costs, coupled with the intensification of strategic competition due to feedback information, implies higher extraction rates as compared to the socially efficient solution.[6] More explicitly, the

---

[6] Although Fujiwara (2011) does not mention it, a role in this respect is also played by the voracity effect already mentioned in Lane and Tornell (1996) and Tornell and Lane (1999) in other contexts, and outlined in this model by Benchekroun (2008) and Lambertini and Mantovani (2014).

'dynamic' (and negative) effect associated with overexploitation more than offsets the 'static' (and positive) effect associated with the output expansion and the resulting decrease in price. That is, the feedback effect matters more than the price effect in determining the ultimate consequences of firms' behaviour on welfare.

The natural complement to the above Proposition is

Corollary 8.10 *Under linear feedback strategies, increasing the number of any group of firms reduces the steady state level of global welfare.*

This contradicts a well-known argument put forward by Lahiri and Ono (1988), whereby removing one or more inefficient firms from a market is a welfare-enhancing policy. The reason is that their point rests on predictions yielded by a static model, where the feedback motive is entirely absent. Indeed, the conclusion reached by Lahiri and Ono (1988) remains true for all $X \geq \tilde{X}_j$, i.e., in the subset of the state space in which firms adopt the static Cournot solution.

8.2.3 Trading Polluting Nonrenewables

In Chapter 7 I haven't devoted any space to games describing the interplay between natural resource exploitation and polluting emission. Intuitively, this is an extremely relevant theme when it comes to nonrenewables such as fossil fuels, and it has inevitably attracted the attention of researchers working in the field of differential game theory.

The cornerstone of the comparative small but very insightful debate existing in this area is in Wirl (1994), getting three eggs in a single basket.

The game takes place over an infinite horizon between a firm based in country 1, holding monopoly access to a nonrenewable resource whose stock is $\overline{X} > 0$, and the government of country 2, importing the resource from abroad. Pollution has two sources, stock $S(t)$ and flow $q(t)$. Hence the instantaneous total environmental damage suffered by country 2 is

$$D_2(t) = \frac{\varsigma S^2(t)}{2} + \frac{\varphi q^2(t)}{2} \tag{8.46}$$

where ς and φ are positive parameters. Country 2's demand has the usual linear form, and the government adopts a unit tax or import tariff $\tau_2(t)$, whose double nature is intuitive in view of the environmental implications of imports. For simplicity, the marginal extraction costs is constant and posed equal to zero (this, by the way, entails that the monopolist is one of the efficient firms considered by Fujiwara, 2011).

As a result, the instantaneous profits of the exporting monopolist are $\pi_1(t) = p_1(t)q(t) = p_1(t)[a - p_1(t) - \tau(t)]$. This expression also measures the relevant 'welfare' function for country 1 (observe that this assumption amounts to saying that pollution is not transboundary). Conversely, country 2 has a proper instantaneous welfare function written as follows:

$$SW_2(t) = CS_2(t) + \tau_2(t)q(t) - D(t) = \tag{8.47}$$

$$\frac{[a - p_1(t) - \tau_2(t)]^2}{2} + \tau_2(t)[a - p_1(t) - \tau_2(t)] - \frac{\varsigma S^2(t)}{2} - \frac{\varphi[a - p_1(t) - \tau_2(t)]^2}{2}$$

Now suppose the stock of pollution is the same as accumulated extraction. If so, emissions evolve according to $\dot{S} = q(t)$, which is the dynamic constraint common to both players. Their respective controls are $p_1(t)$ and $\tau_2(t)$.

The game is played simultaneously under feedback information.[7] If players choose feedback strategies $p_1 = f_1(S)$ and $\tau_2 = f_2(S)$, their respective Bellman equations are

$$\rho V_1(S) = \max_{p_1} \{p_1[a - p_1 - f_2(S)] + V_1'(S)[a - p_1 - f_2(S)]\} \tag{8.48}$$

for the firm, and

$$\rho V_2(S) = \max_{\tau_2} \left\{ \frac{[a - f_1(S) - \tau_2]^2}{2} + \tau_2[a - f_1(S) - \tau_2] \right. \tag{8.49}$$
$$\left. - \frac{\varsigma S^2(t)}{2} - \frac{\varphi[a - f_1(S) - \tau_2]^2}{2} + V_2'(S)[a - f_1(S) - \tau_2] \right\}$$

for the government. Both (8.48) and (8.49) reflect the view of the relevant player who expects the rival to adopt a strategy defined in terms of the single relevant state.

Wirl (1994) solves this game under linear feedback strategies and then compares the outcome with that of the cooperative solution in which a hypothetical planner uses the sum of firm 1's profits and country 2's welfare as the relevant instantaneous payoff. In this case, the model defines an optimal control problem in which the planner must pick the price and tariff to maximise the following Hamiltonian function:

$$\mathcal{H}^{SP} = e^{-\rho t} \left\{ \pi_1 + CS_2 + \tau_2 q - D + \lambda \dot{S} + \theta \left(\overline{X} - S \right) \right\} \tag{8.50}$$

in which θ is the Lagrange multiplier attached to the constraint posed by the existing stock of the nonrenwable resource.

The comparative evaluation of the two solutions reveals

Proposition 8.11 *Cooperative and noncooperative equilibria are observationally equivalent in terms of the steady state stock of polluting emissions. However, the profit-maximising monopolist delays the stock externality and reduces the flow externality along some portion of the path to the steady state of the noncooperative game.*

That is to say, Wirl's (1994) model provides a confirmation of Hotelling's (1931) original idea that monopoly favours the preservation of natural resources and further extends it to include also the quality of the environment, if extraction and pollution are closely connected to each other, because of the obvious output restriction associated with market power. Moreover, Wirl (1994, pp. 11–13) illustrates the existence of infinitely many equilibria attained adopting nonlinear feedback strategies. This continuum of equilibria, however, turns out to be Pareto-dominated by the one reached through linear feedback strategies. This property makes the linear feedback solution entirely representative of the players' behaviour.

---

[7] It is worth observing that Stackelberg play is ruled out, for good reasons. The first is that the government and the firm do not belong to the same country. The second is that the analysis focusses upon the bearings of emission taxation on the market price practiced by the exporting firm (cf. Wirl, 1984, p. 2).

An additional remark (which of course is absent in Wirl, 1994) is in order, concerning the implications of the result stated in the above proposition on the possible arising of the green paradox (Sinn, 2012). Somewhat counterintuitively, the path which would be chosen by the planner being above that chosen by a strategic firm at least over a relevant part of the time horizon, a presumed 'command optimum' myopically leaving aside the green paradox scenario could in fact contribute to create it, while the opposite might be true of a self-interested entrepreneur.

Further Reading

An assessment of the relative performance of tariffs and quotas in a model where the domestic market is a monopoly can be found in Sweeney et al. (1977). An early dynamic approach to trade and technology policies in the spirit of Brander and Spencer (1985) is in Cheng (1987). A dynamic game of trade with tariff policies is in Lapham (1995). Pomfret (1989) contains a comprehensive survey of the literature on voluntary export restraints. Additional insights on VERs and the effects of feedback information on market integration is in Fujiwara (2010), Fujiwara and Shinozaki (2010) and Fujiwara et al. (2011). The choice between environmental standards and emission taxes under international trade is also treated in Feenstra et al. (1996). Essential references for our understanding of the exploitation of natural resources under fee trade are Kemp and Long (1980, 1984). For more on international fishery games, see Crabbé and Long (1993), Brander and Taylor (1997), Benchekroun and Long (2002) and Long (2010, 2011). Further research in the vein of the Wirl (1994) model can be found in Wirl (1995), Wirl and Dockner (1995) and Tahvonen (1996). Recently, also, corporate social responsibility (CSR) has been used as an additional ingredient of differential games on trade and the environment. In Yanase (2012), intraindustry trade takes place among a large number of countries in which firms have adopted a CSR stance. A similar game in Jinji (2013) includes both CSR and different trade policies in the picture.

Bibliography

Benchekroun, H. (2003), "Unilateral Production Restrictions in a Dynamic Duopoly", *Journal of Economic Theory*, **111**, 214–39.

Benchekroun, H. (2008), "Comparative Dynamics in a Productive Asset Oligopoly", *Journal of Economic Theory*, **138**, 237–61.

Benchekroun, H. and A.R. Chauduri (2014), "Transboundary Pollution and Clean Technologies", *Resource and Energy Economics*, **36**, 601–19.

Benchekroun, H. and N.V. Long (1998), "Efficiency Inducing Taxation for Polluting Oligopolists", *Journal of Public Economics*, **70**, 325–42.

Benchekroun, H. and N.V. Long (2002), "Transboundary Fishery: A Differential Game Model", *Economica*, **69**, 207–21.

Bhagwati, J. (1965), "On the Equivalence of Tariffs and Quotas", in R. Baldwin et al. (eds), *Trade, Growth, and the Balance of Payments. Essays in Honor of Gottfried Haberler*, Chicago, Rand McNally.

Bhagwati, J. (1968), "More on the Equivalence of Tariffs and Quotas", *American Economic Review*, **58**, 142–46.

Bhagwati, J. (1987), "VERs, Quid pro Wuo DFI, and VIEs: Political Economy-Theoretical Analysis", *International Economic Journal*, **1**, 1–14.

Bjorksten, N. (1994), "Voluntary Import Expansions and Voluntary Export Restraints in an Oligopoly Model with Capacity Constraints", *Canadian Journal of Economics*, **27**, 446–57.

Brander, J. (1981), "Intra-Industry Trade in Identical Commodities", *Journal of International Economics*, **11**, 1–14.

Brander, J. (1995), "Strategic Trade Policy", in G.M. Grossman and K. Rogoff (eds), *Handbook of International Economics*, vol. 3, Amsterdam, North-Holland.

Brander, J. and P. Krugman (1983), "A 'Reciprocal Dumping' Model of International Trade", *Journal of International Economics*, **15**, 311–21.

Brander, J. and B. Spencer (1985), "Export Subsidies and International Market Share Rivalry", *Journal of International Economics*, **18**, 83–100.

Brander, J. and S.M. Taylor (1997), "International Trade and Open Access Renewable Resources: The Small Open Economy Case", *Canadian Journal of Econonomics*, **30**, 526–52.

Bresnahan, T. (1981), "Duopoly Models with Consistent Conjectures", *American Economic Review*, **71**, 934–45.

Calzolari, G. and L. Lambertini (2006), "Tariffs vs Quotas in a Trade Model with Capital Accumulation", *Review of International Economics*, **14**, 632–44.

Calzolari, G. and L. Lambertini (2007), "Export Restraints in a Model of Trade with Capital Accumulation", *Journal of Economic Dynamics and Control*, **31**, 3822–42.

Cellini, R., and L. Lambertini (1998), "A Dynamic Model of Differentiated Oligopoly with Capital Accumulation", *Journal of Economic Theory*, **83**, 145–55.

Cheng, L. (1987), "Optimal Trade and Technology Policies: Dynamic Linkages", *International Economic Review*, **28**, 757–76.

Chiarella, C., M.C. Kemp, N.V. Long and K. Okuguchi (1984), "On the Economics of International Fisheries", *International Economic Review*, **25**, 85–92.

Clark, C.W. and G.R. Munro (1975), "The Economics of Fishing and Modern Capital Theory", *Journal of Environmental Econonomics and Management*, **2**, 92–106.

Copeland, B.R. and M.S. Taylor (2003), *Trade and the Environment: Theory and Evidence*, Princeton, NJ, Princeton University Press.

Copeland, B.R. and M.S. Taylor (2004), "Trade, Growth, and the Environment", *Journal of Economic Literature*, **42**, 7–71.

Copeland, B.R. and M.S. Taylor (2009), "Trade, Tragedy, and the Commons", *American Economic Review*, **99**, 725–49.

Crabbé, P. and N.V. Long (1993), "Entry Deterrence and Overexploitation of the Fishery", *Journal of Economic Dynamics and Control*, **17**, 679–704.

Dinopoulos, E., and M.E. Kreinin (1990), "An Analysis of Import Expansion Policies", *Economic Inquiry*, **28**, 98–108.

Dockner, E. and A. Haug (1990), "Tariffs and Quotas under Dynamic Duopolistic Competition", *Journal of International Economics*, **29**, 147–59.

Dockner, E. and A. Haug (1991),"The Closed Loop Motive for Voluntary Export Restraints", *Canadian Journal of Economics*, **3**, 679–85.

Driskill, R. (2001), "Durable Goods Oligopoly", *International Journal of Industrial Organization*, **19**, 391–413.

Driskill, R.. and A. Horowitz (1996),"Durability and Strategic Trade: Are There Rents to Be Captured?," *Journal of International Organization*, **41**, 179–94.

Driskill, R.. and S. McCafferty (1989), "Dynamic Duopoly with Output Adjustment Costs in International Markets: Taking the Conjecture out of Conjectural Variations", in R.C. Feenstra (ed.), *Trade Policies for International Competitiveness*, NBER Conference Report series, Chicago, University of Chicago Press.

Driskill, R.. and S. McCafferty (1996),"Industrial Policy and Duopolistic Trade with Dynamic Demand," *Review of Industrial Organization*, **11**, 355–73.

Dutta, P.K. and R. Radner (2006), "Population Growth and Technological Change in a Global Warming Model", *Economic Theory*, **29**, 251–70.

Eaton, J. and G.M. Grossman (1986), "Optimal Trade and Industrial Policy under Oligopoly", *Quarterly Journal of Economics*, **101**, 383–406.

Feenstra, T., P. Kort and A. de Zeeuw (2001), "Environmental Policy Instruments in an International Duopoly with Feedback Investment Strategies", *Journal of Economic Dynamics and Control*, **25**, 1665–87.

Feenstra, T., P. Kort, P. Verheyen and A. de Zeeuw (1996), "Standards versus Taxes in a Dynamic Duopoly Model of Trade", in A. Xepapadeas (ed.), *Economic Policy for the Environment and Natural Resources*, Cheltenham, Edward Elgar.

Fershtman, C. and M. Kamien (1987), "Dynamic Duopolistic Competition with Sticky Prices", *Econometrica*, **55**, 1151–64.

Fujiwara, K. (2008), "Duopoly Can Be More Anti-Competitive than Monopoly", *Economics Letters*, **101**, 217–19.

Fujiwara, K. (2009a), "Gains from Trade in a Differential Game Model of Asymmetric Oligopoly", *Review of International Economics*, **17**, 1066–73.

Fujiwara, K. (2009b), "Why Environmentalists Resist Trade Liberalization", *Environmental and Resource Economics*, **44**, 71–84.

Fujiwara, K. (2010), "When Are Voluntary Export Restraints Voluntary? A Differential Game Approach", *Australian Economic Papers*, **49**, 101–10.

Fujiwara, K. (2011), "Losses from Competition in a Dynamic Game Model of a Renewable Resource Oligopoly", *Resource and Energy Economics*, **33**, 1–11.

Fujiwara, K. and T. Shinozaki (2010), "The Closed-Loop Effects of Market Integration in a Dynamic Duopoly", *Australian Economic Papers*, **49**, 1–12.

Fujiwara, K., T. Shinozaki and A. Yanase (2011), "Dynamic Interactions in Trade Policy in a Differential Game Model of Tariff Protection", *Review of Development Economics*, **15**, 689–98.

Greaney, T. (1996), "Import Now! An Analysis of Market-Share Voluntary Import Expansions (VIEs)", *Journal of International Economics*, **40**, 149–63.

Greaney, T. (1999), "Manipulating Market Shares: The Indirect Effects of Voluntary Import Expansions (VIEs)", *Japan and the World Economy*, **11**, 95–113.

Grossman, G.M. (1992, ed.), *Imperfect Competition and International Trade*, Cambridge, MA, MIT Press.

Harris, R. (1985), "Why Voluntary Export Restraints Are 'Voluntary'", *Canadian Journal of Economics*, **18**, 799–809.

Helpman, E. and P. Krugman (1985), *Market Structure and Foreign Trade: Increasing Returns, Imperfect Competition, and the International Economy*, Cambridge, MA, MIT Press.

Helpman, E. and P. Krugman (1989), *Trade Policy and Market Structure*, Cambridge, MA, MIT Press.

Hotelling, H. (1931), "The Economics of Exhaustible Resources", *Journal of Political Economy*, **39**, 137–75.

Hwang, H. and C.-C. Mai (1988), "On the Equivalence of Tariffs and Quotas under Duopoly", *Journal of International Economics*, **24**, 373–80.

Itoh, M. and Y. Ono (1982), "Tariffs, Quotas and Market Structure", *Quarterly Journal of Economics*, **97**, 295–305.

Itoh, M. and Y. Ono (1984), "Tariffs vs Quotas under Duopoly of Heterogeneous Goods", *Journal of International Economics*, **17**, 359–73.

Jinji, N. (2013), "Is Corporate Environmentalism Good for Domestic Welfare?", *Review of International Economics*, **21**, 901–11.

Kamien, M. and N. Schwartz (1983), "Conjectural Variations", *Canadian Journal of Economics*, **16**, 191–211.

Kemp, M.C. and N.V. Long (1980), *Exhaustible Resources, Optimality, and Trade*, Amsterdam, North-Holland.

Kemp, M.C. and N.V. Long (1984), "The Role of Natural Resources in Trade Models", in R.W. Jones and P. Kenen (eds), *Handbook of Internatioanl Economics*, vol. 1, Amsterdam, North-Holland.

Khalitbari, F. (1977), "Market Imperfections and the Optimum Rate of Depletion of Natural Resources", *Economica*, **44**, 409–14.

Klemperer, P. and M. Meyer (1988), "Consistent Conjectures Equilibria: A Reformulation Showing Non-Uniqueness", *Economics Letters*, **27**, 111–15.

Kreps, D. and J. Scheinkman (1983), "Quantity Precommitment and Bertrand Competition Yield Cournot Outcomes", *Bell Journal of Economics*, **14**, 326–37.

Krishna, K. (1989), "Trade Restrictions as Facilitating Practices", *Journal of International Economics*, **26**, 251–70.

Lahiri, S. and Y. Ono (1988), "Helping Minor Firms Reduces Welfare", *Economic Journal*, **98**, 1199–1202.

Lambertini, L. (2017), "Green Innovation and Market Power", *Annual Review of Resource Economics*, **9**, 231–52.

Lambertini, L. and Mantovani, A. (2014), "Feedback Equilibria in a Dynamic Renewable Resource Oligopoly: Pre-emption, Voracity and Exhaustion", *Journal of Economic Dynamics and Control*, **47**, 115–22.

Lambertini, L. and A. Mantovani (2016), "On the (In)stability of Nonlinear Feedback Solutions in a Dynamic Duopoly with Renewable Resource Exploitation", *Economics Letters*, **143**, 9–12.

Lane, P.R. and A. Tornell (1996), "Power, Growth, and the Voracity Effect", *Journal of Economic Growth*, **1**, 213–41.

Lapham, B. (1995), "Tariffs and Welfare In A Dynamic Differentiated Oligopoly", *Review of International Economics*, **3**, 60–74.

Levhari. D. and L. Mirman (1980), "The Great Fish War: An Example Using a Dynamic Cournot-Nash Solution", *Bell Journal of Economics*, **11**, 322–34.

Long, N.V. (2010), *A Survey of Dynamic Games in Economics*, Singapore, World Scientific.

Long, N.V. (2011), "Dynamic Games in the Economics of Natural Resources: A Survey", *Dynamic Games ands Applications*, **1**, 115–48.

Mai, C. and H. Hwang (1988), "Why Voluntary Export Restraints Are Voluntary: An Extension", *Canadian Journal of Economics*, **21**, 877–82.

Perry, M. (1982), "Oligopoly and Consistent Conjectural Variations", *Bell Journal of Economics*, **13**, 197–205.

Pollak, R.A. (1970), "Habit Formation and Dynamic Demand Functions", *Journal of Political Economy*, **78**, 745–63.

Pomfret, R. (1989), "The Economics of Voluntary Export Restraints Agreements", *Journal of Economic Surveys*, 3, 199–211.

Ramsey, F. (1928), "A Mathematical Theory of Saving", *Economic Journal*, **38**, 543–59.

Requate, T. (2005), "Dynamics Incentives by Environmental Policy Instruments – A Survey", *Ecological Economics*, **54**, 175–95.

Requate, T. and W. Unold (2003), "Environmental Policy Incentives to Adopt Advanced Abatement Technology – Will the True Ranking Please Stand Up?", *European Economic Review*, **47**, 125–46.

Reynolds, S. (1987), "Capacity Investment, Preemption and Commitment in an Infinite Horizon Model", *International Economic Review*, **28**, 69–88.

Shibata, H. (1968), "A Note on the Equivalence of Tariffs and Quotas", *American Economic Review*, **58**, 137–42.

Simaan, M. and T. Takayama (1978), "Game Theory Applied to Dynamic Duopoly Problems with Production Constraints", *Automatica*, **14**, 161–66.

Singh, N. and X. Vives (1984), "Price and Quantity Competition in a Differentiated Duopoly", *RAND Journal of Economics*, **15**, 546–54.

Sinn, H.W. (2012), *The Green Paradox*, Cambridge, MA, MIT Press.

Suzumura, K. and J. Ishikawa (1997), "Voluntary Export Restraints and Economic Welfare", *Japanese Economic Review*, **48**, 176–86.

Sweeney, R.Y., E. Tower and T.D. Willett (1977), "The Ranking of Alternative Tariff and Quota Policies in the Presence of Domestic Monopoly", *Journal of International Economics*, **7**, 246–62.

Tahvonen, O. (1996), "Trade with Polluting Non-Renewable Resources", *Journal of Environmental Economics and Management*, **30**, 1–17.

Tornell, A. and P.R. Lane (1999), "The Voracity Effect", *American Economic Review*, **89**, 22–46.

Ulph, A. (1992), "The Choice of Environmental Policy Instruments and Strategic International Trade", in R. Pethig (ed.), *Conflicts and Cooperation in Managing Environmental Resources*, Berlin, Springer.

Wirl, F. (1994), "Pigouvian Taxation of Energy for Flow and Stock Externalities and Strategic, Noncompetitive Energy Pricing", *Journal of Environmental Economics and Management*, **26**, 1–18.

Wirl, F. (1995), "The Exploitation of Fossil Fuels under the Threat of Global Warming and Carbon Taxes: A Dynamic Game Approach", *Environmental and Resource Economics*, **5**, 333–52.

Wirl, F. and E. Dockner (1995), "Leviathan Governments and Carbon Taxes: Costs and Potential Benefits", *European Economic Review*, **39**, 1215–36.

Yanase, A. (2007), "Dynamic Games of Environmental Policy in a Global Economy: Taxes versus Quotas", *Review of International Economics*, **15**, 592–611.

Yanase, A. (2012), "Trade and Global Pollution in Dynamic Oligopoly with Corporate Environmentalis", *Review of International Economics*, **20**, 924–43.

Yin, X. (2004), "Voluntary Import Expansions with Non-Stationary Demand", *Canadian Journal of Economics*, **37**, 1084–96.

9   Stackelberg Games

Stackelberg equilibria are a delicate matter in game theory in general and in differential game theory in particular, where the critical aspects of hierarchical play become evident in terms of the time inconsistency issue that usually affects these structures. Consequently, this chapter is not a recollection of Stackelberg games in IO, but rather a reconstruction of what differential game theory can say about the solution of dynamic Stackelberg models, complemented by the exposition of a few applications in the field covered by this volume. In a sense, the following treatment of this subject can be taken as an invitation to intensify the implementation of Markovian Stackelberg solutions along a number of different directions where this approach could yield relevant results but its technical difficulties have long prevented its adoption.

As stated in Chapter 1 (Section 1.5), differential game theory becomes aware of the time inconsistency affecting open-loop Stackelberg solutions from Simaan and Cruz (1973a,b) and Kydland (1977) onwards, and quite quickly relevant applications appear in the literature on economic policy (Kydland and Prescott, 1977; Calvo, 1978; Barro and Gordon, 1983a,b), in a debate focussing upon rules versus discretion in manoeuvring monetary and fiscal policy instruments.

A very important aspect which I would like to stress most explicitly is that the presence of time inconsistency affecting an open-loop Stackelberg outcome (note that I'm avoiding the use of the term 'equilibrium') implies that we cannot expect to observe the realization of that outcome, except at most for an instant (in the model) or a very restricted time interval (in the real world) because players will deviate from it either immediately (again, in the theoretical model) or very quickly (again, in real world situations).

In the context of games dealing with monetary and fiscal policies, this problem clearly emerges in Cohen and Michel (1988, pp. 267–68):

The time-inconsistency ... meant that the optimal policy chosen by the government did not have the characteristic of being optimal after the initial instant when it was chosen. Technically speaking, this meant that it did not satisfy the dynamic programming principle of Bellman (1957).

The nature of the problem can be easily grasped from the original static formulation of the sequential play Cournot game in Stackelberg (1934). The subject matter of the game can be spelled out in the following terms. Suppose a market is supplied by two firms selling a homogeneous good, whose demand function is $p = a - q_1 - q_2$. Firms use the same constant returns technology, with a cost function $C_i = cq_i$, $c \in [0, a)$. The game takes place under symmetric, complete and perfect information, whereby firm 1 is the leader and chooses its output correctly anticipating the reaction of firm 2, the follower, along the latter's best reply function. As it turns out, the first mover advantage puts the leader in a dominant position.[1]

The problem of the leader consists in maximising profits under the linear constraint posed by the follower's best reply:

$$\max_{q_1} \pi_1 = (a - q_1 - q_2 - c) \, q_1$$

$$s.t. : q_2^*(q_1) = \frac{a - q_1 - c}{2} \tag{9.1}$$

and of course can be solved by substitution:

$$\max_{q_1} \pi_1 = \left[a - q_1 - \frac{a - q_1 - c}{2} - c \right] q_1 \tag{9.2}$$

This yields the necessary condition

$$\frac{\partial \pi_i}{\partial q_i} = \frac{a - c - 2q_i}{2} = 0 \tag{9.3}$$

which is satisfied by the same optimal output $q^{CL} = (a - c)/2$ as in a pure monopoly model with the same demand and cost functions, where superscript CL identifies the *Cournot leader*. The follower's output is therefore $q^{CF} = (a - c)/4$ (where CF stands for *Cournot follower*), with $q^{CL} = 2q^{CF}$. Equilibrium profits are

$$\pi^{CL} = \frac{(a - c)^2}{8} \; ; \pi^{CF} = \frac{(a - c)^2}{16} \tag{9.4}$$

with, again, $\pi^{CL} = 2\pi^{CF}$.

Even if the linear Cournot game is simple enough to allow for a solution based on the substitution method, it remains true that (9.1) defines a tangency solution, as it appears from Figure 9.1, in which point $CS1$ has coordinates (q^{CL}, q^{CF}), while CN is the symmetric Cournot–Nash equilibrium $q_1 = q_2 = q^{CN} = (a - c)/3$.

Tangency implies that the follower is on its best reply and therefore has no unilateral incentive to deviate, while the opposite holds for the leader, which is not on its best reply. It is easily seen that its best reply to q^{CF}, along $q_1^*(q_2)$ is lower than q^{CL} and this would in turn cause another deviation by firm 2, etc.; this process would ultimately converge to the Cournot–Nash equilibrium at the intersection of reaction functions. This, in the static hierarchical game, happens because the Stackelberg outcome is unstable, as can be ascertained from the Jacobian matrix. Another way of saying the same thing and, which, by the way, creates a connection with the debate on the time inconsistency of economic policy, is that what appears to be optimal as soon as one solves the leader's problem

---

[1] Admitting product differentiation, as in Singh and Vives (1984), one can also solve à la Stackelberg the alternative cases of Bertrand competition (where the follower outperforms the leader under any degree of imperfect product substitutability, by the usual undercutting argument) and 'mixed' competition, where one firm is a quantity setter and the other is a price setter. This spectrum of games has spurred the analysis of the choice of roles in Stackelberg games. For more, see Boyer and Moraux (1987a,b) and Hamilton and Slutsky (1990), *inter alia.*

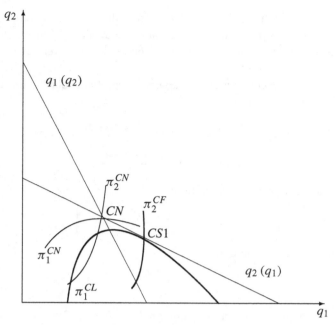

Figure 9.1 The Cournot-Stackelberg outcome with firm 1 leading

to find the tangency point ceases to be optimal when one looks at the leader's reaction function, taking the follower's output as given. The point is that the Stackelberg solution is not subgame perfect because it relies on backward induction, but it also implies that one of the players (the leader) is not along its best reply – which is a requirement for subgame perfection since Selten (1965, 1975). In plain words, *the Stackelberg strategy profile does not constitute a Nash equilibrium of a perfect information game and therefore cannot be subgame perfect.* This is the reason why a dynamic game solved through the same procedure under open-loop information cannot, in general, meets Bellman's (1957) optimality principle.

In a static Stackelberg game, one might be tempted to think that the one-shot nature of the game and the absence of calendar time (in fact, there's only a logical timing corresponding to the possibility for a player to incorporate in its own problem the rival's reaction function as a constraint) altogether eliminate the problem of the aforementioned chain of deviations. This escape route, however, is incompatible with the idea that a game like the Cournot-Stackelberg one should describe the acquisition of a dominant position which in turn should persist over some blackboxed time horizon. One cannot buy both stories at the same time. Another way out has consisted in discussing the possible existence of commitment devices sustaining a Stackelberg equilibrium (note the analogy with the role commitment technologies should play in open-loop differential games, whose solution, however, is at least weakly time consistent).

As we are about to see, the problem is magnified in a dynamic game (in particular, a differential one, but the distinction between discrete and continuous time is inessential), where, in general, sequential play is affected by two related issues: *controllability* and *time inconsistency*. And the task of researchers is to construct Stackelberg games in which commitment devices need not be invoked, the leader's strategy is *credible* (i.e., either really subgame perfect or at least state-linear as in global Stackelberg equilibria) and the descriptive and prescriptive power of the model is not compromised by oversimplifying assumptions. Section 9.1 defines the concept of (un)controllable differential game under open-loop information and outlines the requirements that an open-loop game must satisfy to be uncontrollable by the leader(s). It also points out the condition whereby Nash and Stackelberg solutions coincide in a feedback game, and illustrates a simple game which may or may not be affected by controllability depending on the exact specification of one of its building blocks. Then, an example illustrates the design of a *global Stackelberg equilibrium*. The remainder of the chapter deals with oligopoly games (Section 9.2), advertising campaigns (Section 9.3), supply chain coordination (Section 9.4) and optimal emission taxation in a polluting monopoly (Section 9.5), having the property of generating time-consistent equilibria which can be analytically characterised using different techniques.

9.1   (Un)controllability, Time (In)consistency and the Global Stackelberg Equilibrium

The concept of controllability in Stackelberg games can be intuitively grasped from the above static example: a hierarchical game is said to be controllable by the leader if the leader's control appears in the follower's FOC (or best reply). If this is the case, then the leader can strategically manipulate the follower's reaction at will. The definition of a controllable Stackelberg differential game under open-loop information is due to Xie (1993):

> **Definition 9.a (Controllability)** *Consider a two-player differential game with sequential play at every instant, in which players control $u_i(t)$, $i = 1, 2$, and a single state $x(t)$ is present and follows the kinematic equation $\dot{x} = f(x(t), \mathbf{u}(t))$. Such a game is controllable by the leader – say, player i – if the follower's best reply exhibits the property $\partial u_j^*(u_i) / \partial u_i(t) \neq 0$, either because*
>
> $$\frac{\partial^2 \mathcal{H}_j(t)}{\partial u_j(t) \partial u_i(t)} \neq 0$$
>
> *from j' Hamiltonian, or after substituting the expression of the optimal costate variable into j's FOC.*

Note that the above definition implies that one has to check for the presence of $u_i(t)$ in both $\partial \mathcal{H}_j(t) / \partial u_j(t)$ and in the adjoint equation describing the costate dynamics $\dot{\lambda}_j$, whose solution yields the correct value of $\lambda_j(t)$ at any time.

A structure yielding an uncontrollable open-loop Stackelberg game is the following, originally illustrated by Xie (1993), then expanded upon by Karp and Lee (2003) and also illustrated in Dockner *et al.* (2000, chapter 5) and Cellini and Lambertini (2007).

The model describes a perfectly competitive Ramsey economy over $t \in [0, \infty)$, in which an atomistic representative agent has the following instantaneous utility function:

$$U(t) = \ln c(t) + \ln g(t) \tag{9.5}$$

in which $c(t)$ is consumption and $g(t)$ is public expenditure. Productive capital $k(t)$ enters a linear production function whose output is $q(t) = Ak(t)$, $A > 0$. The other relevant agent is the government controlling the tax rate $\tau(t) \in [0, 1]$ to collect the funds needed to finance the public expenditure. It is assumed that $g(t) = \tau(t) q(t)$ at all times. Hence, taxation enters the state equation:

$$\dot{k} = [1 - \tau(t)] q(t) - c(t) = A[1 - \tau(t)] k(t) - c(t). \tag{9.6}$$

The representative consumer chooses $c(t)$ to maximise the discounted utility flow

$$\mathbf{U}(t) = \int_0^\infty \left[\ln c(t) + \ln g(t) \right] e^{-\rho t} dt \tag{9.7}$$

subject to the state equation (9.6) and the initial condition $k_0 > 0$.

The government is leading,while the agent is following taking the government's tax policy $\tau(t)$ as given. From the consumer's Hamiltonian, one obtains the FOC

$$\frac{1}{c(t)} - \lambda(t) = 0 \tag{9.8}$$

where $\lambda(t)$ is the costate appearing in the consumer's Hamiltonian function. The associated costate equation is

$$\dot{\lambda} = \lambda(t) [\rho - A(1 - \tau(t))] \tag{9.9}$$

From (9.8), dropping the time argument for simplicity, we have $c^* = 1/\lambda$. Now, substitute c^* into (9.6) and multiply all terms by λ to obtain the following equation:

$$\lambda \dot{k} = A(1 - \tau) \lambda k - 1 \tag{9.10}$$

Then, take (9.9) and multiply all of its terms by k, to obtain

$$k \dot{\lambda} = k \lambda [\rho - A(1 - \tau(t))] \tag{9.11}$$

Note that the sum of (9.10) and (9.11),

$$k \dot{\lambda} + \lambda \dot{k} = \lambda k \rho - 1 \tag{9.12}$$

is the derivative of $k\lambda$ w.r.t. t. Solving (9.12) yields $k\lambda = 1/\rho + Ce^{\rho t}$, in which C is an integration constant which must be nil for the transversality condition $\lim_{t \to \infty} e^{-\rho t} \lambda k = 0$ to be satisfied. This implies $k\lambda = 1/\rho$, and therefore $c^* = \rho k$. Additionally, $\lambda_0 = 1/(\rho k_0)$, which is independent of the government's control path, which in turn proves the costate variable is independent of τ at all times. The foregoing analysis implies that this game is indeed *uncontrollable* by the leader, and consequently also that the open-loop Stackelberg solution is time consistent.

Now consider that, as we know from Chapter 1 (Section 1.4.1), the open-loop Nash equilibrium is strongly time consistent if the game is perfect, i.e., either state-separable, which requires

$$\left.\frac{\partial^2 \mathcal{H}_i}{\partial u_i \partial x}\right|_{\frac{\partial \mathcal{H}_i}{\partial u_i}=0} = 0 \text{ and } \frac{\partial^2 \mathcal{H}_i}{\partial x_j^2} = 0 \tag{9.13}$$

or state-redundant, which requires

$$\left.\frac{\partial^2 \mathcal{H}_i}{\partial u_i \partial x}\right|_{\lambda_i=\lambda_i^*} = 0 \tag{9.14}$$

and any perfect game not originally defined in a state-redundant form can be reformulated as a state-redundant one (Mehlmann and Willing, 1983).

Hence, as stressed in Cellini *et al.* (2005, pp. 188–89), there emerges an inherent relationship between the two following Lemmas:

Lemma 9.1 *If a differential game is state-redundant, all of its open-loop Nash equilibria are strongly time consistent.*

Lemma 9.2 *If a differential game is uncontrollable by all of the players involved, then all of its open-loop Stackelberg equilibria are time consistent.*

The first lemma comes from Mehlmann and Willing (1983), Dockner *et al.* (1985) and Fershtman (1987). The second results from Xie (1993) and Karp and Lee (2003). Their relevant implication can be formulated as follows (Cellini *et al.*, 2005, p. 188):

Proposition 9.3 *If a differential game is uncontrollable by all players and state-redundant, then all of its Stackelberg open-loop solutions are strongly time consistent. If it is state-redundant but controllable by at least one player, then the open-loop Stackelberg outcome with that player leading is time inconsistent.*

Moreover (Cellini *et al.*, 2005, p. 189),

Corollary 9.4 *A sufficient condition for the joint presence of state-redundancy and strong time consistency under open-loop information is the additive separability of all the players' Hamiltonian functions w.r.t. all state and control variables.*

This may indeed look like a very demanding requirement, but consider that it defines a sufficient condition, not a necessary one.

The next step is in Rubio (2006), who shows – in two-player games – that the orthogonality of instantaneous reaction entails that feedback Nash and Stackelberg equilibria coincide. Interestingly, this may apply also in cases where the open-loop game is not state-redundant and therefore the open-loop Stackelberg solution is not subgame perfect. The last development of the line of research seeking for strongly time-consistent Stackelberg equilibria is in Bacchiega *et al.* (2010), where Rubio's (2006) result is generalised to the *n*-player setting and it is shown that, if the open-loop Nash equilibrium is strongly time consistent, then the presence of orthogonal best replies and state-redundancy entails that the open-loop Nash solution and the feedback Stackelberg solution are indeed the same thing and are both strongly time consistent. This also encompasses the analysis contained in Cellini *et al.* (2005), in particular the above corollary.[2]

To help fixing ideas, we can examine the properties of the Stackelberg solutions of two different versions of a game of renewable resource extraction which is a modified version of the model used by Benchekroun (2003), Fujiwara (2008) and several others, examined in detail in Chapter 7. Two identical firms exploit a common pool resource whose evolution follows the kinematic equation

$$\dot{X} = \delta X(y) - q_1(t) - q_2(t) \tag{9.15}$$

Each firm bears instantaneous total extraction costs $C_i(t) = bq_i^2(t)$, and the market price is determined by a demand function $p(t) = a - q_1(t) - q_2(t)$.

Firm i's current value Hamiltonian function

$$\mathcal{H}_i(t) = e^{-\rho t} \left\{ \left[a - q_i(t) - q_j(t) - bq_i(t) \right] q_i(t) + \lambda_i \left[\delta X(y) - q_i(t) - q_j(t) \right] \right\} \tag{9.16}$$

obviously reveals that the game has a linear state structure, and therefore its open-loop Nash equilibrium is strongly time consistent (just leave aside stability as this is not the focus of the analysis here). However, the FOC

$$\frac{\partial \mathcal{H}_i}{\partial q_i} = a - 2q_i(1+c) - q_j - \lambda_i = 0 \tag{9.17}$$

features both controls, which makes the game controllable by the leader, should firms adopt hierarchical play, notwithstanding the fact that the adjoint equation $\dot{\lambda}_i = \lambda_i(\rho - \delta)$ admits the nil solution at all times – this, by the way, implies that controllability is exactly the same as in the static Cournot setup.

The alternative version envisages an exogenous and time-invariant price $\bar{p}$, so that the instantaneous individual profit becomes $\pi_i(t) = \bar{p} \left[1 - bq_i \right] q_i$, which is independent of q_j, and the FOC writes now as follows:[3]

$$\frac{\partial \mathcal{H}_i}{\partial q_i} = p - 2cq_i - \lambda_i = 0 \tag{9.18}$$

accompanied by the same costate equation as in the previous version, so that $\lambda = 0$ always. In this form, the game features instantaneous best replies which are orthogonal to each other in the control space, i.e., $\partial q_i^*/\partial q_j = 0$, and optimal controls are independent of the unique state variable throughout the open-loop game. Hence, this

---

[2] A recent extension of the stream of research on open-loop hierarchical play in differential games is in Buratto *et al.* (2012). They revisit the time consistency issue of open-loop Stackelberg strategies in linear-state games adding the possibility that a final-state constraint appears in the leader's problem (while the usual approach is to consider a free final state). Buratto *et al.* (2012) prove that the resulting Stackelberg outcome satisfies a weaker concept of subgame perfection, which they label as ϵ-subgame perfectness, where the 'ϵ' indicates that the equilibrium is robust to sufficiently small perturbations and keeps satifying the condition on the final state.

[3] The necessity of producing FOC (9.18) explains the elementary modification of the model in terms of the presence of decreasing returns to scale in the extractive technology.

version is state-redundant as well as uncontrollable, and its open-loop Stackelberg and Nash equilibria coincide and are both strongly time consistent. Intuitively, analogous considerations apply for the companion model where the natural resource is replaced by polluting emissions, as in Benchekroun and Long (1998) and its follow-ups, to which I will return in Section 9.5.

There remains to outline the strategies associated with the global Stackelberg equilibrium, recalling from Chapter 1 that this involves the adoption on the part of the leader of a control strategy defined as a function of the relevant state of the system. This is a (nondegenerate) Markovian strategy which is time consistent. Consider a two-player game, with two controls and one state, and suppose player 1 leads and announces the strategy to be adopted during the whole game. Such a strategy is defined as $u_1 = f(x)$. The follower, taking $f(x)$ as given, chooses its control u_2 to maximize its discounted flow of payoffs under the constraint posed by the relevant state equation. The following example, based on a simultaneous play game in Cornes et al. (1995), is borrowed from Dockner et al. (2000, chapter 5) and Rubio (2006).

The instantaneous payoff of i is $\pi_i(t) = [x(t) u_i(t)]^\alpha$, with $\alpha \in (0, 1/2)$, and the state equation is

$$\dot{x} = \begin{cases} -u_1(t) - u_2(t) \ \forall x(t) > 0 \\ 0 \ \forall x(t) \leq 0 \end{cases} \tag{9.19}$$

so that the HJB equation of player i is

$$\rho V_i(x(t)) = \max_{u_i(t)} \left\{ [x(t) u_i(t)]^\alpha - V_i'(x(t)) [u_1(t) + u_2(t)] \right\} \tag{9.20}$$

and the FOC yields

$$u_i^* = \left[\frac{\alpha x^\alpha}{V_i'(x)} \right]^{1/(1-\alpha)} \tag{9.21}$$

Then, adopting the value function $V_i(x) = \varepsilon x^{2\alpha}$, the unknown parameter ε can be univocally determined to yield the symmetric linear feedback Nash strategy $u^{LF} = \rho x / [2(1 - 2\alpha)]$.

Examine now the alternative scenario in which 1 is leading. This player poses $u_1(t) = \beta x(t)$, where the slope β must be chosen by the leader to maximise its objective and kept constant throughout the game. The follower, being aware of that, has to solve the HJB equation

$$\rho V_2(x(t)) = \max_{u_2(t)} \left\{ [x(t) u_2(t)]^\alpha - V_2'(x(t)) [\beta x(t) + u_2(t)] \right\} \tag{9.22}$$

whose FOC yields the same control as in (9.21), but using the same form for the value function, $V_2(x) = \varepsilon x^{2\alpha}$, the feedback strategy of the follower writes as $u_2 = (\rho + 2\alpha\beta) x / [2(1 - \alpha)]$, which does not coincide with u^{LF}.

Now let's go back to the problem of the leader, who has to choose β optimally. The HJB equation is

$$\rho V_1(x) = \max_{\beta} \left\{ \beta^\alpha x^{2\alpha} - V_1'(x) \left[\beta + \frac{\rho + 2\alpha\beta}{2(1 - \alpha)} \right] x \right\} \tag{9.23}$$

which generates the FOC

$$\alpha\beta^{\alpha-1}x^{2\alpha} - V_1'(x)\left[1 + \frac{2\alpha}{2(1-\alpha)}\right]x = 0 \tag{9.24}$$

in turn implying that the resulting strategy of the leader will differ from optimal one under simultaneous play. The problem associated with this solution is that while the follower's strategy is a real feedback strategy, that of the leader is Markovian and time consistent but restricted to a family of strategies with a defined structure. In fact, several authors, including Dockner et al. (2000) and Rubio (2006), stress that the leader's strategy could be seen as quasi-open-loop. Personally, I am more positive in this regard, as this method allows us to solve games which are neither state-redundant nor uncontrollable in a time-consistent way. One such example is the polluting oligopoly with emission taxation of Benchekroun and Long (1998) which is summarised in Chapter 7. Another relevant case is in the last section.

9.2   Oligopoly Games

The first example, the oligopoly game with firms choosing output levels under sticky price dynamics as in Simaan and Takayama (1978) and Fershtman and Kamien (1987), is considered by Rubio (2006, pp. 217–20) because it is an example of a game in which, under feedback rules, feedback Nash and Stackelberg equilibria coincide. Suppose for simplicity that there are only two firms (but what follows is independent of the number of firms as well as their partition into sets of leaders and followers). The aforementioned property is easily verified by checking that (1) the Bellman equation of firm i,

$$\rho V_i(p) = \max_{q_i}\left\{\left(p - c - \frac{q_i}{2}\right)q_i + V_i'(p)s\left(a - q_i - q_j - p\right)\right\} \tag{9.25}$$

is additively separable w.r.t. controls, so that provided the optimal output is positive, i.e., $q_i^* = p - c - sV_i'(p)$, best replies are orthogonal to each other and the game is solvable instant by instant in dominant strategies, because $\partial q_i^*/\partial q_j = 0$ at all times. Then, (2) it is also quickly seen that, by virtue of additive separability, plugging q_i^* into firm j's HJB equation and then differentiating it w.r.t. q_j yields the FOC

$$p - c - q_j - sV_j'(p) = 0 \tag{9.26}$$

which is exactly the same as under simultaneous play. Of course this property extends to any games where orthogonality characterises the map of best replies. In fact, it is quite easy to construct differential games (especially in linear-quadratic form) solvable in dominant strategies, and this induces Rubio (2003, p. 203) to say that

The conclusion is that the feedback Stackelberg solution is generally not useful to investigate leadership in the framework of a differential game, at least for a good number of economic applications.

The understandable reason for his regret is that the first mover advantage disappears, thereby seemingly making the model poorer, in some sense. My personal view is that, on the other hand, we obtain the prize of having an entire class of models in which the linear feedback equilibrium is unique and timing is not an issue.[4] The point is that the set of games which do not enjoy this property is far larger than the class considered in this section. In fact, it suffices to go back to the Cournot–Ramsey game (Cellini and Lambertini, 1998), also appearing in Chapter 3, to ascertain immediately that, although its open-loop Nash solution is strongly time consistent because the game is state-redundant, the open-loop Stackelberg outcome is time inconsistent, due to controllability, precisely because it is quasi-static in nature; and therefore the coincidence between the two solution concepts under feedback rules cannot arise.

9.3 An Advertising Game

This section contains an example of an uncontrollable state-redundant game in which the open-loop Stackelberg equilibrium is strongly time consistent. That is, here the focus is on the technical properties put into evidence by Bacchiega et al. (2010), whereby the feedback Stackelberg equilibrium coincides with the open-loop Nash equilibrium.

The setup, appearing in Bacchiega et al. (2010, pp. 423–26) is a modified version of the advertising game by Leitmann and Schmitendorf (1978) and Feichtinger (1983). Consider a duopoly where the individual market shares changes over time as a function of firms' advertising efforts and to a fixed decay rate:

$$\dot{\sigma}_i(t) = k_i(t) + sk_j(t) - \delta\sigma_i(t). \tag{9.27}$$

In (9.27), parameter $s \in [-1, 1]$ measures an externality from the investment of firm j onto the market share of firm i but the r.h.s. is additively separable in all endogenous variables. Individual instantaneous profits are $\pi_i(t) = p\sigma_i(t) - bk_i^2$, where p and b are positive constants. The current value Hamiltonian is:

$$\mathcal{H}_i = p\sigma_i - bk_i^2 + \lambda_{ii}\left(k_i + sk_j - \delta\sigma_i\right) + \lambda_{ij}\left(k_j + sk_i - \delta\sigma_j\right). \tag{9.28}$$

Take a look at the open-loop Nash solution. The necessary conditions are

$$\frac{\partial \mathcal{H}_i}{\partial k_i} = -2bk_i + \lambda_{ii} + s\lambda_{ij} = 0 \tag{9.29}$$

$$\dot{\lambda}_{ii} = (\delta + \rho)\lambda_{ii} - p \tag{9.30}$$

$$\dot{\lambda}_{ij} = (\delta + \rho)\lambda_{ij} \tag{9.31}$$

From (9.29–9.31) we learn that, the game being in a state linear form, (1) the open-loop Nash strategies are subgame perfect; (2) the solution $\lambda_{ij} \equiv 0$ is admissible at all times; and therefore (3) the optimal instantaneous control is $k_i^* = \lambda_{ii}/(2b)$, independent of states and the rival's control. So to speak, the optimal advertising effort is 'flat' in all directions in the state-control space. As a consequence, the game is both state-redundant and uncontrollable.

---

[4] Economic games belonging to this class, and cited in Rubio (2006), are Başar et al. (1985), van der Ploeg and de Zeeuw (1990), Gradus (1991) and Rubio and Escriche (2001).

But there is more to it. Since the control equation is $\dot{k}_i = \lambda_{ii}/(2b)$, the open-loop strategy is

$$k^*(t) = \left[k_0 - \frac{p}{2b(\delta + \rho)}\right] e^{(\delta + \rho)t} + \frac{p}{2b(\delta + \rho)} \tag{9.32}$$

Expression (9.32) confirms that the point of coordinates (u_1^*, u_2^*) is simultaneously the open-loop Nash and Stackelberg subgame perfect equilibrium.

We can now turn to the feedback game, considering a linear value function $V_i(\sigma_i) = \varepsilon_1 \sigma_i + \varepsilon_2$. The FOC yields $k_i^F = \varepsilon_1/(2b)$. Since this is a linear state game,

$$\varepsilon_1 = \frac{\partial V_i}{\partial \sigma_i} = \lambda_{ii} \tag{9.33}$$

because the costate variable λ_{ii} is indeed the shadow price coinciding with the partial derivative of the value function w.r.t. σ_i. Hence, (1) the feedback Stackelberg equilibrium coincides with the open-loop Stackelberg equilibrium, and (2) both coincide with the open-loop Nash solution.[5] To conclude this section, it is worth noting that in the sticky price game there exists no equivalent of (9.33), as the game is not state-redundant, although best replies are orthogonal.

9.4   Supply Chain Coordination

An alternative title would have been *vertical relations*, or *vertical integration versus separation*, a theme that commonly takes an entire chapter of its own in leading textbook in IO (e.g., Chapter 4 in Tirole, 1988). The *leitmotiv* of this topic, which is equally relevant in IO and business & management, is double marginalization along a vertical channel involving (at least) two firms. If such firms (say, a manufacturer and a retailer) control only output and prices (the transfer or wholesale price and the market price), then the double marginalization problem can be easily solved through the adoption of an elementary two-part tariff (*TPT* henceforth).

This can be seen by resorting to a standard toy model. Consider a vertical relation between a manufacturer, firm m, and a retailer, firm r. Assume the manufacturer uses a constant returns to scale technology with a unit production cost $c > 0$ to supply the final good. The market demand function is $Q = a - p$, and the unit price paid by the retailer to the manufacturer is w. Under the same demand and cost conditions, the vertically integrated monopolist gets profits $\pi_M = (a - c)^2/4$, which can be replicated by the vertically separated supply chain by adopting a *TPT* establishing that the transfer price is $w = c + F/Q$, whereby each unit is sold by the manufacturer at marginal cost c but the retailer has to pay also a fixed fee F. Hence, the two-part tariff is written as $TPT = cQ + F$. If $F = (a - c)^2/4$, then in equilibrium the retailer is forced to practice the pure monopoly price in order to obtain $\pi_r = 0$, full monopoly profits accruing to the manufacturer, with $\pi_m = F = \pi_M$. Actually, the surplus appropriated by the supply

---

[5] The proof contained in Bacchiega *et al.* (2010) is more detailed, but the implications of the equivalence illustrated in (9.33) is sufficiently intuitive.

chain can be distributed across firms using a Nash bargaining solution sustained by threats defined in terms of the disagreement payoffs, but what really matters here is that overall channel profits with vertical separation may indeed be the same as under vertical integration. This is a consolidated result in the acquired wisdom on vertical relations and supply chain coordination (see, e.g., Cachon, 2003; Ingene and Parry, 2004, *inter alia*).

The problem is complicated by the addition of other variables related to R&D, capacity or advertising – that is, any investments which could be carried out by the firms along the supply chain. The reason is that there immediately appears another issue, known as the *hold-up problem*, whereby uncoordinated (i.e., strictly noncooperative) vertical separation hinders the firms' incentives to invest (in particular, those of upstream firms) and therefore causes a sharp drop in the channel's total profits as hold-up combines with double marginalisation.

Intuitively, the problem of coordinating supply chain activities largely overlaps with contract theory and the theory of the firm, as it poses the problem of specifying the equilibrium contract (or a nexus of optimal contracts) which, in principle, should account for each and every relevant feature of the vertical relation as well as any contingency which could affect its performance in some way (cf. Klein *et al.*, 1978; Zusman and Etgar, 1981; Grout, 1984; Cachon and Lariviere, 2005, to mention just a few). And, again naturally, there exists a close connection between this coordination problem and the concepts of *opportunistic behaviour* or *moral hazard* affecting any agency relationship inside a firm (cf. Williamson, 1971, 1975; Joskow, 1985, 1987, 2005; Grossman and Hart, 1986; Hart and Moore, 1990, among many others). The role of incomplete information about demand and buyers' willingness to pay is also accounted for in the latest contributions in this area (Calzolari and Denicolò, 2013, 2015).

Here, I want to reconstruct the issue of coordinating advertising efforts along a supply chain under full information, dating back to the static models illustrated in Jeuland and Shugan (1983, 1988a,b) and Moorthy (1987) and then revisited in differential games played under feedback information which can be found in Zaccour (2008) and Lambertini (2014).

9.4.1   The Static Game

The static benchmark is adapted from Zaccour (2008), except for some notational details, and captures the essence of the original model by Jeuland and Shugan (1983). Consider a marketing channel made up by two firms, a manufacturer and a retailer, who may invest in advertising to enhance goodwill or brand equity, which, in this case, translates into an expansion of the output demanded at any price level. Hence, market demand is $Q = a + k_m + k_r - bp$, where parameter $b > 1$, and k_i, $i = m, r$, is the advertising investment of firm i. This effort entails a quadratic cost $C_i = k_i^2/2$. Consequently, firms' profit functions are

$$\pi_m = (w - c) Q - \frac{k_m^2}{2} \, ; \, \pi_r = (p - w) Q - \frac{k_r^2}{2} \qquad (9.34)$$

if they are independent. Otherwise, under vertical integration, m and r are the two divisions of a single monopolistic firm, whose profit function is:

$$\pi_{vi} = (p - c) Q - \frac{k_m^2}{2} - \frac{k_r^2}{2} \qquad (9.35)$$

subscript vi standing for vertical integration. The characterisation of the vertically integrated solution is straightforward. The following system of simultaneous FOCs

$$\frac{\partial \pi_{vi}}{\partial p} = a + k_M + k_R - b (2p - c) = 0$$

$$\frac{\partial \pi_{vi}}{\partial k_m} = p - c - k_m = 0 \qquad (9.36)$$

$$\frac{\partial \pi_{vi}}{\partial k_r} = p - c - k_m = 0$$

delivers the coordinates of the equilibrium

$$p^* = \frac{a - c (b - 2)}{2 (b - 1)} \; ; \; k_m^* = k_r^* = \frac{a - bc}{2 (b - 1)} \qquad (9.37)$$

while equilibrium output and profits are $Q_{vi}^* = b (a - bc) / [2 (b - 1)]$ and $\pi_{vi}^* = (a - bc)^2 / [4 (b - 1)]$, respectively.

The problem of independent firms m and r is twofold. To begin with, theirs is a Stackelberg game with the retailer in the follower's role. Indeed, under vertical separation, firm r's FOCs

$$\frac{\partial \pi_r}{\partial p} = a - b (2p - w) + k_m + k_r = 0$$

$$\frac{\partial \pi_r}{\partial k_r} = p - w - k_r = 0 \qquad (9.38)$$

reveal at first sight the underlying inconsistency problem created by the presence of k_m in the first FOC, which affects the price, whose distortion enters the second FOC w.r.t. k_r.

Additionally, firms might look for a way of replicating the performance of the vertically integrated monopolist. To this purpose, we can set out analysing the performance of a *TPT* featuring an exogenous fixed fee. This can be done using a standard backward induction produce. The maximization of

$$\pi_r = (p - w) (a + k_m + k_r - bp) - \frac{k_r^2}{2} - F \qquad (9.39)$$

yields

$$p^{TPT} = \frac{a + c (b - 1) + k_m}{2b - 1} \; ; \; k_r^{TPT} = \frac{a - bc + k_m}{2b - 1} \qquad (9.40)$$

Substituting these expressions and $w = c$ into π_m reveals that firm m's profit function collapses to $\pi_m = F - k_m^2/2$, whose partial derivative w.r.t. k_m is obviously negative and implies that this *TPT* cancels any investment incentives upstream. However, taking the alternative route of endogenising the fixed fee, which can be written as $F = \alpha + \beta k_m$, solves the problem of coordinating activities along the channel, because the manufacturer profits are now $\pi_m = \alpha + k_m (\beta - k_m/2)$ and the FOC yields $k_m^{TPT} = \beta > 0$ for all $\beta > 0$. Then, we have

$$k_m^{TPT} + k_r^{TPT} = \frac{a + b(2\beta - c)}{2b - 1} = \frac{a - bc}{b - 1} = k_m^* + k_r^* \tag{9.41}$$

for $\beta = (a - bc)/[2(b - 1)] = k_m^* = k_m^*$. Therefore, we see that the slope of the fixed fee must coincide with the equilibrium investment of a single division under vertical integration, in order for the vertically separated supply chain to replicate the optimal advertising efforts of a pure monopolist with two divisions. Additionally, observing the profits generated by such fee, we learn that

$$\pi_m^{TPT} + \pi_r^{TPT} = \pi_{vi}^* = \frac{(a - bc)^2}{4(b - 1)} \tag{9.42}$$

and

$$\pi_r^{TPT} = \frac{(a - bc)^2 (2b - 3) - 8\alpha (b - 1)^2}{8(b - 1)^2} \tag{9.43}$$

Taken together, (9.42–9.43) imply the following result:

Proposition 9.5 *There exist a continuum of infinitely many optimal contracts $\left(\alpha \in \{\alpha | \pi_r^{TPT} \geq 0\}; \beta = (a - bc)/[2(b - 1)]\right)$ allowing the supply chain to perform efficiently. If $\alpha = (a - bc)^2 (2b - 3)/[8(b - 1)^2]$, the whole profit generated by the efficient supply chain is appropriated by the manufacturer.*

Before continuing, a remark is in order. The functional form of the efficient fixed fee is linear in the manufacturer's investment, because (1) this modifies in the desired direction the FOC, and (2) this being a static game, by definition it lacks a state variable. This instead kicks in when we look at the dynamic version of the game, allowing for the reproduction of a contract which relies on the concept of global Stackelberg equilibrium.

9.4.2   The Differential Game

The corresponding dynamic problem is defined for $t \in [0, \infty)$, stipulating that firms use the same $\rho > 0$. Advertising controls and costs are the same as above, except for the appearance of the time argument. The dynamics of goodwill is

$$\dot{G} = k_m(t) + k_r(t) - \delta G(t) \tag{9.44}$$

with the initial condition $G_0 > 0$. The instantaneous demand function is $Q(t) = a + G(t) - bp(t)$, with $b > 1/[\delta(\delta + \rho)]$, which is required to ensure stability and the non-negativity of relevant equilibrium magnitudes.

The vector of optimal controls for the vertically integrated monopolist is:

$$p^*(B) = \frac{a + G + bc}{2b} \tag{9.45}$$

$$k_i^*(B) = \varepsilon_1 G + \varepsilon_2, \quad i = m, r$$

where

$$\varepsilon_1 = \frac{b(2\delta + \rho) - \sqrt{b\left[b(2\delta + \rho)^2 - 4\right]}}{4\alpha}$$

$$\varepsilon_2 = \frac{a - bc}{2b(2\varphi_1 - \delta - \rho)} \tag{9.46}$$

$$\varepsilon_3 = \frac{4b\varphi_2^2 - (a - bc)^2}{4b\rho}$$

are the expressions of the optimal coefficients of the value function $V(G) = \varepsilon_1 G^2/2 + \varepsilon_2 B + \varepsilon_3$. The resulting steady state level of brand equity is

$$G^* = \frac{a - bc}{b\delta(\delta - \rho) - 1} \tag{9.47}$$

Once again, it turns out that an exogenous fixed fee cannot do the job, for the very same reason as above. Therefore, the fee must be designed anew in terms of endogenous variables; the obvious candidate is the stock of goodwill G. Yet, for the moment, let's stick to the initial form $w = c + F/Q$. If the retailer's value function as $V_r(G) = \xi_1 G^2/2 + \xi_2 G + \xi_3$, the downstream firm's Bellman equation is

$$\rho V_r(G) = \max_{p,k_r} \left[\left(p - \frac{F}{a + G - bp} \right)(a + G - bp) \right.$$
$$\left. - \frac{k_r^2}{2} + (\xi_1 G + \xi_2)(k_m + k_r - \delta G) \right] \tag{9.48}$$

and optimal state-linear controls are

$$p^{TPT}(G) = \frac{a + G + bc}{2b} \; ; \; k_r^{TPT} = \xi_1 G + \xi_2 \tag{9.49}$$

which can be substituted back into (9.48) to identify the coefficients of the value function through the usual method:

$$\xi_3 = \frac{b^2 c^2 + a^2 + 2b\left[\xi_2(\xi_2 + 2k_m) - ac - 2F\right]}{4b\rho}$$

$$\xi_2 = \frac{a + b(2\xi_1 k_m - c)}{4b\rho} \tag{9.50}$$

$$\xi_1 = \frac{b(2\delta + \rho) - \sqrt{b\left[b(2\delta + \rho)^2 - 2\right]}}{2b}$$

Now we can make the functional form of the fixed fee explicit, and use $F = \alpha + \beta G$, so that the Bellman equation of the manufacturer becomes

$$\rho V_m(G) = \max_{k_m} \left[\alpha + \beta G - \frac{k_m^2}{2} + V_m'(G)\left(k_m + k_r^{TPT} - \delta GB\right) \right] \tag{9.51}$$

in which $k_r^{TPT} = \xi_1 G + \xi_2$ as in (9.49) and (ξ_1, ξ_2) are as in (9.50). We can Define the manufacturer's value function as $V_m(G) = \psi_1 G^2/2 + \psi_2 G + \psi_3$, and write the FOC w.r.t. k_m, to obtain $k_m^{TPT}(G) = V_m'(G)$. Simplifying and solving the HJB equation of the manufacturer to identify the triple of parameters (ψ_1, ψ_2, ψ_3) ensuring concavity and stability, we arrive at the steady state stock of goodwill

$$B = \frac{(a - bc)[1 - 2b\delta(\delta + \rho)]^2 + 4b^2(\delta + \rho)^2[b(2\delta(\delta + \rho) + \rho^2) - 1 - \rho\Omega]\beta}{[2b\delta(\delta + \rho) - 1]^3}$$

(9.52)

where $\Omega \equiv \sqrt{b(b(2\delta + \rho)^2 - 2)}$. Then, posing

$$\beta = \frac{\delta(a - bc)[1 - 2b\delta(\delta + \rho)]^2}{4b(\delta + \rho)[b\delta(\delta + \rho) - 1][b(2\delta(\delta + \rho) + \rho^2) - 1 - \rho\Omega]}$$

(9.53)

yields (i) $k_m^{TPT} + k_r^{TPT} = k_m^* + k_r^*$; (ii) $k_m^{TPT} = k_m^*$; (iii) $G^{TPT} = G^*$; and then also (iv) $\pi_m^{TPT} + \pi_r^{TPT} = \pi^*$. Moreover,

$$\alpha = \frac{\delta(a - bc)^2[2(1 + b^2\delta(\delta + \rho)^3) - b(5\delta(\delta + \rho) + 2\rho^2) - 2\rho\Omega]}{8b(\delta + \rho)[b\delta(\delta + \rho) - 1]^2}$$

(9.54)

delivers the whole of channel profits to the manufacturer, as it solves $\pi_m^{TPT} = \pi^*$ and $\pi_r^{TPT} = 0$. The following Proposition summarises the foregoing discussion:

Proposition 9.6 *The marketing channel can replicate the efficient outcome attained by a vertically integrated monopolist through the adoption of a two-part tariff in which the fixed fee is linear in the stock of brand equity. As in the static game, there are infinitely many TPT's performing this task, but only one which allocates the entire channel profit to the manufacturer.*

9.5   Taxing Emissions in a Polluting Monopoly

This model is in Benchekroun and Long (2002). The basic layout is the same as in Section 2.2. Consider a monopolistic industry in which the firm faces a linear demand function $p(t) = a - Q(t)$ for the final good, whose production takes place through a technology characterised by constant returns to scale, with production costs $C(t) = cQ(t)$, and pollutes the environment. Emissions follow the state equation

$$\dot{S}(t) = Q(t) - \delta S(t)$$

(9.55)

The policy maker intervenes by taxing every unit of output at the rate $\tau(S) = \alpha + \beta S(t)$, so that the total costs borne by the monopolist increase by the amount $\mathfrak{T}(t) = [\alpha + \beta S(t)]Q(t)$, and instantaneous profits are

$$\pi(t) = [p(t) - c - \tau(S)]Q(t)$$

(9.56)

The objective of the firm (the follower) is to maximise the discounted profit flow

$$\Pi(t) = \int_0^\infty [p(t) - c - \tau(S)]Q(t)e^{-\rho t}dt$$

(9.57)

w.r.t. $Q(t)$, under the constraint (9.55) and taking the policy instruments α and β as given.

Conversely, the objective of the government is to choose once and for all the intercept α and the slope β of its tax rule $\tau(S)$ so as to induce the monopolist to follow the same production path and attain the same steady state equilibrium as under the command optimum (or, social planning), with the public authority solving the following problem:

$$\max_{Q(t)} \int_0^\infty SW(t) e^{-\rho t} dt = \int_0^\infty \left[(p(t) - c) Q(t) + \frac{Q^2(t)}{2} - \frac{\varsigma S^2(t)}{2} \right] e^{-\rho t} dt \quad (9.58)$$

This would yield the optimal control

$$Q^{SP}(S) = \omega S(t) - (\delta - \rho) S^{SP} \quad (9.59)$$

where

$$\omega = \frac{2\delta + \rho - \sqrt{(2\delta + \rho)^2 + 4\varsigma}}{2} \quad (9.60)$$

The socially efficient control path in (9.59) leads to the steady state emission stock

$$S^{SP} = \frac{(a - c)(\delta + \rho)}{\delta(\delta + \rho) + \varsigma} \quad (9.61)$$

Note that this problem replicates the social optimum illustrated in Section 7.2, for the obvious reason that production costs are linear in the output level.

Hence, without replicating the solution of the monopoly problem under environmental regulation (which is a special case of the analogous oligopoly problem except that $n = 1$), I may confine myself to specify the expressions of the intercept and slope of $\tau(S)$ which induce the profit-seeking monopolist to reproduce both (9.59) and (9.61):

$$\alpha^{SP} = \frac{\left[\varsigma - \delta(\delta + \rho) - \beta^{SP}(2\delta + \rho) \right] S^{SP}}{\delta + \rho} \; ; \; \beta^{SP} = \frac{2\varsigma}{2\delta + \rho} \quad (9.62)$$

The material exposed in the last two sections deserves a few comments to reconstruct the picture emerging from the models. A global Stackelberg equilibrium comes out of a game in which the leader uses a control policy defined as a function of the relevant state(s). If there is a single state variable and the game is linear quadratic like this one, then the leader's control is linear in the state. Then, the prescription for the leader is to choose the intercept and slope of the state-linear control to maximise its objective functional. Now, apparently, this seems not to correspond to what I have illustrated in this example dealing with the coordination of activities along a supply chain. However, observe that, at the outset, the leader has three controls, w, F and k_m, but one (the wholesale price) is immediately fixed by the definition of the two-part tariff. Hence, since there is only one state, the matter reduces to deciding which one has to be transformed into a function of the state, and it turns out that there is a route which (1) allows the marketing channel to reproduce the efficient outcome and (2) maximises the leader's profits without requiring the assessment of derivatives and FOCs taken w.r.t. α and β. This would have been the case if the differential game version of the Stackelberg game had been solved stipulating that $k_m = \alpha + \beta G$. Additional details and alternative solutions of both the static and the dynamic game are in Lambertini (2013).

The same considerations holds in the polluting monopoly setup, where again the leader (in this case, the regulator) does not use FOCs to maximise its objective function. However, also in this case, the first mover advantage is properly exploited to produce the desired outcome without controlling the follower directly, but rather through the appropriate stimulus of a state-linear rule. Also note that, in both cases, not only the desired steady state outcome but also the path leading to it are fully replicating those that the leader judges optimal (either for the marketing channel or for society).

Further Reading

For the stability analysis of the Cournot game, see Fudenberg and Tirole (1991). An exhaustive perspective on the debate about the time inconsistency of macroeconomic policy instruments is in Petit (1990) and Persson and Tabellini (1990, 2000). The literature on supply chain is reviewed in Lariviere (1999). Comprehensive surveys of dynamic games involving supply chains are in Jørgensen and Zaccour (2004) and Long (2010). An updated overview of the debate spurred by Jeuland and Shugan (1983) is in Ingene *et al.* (2012). A way out of the conundrum of Stackelberg play in oligopoly is managerialisation *à la* Vickers (1985), which hosts vertical relations as well as a relevant application (Bonanno and Vickers, 1988). For the connection between vertical integration, strategic delegation and the theory of the firm, see Lambertini (2017).

Bibliography

Bacchiega, E., L. Lambertini and A. Palestini (2010), "On the Time Consistency of Equilibria in a Class of Additively Separable Differential Games", *Journal of Optimization Theory and Applications*, **145**, 415–27.

Barro, R.J. and D.B. Gordon (1983a), "A Positive Theory of Monetary Policy in a Natural Rate Model", *Journal of Political Economy*, **91**, 589–610.

Barro, R.J. and D.B. Gordon (1983b), "Rules, Discretion and Reputation in a Model of Monetary Policy", *Journal of Monetary Economics*, **12**, 101–21.

Başar, T., A. Haurie and G. Ricci (1985), "On the Dominance of Capitalism Leadership in a Feedback-Stackelberg Solution of a Differential Game Model of Capitalism", *Journal of Economic Dynamics and Control*, **9**, 101–25.

Bellman, R.E. (1957), *Dynamic Programming*, Princeton, NJ, Princeton University Press.

Benchekroun, H. (2003), "Unilateral Production Restrictions in a Dynamic Duopoly", *Journal of Economic Theory*, **111**, 214–39.

Benchekroun, H. and N.V. Long (1998), "Efficiency Inducing Taxation for Polluting Oligopolists", *Journal of Public Economics*, **70**, 325–42.

Benchekroun, H. and N.V. Long (2002), "On the Multiplicity of Efficiency-Inducing Tax Rules", *Economics Letters*, **76**, 331–36.

Bonanno, G. and J. Vickers (1988), "Vertical Separation", *Journal of Industrial Economics*, **36**, 257–65.

Boyer, M. and Moreaux, M. (1987a), "Being a Leader or a Follower: Reflections on the Distribution of Roles in Duopoly", *International Journal of Industrial Organization*, **5**, 175–92.

Boyer, M. and Moreaux, M. (1987b), "On Stackelberg Equilibria with Differentiated Products: The Critical Role of the Strategy Space", *Journal of Industrial Economics*, **36**, 217–30.

Buratto, A., L. Grosset and B. Viscolani (2012), "∈-Subgame Perfectness of an Open-Loop Stackelberg Equilibrium in Linear-State Games", *Dynamic Games and Applications*, **2**, 269–79.

Cachon, G.P. (2003), "Supply Chain Coordination with Contracts", in S. Graves and T. de Kok (eds), *Handbook in Operation Research and Management Science: Supply Chain Management*, Amsterdam, North-Holland.

Cachon, G.P. and M.A. Lariviere (2005), "Supply Chain Coordination with Revenue-Sharing Contracts: Strengths and Limitations", *Management Science*, **51**, 30–44.

Calvo, G. (1978), "On the Time Consistency of Optimal Policy in a Monetary Economy", *Econometrica*, **46**, 1411–28.

Calzolari, G. and V. Denicolò (2013), "Competition with Exclusive Contracts and Market-Share Discounts", *American Economic Review*, **103**, 2384–411.

Calzolari, G. and V. Denicolò (2015), "Exclusive Contracts and Market Dominance", *American Economic Review*, **105**, 3321–51.

Cellini, R., and L. Lambertini (1998), "A Dynamic Model of Differentiated Oligopoly with Capital Accumulation", *Journal of Economic Theory*, **83**, 145–55.

Cellini, R. and L. Lambertini (2007), "Time Consistent Fiscal Policies in a Ramsey Economy", *Mathematical Social Sciences*, **53**, 296–313.

Cellini, R., L. Lambertini and G. Leitmann (2005), "Degenerate Feedback and Time Consistency in Differential Games", in E.P. Hofer and E. Reithmeier (eds), *Modeling and Control of Autonomous Decision Support Based Systems. Proceedings of the 13th International Workshop on Dynamics and Control*, Aachen, Shaker Verlag, 185–92.

Cohen, D. and P. Michel (1988), "How Should Control Theory Be Used to Calculate a Time-Consistent Government Policy?", *Review of Economic Studies*, **55**, 263–74.

Cornes, R., N.V. Long and K. Shimomura (1995), "Drugs and Pests: Intertemporal Productive Externalities", wp, Australian National University, Canberra.

Dockner, E.J., G. Feichtinger and S. Jørgensen (1985), "Tractable Classes of Nonzero-Sum Open-Loop Nash Differential Games: Theory and Examples", *Journal of Optimization Theory and Applications*, **45**, 179–97.

Dockner, E., S. Jørgensen, N.V. Long and G. Sorger (2000), *Differential Games in Economics and Management Science*, Cambridge, Cambridge University Press.

Feichtinger, G. (1983), "The Nash Solution of an Advertising Differential Game: Generalization of a Model by Leitmann and Schmitendorf", *IEEE Transactions on Automatic Control*, **28**, 1044–1048.

Fershtman, C. (1987), "Identification of Classes of Differential Games for Which the Open-Loop Is a Degenerate Feedback Nash Equilibrium", *Journal of Optimization Theory and Applications*, **55**, 217–31.

Fershtman, C. and M.I. Kamien (1987), "Dynamic Duopolistic Competition with Sticky Prices", *Econometrica*, **55**, 1151–64.

Fudenberg, D. and J. Tirole (1991), *Game Theory*, Cambridge, MA, MIT Press.

Fujiwara, K. (2008), "Duopoly Can Be More Anti-Competitive than Monopoly", *Economics Letters*, **101**, 217–19.

Gradus, R. (1991), "Optimal Dynamic Profit Taxation: The Derivation of Feedback Stackelberg Equilibria", *Metroeconomica*, **42**, 157–77.

Grossman, S. and O. Hart (1986), "The Costs and Benefits of Ownership: A Theory of Vertical and Lateral Integration", *Journal of Political Economy*, **94**, 691–719.

Grout, P. (1984), "Investment and Wages in the Absence of Binding Contracts: A Nash Bargining Approach", *Econometrica*, **52**, 449–60.

Hamilton, J. and S. Slutsky (1990), "Endogenous Timing in Duopoly Games: Stackelberg or Cournot Equilibria", *Games and Economic Behavior*, **2**, 29–46.

Hart, O. and J. Moore (1990), "Property Rights and the Nature of the Firm", *Journal of Political Economy*, 98, 1119–58.

Ingene, C.A. and M.E. Parry (2004), *Mathematical Models of Distribution Channels*, Boston, MA, Kluwer Academic Publishers.

Ingene, C.A., S. Taboubi and G. Zaccour (2012), "Game-Theoretic Coordination Mechanisms in Distribution Channels: Integration and Extensions for Models Without Competition", *Journal of Retailing*, **88**, 476–96.

Jeuland, A.P. and S.M. Shugan (1983), "Managing Channel Profits", *Marketing Science*, **2**, 239–72.

Jeuland, A.P. and S.M. Shugan (1988a), "Reply To: Managing Channel Profits: Comment", *Marketing Science*, **7**, 103–06.

Jeuland, A.P. and S.M. Shugan (1988b), "Channel of Distribution Profits When Channel Members Form Conjectures", *Marketing Science*, **7**, 202–10.

Jørgensen, S. and G. Zaccour (2004), *Differential Games in Marketing*, Kluwer, Dordrecht.

Joskow, P. (1985), "Vertical Integration and Long Term Contracts: The Case of Coal-Burning Electric Generating Stations", *Journal of Law, Economics and Organization*, **1**, 33–80.

Joskow, P. (1987), "Contract Duration and Relationship-Specific Investments: Empirical Evidence from Coal Markets", *American Economic Review*, **67**, 168–85.

Joskow, P. (2005), "Vertical Integration", in C. Menard and M. Shirley (eds), *Handbook of New Institutional Economics*, Heidelberg, Springer.

Karp, L. and I.H. Lee (2003), "Time-Consistent Policies", *Journal of Economic Theory*, **112**, 353–64.

Klein, B., R. Crawford and A. Alchian (1978), "Vertical Integration, Appropriable Rents, and the Competitive Contracting Process", *Journal of Law and Economics*, **21**, 297–326.

Kydland, F. (1977), "Equilibrium Solutions in Dynamic Dominant-Player Models", *Journal of Economic Theory*, **15**, 307–24.

Kydland, F. and E. Prescott (1977), "Rules rather than Discretion: The Inconsistency of Optimal Plans", *Journal of Political Economy*, **85**, 473–92.

Lambertini, L. (2013), "Coordinating Static and Dynamic Supply Chains with Advertising through Two-Part Tariffs", Working Paper no. 874, Department of Economics, University of Bologna.

Lambertini, L. (2014), "Coordinating Static and Dynamic Supply Chains with Advertising through Two-Part Tariffs", *Automatica*, **50**, 565–69.

Lambertini, L. (2017), *An Economic Theory of Managerial Firms: Strategic Delegation in Oligopoly*, London, Routledge, forthcoming.

Lariviere, M.A. (1999), "Supply Chain Contracting and Coordination with Stochastic Demand", in S. Tayur, R. Ganeshan and M. Magazine (eds), *Quantitative Models for Supply Chain Management*, Boston, Kluwer Academic Publishers.

Leitmann, G. and W.E. Schmitendorf (1978), "Profit Maximization Through Advertising: A Nonzero Sum Differential Game Approach", *IEEE Transactions on Automatic Control*, **23**, 646–50.

Long, N.V. (2010), *A Survey of Dynamic Games in Economics*, Singapore, World Scientific.

Mehlmann, A. and R. Willing (1983), "On Nonunique Closed-Loop Nash Equilibria for a Class of Differential Games with a Unique and Degenerate Feedback Solution", *Journal of Optimization Theory and Applications*, **41**, 463–72.

Moorthy, K.S. (1987), "Managing Channel Profits: Comment", *Marketing Science*, **6**, 375–79.

Persson, T. and G. Tabellini (1990), *Macroeconomic Policy, Credibility and Politics*, Chur, Harwood Academic Publishers.

Persson, T. and G. Tabellini (2000), *Political Economics. Explaining Economic Policy*, Cambridge, MA, MIT Press.

Petit, M.L. (1990), *Control Theory and Dynamic Games in Economic Policy Analysis*, Cambridge, Cambridge University Press.

Rubio, S. (2006), "On Coincidence of Feedback Nash Equilibria and Stackelberg Equilibria in Economic Applications of Differential Games", *Journal of Optimization Theory and Applications*, **128**, 203–21.

Rubio, S. and L. Escriche (2001), "Strategic Pigouvian Taxation, Stock Externalities, and Polluting Nonrenewable Resources", *Journal of Public Economics*, **79**, 297–313.

Selten, R. (1965), "Spieltheoretische Behandlung eines Oligopolmodells mit Nachfrageträgheit, Teil I: Bestimmung des Dynamischen Preisgleichgewichts", *Zeitschrift für die gesamte Staatswissenschaft / Journal of Institutional and Theoretical Economics*, **121**, 301–24.

Selten, R. (1975), "Reexamination of the Perfectness Concept for Equilibrium Points in Extensive Games", *International Journal of Game Theory*, **4**, 25–55.

Simaan, M. and J.B. Cruz, Jr. (1973a), "On the Stackelberg Strategy in Nonzero Sum Games", *Journal of Optimization Theory and Applications*, **11**, 533–55.

Simaan, M. and J.B. Cruz, Jr. (1973b), "Additional Aspects of the Stackelberg Strategy in Nonzero Sum Games", *Journal of Optimization Theory and Applications*, **11**, 613–26.

Simaan, M. and T. Takayama (1978), "Game Theory Applied to Dynamic Duopoly Problems with Production Constraints", *Automatica*, **14**, 161–66.

Singh, N. and X. Vives (1984), "Price and Quantity Competition in a Differentiated Duopoly", *RAND Journal of Economics*, **15**, 546–54.

Stackelberg, H. von (1934), *Marktform und Gleichgewicht*, Berlin and Vienna, Springer-Verlag.

Tirole, J. (1988), *The Theory of Industrial Organization*, Cambridge, MA, MIT Press.

van der Ploeg, F. and A. De Zeeuw (1990), "Perfect Equilibrium in a Model of Competitive Arms Accumulation", *International Economic Review*, **31**, 131–46.

Vickers, J. (1985), "Delegation and the Theory of the Firm", *Economic Journal*, **95** (Conference Papers), 138–47.

Williamson, O.E. (1971), "The Vertical Integration of Production: Market Failure Considerations", *American Economic Review*, **61**, 112–23.

Williamson, O. (1975), *Markets and Hierarchies: Analysis and Antitrust Implications*, New York, Free Press.

Zaccour, G. (2008), "On the Coordination of Dynamic Marketing Channels and Two-Part Tariffs", *Automatica*, **44**, 1233–39.

Zusman, P. and M. Etgar (1981), "The Marketing Channel as an Equilibrium Set of Contracts", *Management Science*, **27**, 284–302.

Xie, D. (1997), "On Time Consistency: A Technical Issue in Stackelberg Differential Games", *Journal of Economic Theory*, **76**, 412–30.

Index